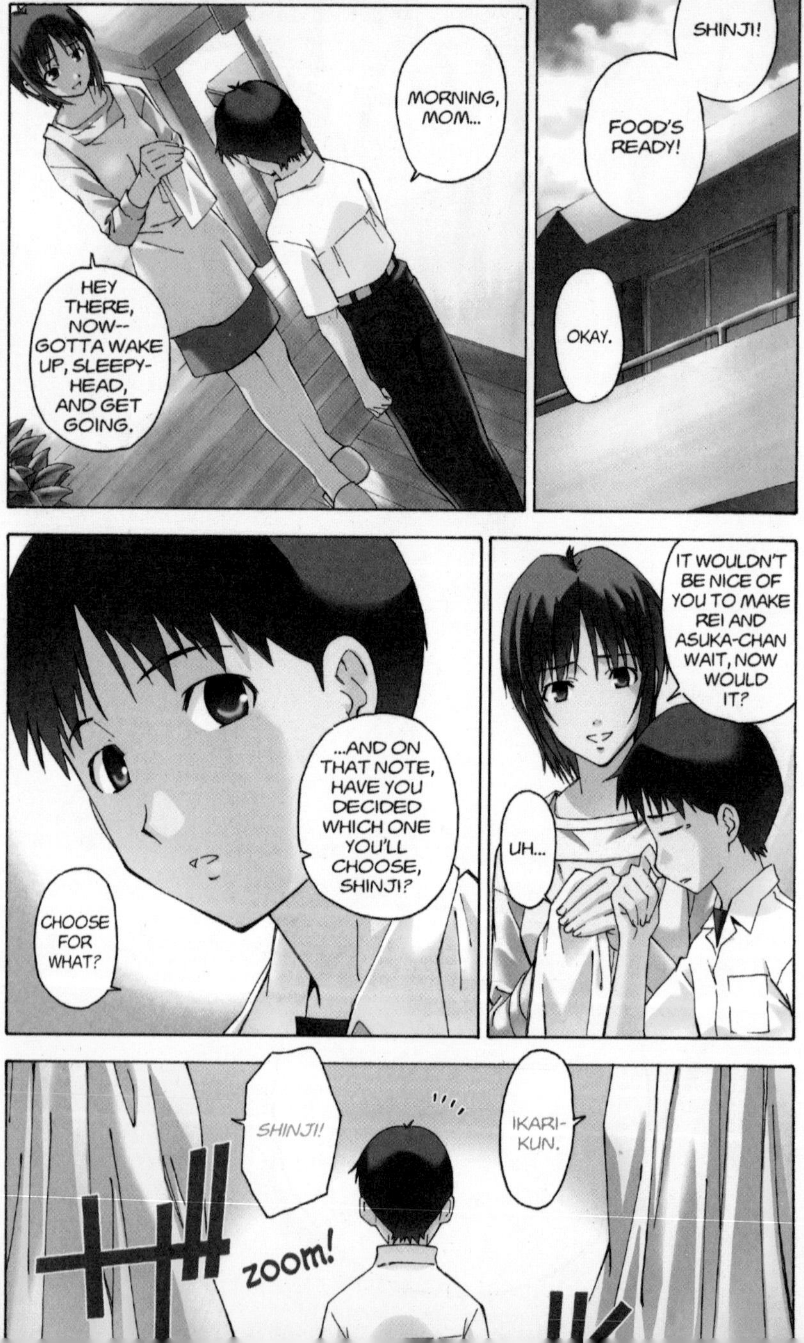
SHINJI!
FOOD'S READY!
OKAY.
MORNING, MOM...
HEY THERE, NOW-- GOTTA WAKE UP, SLEEPY-HEAD, AND GET GOING.
IT WOULDN'T BE NICE OF YOU TO MAKE REI AND ASUKA-CHAN WAIT, NOW WOULD IT?
UH...
...AND ON THAT NOTE, HAVE YOU DECIDED WHICH ONE YOU'LL CHOOSE, SHINJI?
CHOOSE FOR WHAT?
IKARI-KUN.
SHINJI!
zoom!

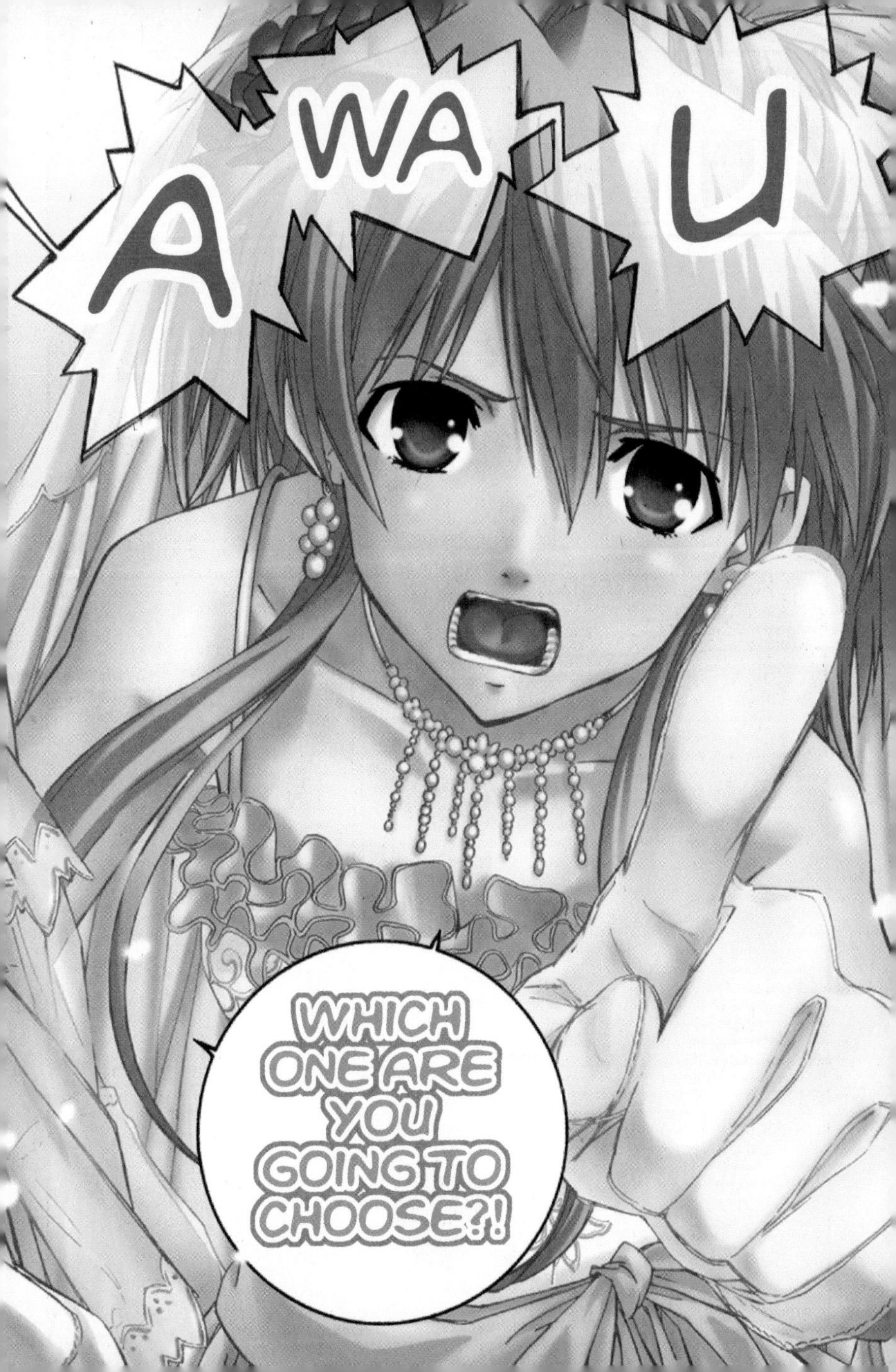
A WA U
WHICH ONE ARE YOU GOING TO CHOOSE?!

NEON GENESIS EVANGELION

THE SHINJI IKARI RAISING PROJECT

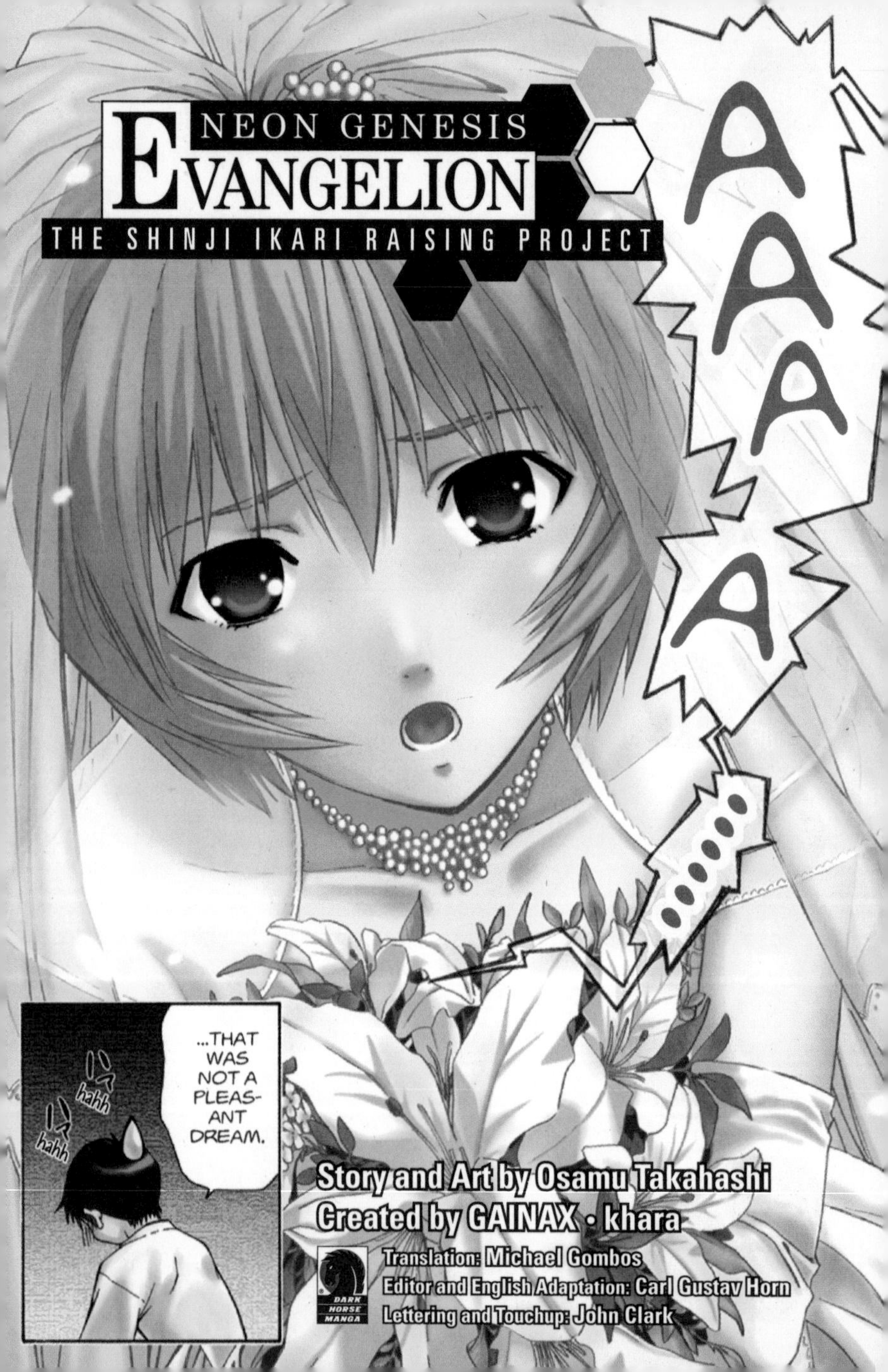
AAAA
......
ハァ hahh
ハァ hahh
...THAT WAS NOT A PLEASANT DREAM.

Story and Art by Osamu Takahashi
Created by GAINAX • khara

Translation: Michael Gombos
Editor and English Adaptation: Carl Gustav Horn
Lettering and Touchup: John Clark

NEON GENESIS EVANGELION
THE SHINJI IKARI
RAISING PROJECT

CONTENTS

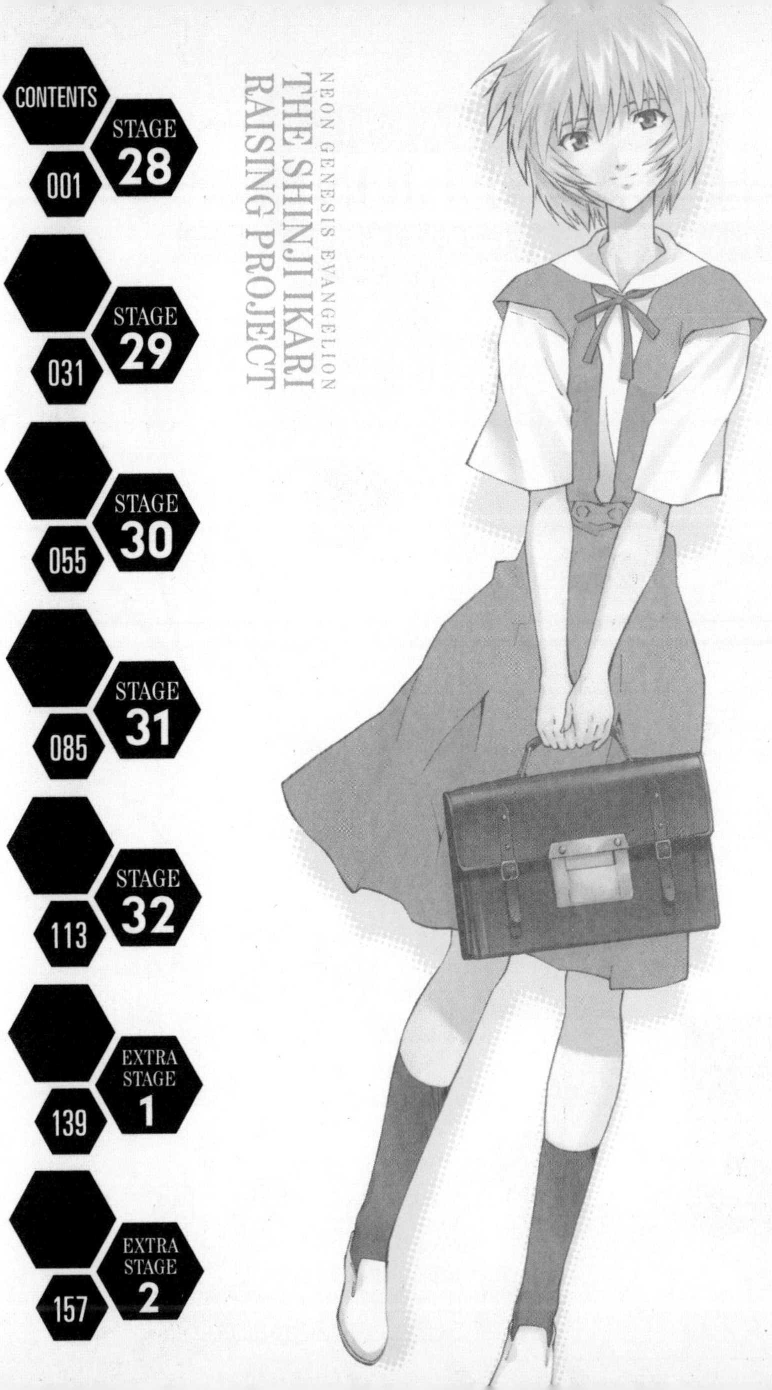

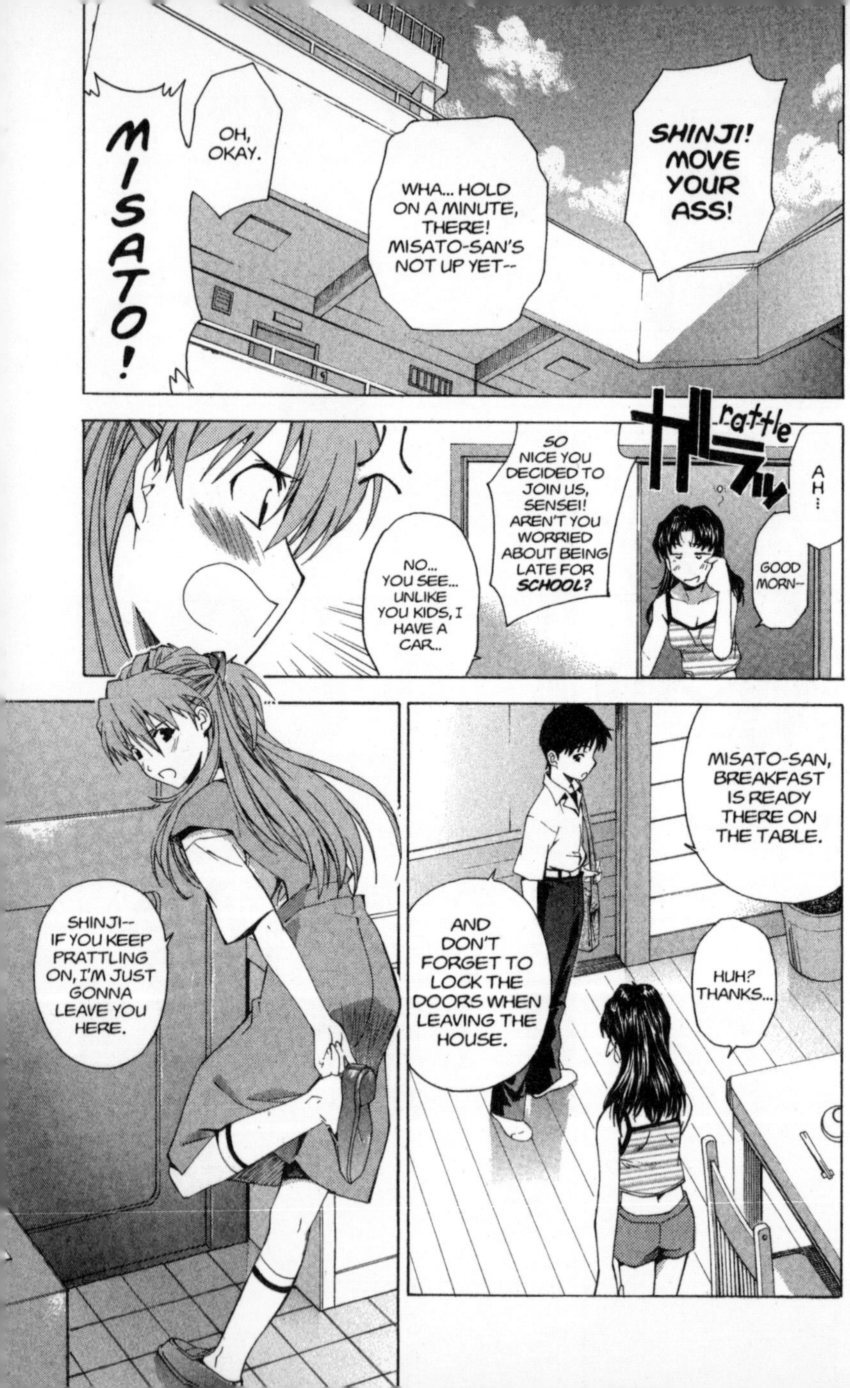
SHINJI! MOVE YOUR ASS!
WHA... HOLD ON A MINUTE, THERE! MISATO-SAN'S NOT UP YET--
OH, OKAY.
MISATO!
rattle
AH...
GOOD MORN--
SO NICE YOU DECIDED TO JOIN US, SENSEI! AREN'T YOU WORRIED ABOUT BEING LATE FOR SCHOOL?
NO... YOU SEE... UNLIKE YOU KIDS, I HAVE A CAR...
MISATO-SAN, BREAKFAST IS READY THERE ON THE TABLE.
HUH? THANKS...
AND DON'T FORGET TO LOCK THE DOORS WHEN LEAVING THE HOUSE.
SHINJI-- IF YOU KEEP PRATTLING ON, I'M JUST GONNA LEAVE YOU HERE.

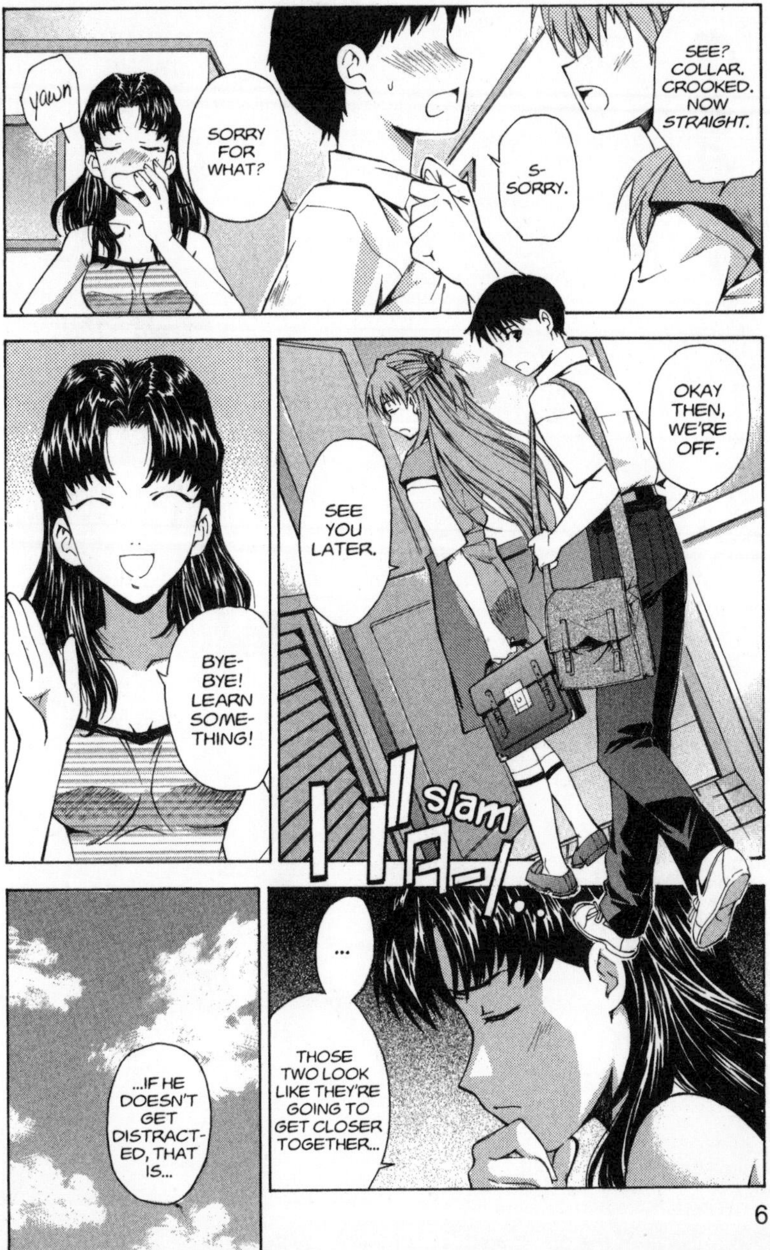
SEE? COLLAR. CROOKED. NOW STRAIGHT.
S-SORRY.
SORRY FOR WHAT?
yawn
OKAY THEN, WE'RE OFF.
SEE YOU LATER.
slam
BYE-BYE! LEARN SOME-THING!
...
THOSE TWO LOOK LIKE THEY'RE GOING TO GET CLOSER TOGETHER...
...IF HE DOESN'T GET DISTRACT-ED, THAT IS...

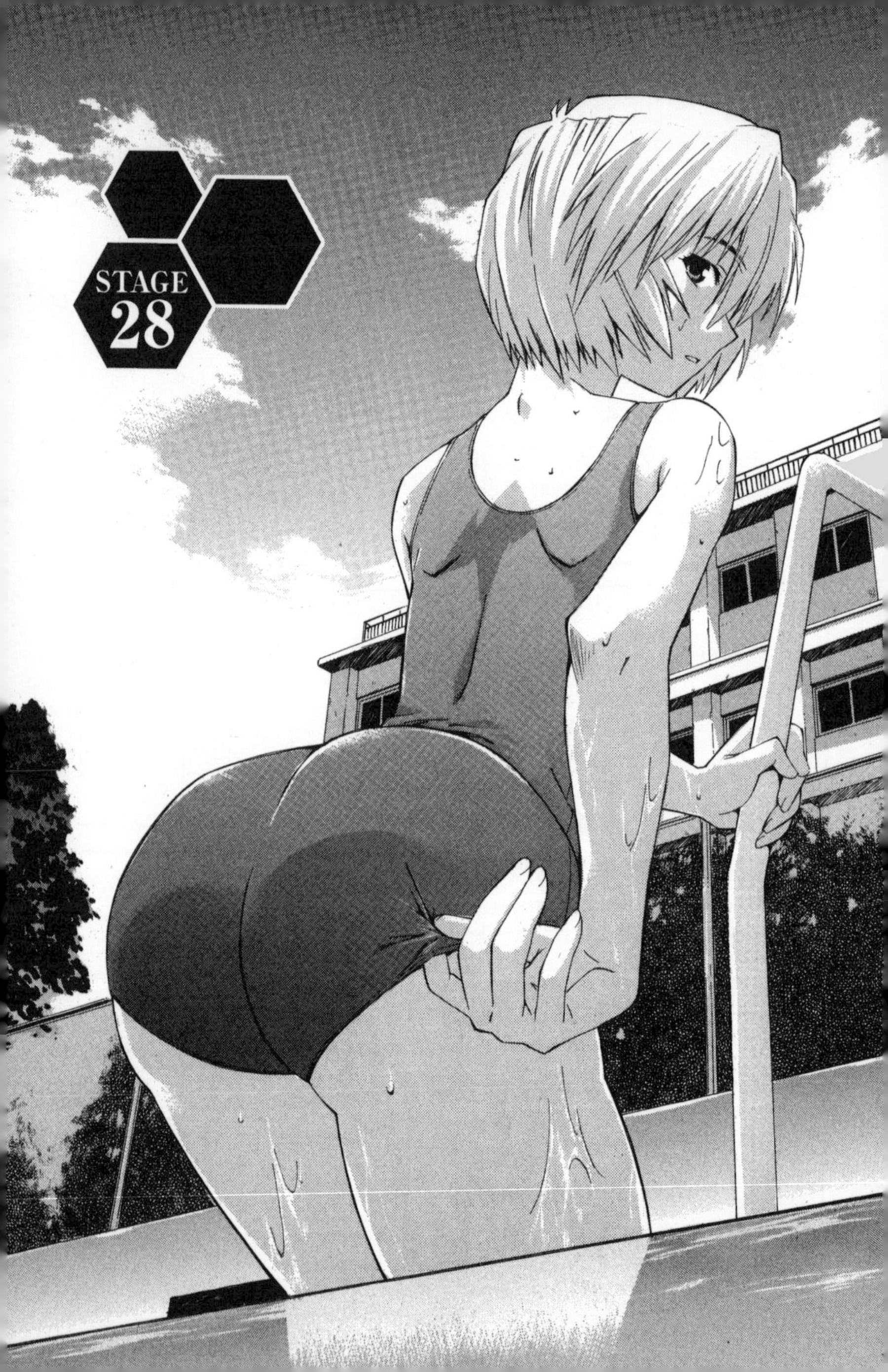
STAGE
28

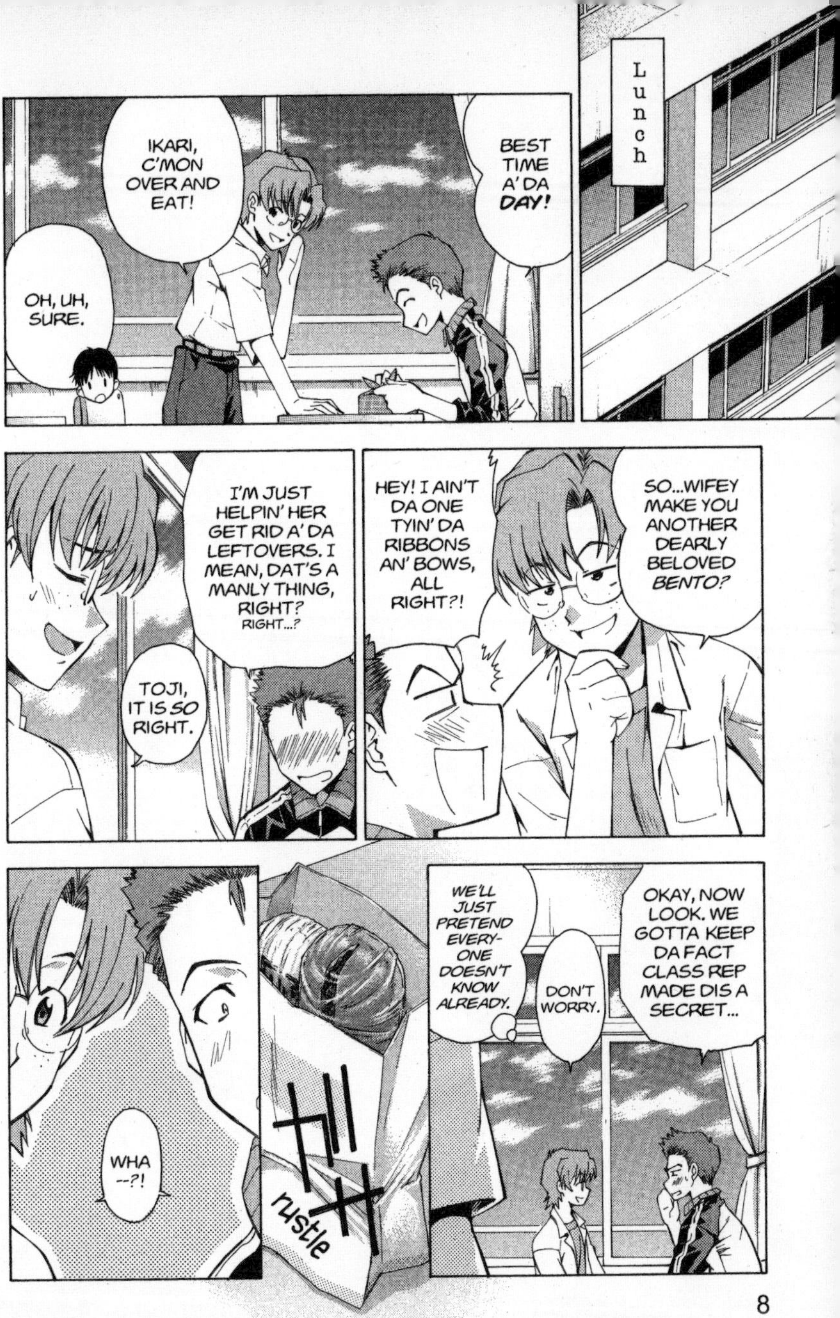
Lunch
BEST TIME A' DA DAY!
IKARI, C'MON OVER AND EAT!
OH, UH, SURE.
SO...WIFEY MAKE YOU ANOTHER DEARLY BELOVED BENTO?
HEY! I AIN'T DA ONE TYIN' DA RIBBONS AN' BOWS, ALL RIGHT?!
I'M JUST HELPIN' HER GET RID A' DA LEFTOVERS. I MEAN, DAT'S A MANLY THING, RIGHT? RIGHT...?
TOJI, IT IS SO RIGHT.
OKAY, NOW LOOK. WE GOTTA KEEP DA FACT CLASS REP MADE DIS A SECRET...
DON'T WORRY.
WE'LL JUST PRETEND EVERY-ONE DOESN'T KNOW ALREADY.
WHA --?!
rustle

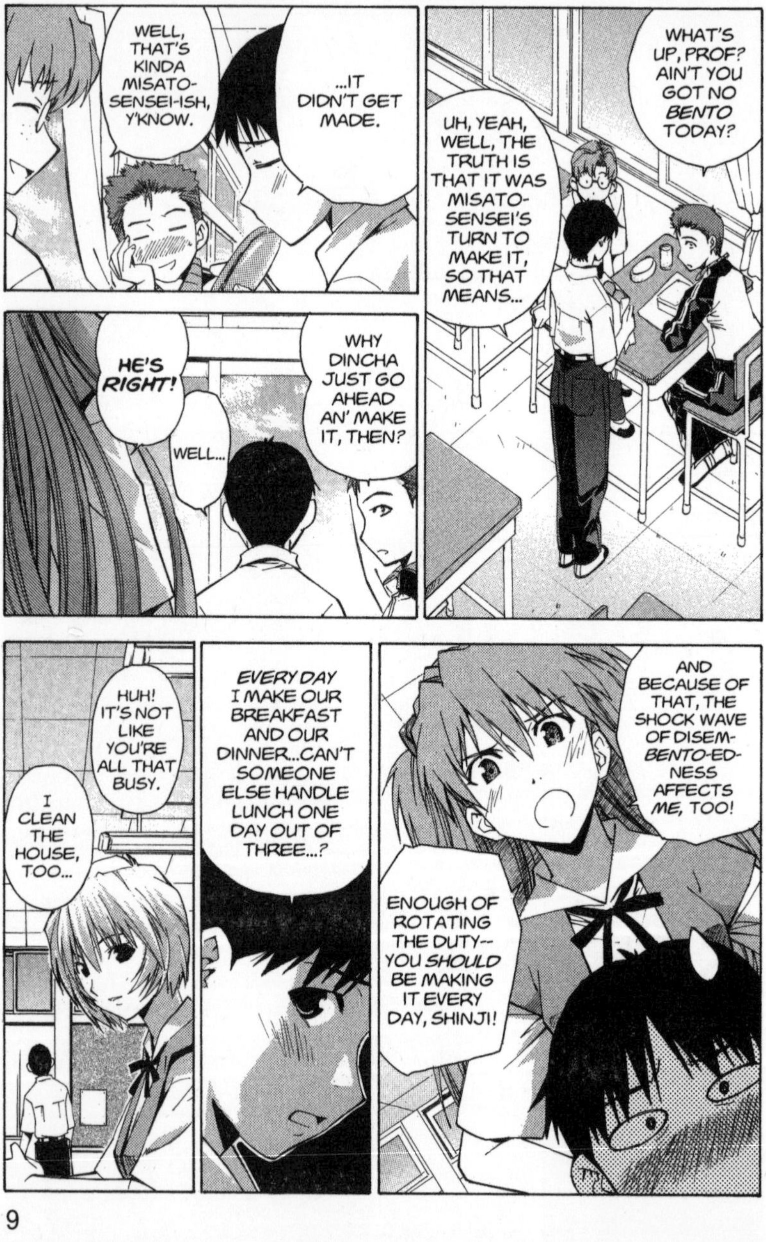
WHAT'S UP, PROF? AIN'T YOU GOT NO *BENTO* TODAY?
UH, YEAH, WELL, THE TRUTH IS THAT IT WAS MISATO-SENSEI'S TURN TO MAKE IT, SO THAT MEANS...
...IT DIDN'T GET MADE.
WELL, THAT'S KINDA MISATO-SENSEI-ISH, Y'KNOW.
WHY DINCHA JUST GO AHEAD AN' MAKE IT, THEN?
HE'S RIGHT!
WELL...
AND BECAUSE OF THAT, THE SHOCK WAVE OF DISEM-BENTO-EDNESS AFFECTS *ME*, TOO!
ENOUGH OF ROTATING THE DUTY-- YOU *SHOULD* BE MAKING IT EVERY DAY, SHINJI!
EVERY DAY I MAKE OUR BREAKFAST AND OUR DINNER...CAN'T SOMEONE ELSE HANDLE LUNCH ONE DAY OUT OF THREE...?
HUH! IT'S NOT LIKE YOU'RE ALL THAT BUSY.
I CLEAN THE HOUSE, TOO...

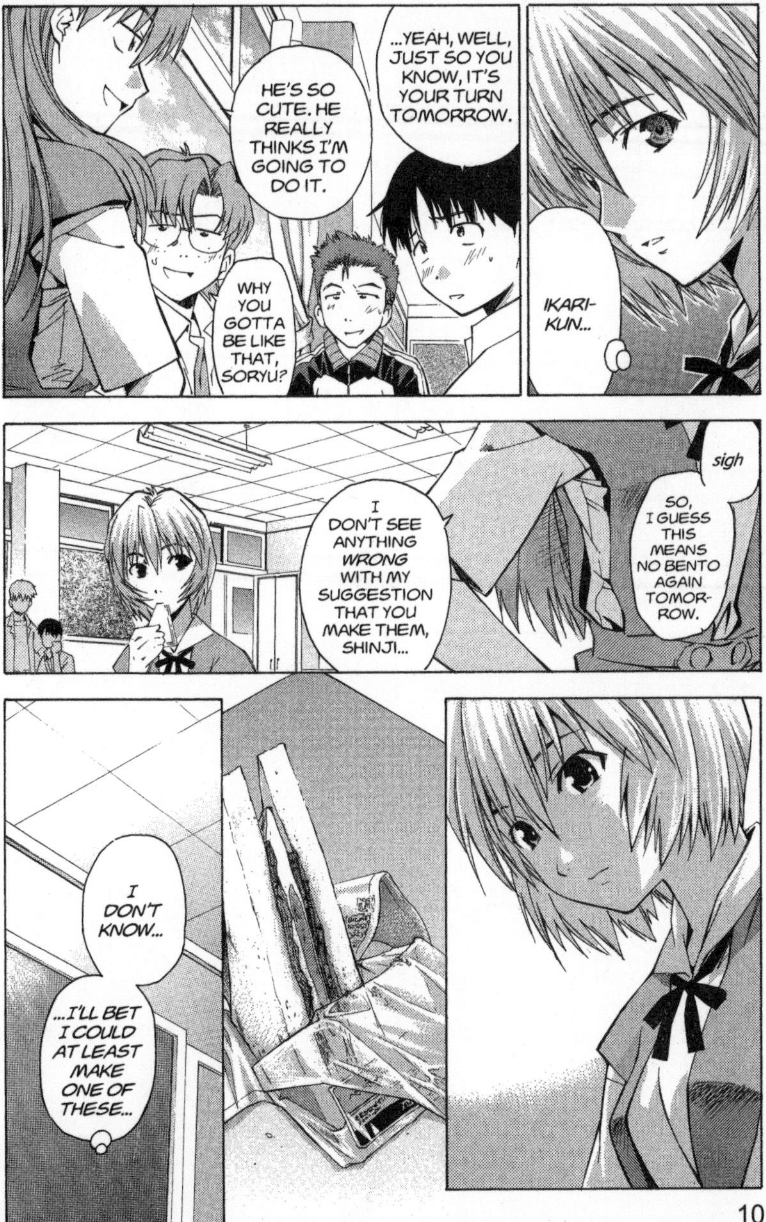
IKARI-KUN...
...YEAH, WELL, JUST SO YOU KNOW, IT'S YOUR TURN TOMORROW.
HE'S SO CUTE. HE REALLY THINKS I'M GOING TO DO IT.
WHY YOU GOTTA BE LIKE THAT, SORYU?
sigh
SO, I GUESS THIS MEANS NO BENTO AGAIN TOMORROW.
I DON'T SEE ANYTHING WRONG WITH MY SUGGESTION THAT YOU MAKE THEM, SHINJI...
I DON'T KNOW...
...I'LL BET I COULD AT LEAST MAKE ONE OF THESE...

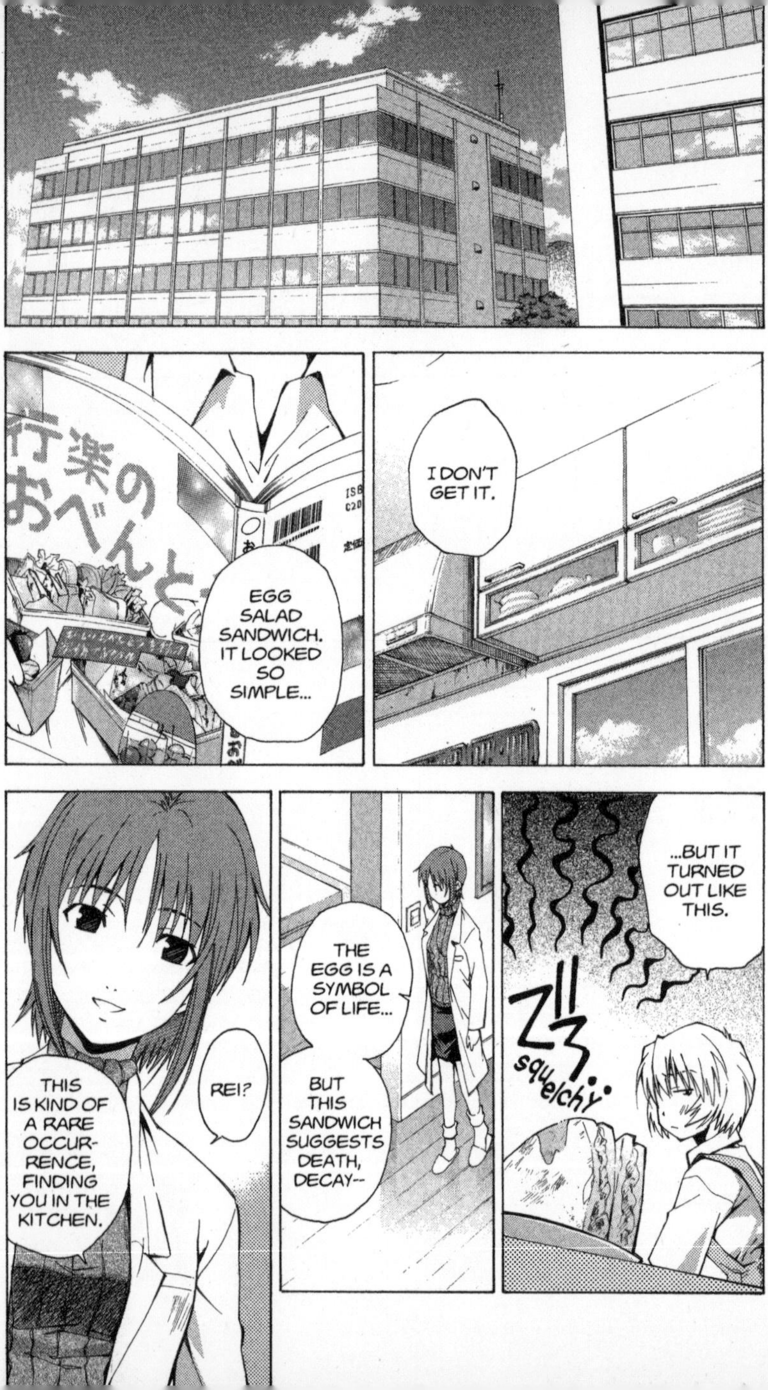
I DON'T GET IT.
行楽の
おべんと
EGG SALAD SANDWICH. IT LOOKED SO SIMPLE...
...BUT IT TURNED OUT LIKE THIS.
squelchy
THE EGG IS A SYMBOL OF LIFE...
BUT THIS SANDWICH SUGGESTS DEATH, DECAY--
REI?
THIS IS KIND OF A RARE OCCURRENCE, FINDING YOU IN THE KITCHEN.

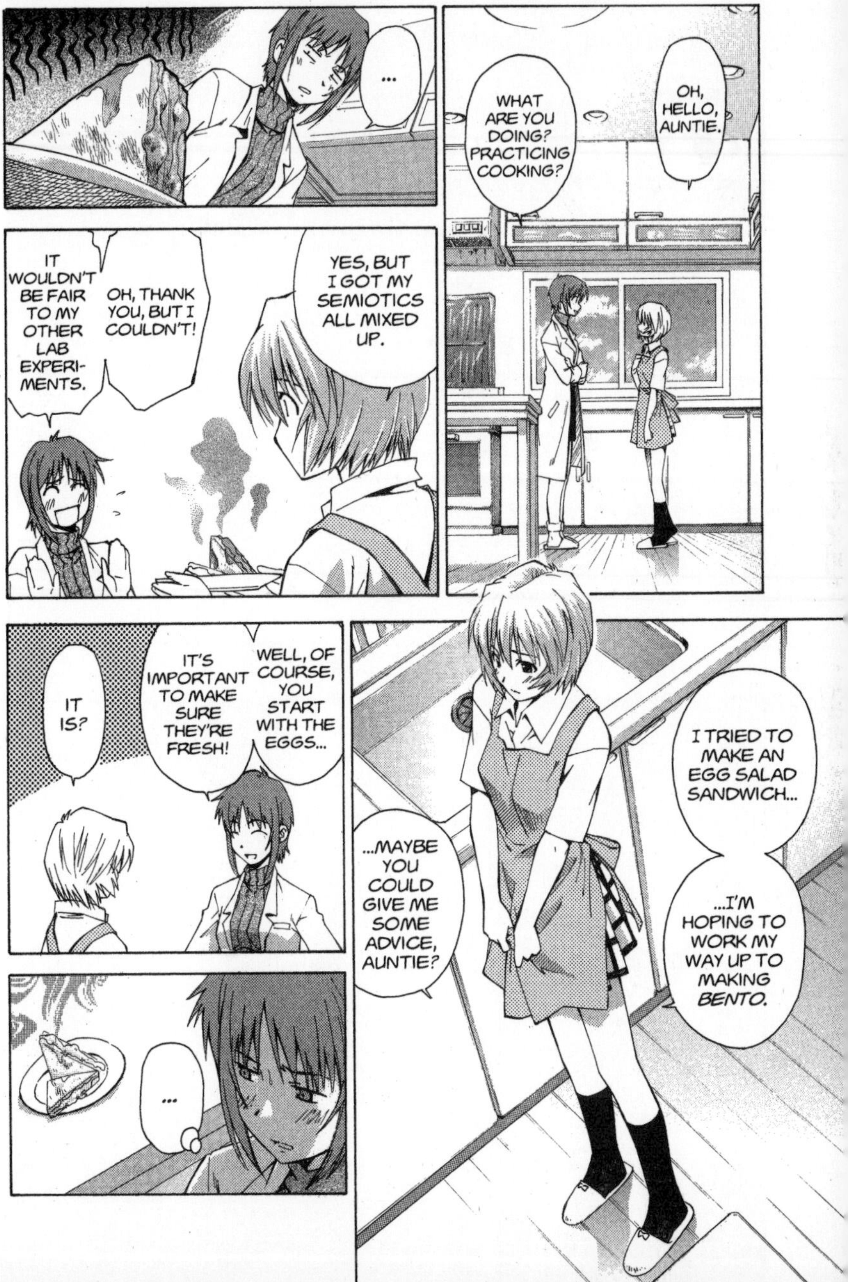
OH, HELLO, AUNTIE.
WHAT ARE YOU DOING? PRACTICING COOKING?
...
YES, BUT I GOT MY SEMIOTICS ALL MIXED UP.
OH, THANK YOU, BUT I COULDN'T!
IT WOULDN'T BE FAIR TO MY OTHER LAB EXPERI-MENTS.
I TRIED TO MAKE AN EGG SALAD SANDWICH...
...I'M HOPING TO WORK MY WAY UP TO MAKING *BENTO*.
...MAYBE YOU COULD GIVE ME SOME ADVICE, AUNTIE?
WELL, OF COURSE, YOU START WITH THE EGGS...
IT'S IMPORTANT TO MAKE SURE THEY'RE FRESH!
IT IS?
...

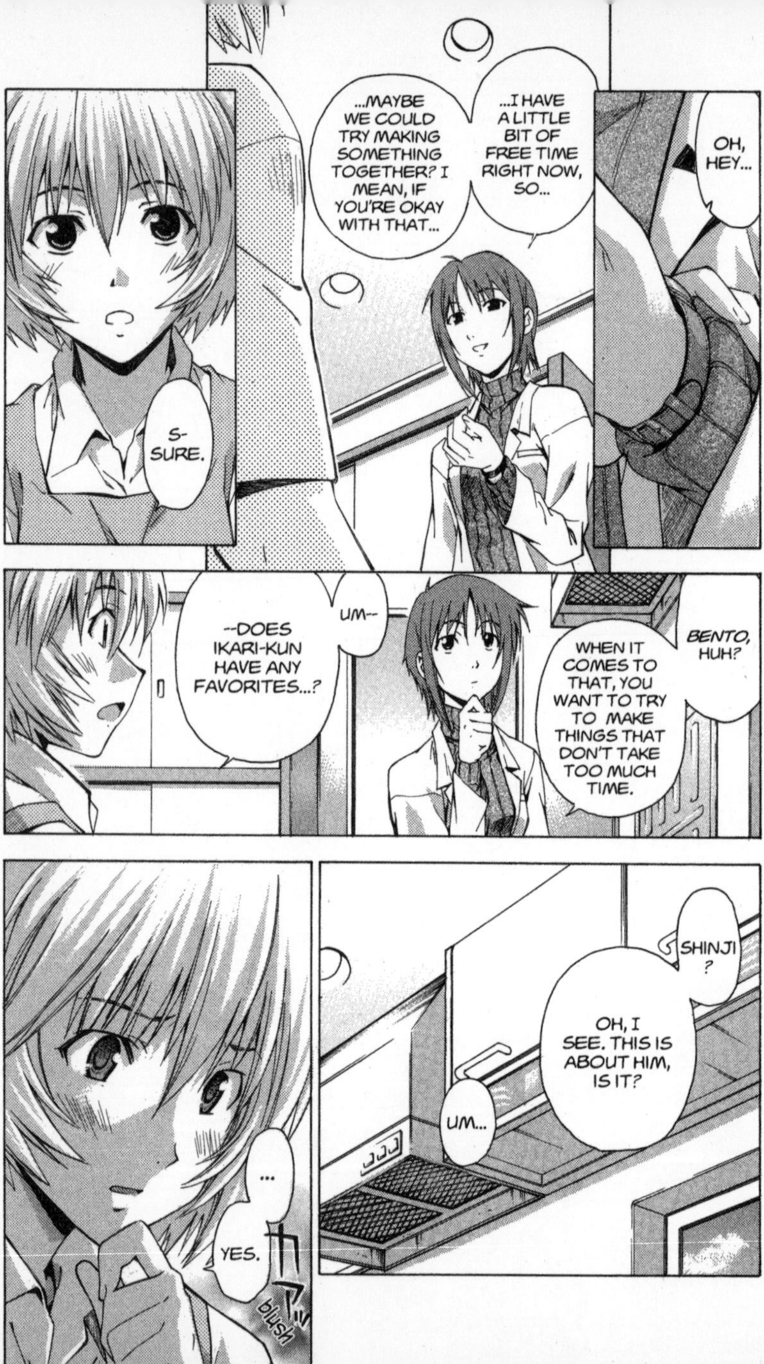
OH, HEY...
...I HAVE A LITTLE BIT OF FREE TIME RIGHT NOW, SO...
...MAYBE WE COULD TRY MAKING SOMETHING TOGETHER? I MEAN, IF YOU'RE OKAY WITH THAT...
S-SURE.
BENTO, HUH?
WHEN IT COMES TO THAT, YOU WANT TO TRY TO MAKE THINGS THAT DON'T TAKE TOO MUCH TIME.
UM--
--DOES IKARI-KUN HAVE ANY FAVORITES...?
SHINJI?
OH, I SEE. THIS IS ABOUT HIM, IS IT?
UM...
...
YES.
blush

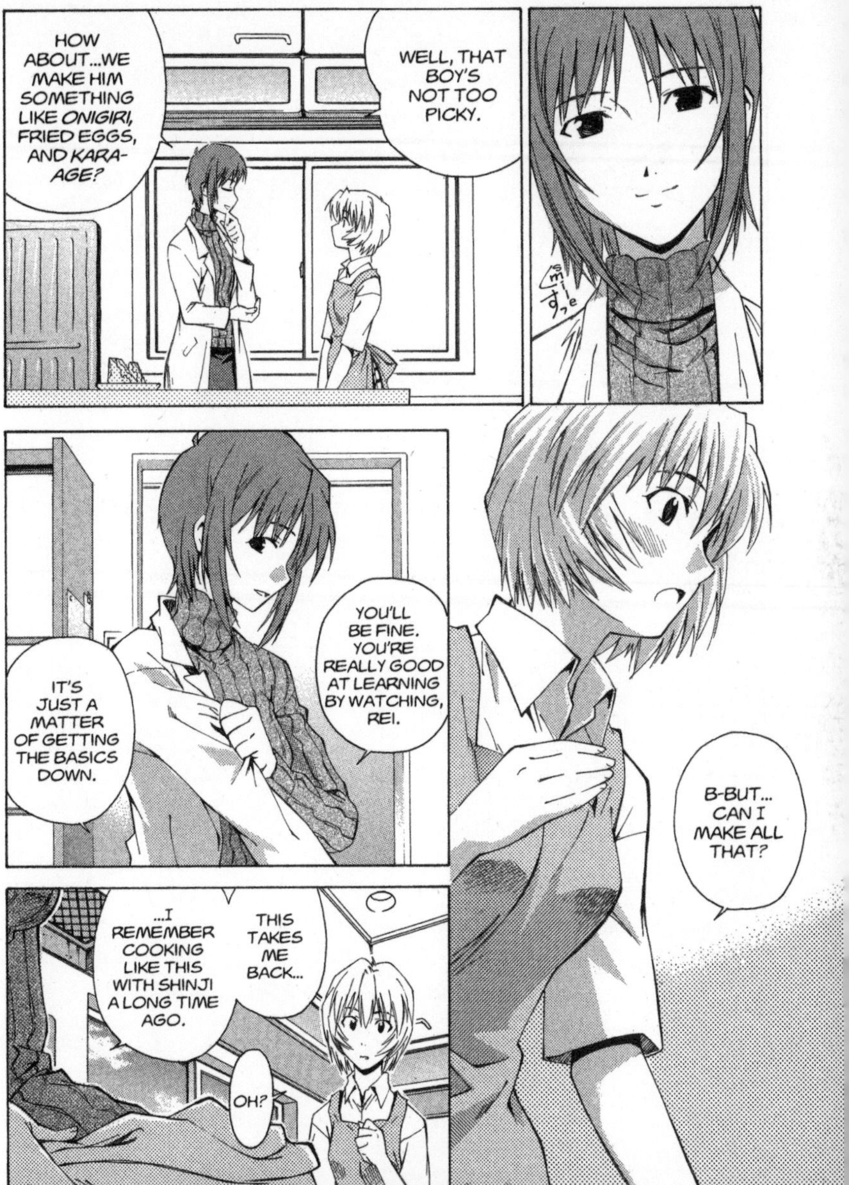
smile
WELL, THAT BOY'S NOT TOO PICKY.
HOW ABOUT...WE MAKE HIM SOMETHING LIKE *ONIGIRI*, FRIED EGGS, AND *KARA-AGE*?
B-BUT... CAN I MAKE ALL THAT?
YOU'LL BE FINE. YOU'RE REALLY GOOD AT LEARNING BY WATCHING, REI.
IT'S JUST A MATTER OF GETTING THE BASICS DOWN.
THIS TAKES ME BACK...
...I REMEMBER COOKING LIKE THIS WITH SHINJI A LONG TIME AGO.
OH?

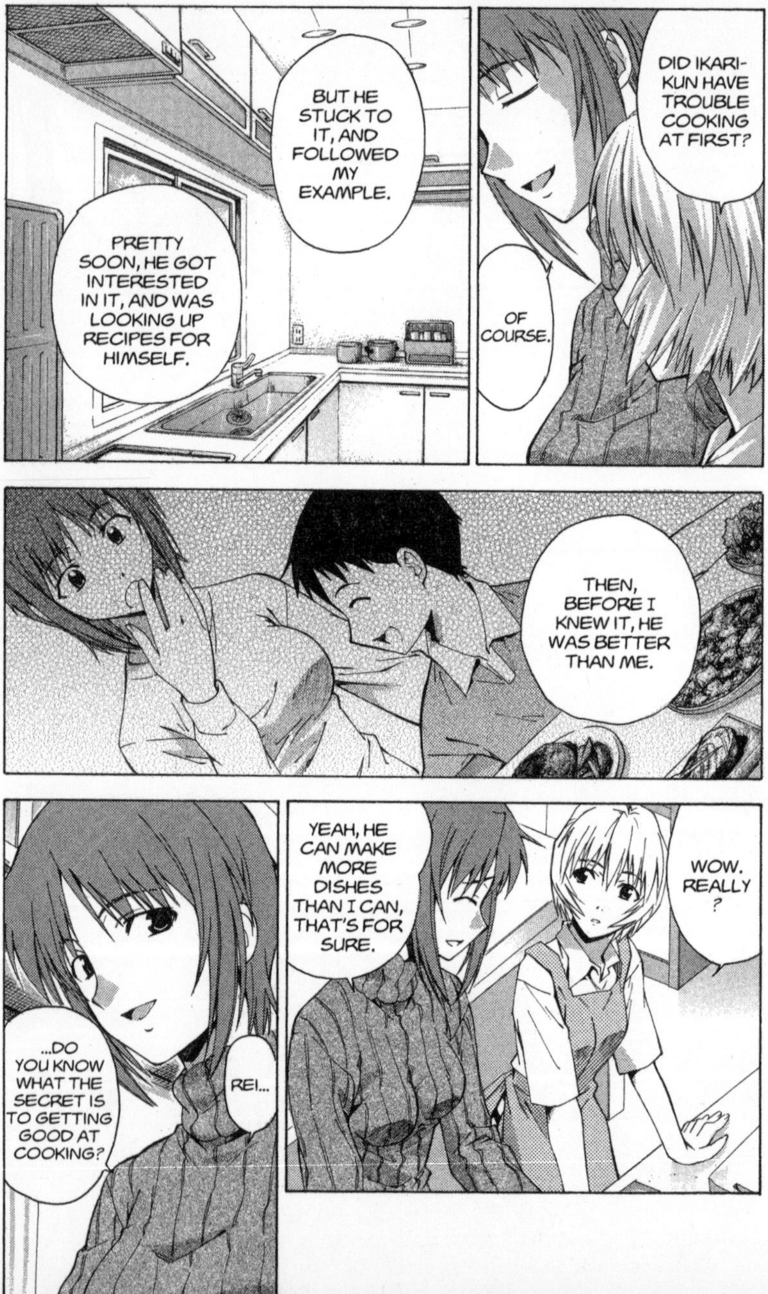
DID IKARI-KUN HAVE TROUBLE COOKING AT FIRST?
OF COURSE.
BUT HE STUCK TO IT, AND FOLLOWED MY EXAMPLE.
PRETTY SOON, HE GOT INTERESTED IN IT, AND WAS LOOKING UP RECIPES FOR HIMSELF.
THEN, BEFORE I KNEW IT, HE WAS BETTER THAN ME.
WOW. REALLY?
YEAH, HE CAN MAKE MORE DISHES THAN I CAN, THAT'S FOR SURE.
REI...
...DO YOU KNOW WHAT THE SECRET IS TO GETTING GOOD AT COOKING?

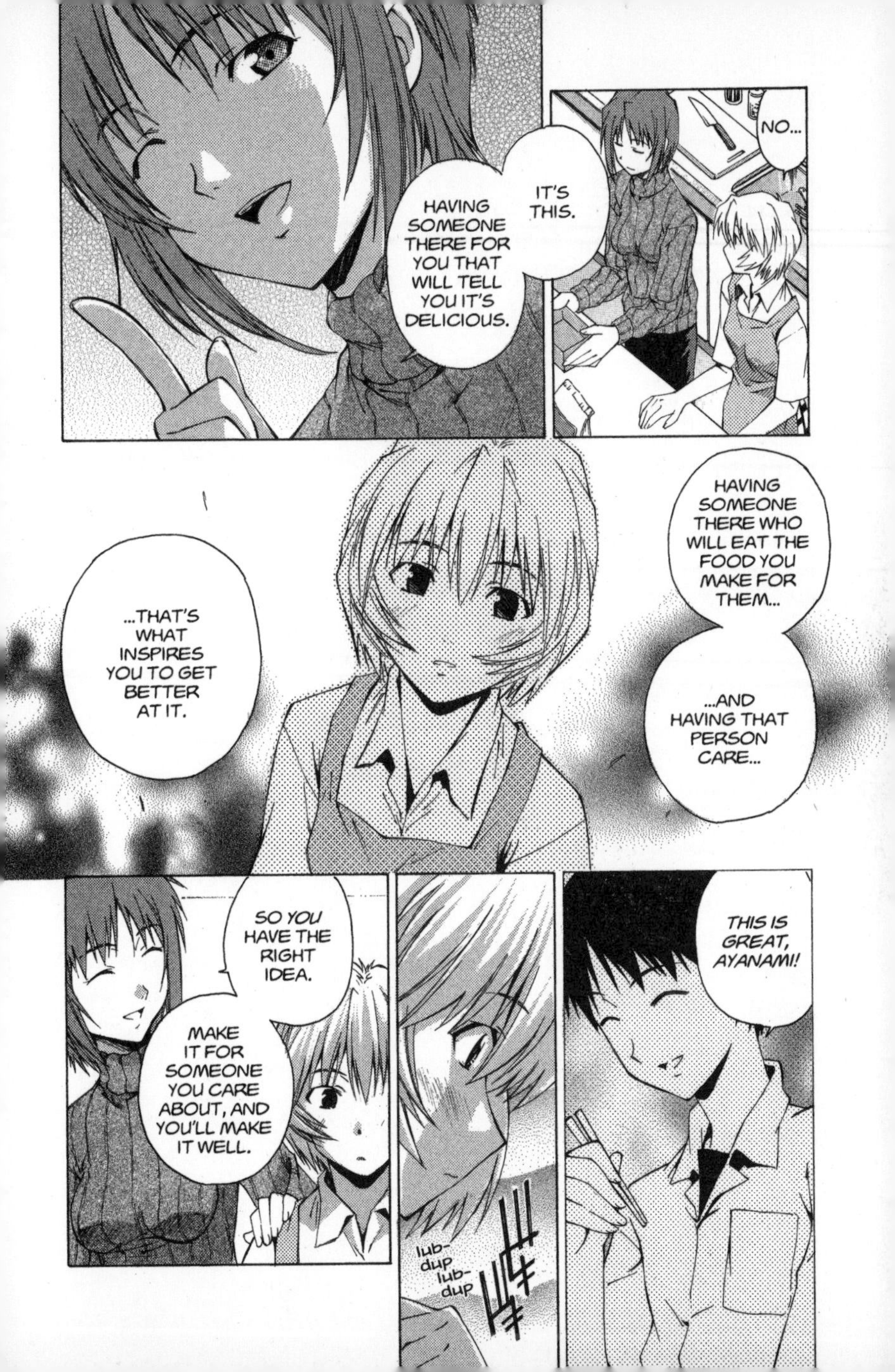
NO...
IT'S THIS.
HAVING SOMEONE THERE FOR YOU THAT WILL TELL YOU IT'S DELICIOUS.
HAVING SOMEONE THERE WHO WILL EAT THE FOOD YOU MAKE FOR THEM...
...AND HAVING THAT PERSON CARE...
...THAT'S WHAT INSPIRES YOU TO GET BETTER AT IT.
THIS IS GREAT, AYANAMI!
lub-dup lub-dup
SO YOU HAVE THE RIGHT IDEA.
MAKE IT FOR SOMEONE YOU CARE ABOUT, AND YOU'LL MAKE IT WELL.

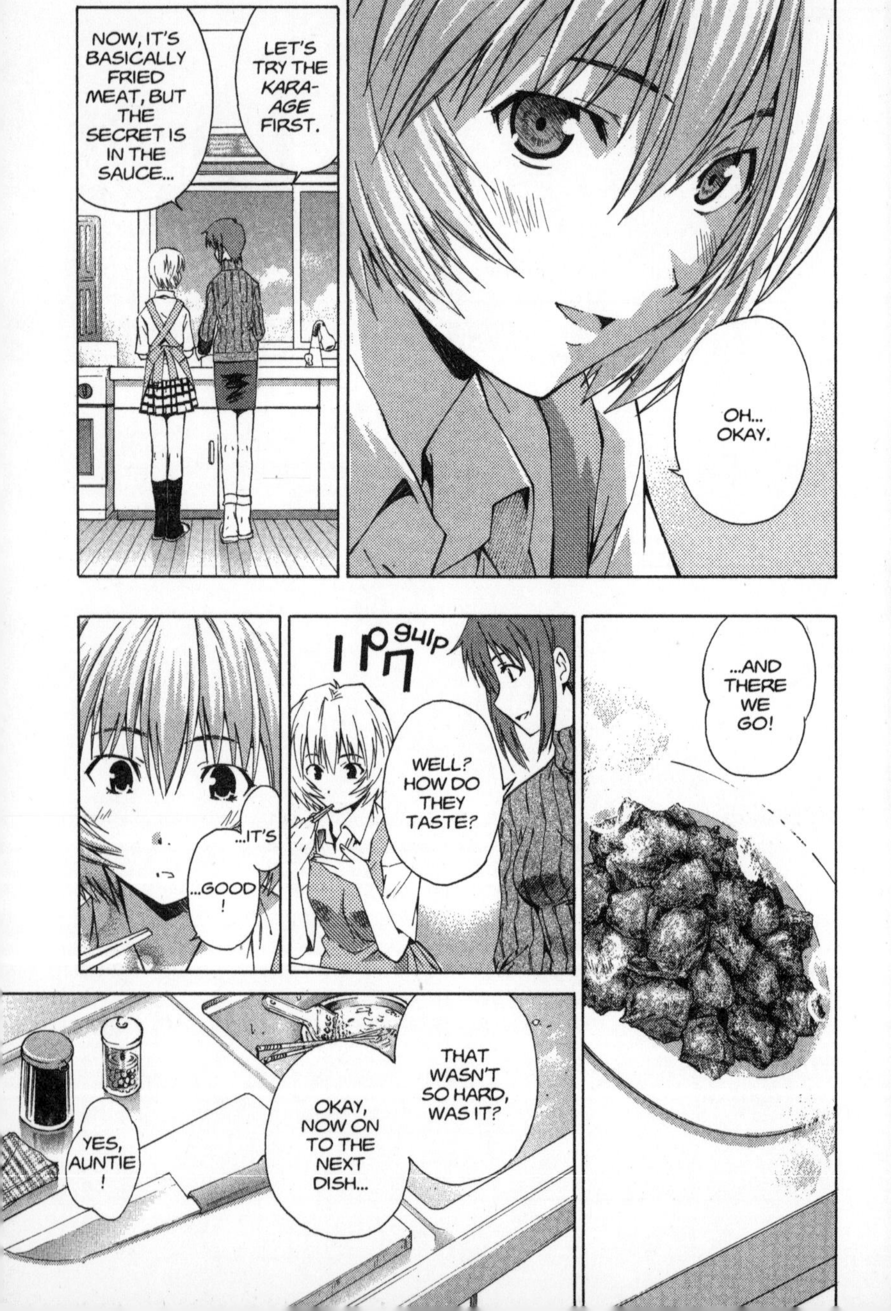
OH... OKAY.
LET'S TRY THE KARA-AGE FIRST.
NOW, IT'S BASICALLY FRIED MEAT, BUT THE SECRET IS IN THE SAUCE...
...AND THERE WE GO!
gulp
WELL? HOW DO THEY TASTE?
...IT'S
...GOOD!
THAT WASN'T SO HARD, WAS IT?
OKAY, NOW ON TO THE NEXT DISH...
YES, AUNTIE!

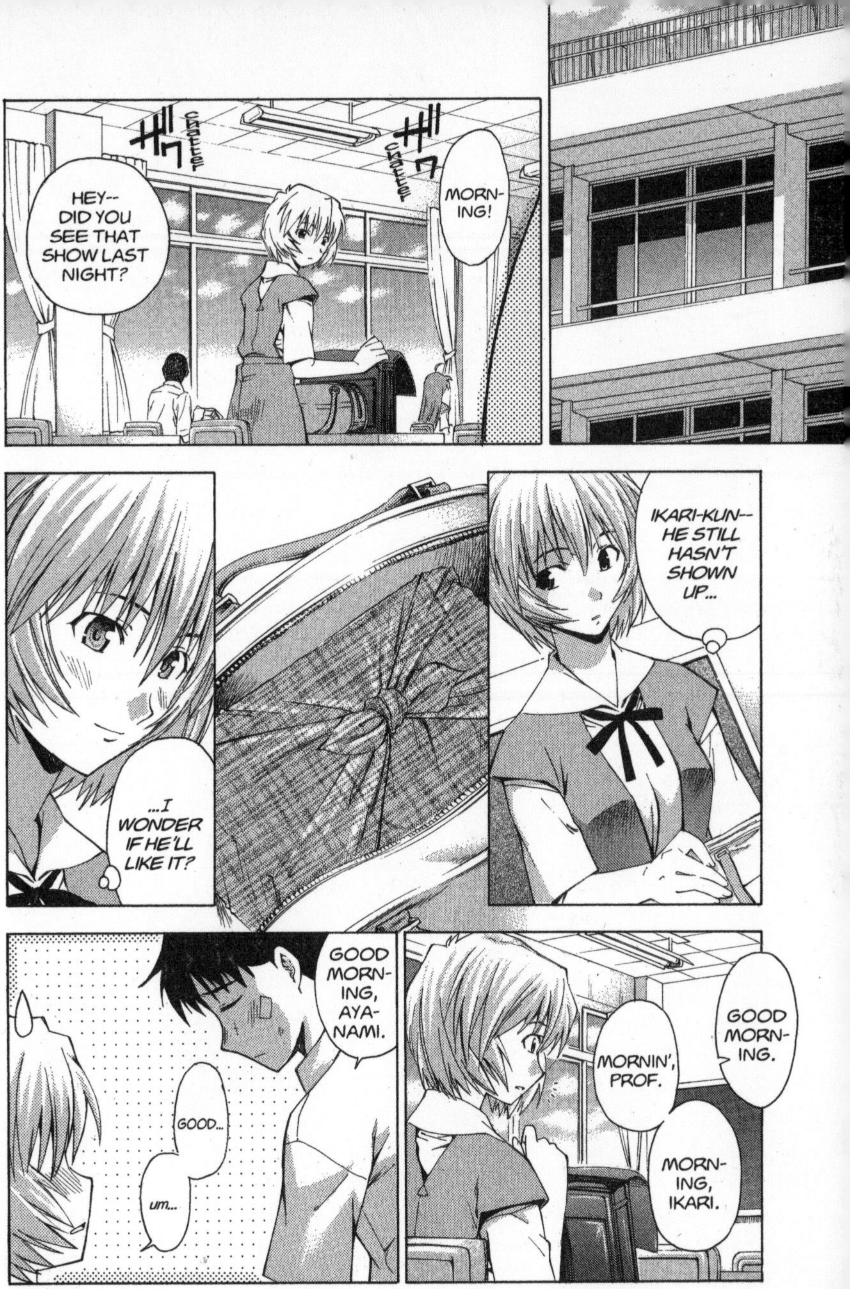
CHATTER
MORNING!
CHATTER
HEY-- DID YOU SEE THAT SHOW LAST NIGHT?
IKARI-KUN-- HE STILL HASN'T SHOWN UP...
...I WONDER IF HE'LL LIKE IT?
GOOD MORNING.
MORNIN', PROF.
MORNING, IKARI.
GOOD MORNING, AYANAMI.
GOOD...
um...

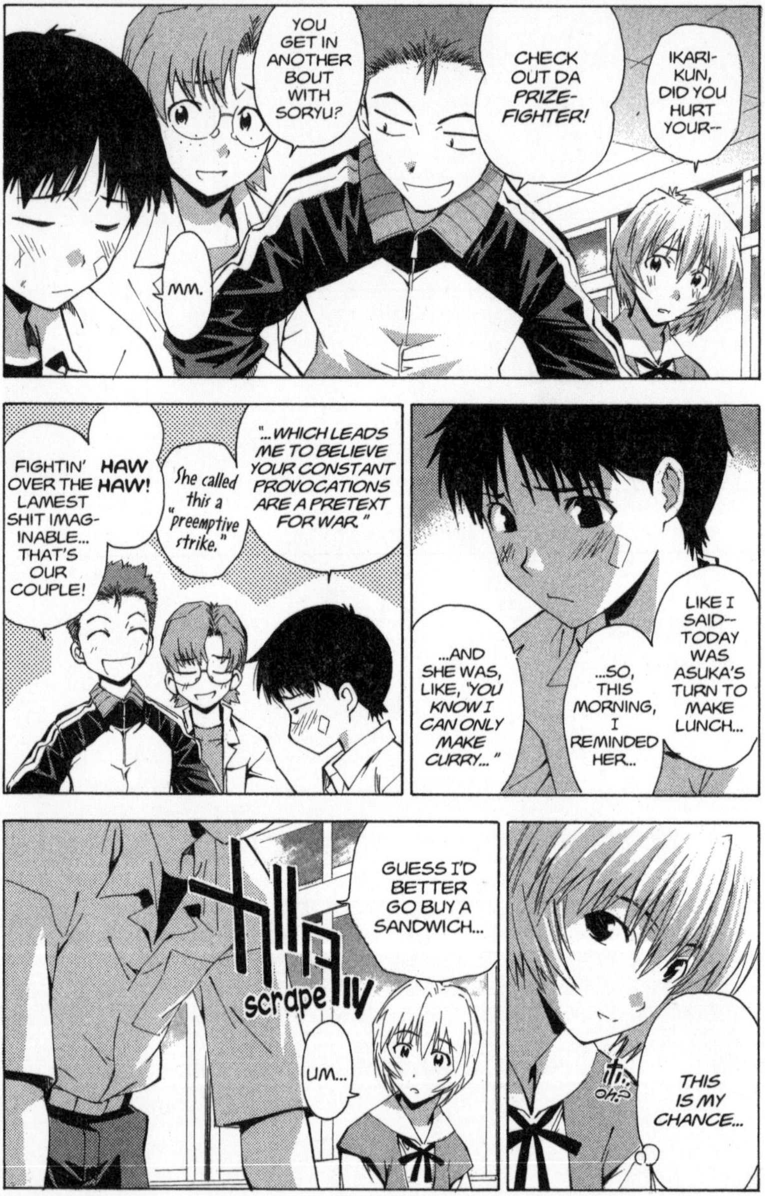
IKARI-KUN, DID YOU HURT YOUR--
CHECK OUT DA PRIZE-FIGHTER!
YOU GET IN ANOTHER BOUT WITH SORYU?
MM.
LIKE I SAID-- TODAY WAS ASUKA'S TURN TO MAKE LUNCH...
...SO, THIS MORNING, I REMINDED HER...
...AND SHE WAS, LIKE, "YOU KNOW I CAN ONLY MAKE CURRY..."
"...WHICH LEADS ME TO BELIEVE YOUR CONSTANT PROVOCATIONS ARE A PRETEXT FOR WAR."
She called this a "preemptive strike."
HAW HAW!
FIGHTIN' OVER THE LAMEST SHIT IMAGINABLE... THAT'S OUR COUPLE!
oh?
THIS IS MY CHANCE...
GUESS I'D BETTER GO BUY A SANDWICH...
scrape
UM...

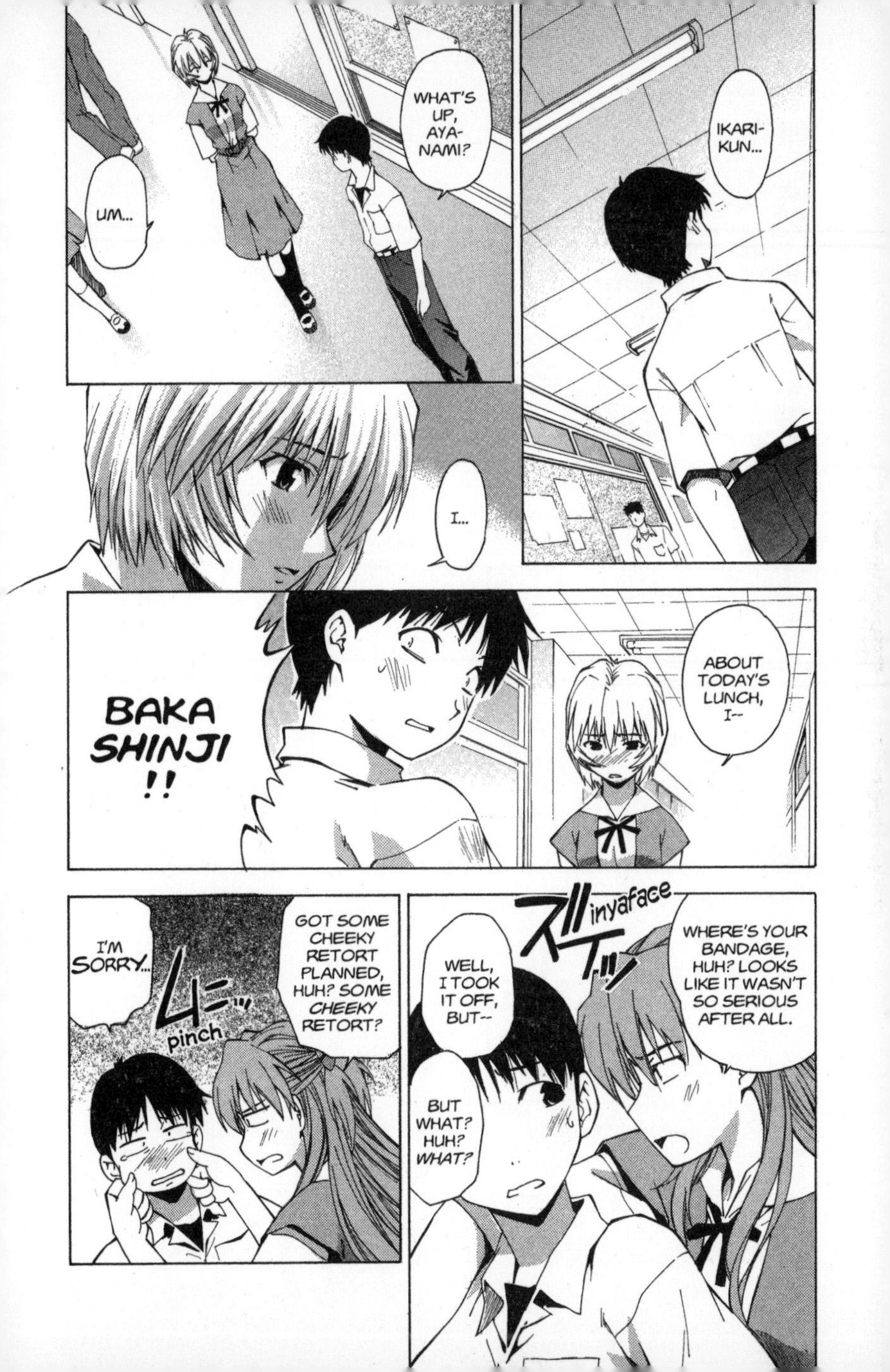
IKARI-KUN...
WHAT'S UP, AYA-NAMI?
UM...
I...
ABOUT TODAY'S LUNCH, I--
BAKA SHINJI!!
inyaface
WHERE'S YOUR BANDAGE, HUH? LOOKS LIKE IT WASN'T SO SERIOUS AFTER ALL.
WELL, I TOOK IT OFF, BUT--
BUT WHAT? HUH? *WHAT?*
GOT SOME CHEEKY RETORT PLANNED, HUH? SOME *CHEEKY* RETORT?
I'M SORRY...
pinch

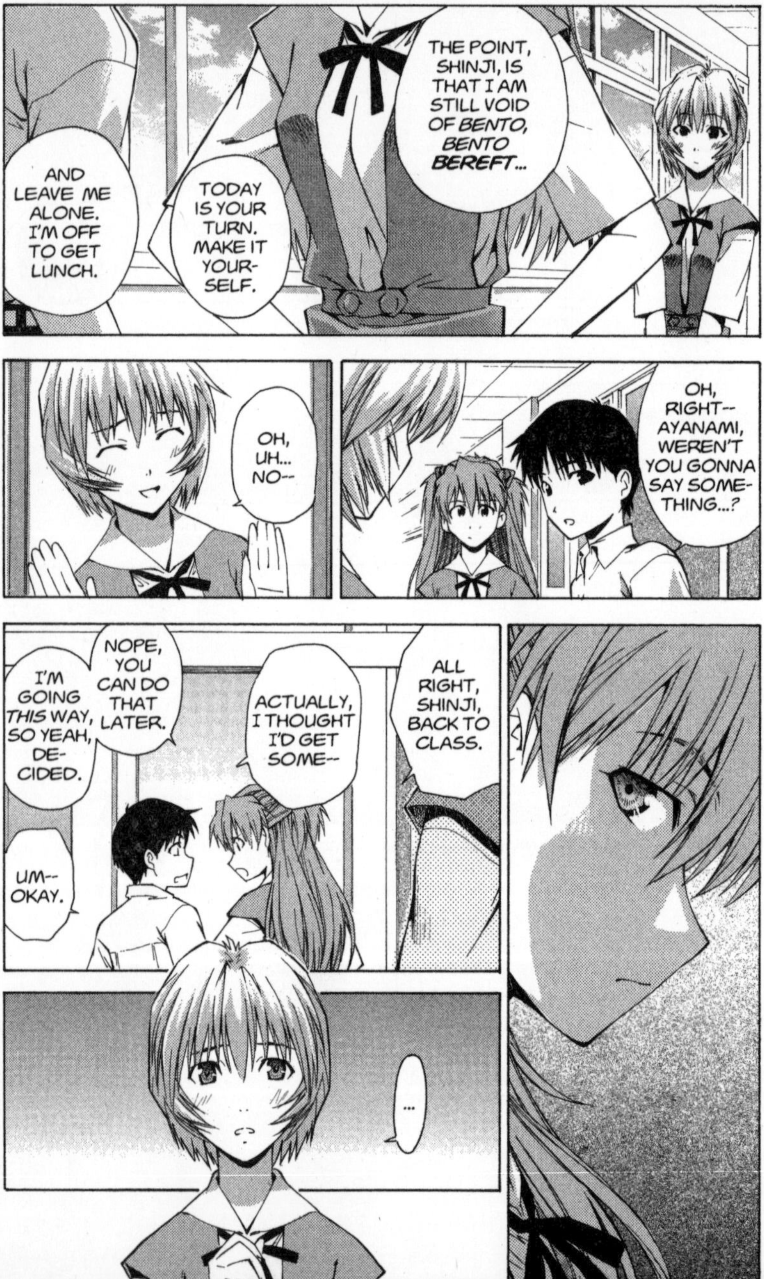
THE POINT, SHINJI, IS THAT I AM STILL VOID OF *BENTO*, *BENTO* ***BEREFT***...
TODAY IS YOUR TURN. MAKE IT YOURSELF.
AND LEAVE ME ALONE. I'M OFF TO GET LUNCH.
OH, RIGHT-- AYANAMI, WEREN'T YOU GONNA SAY SOMETHING...?
OH, UH... NO--
ALL RIGHT, SHINJI, BACK TO CLASS.
ACTUALLY, I THOUGHT I'D GET SOME--
NOPE, YOU CAN DO THAT LATER.
I'M GOING *THIS* WAY, SO YEAH, DECIDED.
UM-- OKAY.
...

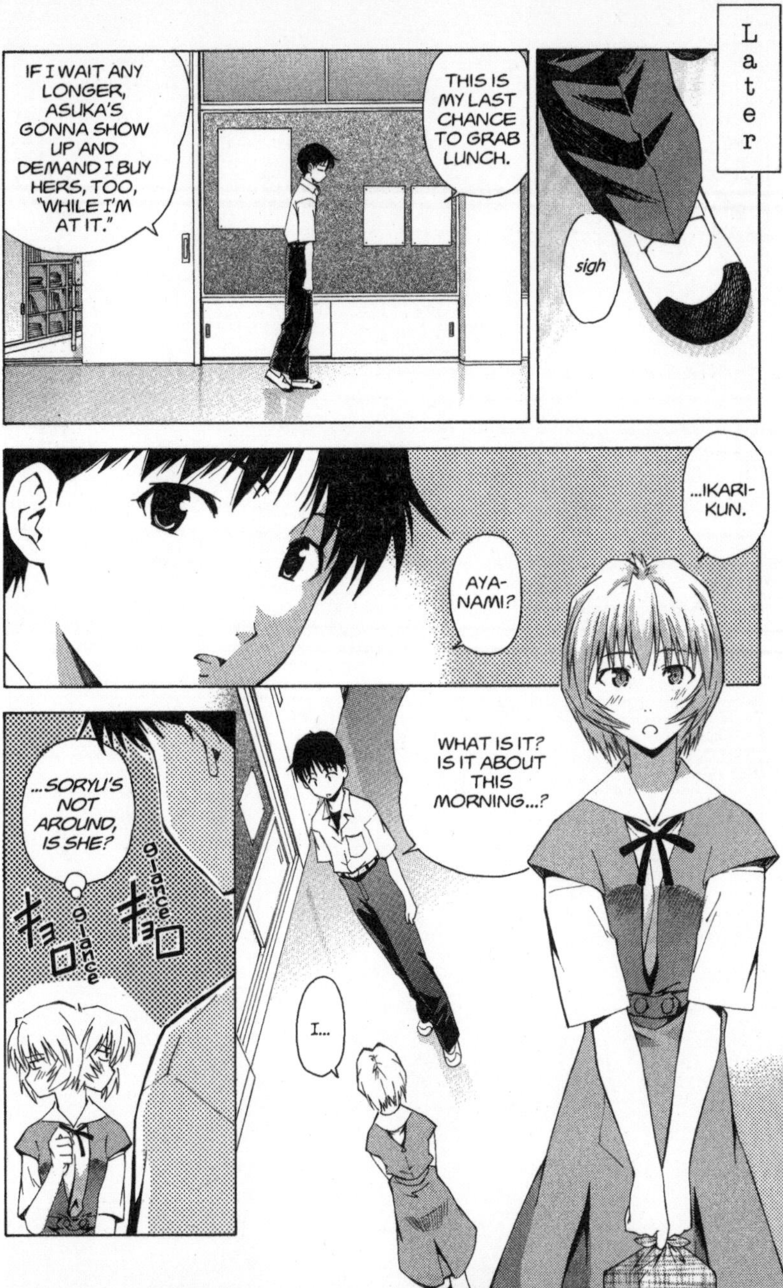
Later
sigh
THIS IS MY LAST CHANCE TO GRAB LUNCH.
IF I WAIT ANY LONGER, ASUKA'S GONNA SHOW UP AND DEMAND I BUY HERS, TOO, "WHILE I'M AT IT."
...IKARI-KUN.
AYA-NAMI?
WHAT IS IT? IS IT ABOUT THIS MORNING...?
I...
...SORYU'S NOT AROUND, IS SHE?
キョロ
glance
キョロ
glance

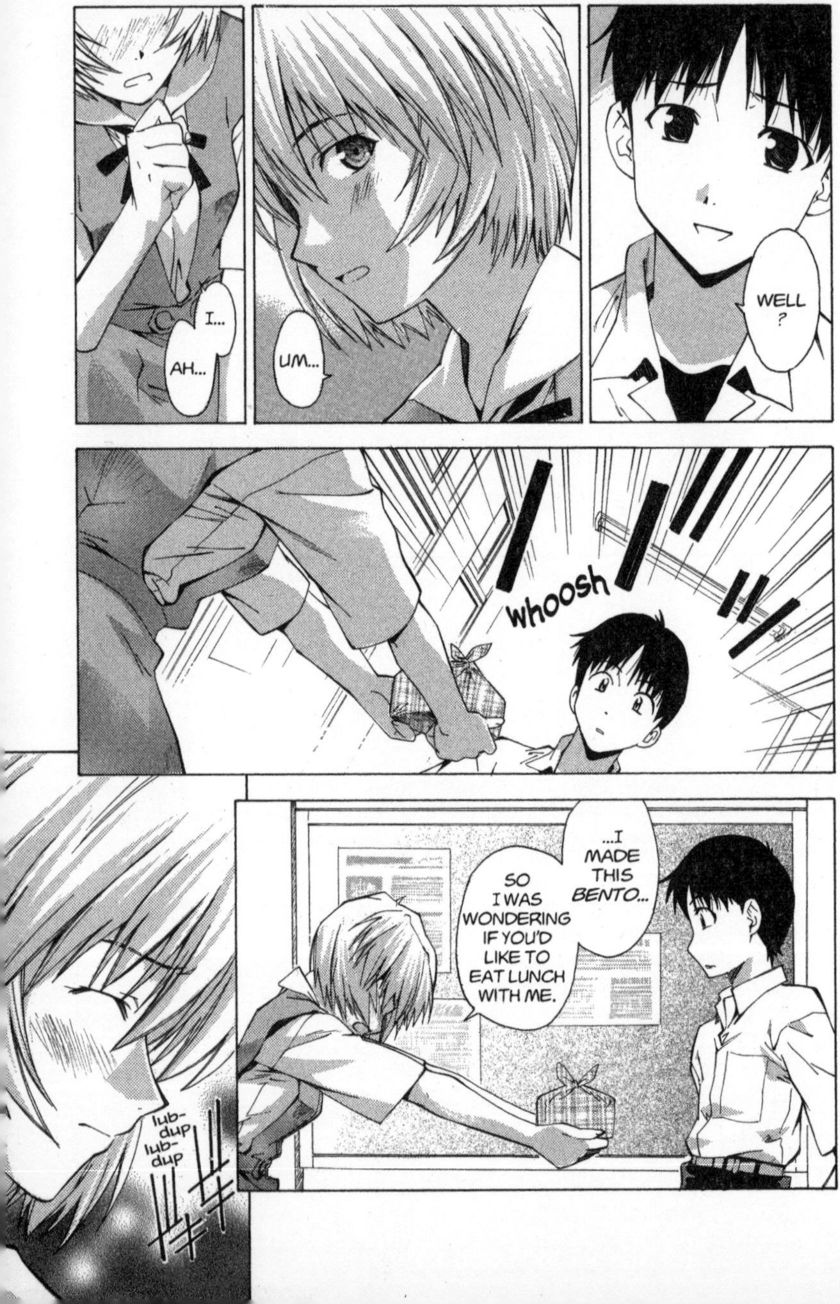
WELL ?
UM...
I...
AH...
whoosh
...I MADE THIS BENTO...
SO I WAS WONDERING IF YOU'D LIKE TO EAT LUNCH WITH ME.
lub-dup lub-dup

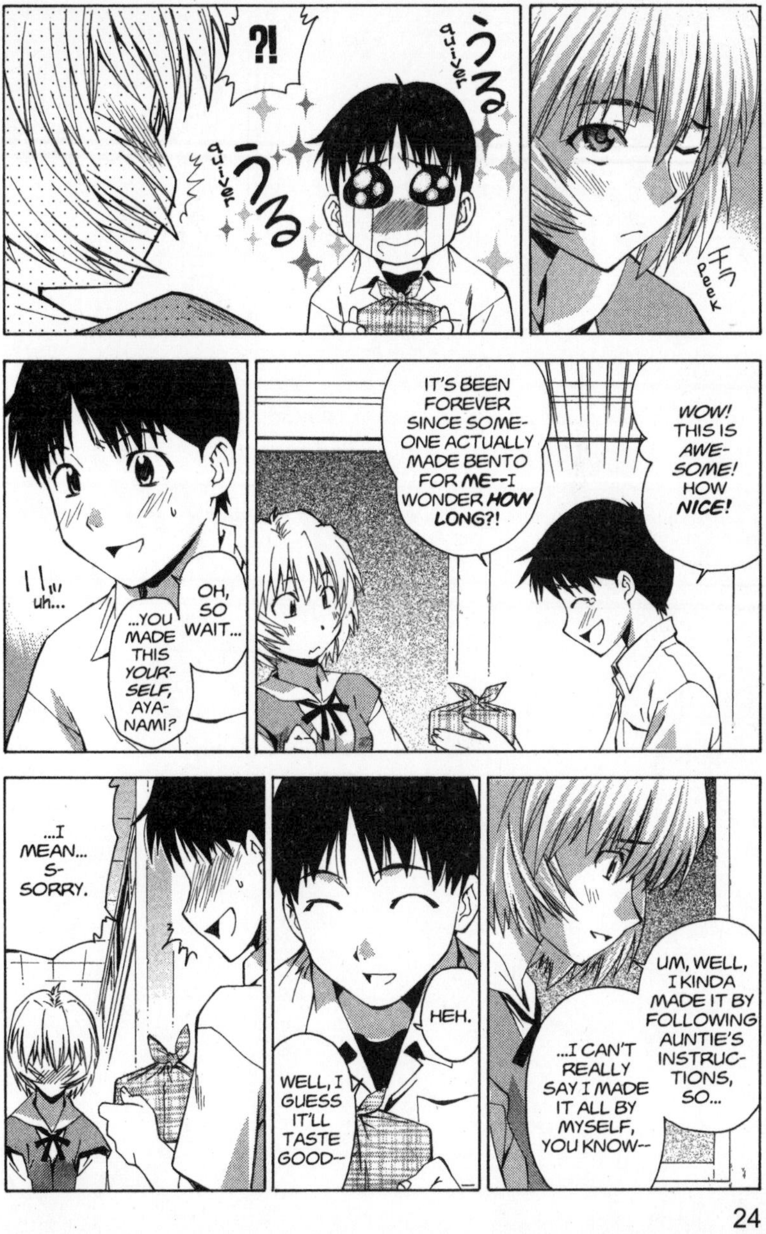
チラ
peek
うる
quiver
?!
うる
quiver
WOW! THIS IS AWESOME! HOW NICE!
IT'S BEEN FOREVER SINCE SOMEONE ACTUALLY MADE BENTO FOR ME--I WONDER HOW LONG?!
OH, SO WAIT...
...YOU MADE THIS YOURSELF, AYANAMI?
uh...
UM, WELL, I KINDA MADE IT BY FOLLOWING AUNTIE'S INSTRUCTIONS, SO...
...I CAN'T REALLY SAY I MADE IT ALL BY MYSELF, YOU KNOW--
HEH.
WELL, I GUESS IT'LL TASTE GOOD--
...I MEAN... S-SORRY.

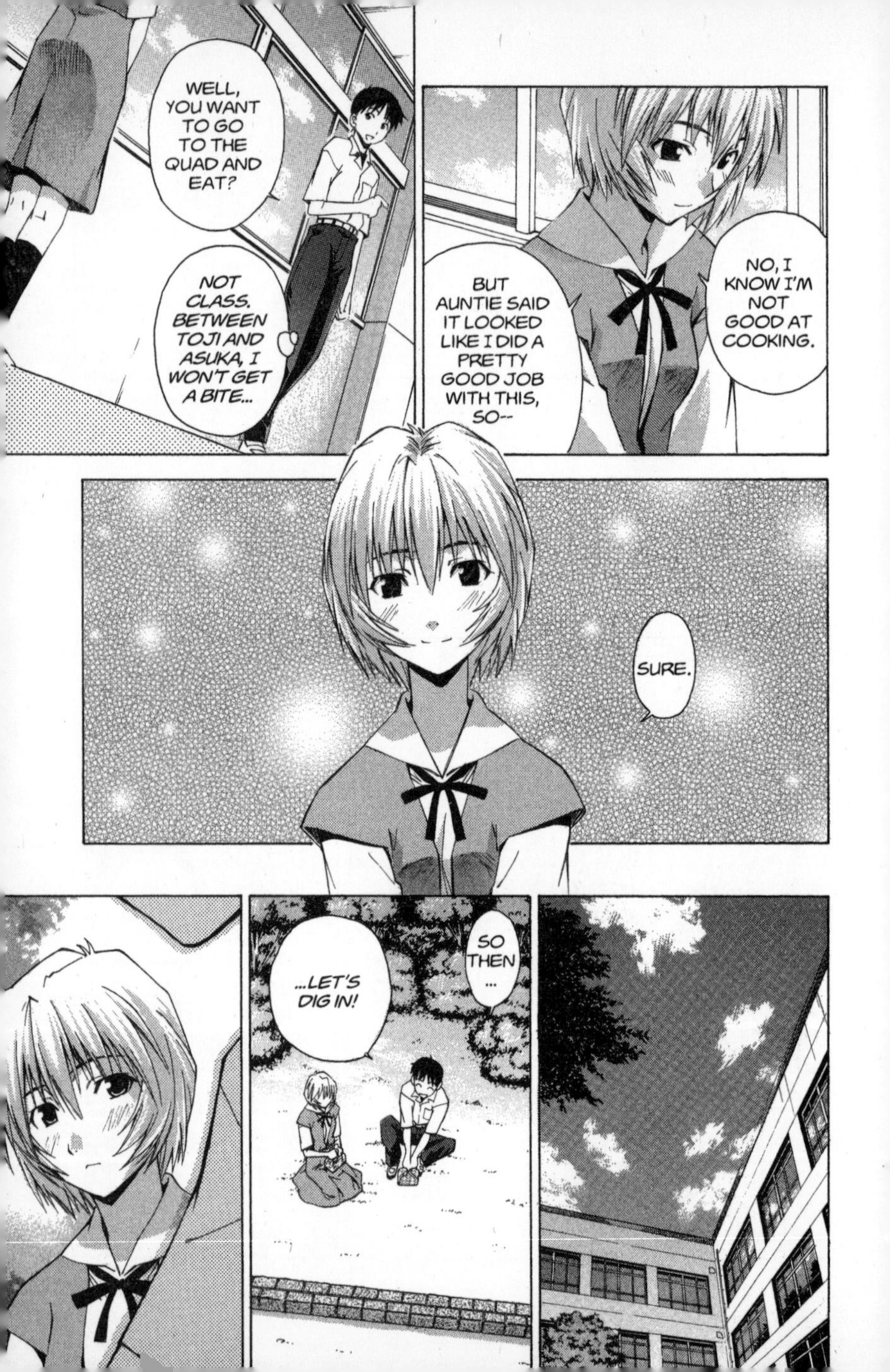
NO, I KNOW I'M NOT GOOD AT COOKING.
BUT AUNTIE SAID IT LOOKED LIKE I DID A PRETTY GOOD JOB WITH THIS, SO--
WELL, YOU WANT TO GO TO THE QUAD AND EAT?
NOT CLASS. BETWEEN TOJI AND ASUKA, I WON'T GET A BITE...
SURE.
SO THEN ...
...LET'S DIG IN!

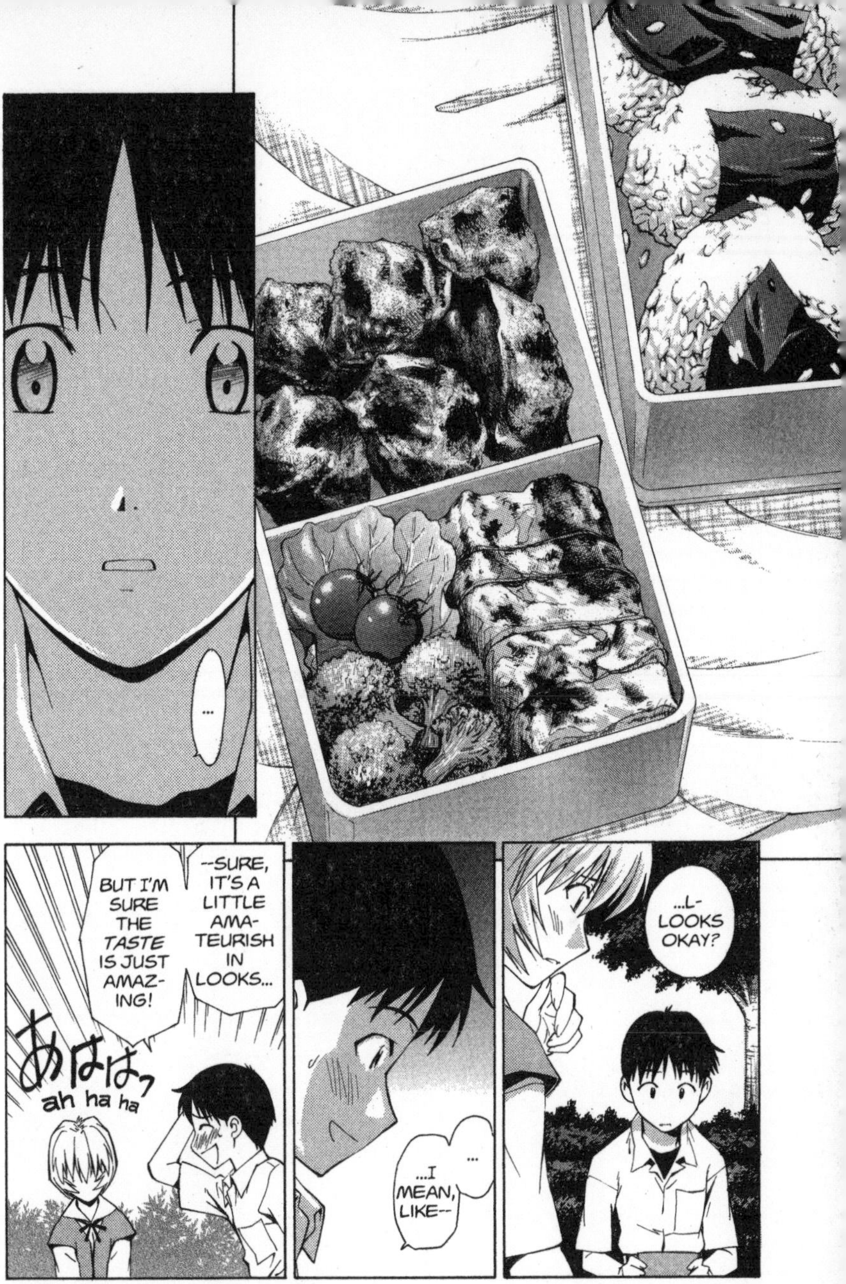
...
...L-LOOKS OKAY?
...
...I MEAN, LIKE--
--SURE, IT'S A LITTLE AMATEURISH IN LOOKS...
BUT I'M SURE THE *TASTE* IS JUST AMAZING!
あははっ
ah ha ha

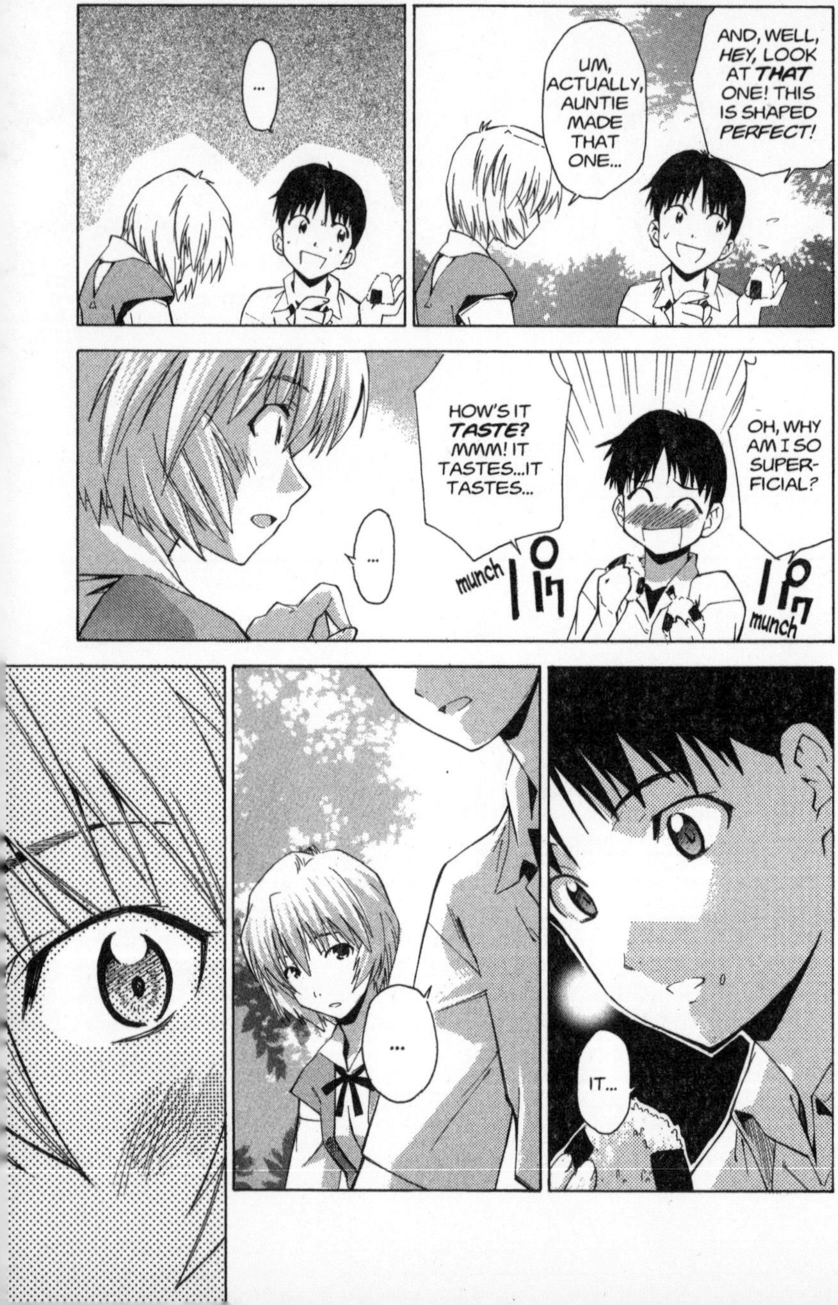
AND, WELL, HEY, LOOK AT THAT ONE! THIS IS SHAPED PERFECT!
UM, ACTUALLY, AUNTIE MADE THAT ONE...
...
OH, WHY AM I SO SUPER-FICIAL?
HOW'S IT TASTE? MMM! IT TASTES...IT TASTES...
munch
munch
...
IT...
...

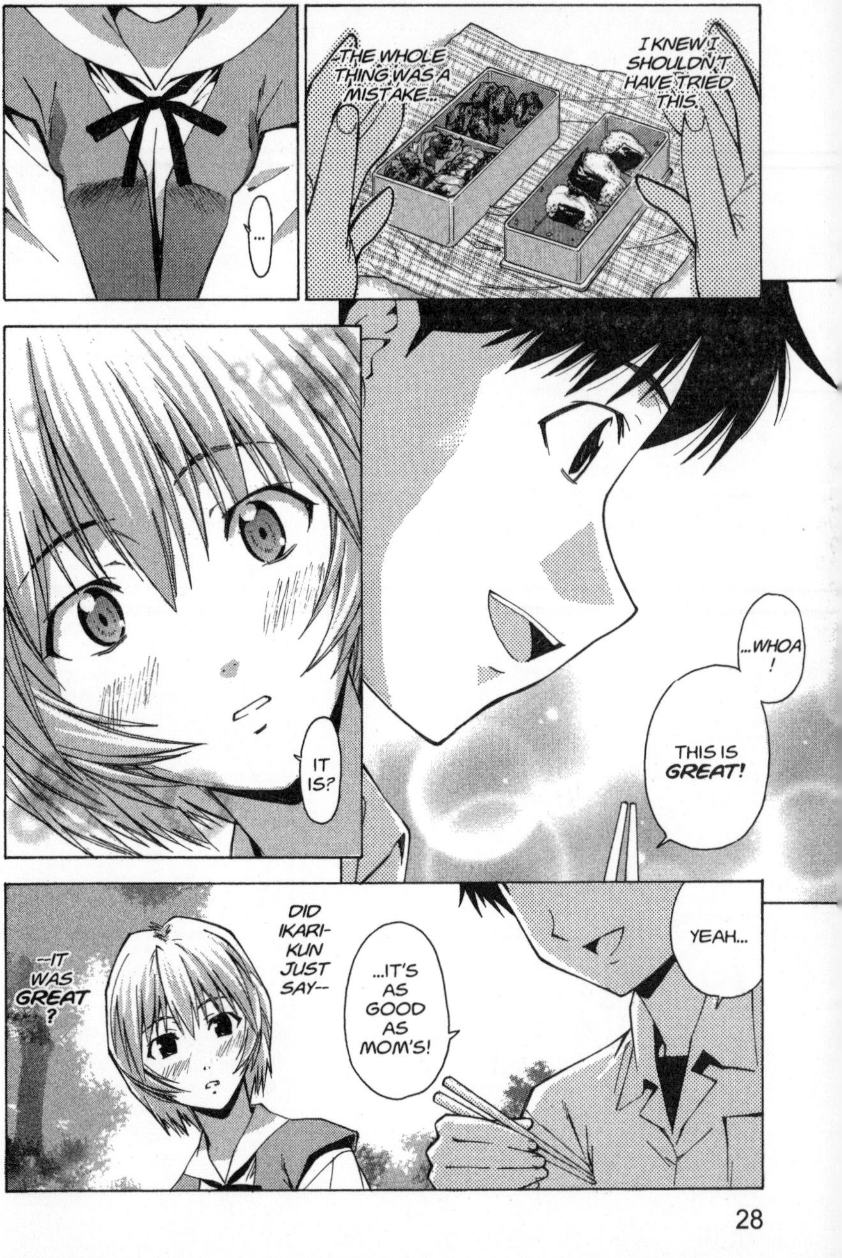
I KNEW I SHOULDN'T HAVE TRIED THIS.
THE WHOLE THING WAS A MISTAKE...
...
...WHOA!
THIS IS GREAT!
IT IS?
YEAH...
...IT'S AS GOOD AS MOM'S!
DID IKARI-KUN JUST SAY--
--IT WAS GREAT?

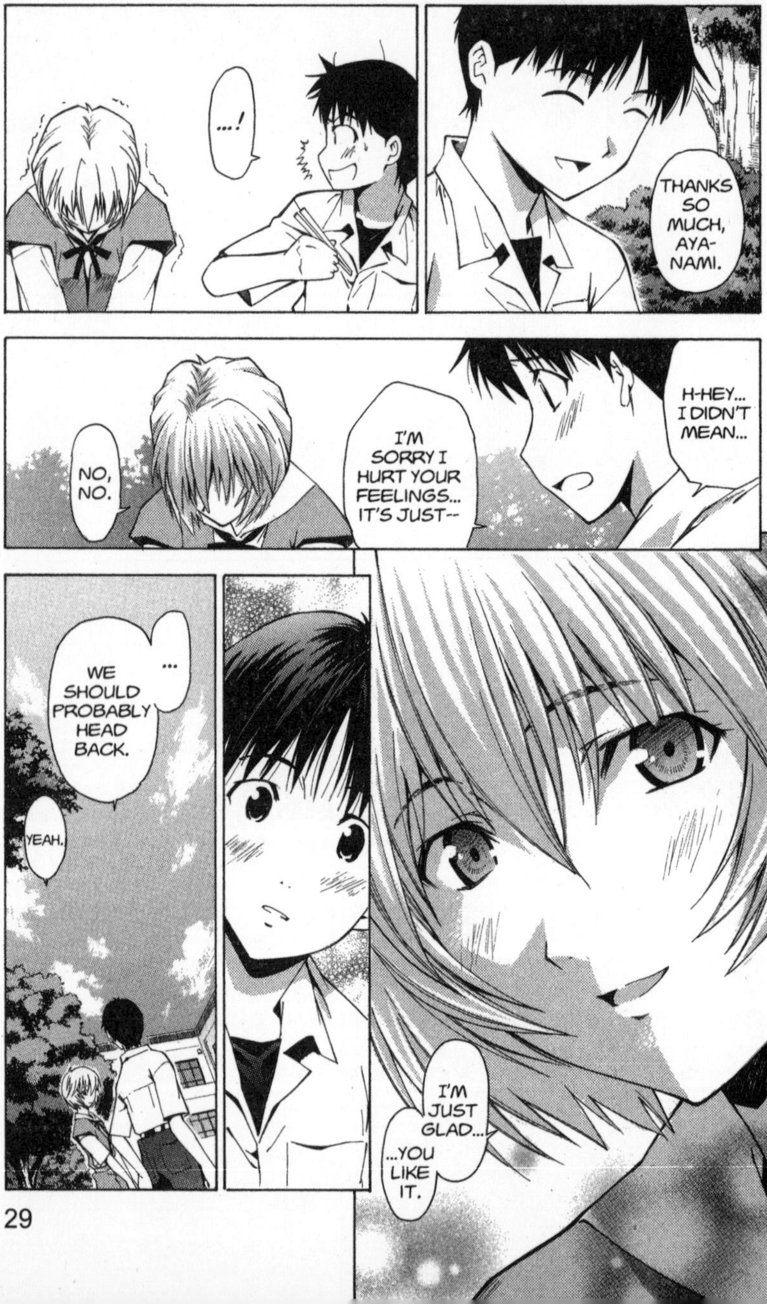
THANKS SO MUCH, AYA-NAMI.
...!
H-HEY... I DIDN'T MEAN...
I'M SORRY I HURT YOUR FEELINGS... IT'S JUST--
NO, NO.
I'M JUST GLAD...
...YOU LIKE IT.
...
WE SHOULD PROBABLY HEAD BACK.
YEAH.

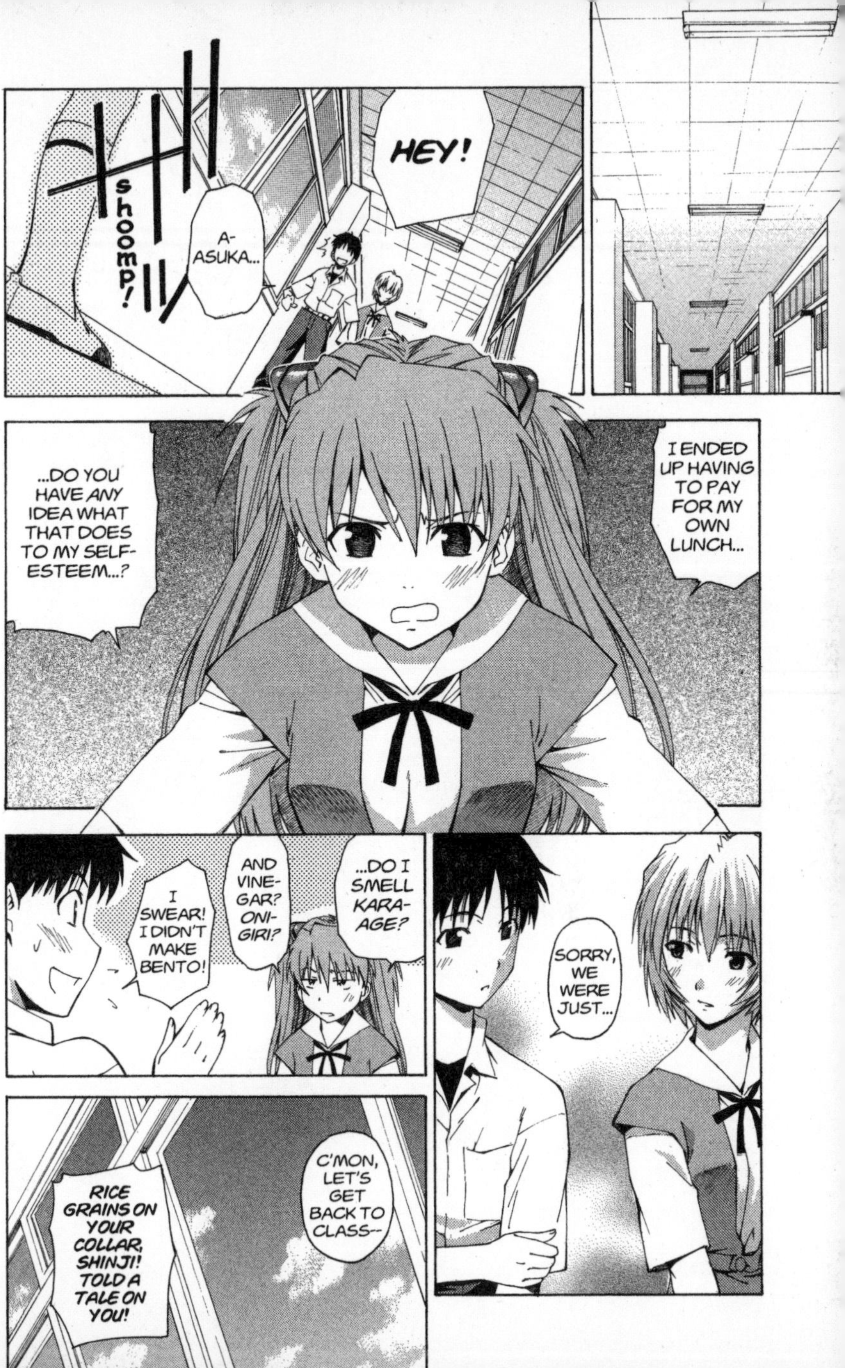
HEY!
A-ASUKA...
shoomp!
I ENDED UP HAVING TO PAY FOR MY OWN LUNCH...
...DO YOU HAVE ANY IDEA WHAT THAT DOES TO MY SELF-ESTEEM...?
SORRY, WE WERE JUST...
...DO I SMELL KARA-AGE?
AND VINEGAR? ONI-GIRI?
I SWEAR! I DIDN'T MAKE BENTO!
C'MON, LET'S GET BACK TO CLASS--
RICE GRAINS ON YOUR COLLAR, SHINJI! TOLD A TALE ON YOU!

STAGE 29

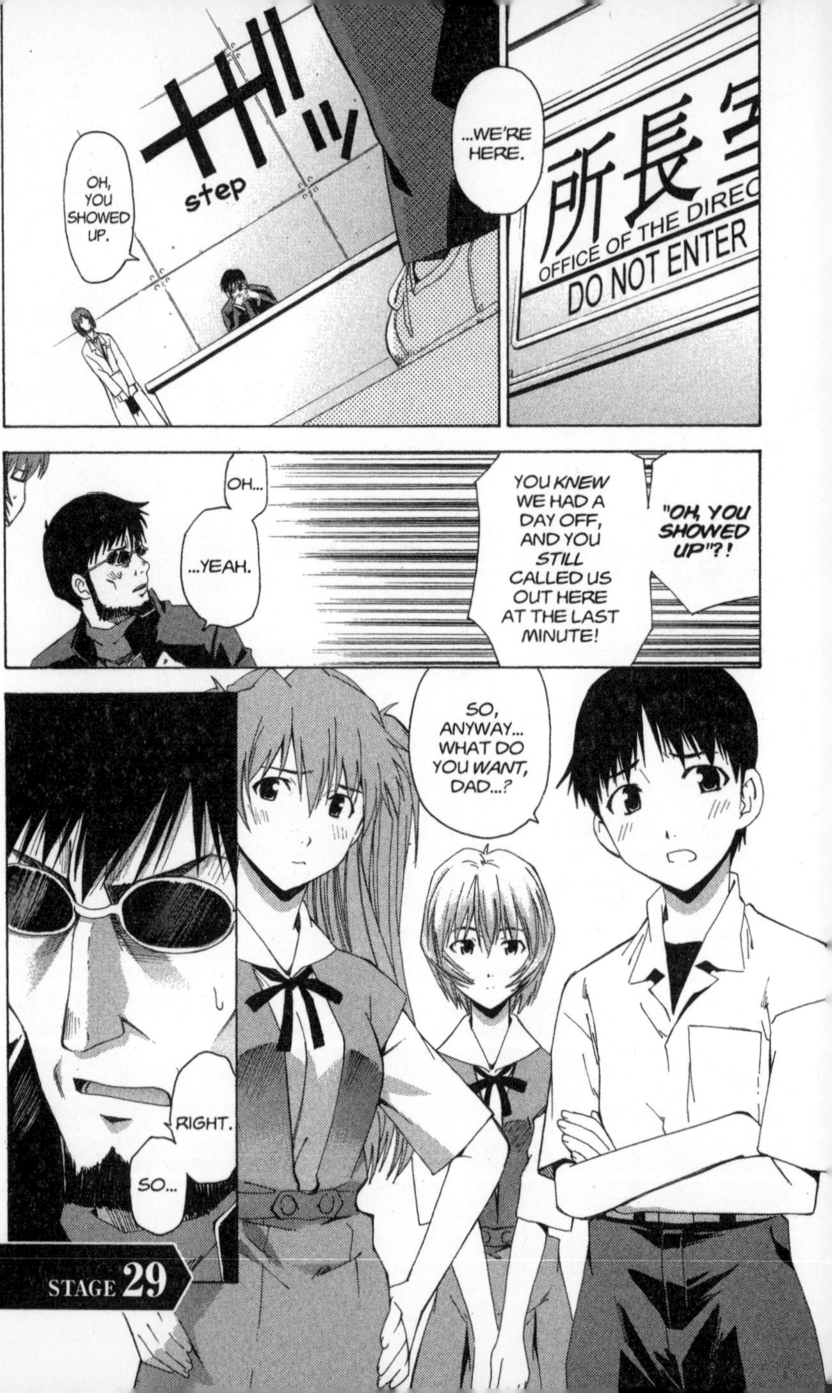
所長室
OFFICE OF THE DIREC
DO NOT ENTER
...WE'RE HERE.
ガッ
step
OH, YOU SHOWED UP.
"OH, YOU SHOWED UP"?!
YOU KNEW WE HAD A DAY OFF, AND YOU STILL CALLED US OUT HERE AT THE LAST MINUTE!
OH...
...YEAH.
SO, ANYWAY... WHAT DO YOU WANT, DAD...?
RIGHT.
SO...

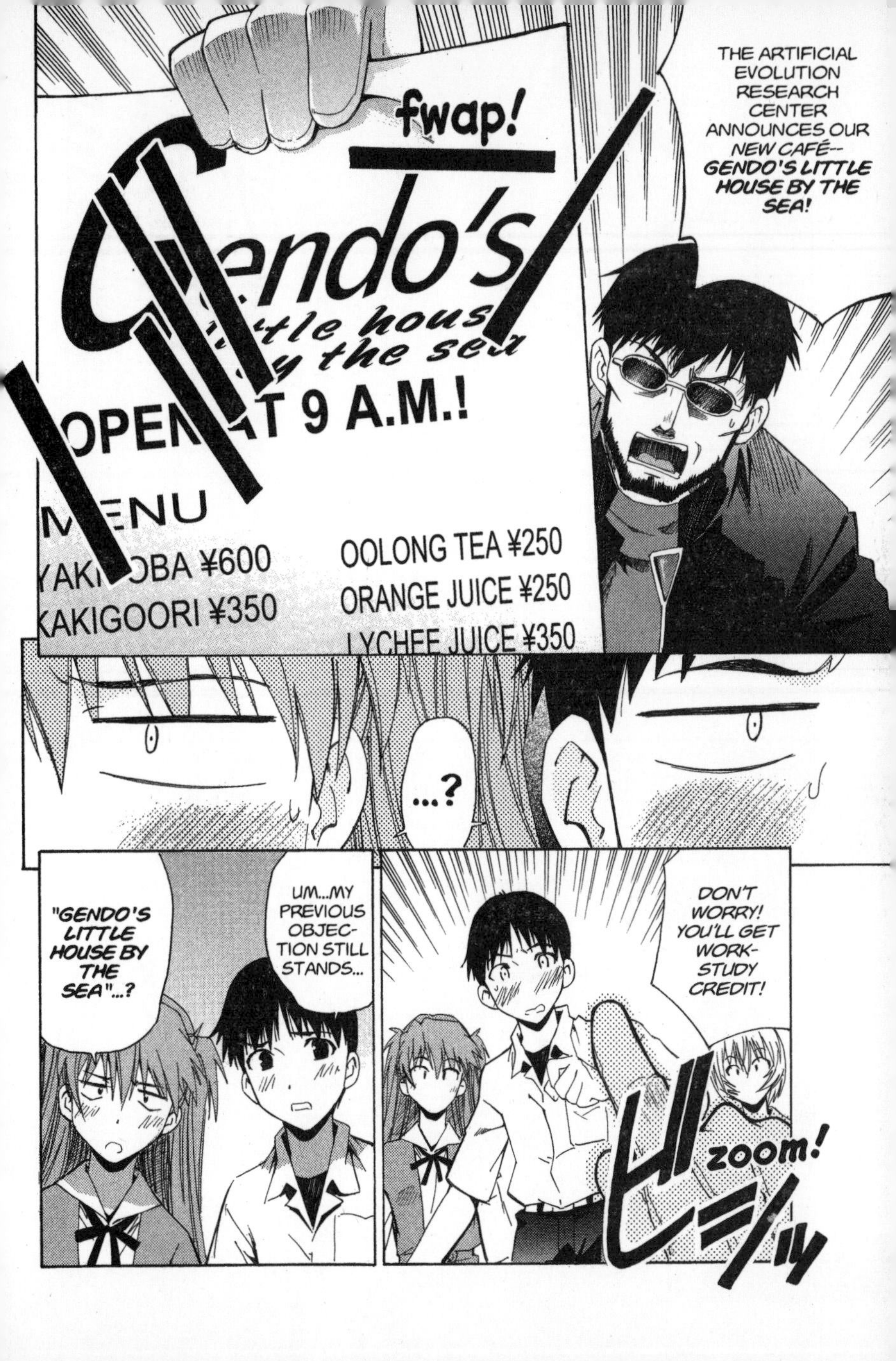
THE ARTIFICIAL EVOLUTION RESEARCH CENTER ANNOUNCES OUR NEW CAFÉ-- GENDO'S LITTLE HOUSE BY THE SEA!
fwap!
endo's
ttle hous
y the sea
OPEN AT 9 A.M.!
MENU
YAKI OBA ¥600
KAKIGOORI ¥350
OOLONG TEA ¥250
ORANGE JUICE ¥250
LYCHEE JUICE ¥350
...?
DON'T WORRY! YOU'LL GET WORK-STUDY CREDIT!
zoom!
UM...MY PREVIOUS OBJECTION STILL STANDS...
"GENDO'S LITTLE HOUSE BY THE SEA"...?

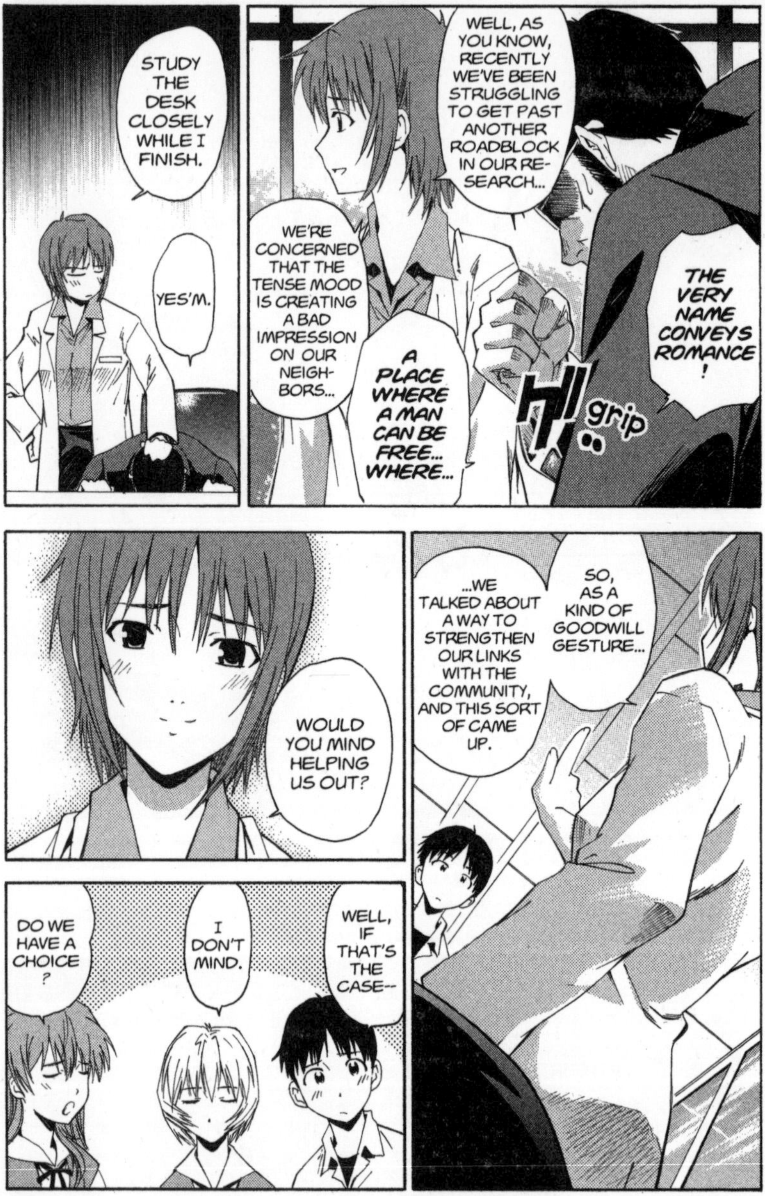
WELL, AS YOU KNOW, RECENTLY WE'VE BEEN STRUGGLING TO GET PAST ANOTHER ROADBLOCK IN OUR RE-SEARCH...
WE'RE CONCERNED THAT THE TENSE MOOD IS CREATING A BAD IMPRESSION ON OUR NEIGH-BORS...
THE VERY NAME CONVEYS ROMANCE!
A PLACE WHERE A MAN CAN BE FREE... WHERE...
grip
STUDY THE DESK CLOSELY WHILE I FINISH.
YES'M.
SO, AS A KIND OF GOODWILL GESTURE...
...WE TALKED ABOUT A WAY TO STRENGTHEN OUR LINKS WITH THE COMMUNITY, AND THIS SORT OF CAME UP.
WOULD YOU MIND HELPING US OUT?
WELL, IF THAT'S THE CASE--
I DON'T MIND.
DO WE HAVE A CHOICE?

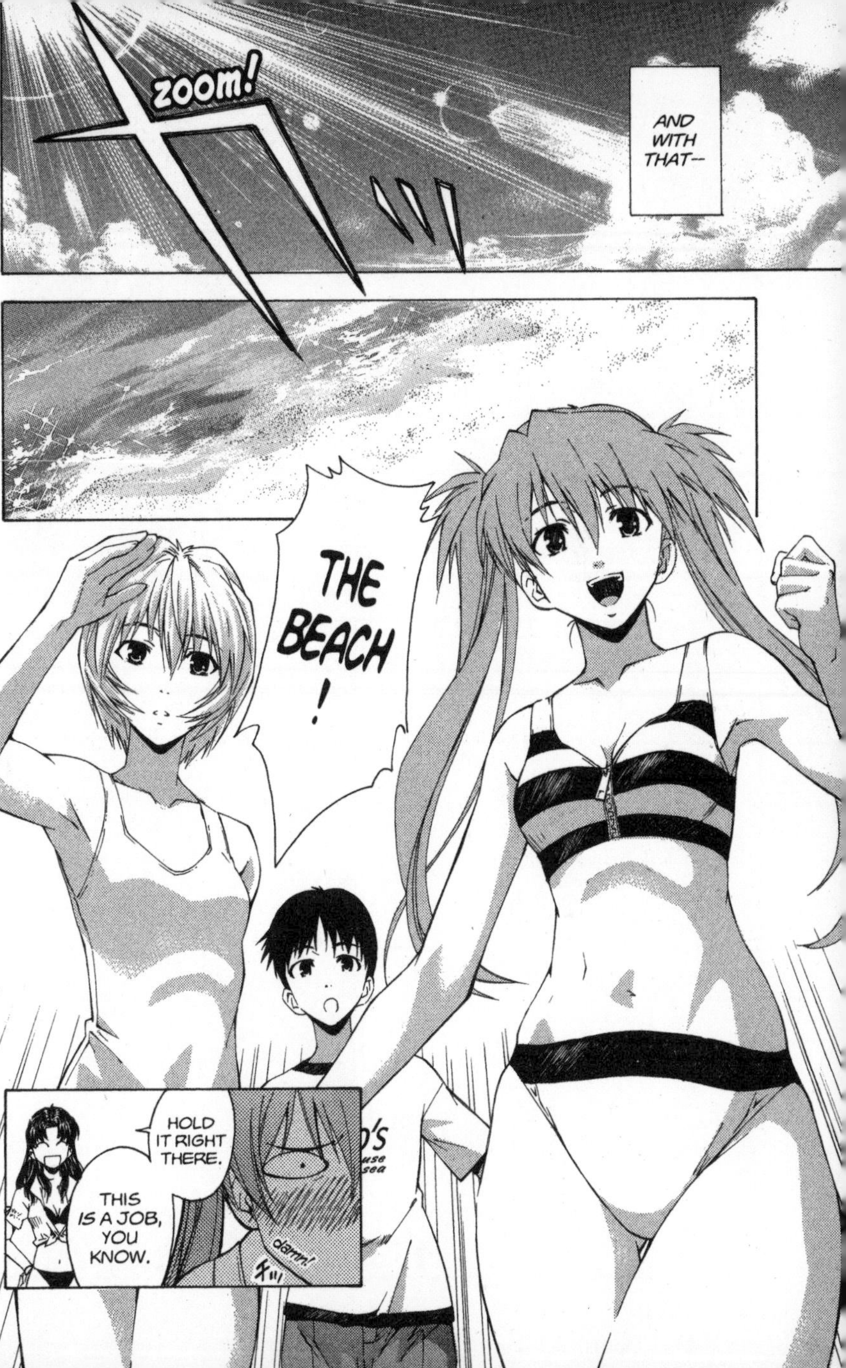
AND WITH THAT--
zoom!
THE BEACH!
HOLD IT RIGHT THERE.
THIS IS A JOB, YOU KNOW.
damn!
チッ

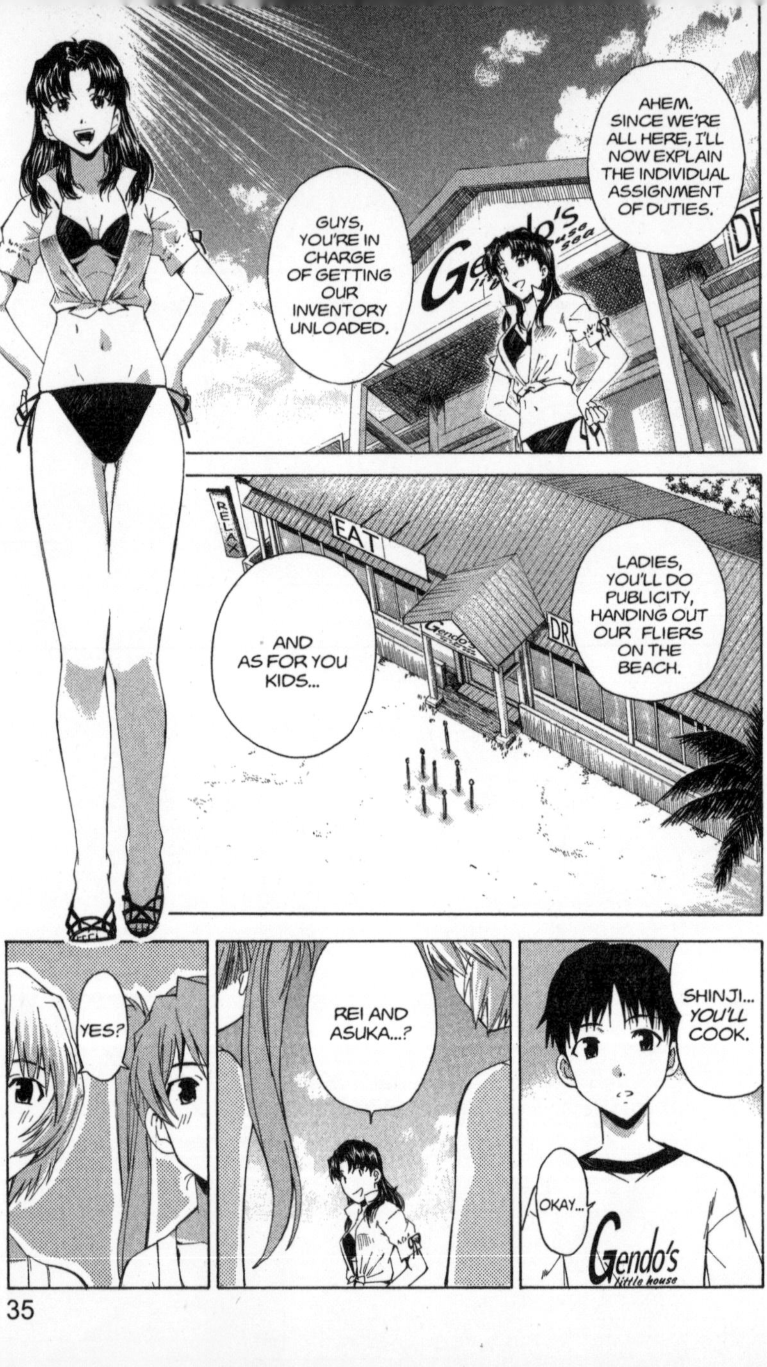
AHEM. SINCE WE'RE ALL HERE, I'LL NOW EXPLAIN THE INDIVIDUAL ASSIGNMENT OF DUTIES.
GUYS, YOU'RE IN CHARGE OF GETTING OUR INVENTORY UNLOADED.
LADIES, YOU'LL DO PUBLICITY, HANDING OUT OUR FLIERS ON THE BEACH.
AND AS FOR YOU KIDS...
RELAX
EAT
SHINJI... YOU'LL COOK.
OKAY...
Gendo's
little house
REI AND ASUKA...?
YES?

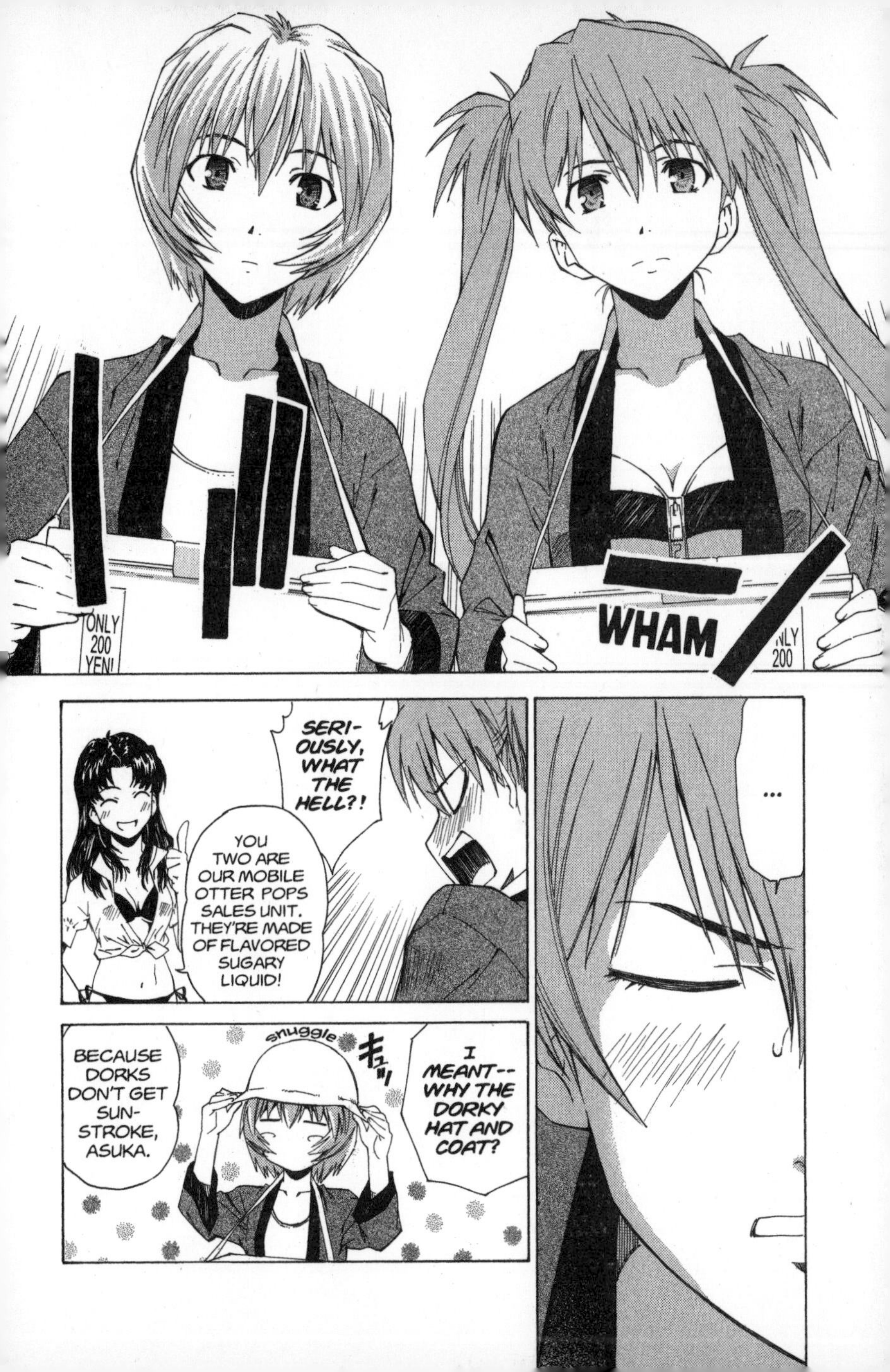
ONLY 200 YEN!
WHAM
NLY 200
...
SERI-OUSLY, WHAT THE HELL?!
YOU TWO ARE OUR MOBILE OTTER POPS SALES UNIT. THEY'RE MADE OF FLAVORED SUGARY LIQUID!
I MEANT-- WHY THE DORKY HAT AND COAT?
snuggle
BECAUSE DORKS DON'T GET SUN-STROKE, ASUKA.

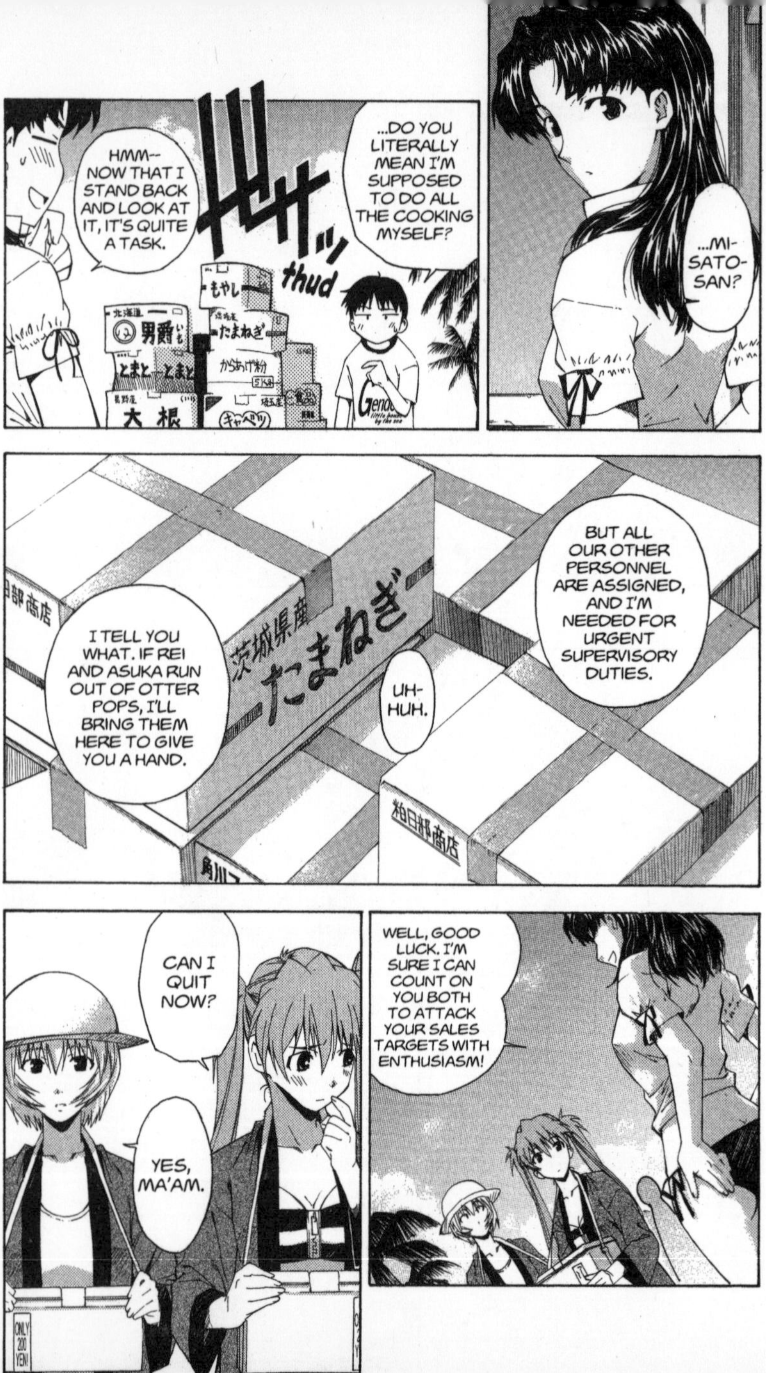
...MI-SATO-SAN?
...DO YOU LITERALLY MEAN I'M SUPPOSED TO DO ALL THE COOKING MYSELF?
thud
HMM-- NOW THAT I STAND BACK AND LOOK AT IT, IT'S QUITE A TASK.
BUT ALL OUR OTHER PERSONNEL ARE ASSIGNED, AND I'M NEEDED FOR URGENT SUPERVISORY DUTIES.
UH-HUH.
茨城県産 たまねぎ
I TELL YOU WHAT. IF REI AND ASUKA RUN OUT OF OTTER POPS, I'LL BRING THEM HERE TO GIVE YOU A HAND.
WELL, GOOD LUCK. I'M SURE I CAN COUNT ON YOU BOTH TO ATTACK YOUR SALES TARGETS WITH ENTHUSIASM!
CAN I QUIT NOW?
YES, MA'AM.
ONLY 200 YEN!

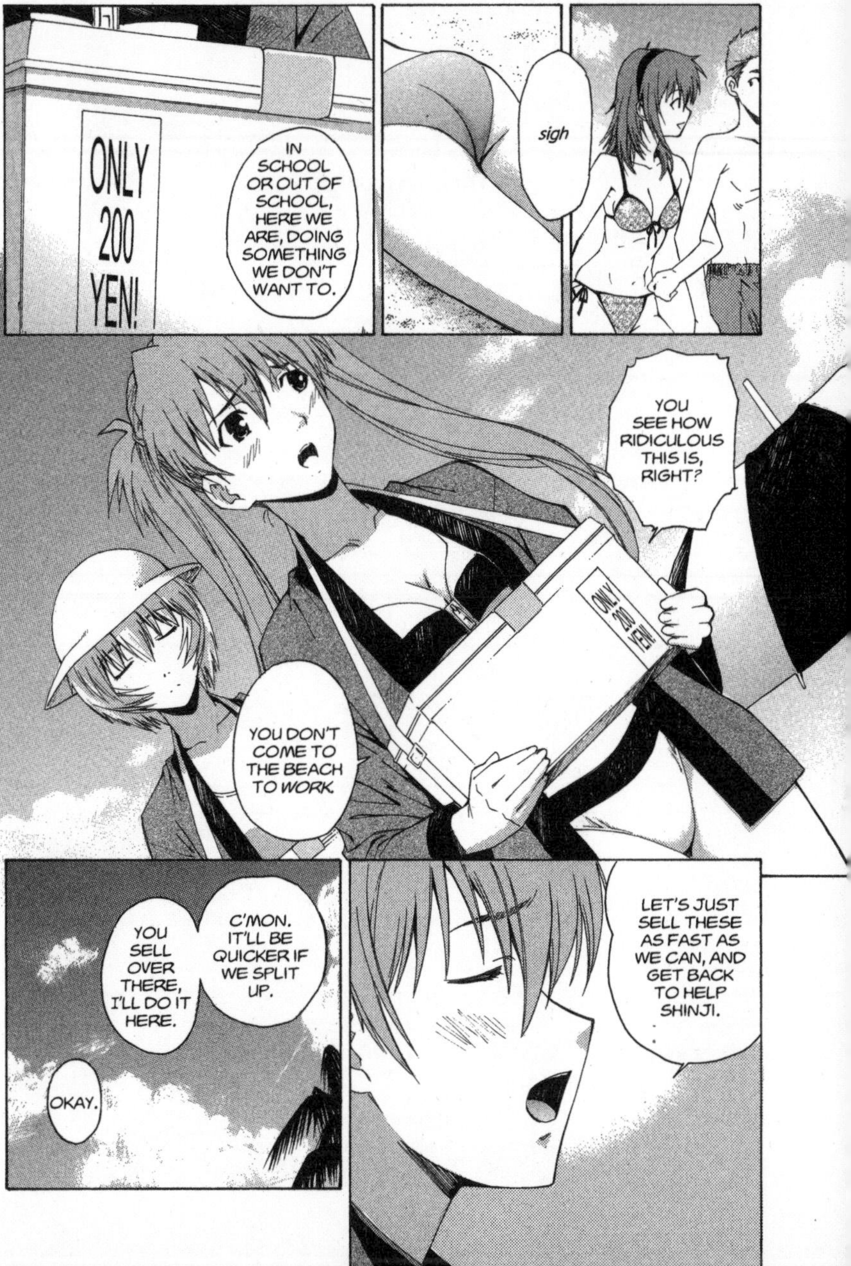
sigh
ONLY 200 YEN!
IN SCHOOL OR OUT OF SCHOOL, HERE WE ARE, DOING SOMETHING WE DON'T WANT TO.
YOU SEE HOW RIDICULOUS THIS IS, RIGHT?
ONLY 200 YEN!
YOU DON'T COME TO THE BEACH TO *WORK.*
LET'S JUST SELL THESE AS FAST AS WE CAN, AND GET BACK TO HELP SHINJI.
C'MON. IT'LL BE QUICKER IF WE SPLIT UP.
YOU SELL OVER THERE, I'LL DO IT HERE.
OKAY.

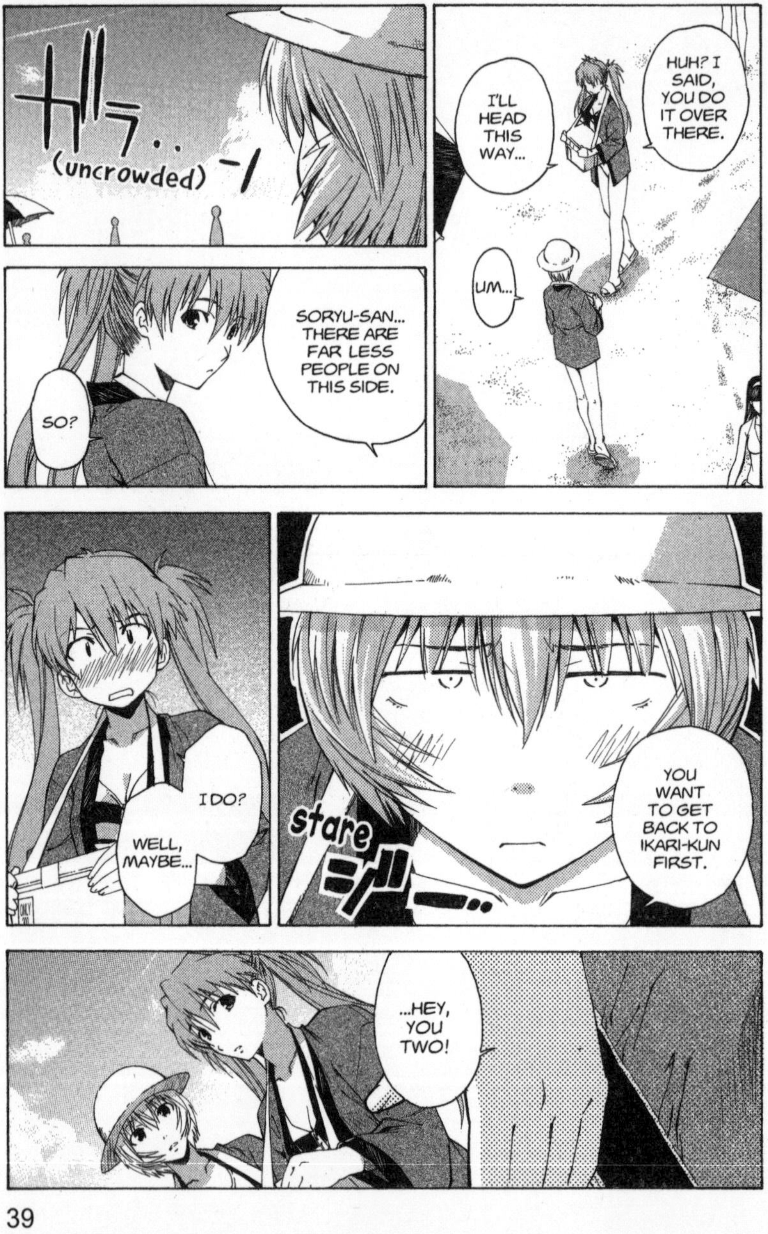
HUH? I SAID, YOU DO IT OVER THERE.
I'LL HEAD THIS WAY...
UM...
(uncrowded)
SORYU-SAN... THERE ARE FAR LESS PEOPLE ON THIS SIDE.
SO?
YOU WANT TO GET BACK TO IKARI-KUN FIRST.
stare
I DO?
WELL, MAYBE...
...HEY, YOU TWO!

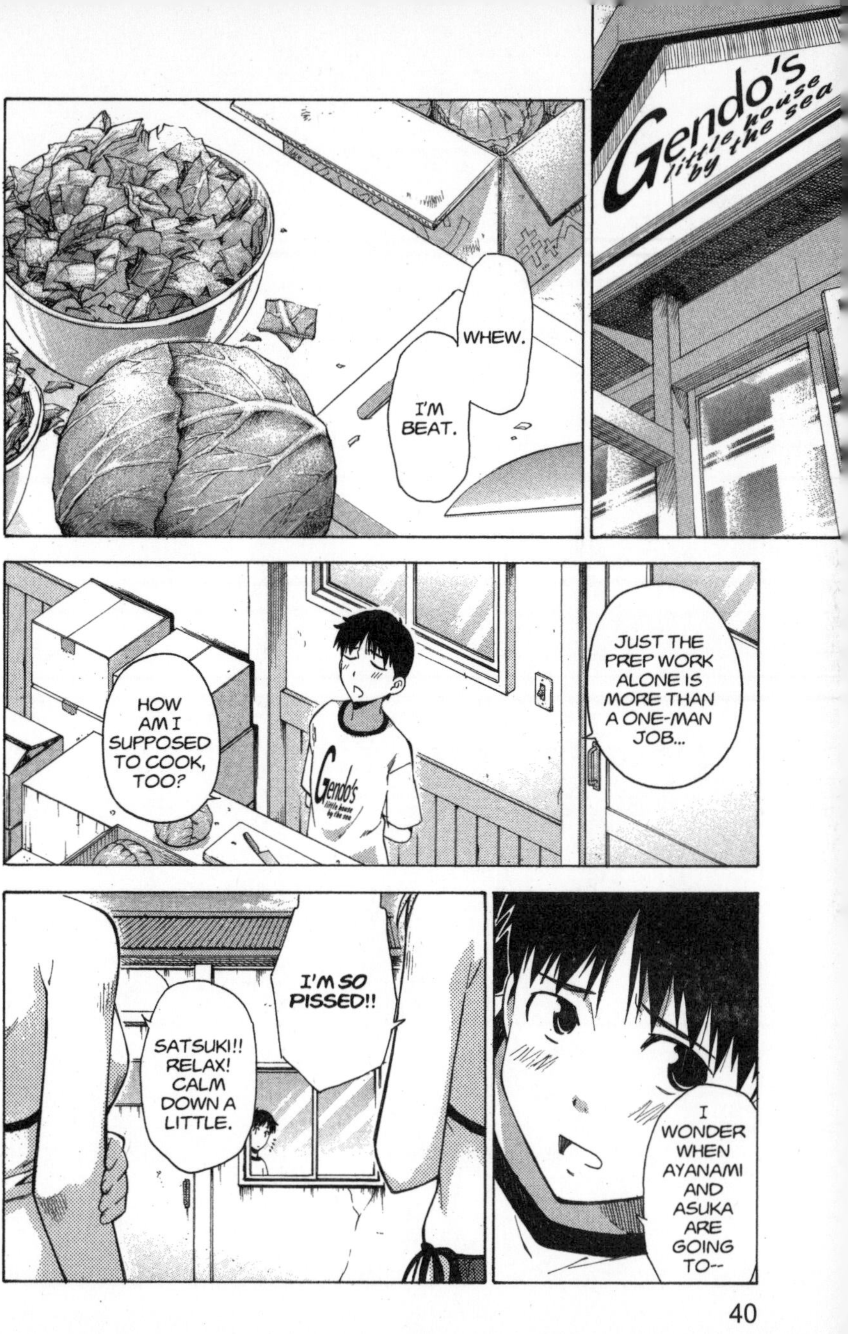
Gendo's
little house by the sea
WHEW.
I'M BEAT.
JUST THE PREP WORK ALONE IS MORE THAN A ONE-MAN JOB...
HOW AM I SUPPOSED TO COOK, TOO?
I WONDER WHEN AYANAMI AND ASUKA ARE GOING TO--
I'M SO PISSED!!
SATSUKI!! RELAX! CALM DOWN A LITTLE.

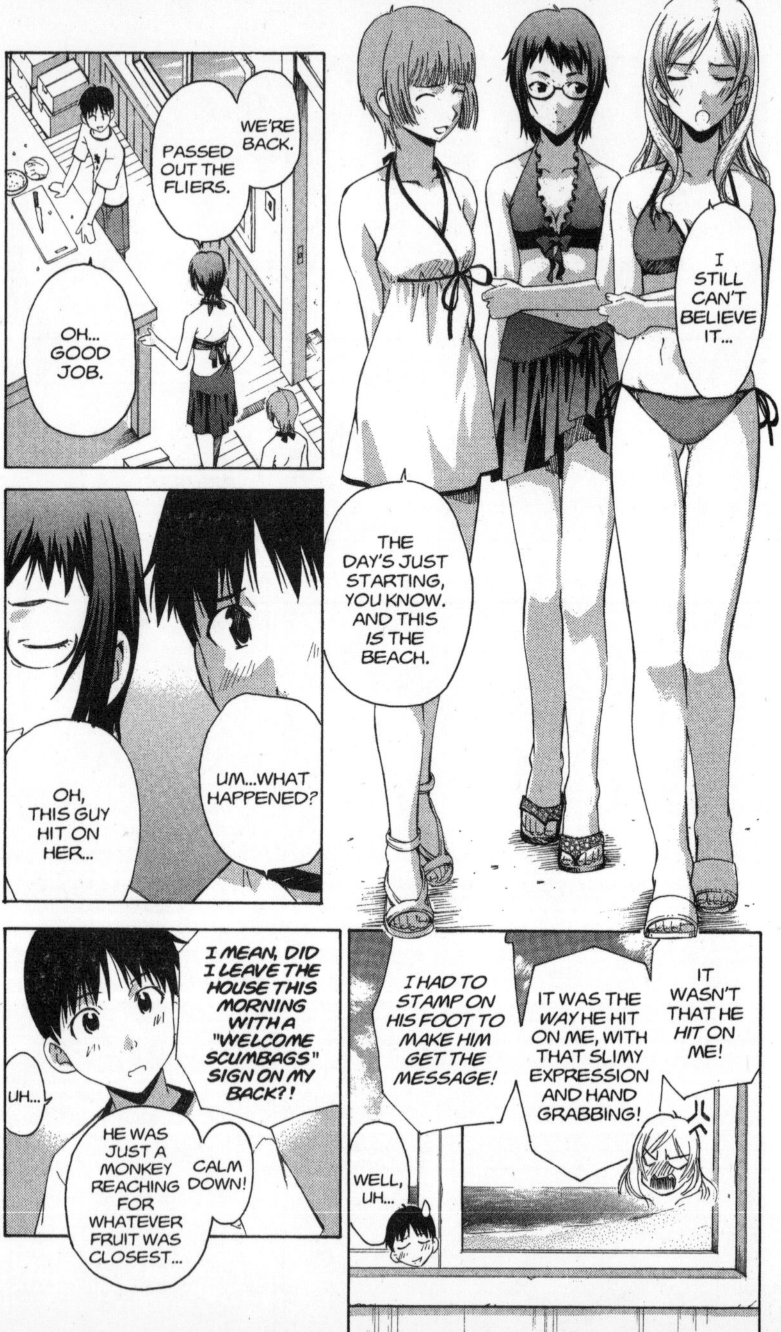
I STILL CAN'T BELIEVE IT...
THE DAY'S JUST STARTING, YOU KNOW. AND THIS *IS* THE BEACH.
WE'RE BACK.
PASSED OUT THE FLIERS.
OH... GOOD JOB.
UM...WHAT HAPPENED?
OH, THIS GUY HIT ON HER...
IT WASN'T THAT HE *HIT ON* ME!
IT WAS THE *WAY* HE HIT ON ME, WITH THAT SLIMY EXPRESSION AND HAND GRABBING!
I HAD TO STAMP ON HIS FOOT TO MAKE HIM GET THE MESSAGE!
WELL, UH...
I MEAN, DID I LEAVE THE HOUSE THIS MORNING WITH A "WELCOME SCUMBAGS" SIGN ON MY BACK?!
UH...
CALM DOWN!
HE WAS JUST A MONKEY REACHING FOR WHATEVER FRUIT WAS CLOSEST...

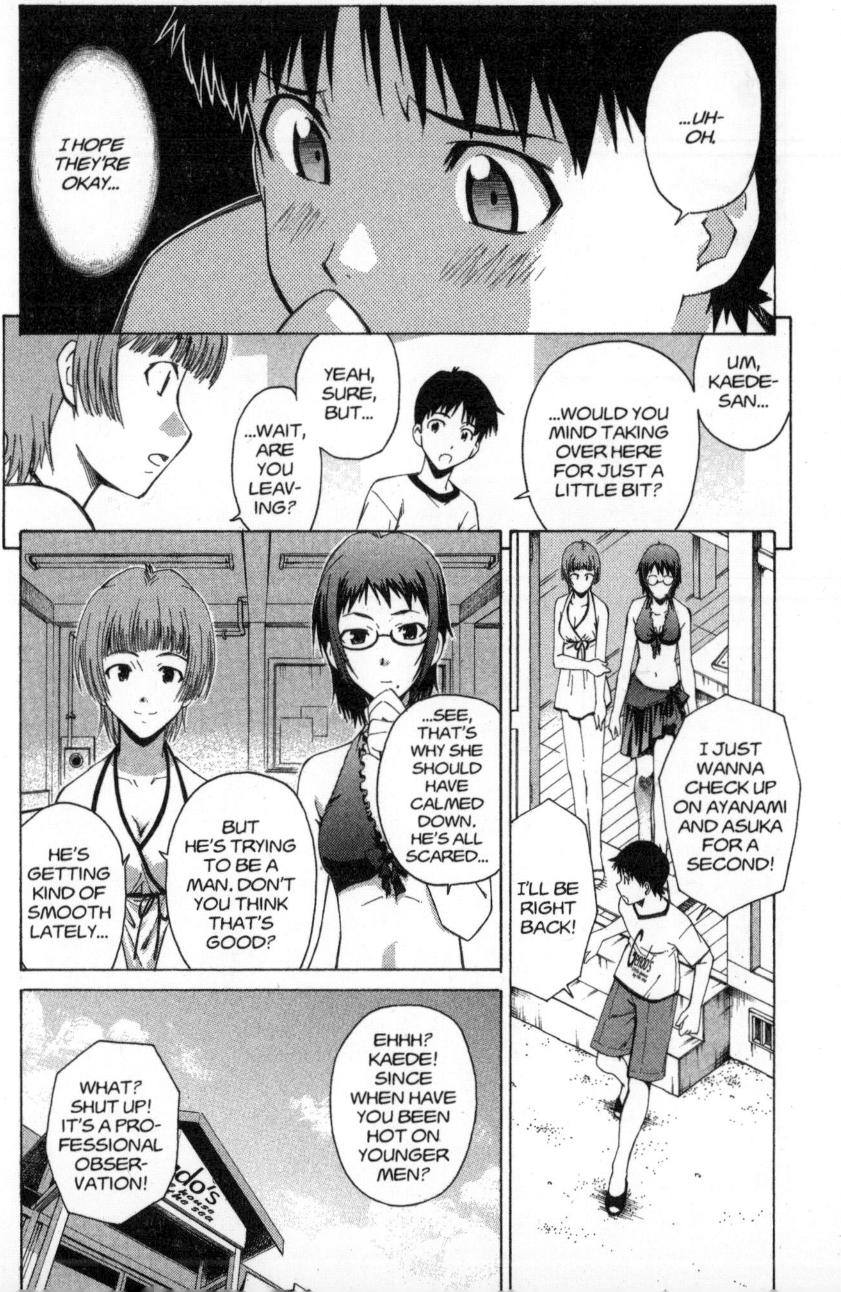
...UH-OH.
I HOPE THEY'RE OKAY...
UM, KAEDE-SAN...
...WOULD YOU MIND TAKING OVER HERE FOR JUST A LITTLE BIT?
YEAH, SURE, BUT...
...WAIT, ARE YOU LEAVING?
I JUST WANNA CHECK UP ON AYANAMI AND ASUKA FOR A SECOND!
I'LL BE RIGHT BACK!
...SEE, THAT'S WHY SHE SHOULD HAVE CALMED DOWN. HE'S ALL SCARED...
BUT HE'S TRYING TO BE A MAN. DON'T YOU THINK THAT'S GOOD?
HE'S GETTING KIND OF SMOOTH LATELY...
EHHH? KAEDE! SINCE WHEN HAVE YOU BEEN HOT ON YOUNGER MEN?
WHAT? SHUT UP! IT'S A PRO-FESSIONAL OBSER-VATION!

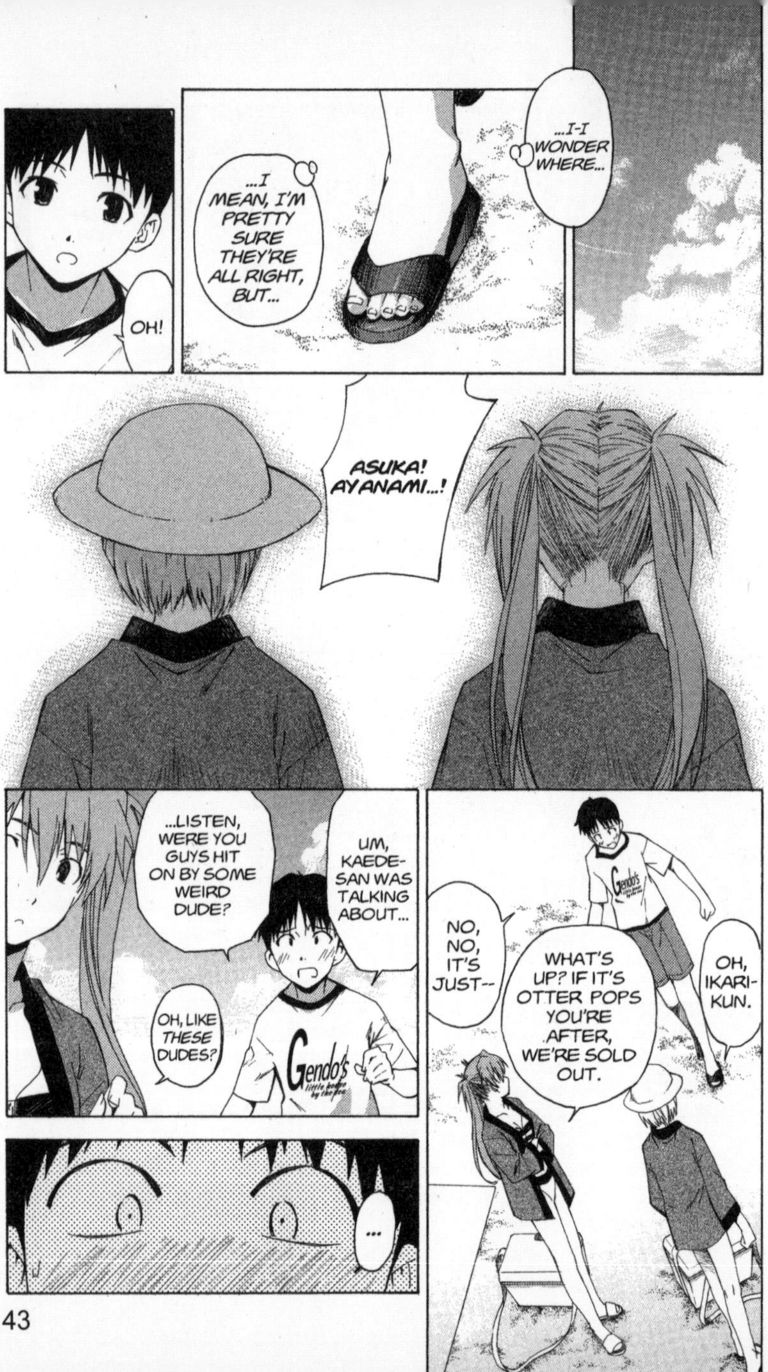

...I-I WONDER WHERE...
...I MEAN, I'M PRETTY SURE THEY'RE ALL RIGHT, BUT...
OH!
ASUKA! AYANAMI...!
OH, IKARI-KUN.
WHAT'S UP? IF IT'S OTTER POPS YOU'RE AFTER, WE'RE SOLD OUT.
NO, NO, IT'S JUST--
UM, KAEDE-SAN WAS TALKING ABOUT...
...LISTEN, WERE YOU GUYS HIT ON BY SOME WEIRD DUDE?
OH, LIKE THESE DUDES?
Gendo's
...

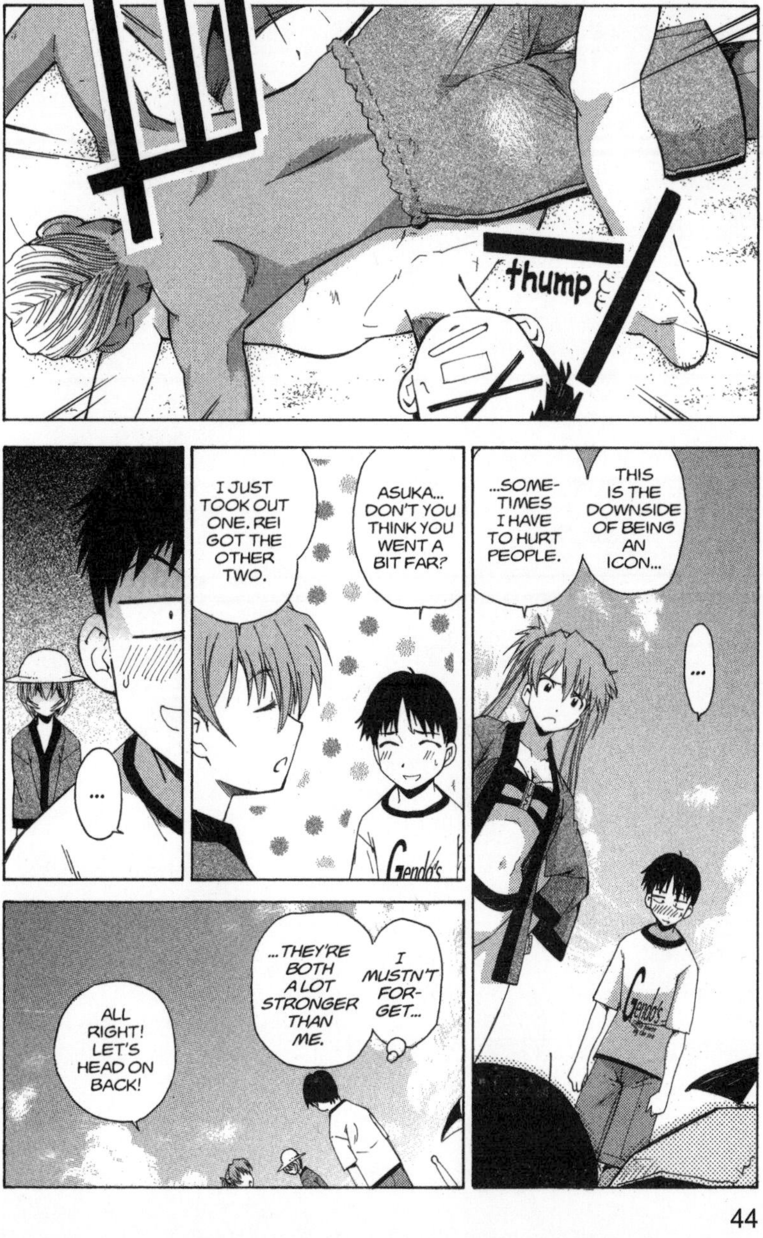
thump
THIS IS THE DOWNSIDE OF BEING AN ICON...
...SOME-TIMES I HAVE TO HURT PEOPLE.
...
Gendo's
ASUKA... DON'T YOU THINK YOU WENT A BIT FAR?
I JUST TOOK OUT ONE. REI GOT THE OTHER TWO.
Gendo's
...
I MUSTN'T FOR-GET...
...THEY'RE BOTH A LOT STRONGER THAN ME.
ALL RIGHT! LET'S HEAD ON BACK!

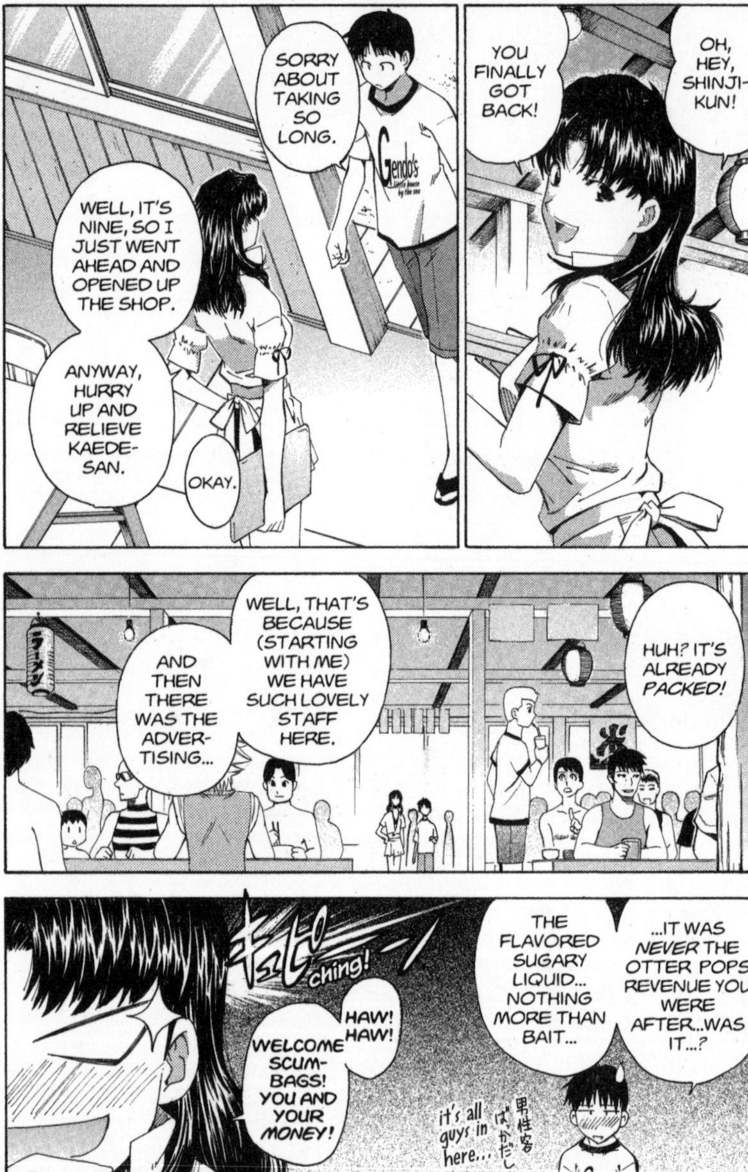
OH, HEY, SHINJI-KUN!
YOU FINALLY GOT BACK!
SORRY ABOUT TAKING SO LONG.
Gendo's Little house by the sea
WELL, IT'S NINE, SO I JUST WENT AHEAD AND OPENED UP THE SHOP.
ANYWAY, HURRY UP AND RELIEVE KAEDE-SAN.
OKAY.
HUH? IT'S ALREADY *PACKED!*
WELL, THAT'S BECAUSE (STARTING WITH ME) WE HAVE SUCH LOVELY STAFF HERE.
AND THEN THERE WAS THE ADVERTISING...
...IT WAS *NEVER* THE OTTER POPS REVENUE YOU WERE AFTER...WAS IT...?
THE FLAVORED SUGARY LIQUID... NOTHING MORE THAN BAIT...
男性客ばっかだし…
it's all guys in here...
ching!
HAW! HAW!
WELCOME SCUM-BAGS! YOU AND YOUR *MONEY!*
Gendo's

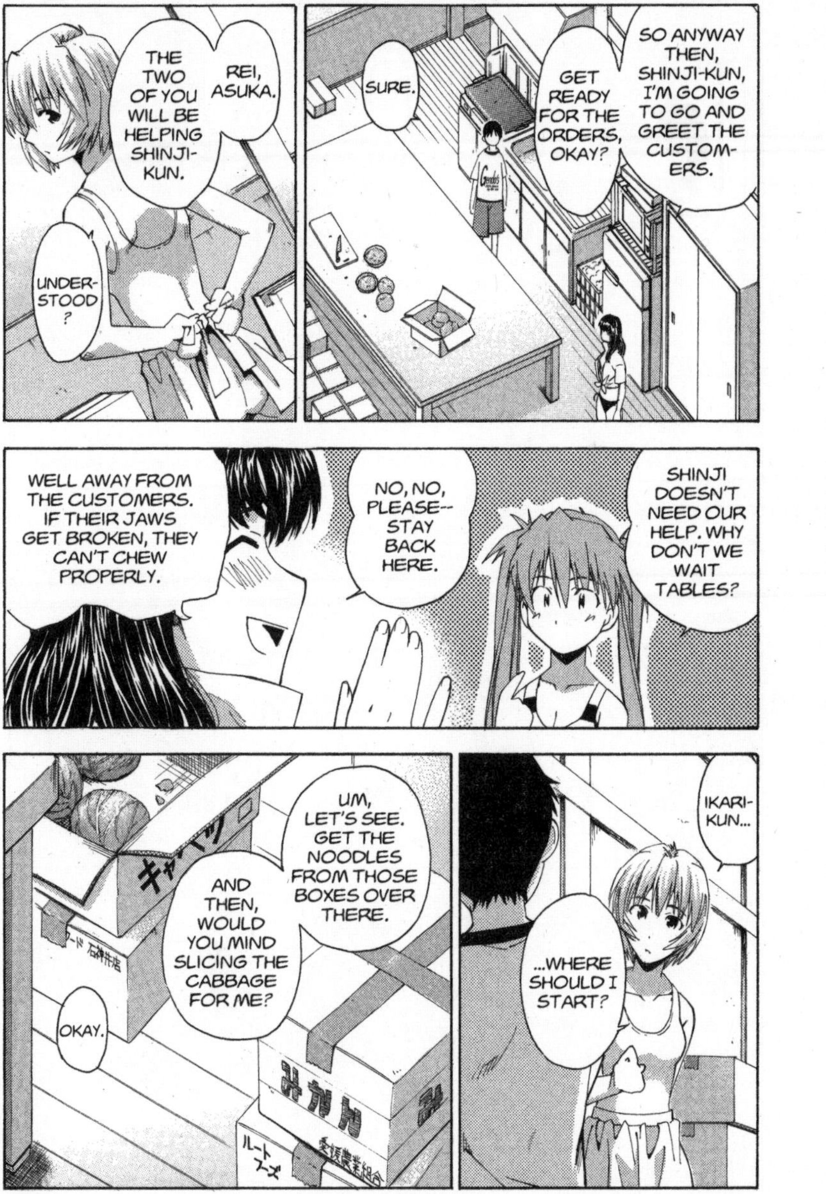
SO ANYWAY THEN, SHINJI-KUN, I'M GOING TO GO AND GREET THE CUSTOM-ERS.
GET READY FOR THE ORDERS, OKAY?
SURE.
REI, ASUKA.
THE TWO OF YOU WILL BE HELPING SHINJI-KUN.
UNDER-STOOD?
SHINJI DOESN'T NEED OUR HELP. WHY DON'T WE WAIT TABLES?
NO, NO, PLEASE-- STAY BACK HERE.
WELL AWAY FROM THE CUSTOMERS. IF THEIR JAWS GET BROKEN, THEY CAN'T CHEW PROPERLY.
IKARI-KUN...
...WHERE SHOULD I START?
UM, LET'S SEE. GET THE NOODLES FROM THOSE BOXES OVER THERE.
AND THEN, WOULD YOU MIND SLICING THE CABBAGE FOR ME?
OKAY.

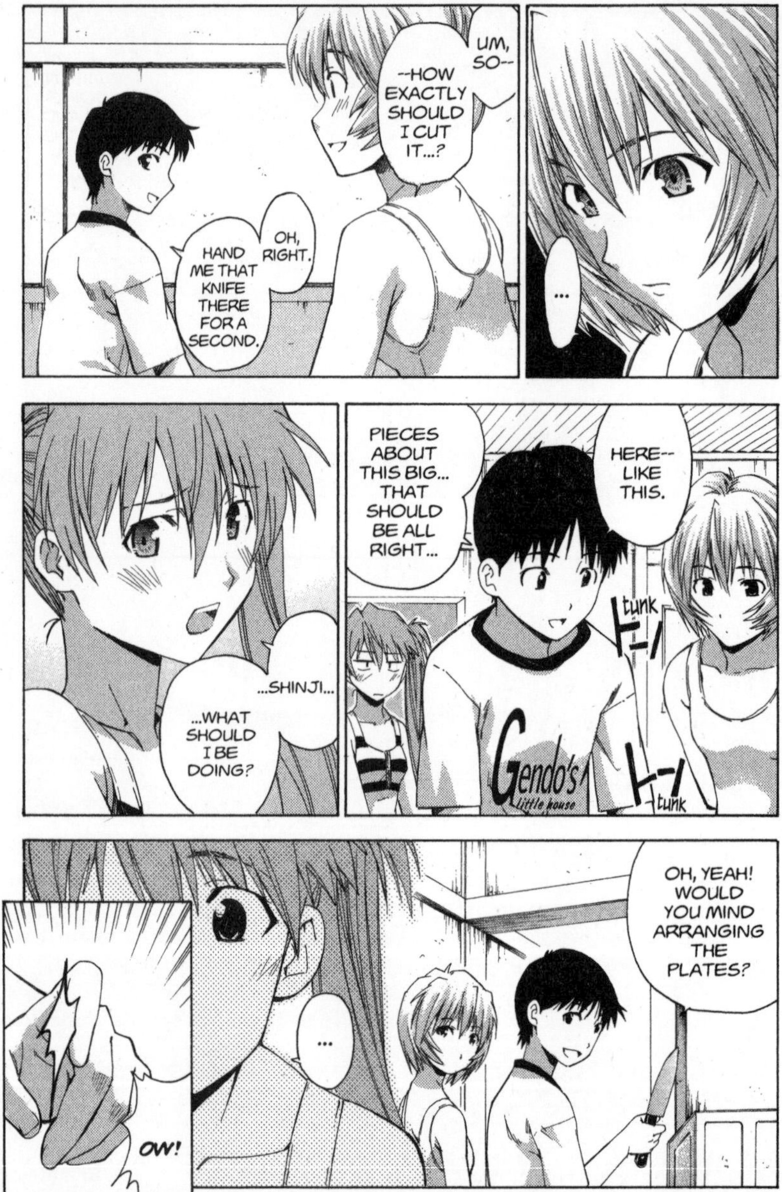
...
UM, SO--
--HOW EXACTLY SHOULD I CUT IT...?
OH, RIGHT.
HAND ME THAT KNIFE THERE FOR A SECOND.
HERE-- LIKE THIS.
PIECES ABOUT THIS BIG... THAT SHOULD BE ALL RIGHT...
tunk
tunk
Gendo's little house
...SHINJI...
...WHAT SHOULD I BE DOING?
OH, YEAH! WOULD YOU MIND ARRANGING THE PLATES?
...
OW!

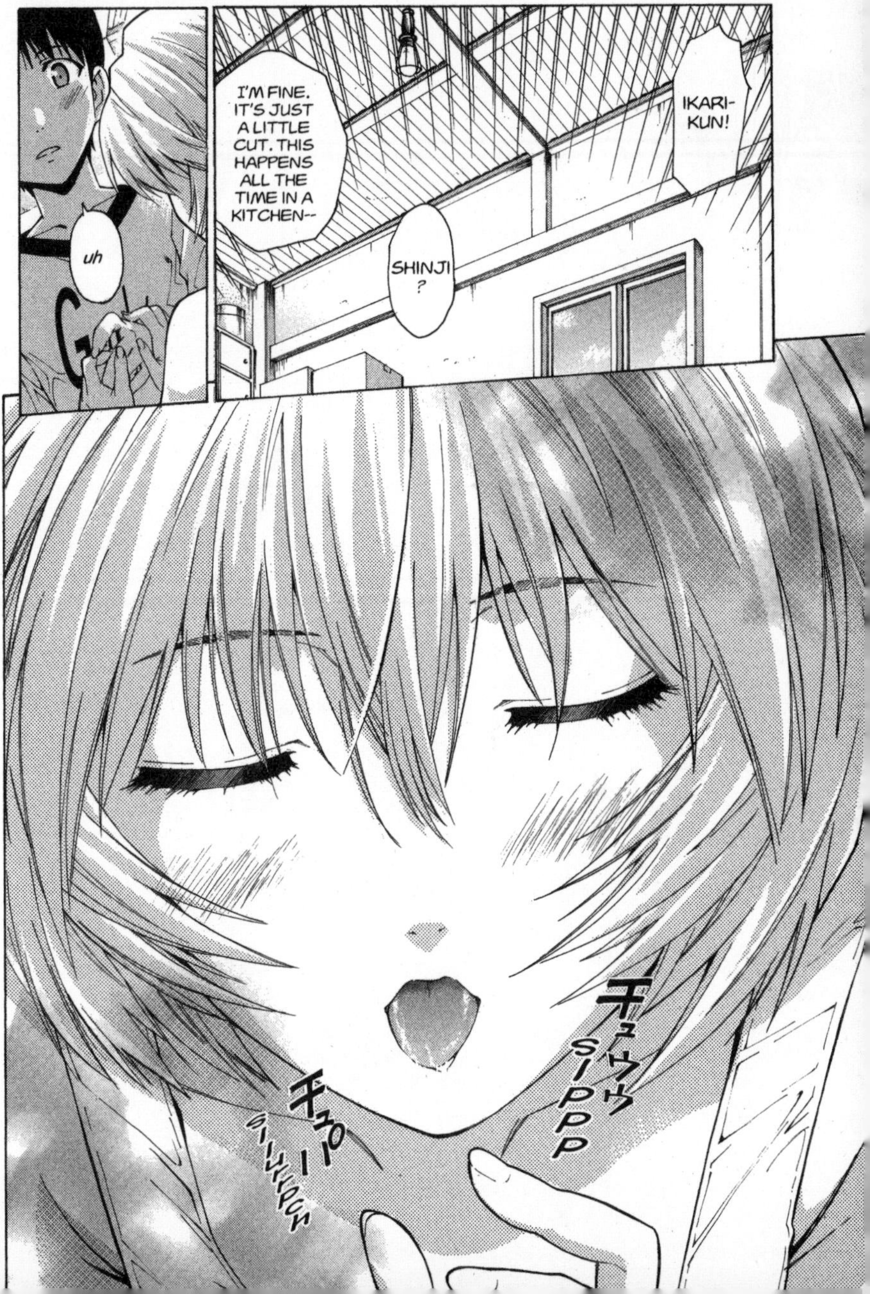
IKARI-KUN!
SHINJI ?
I'M FINE. IT'S JUST A LITTLE CUT. THIS HAPPENS ALL THE TIME IN A KITCHEN--
uh
チュウウ SIPPP
チュプー

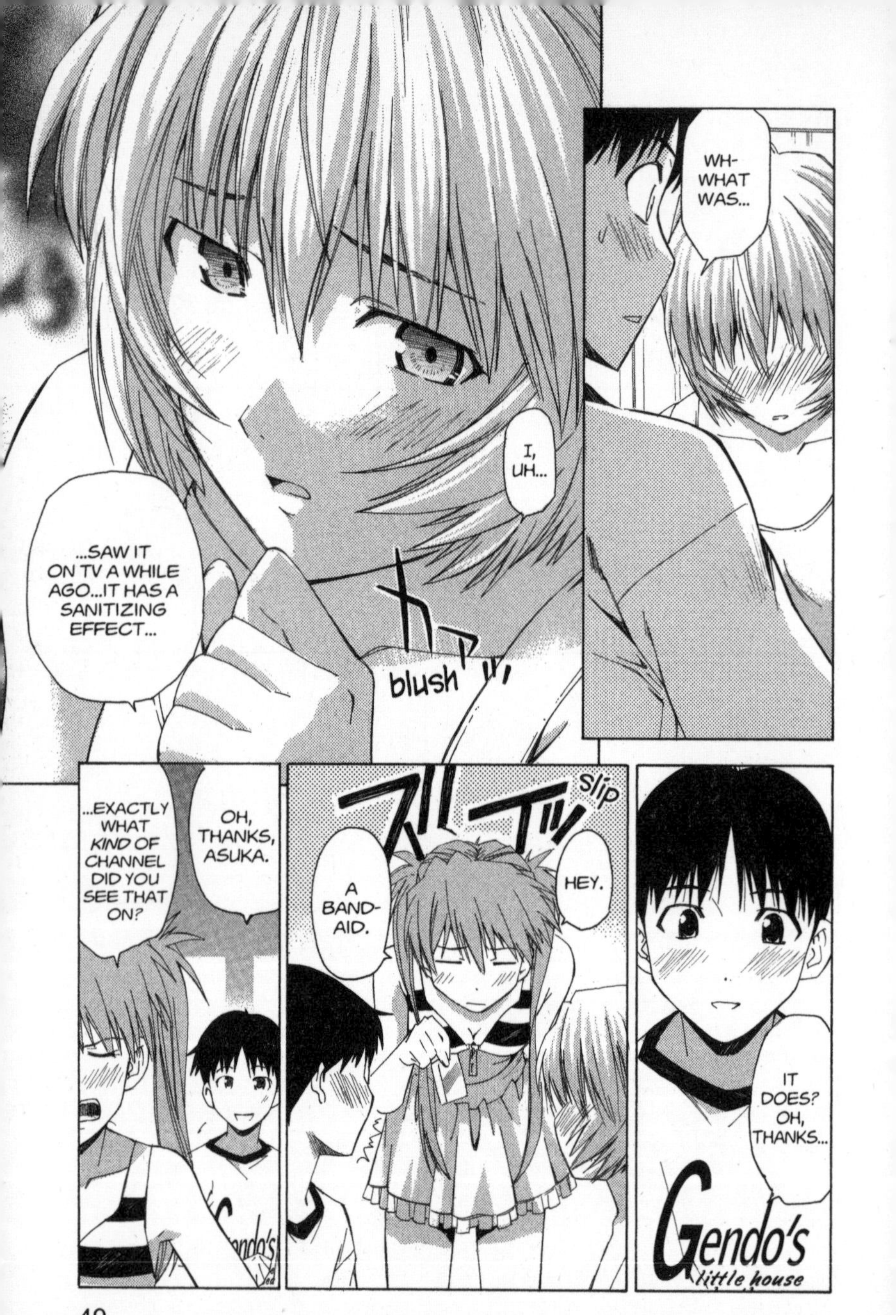
WH-WHAT WAS...
I, UH...
...SAW IT ON TV A WHILE AGO...IT HAS A SANITIZING EFFECT...
blush
IT DOES? OH, THANKS...
Gendo's little house
Slip
HEY.
A BAND-AID.
OH, THANKS, ASUKA.
...EXACTLY WHAT KIND OF CHANNEL DID YOU SEE THAT ON?

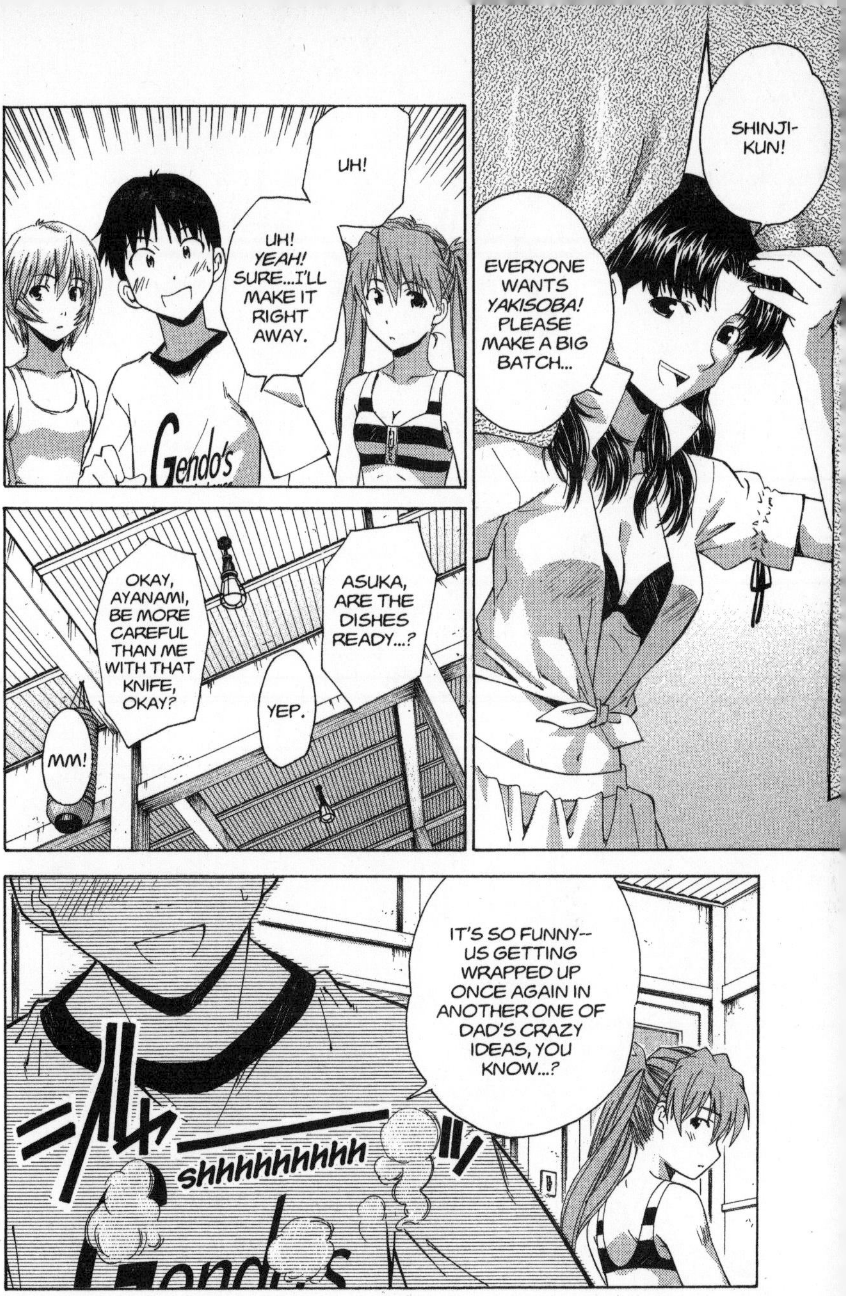
SHINJI-KUN!
EVERYONE WANTS *YAKISOBA!* PLEASE MAKE A BIG BATCH...
UH!
UH! *YEAH!* SURE...I'LL MAKE IT RIGHT AWAY.
ASUKA, ARE THE DISHES READY...?
YEP.
OKAY, AYANAMI, BE MORE CAREFUL THAN ME WITH THAT KNIFE, OKAY?
MM!
IT'S SO FUNNY-- US GETTING WRAPPED UP ONCE AGAIN IN ANOTHER ONE OF DAD'S CRAZY IDEAS, YOU KNOW...?
shhhhhhhhh

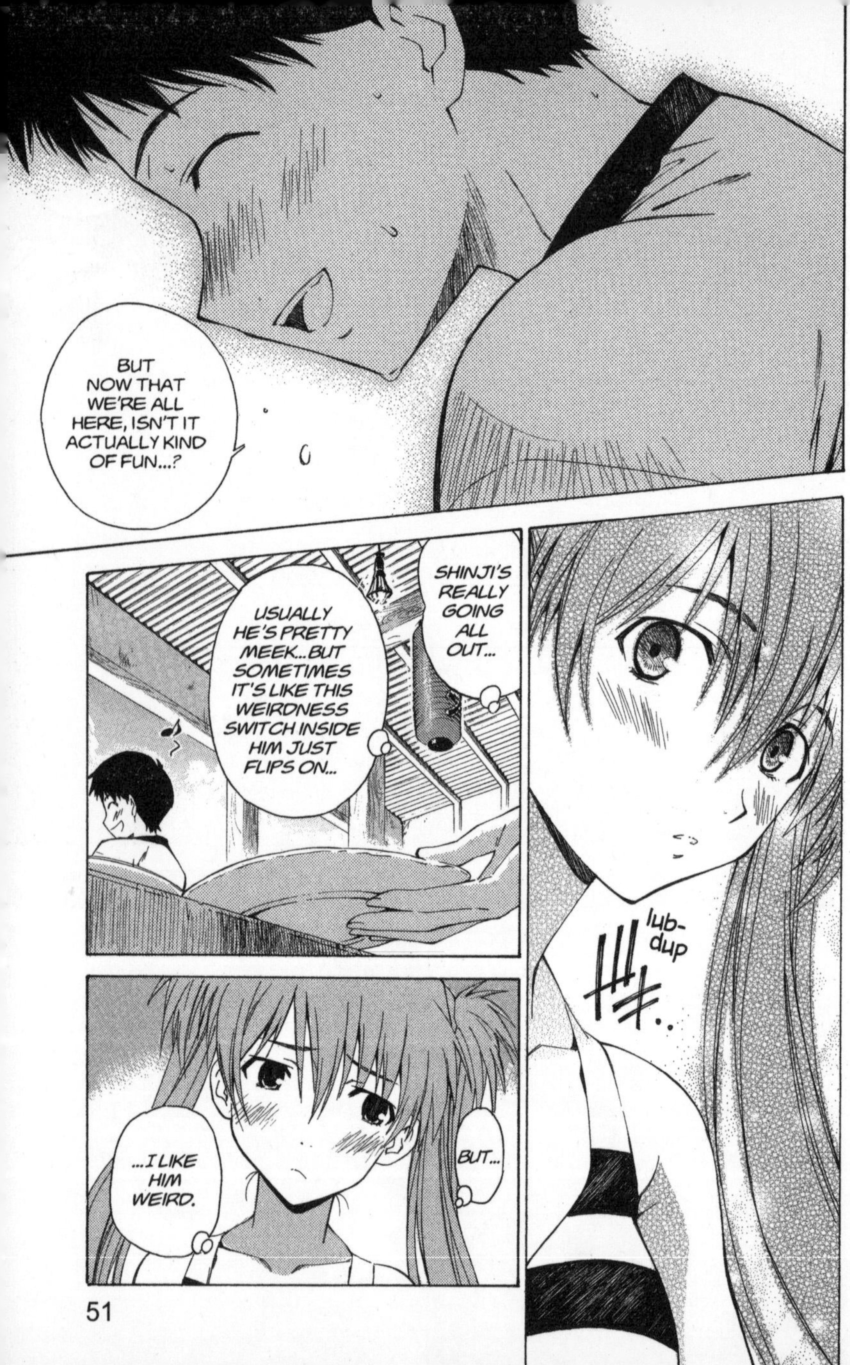
BUT NOW THAT WE'RE ALL HERE, ISN'T IT ACTUALLY KIND OF FUN...?
lub-dup
SHINJI'S REALLY GOING ALL OUT...
USUALLY HE'S PRETTY MEEK...BUT SOMETIMES IT'S LIKE THIS WEIRDNESS SWITCH INSIDE HIM JUST FLIPS ON...
BUT...
...I LIKE HIM WEIRD.

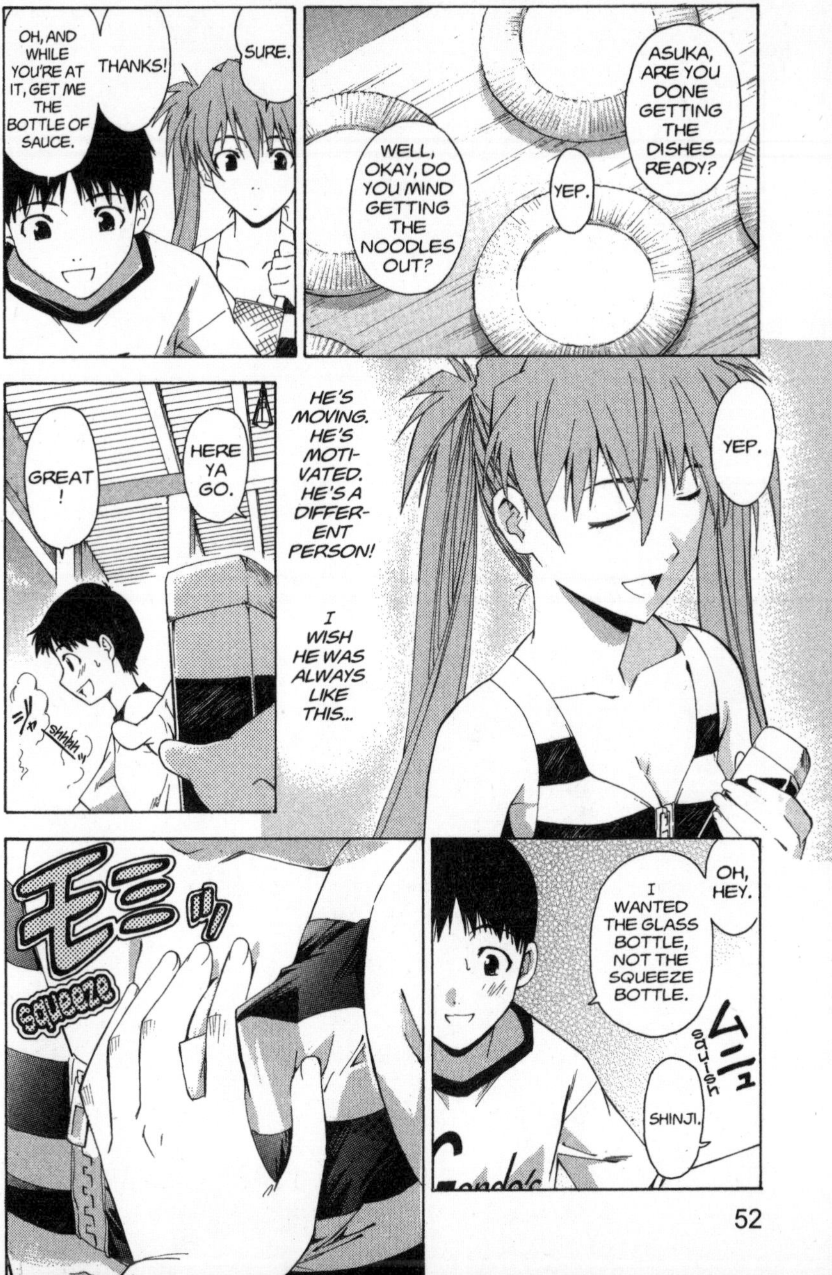
ASUKA, ARE YOU DONE GETTING THE DISHES READY?
YEP.
WELL, OKAY, DO YOU MIND GETTING THE NOODLES OUT?
SURE.
THANKS!
OH, AND WHILE YOU'RE AT IT, GET ME THE BOTTLE OF SAUCE.
YEP.
HE'S MOVING. HE'S MOTI-VATED. HE'S A DIFFER-ENT PERSON!
I WISH HE WAS ALWAYS LIKE THIS...
HERE YA GO.
GREAT!
shhhh
OH, HEY.
I WANTED THE GLASS BOTTLE, NOT THE SQUEEZE BOTTLE.
squish
SHINJI.
squeeze

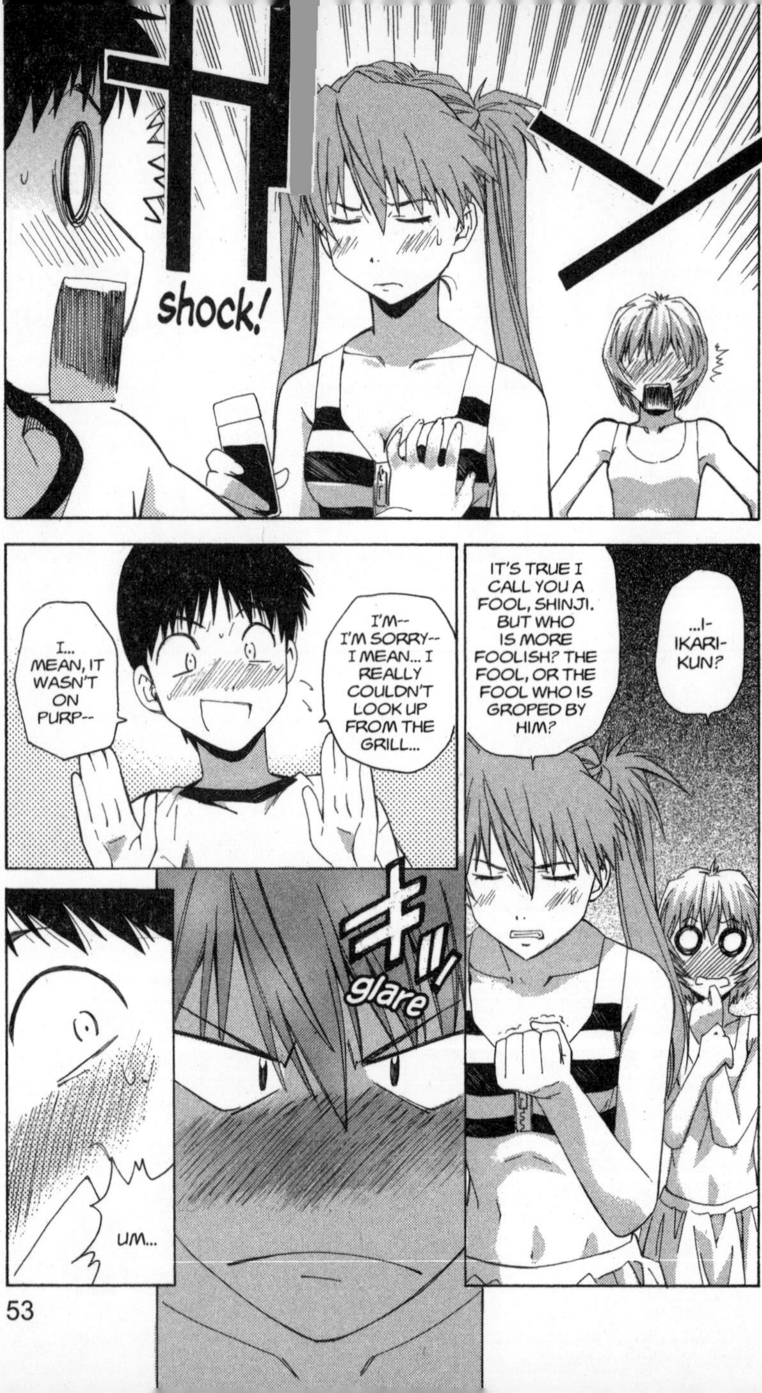
shock!
...I- IKARI- KUN?
IT'S TRUE I CALL YOU A FOOL, SHINJI. BUT WHO IS MORE FOOLISH? THE FOOL, OR THE FOOL WHO IS GROPED BY HIM?
I'M-- I'M SORRY-- I MEAN... I REALLY COULDN'T LOOK UP FROM THE GRILL...
I... MEAN, IT WASN'T ON PURP--
glare
UM...

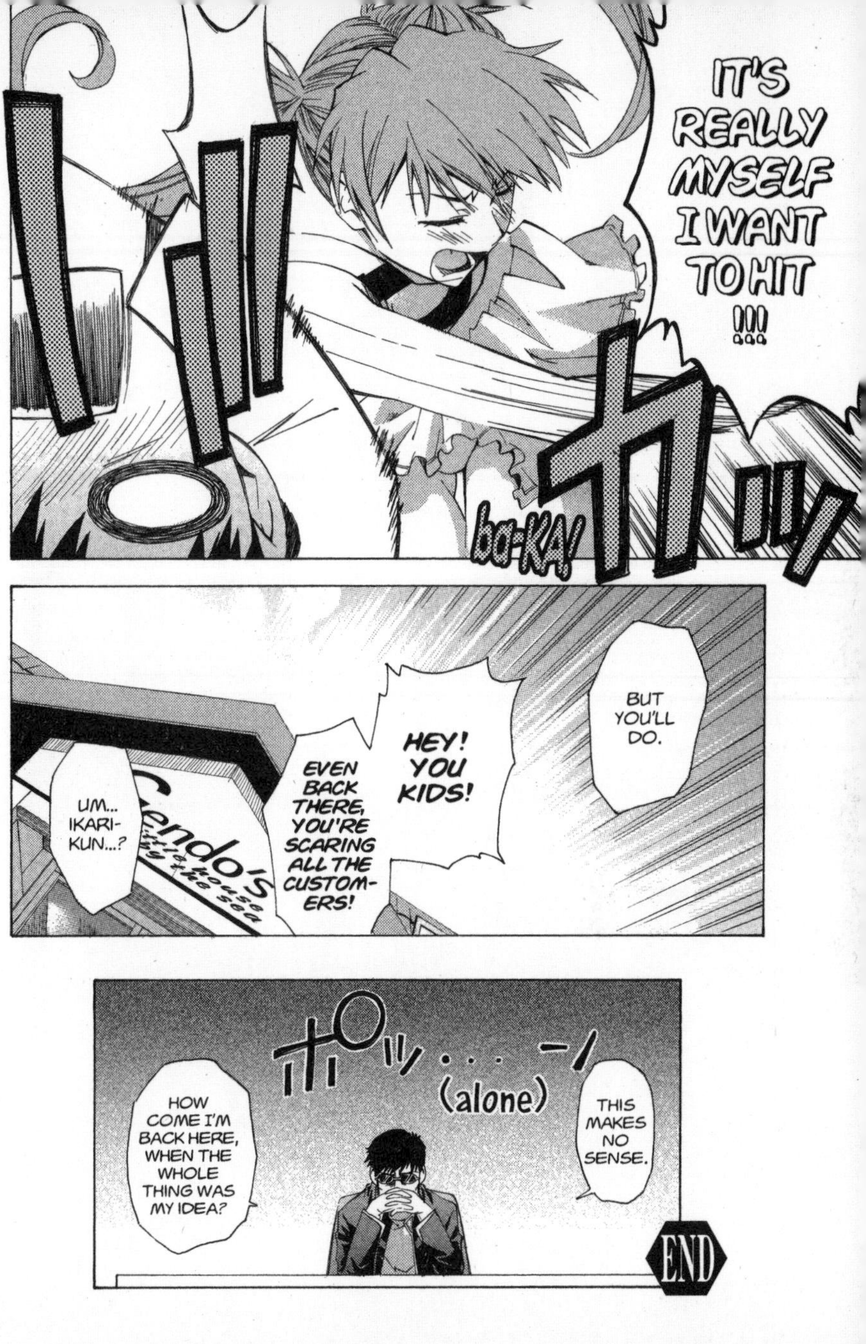
IT'S REALLY MYSELF I WANT TO HIT !!!
ba-KA!
BUT YOU'LL DO.
HEY! YOU KIDS!
EVEN BACK THERE, YOU'RE SCARING ALL THE CUSTOMERS!
UM... IKARI-KUN...?
Gendo's
(alone)
THIS MAKES NO SENSE.
HOW COME I'M BACK HERE, WHEN THE WHOLE THING WAS MY IDEA?
END

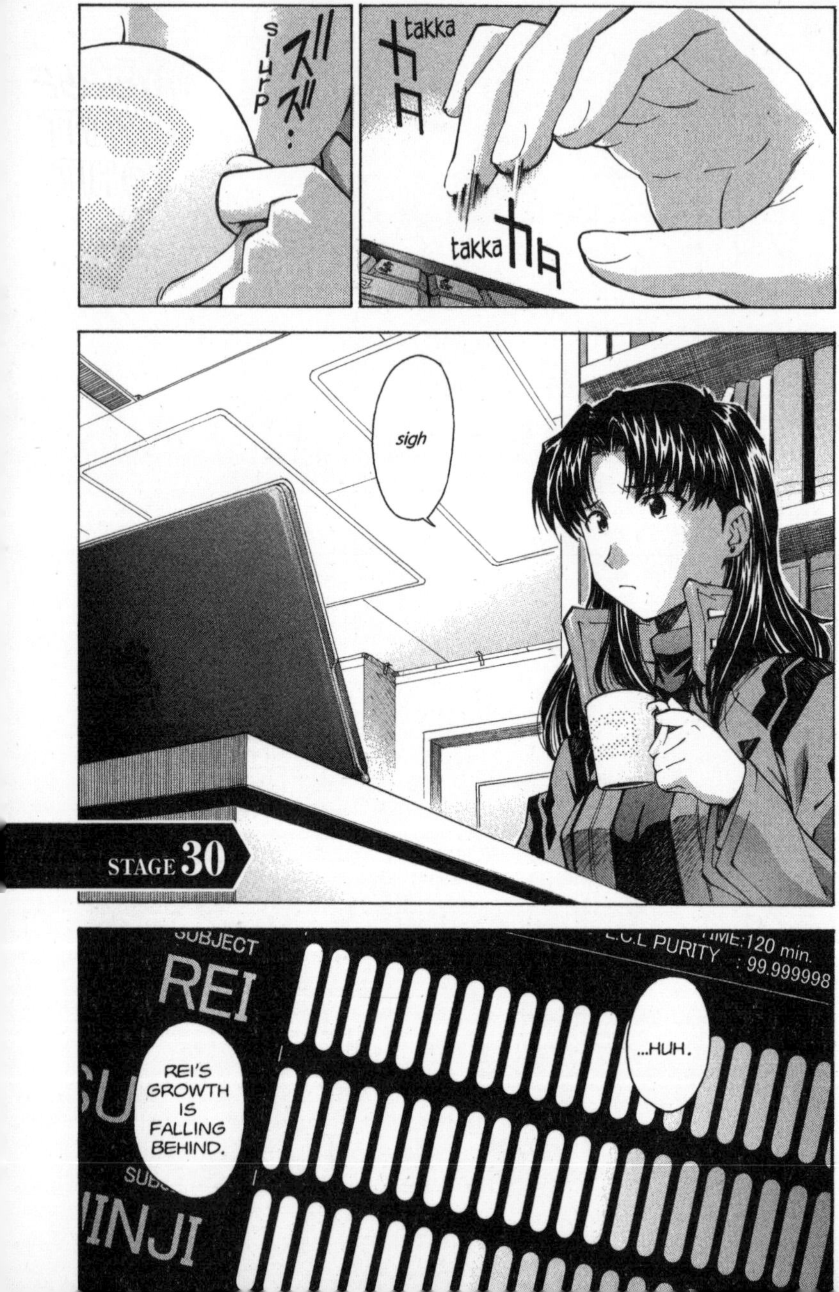
カタ takka
カタ takka
ズズ… slurp
sigh
STAGE 30
SUBJECT
REI
L.C.L PURITY : 99.999998
TIME:120 min.
...HUH.
REI'S GROWTH IS FALLING BEHIND.
INJI

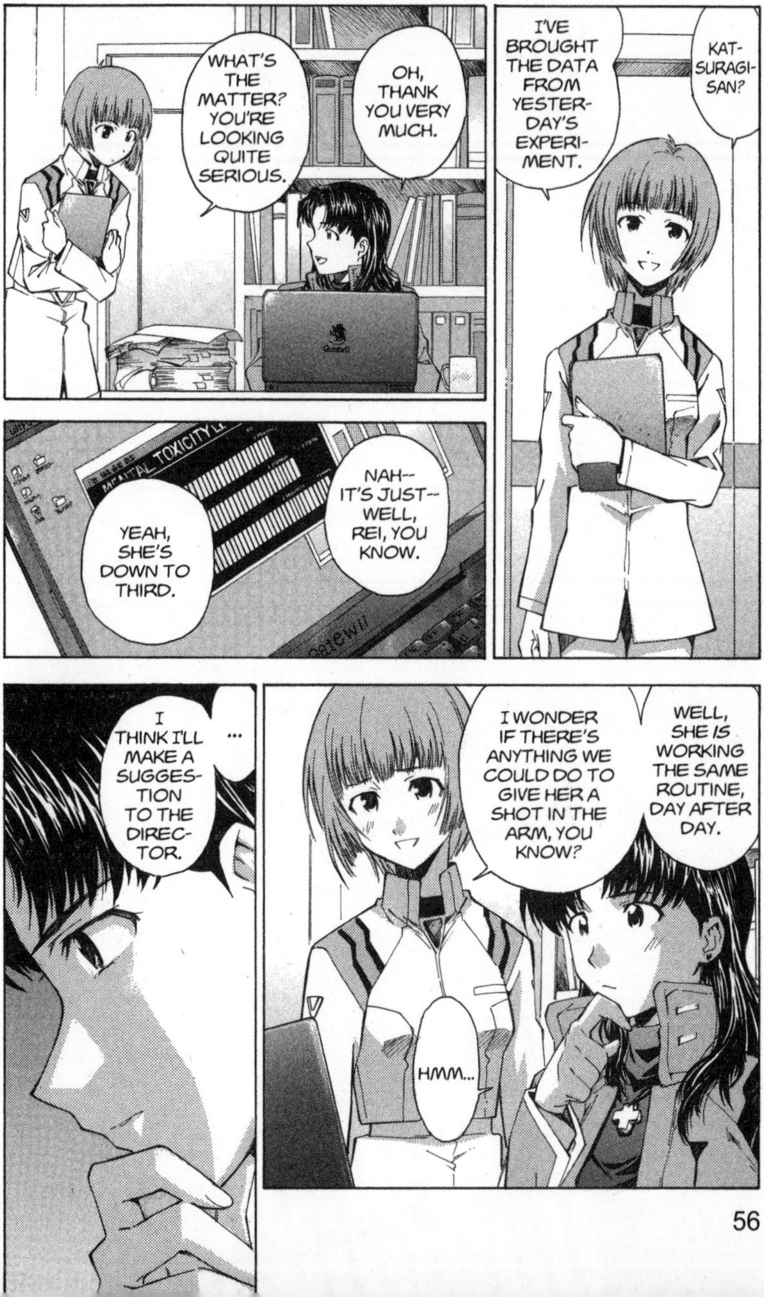

KAT-SURAGI-SAN?
I'VE BROUGHT THE DATA FROM YESTER-DAY'S EXPERI-MENT.
OH, THANK YOU VERY MUCH.
WHAT'S THE MATTER? YOU'RE LOOKING QUITE SERIOUS.
NAH-- IT'S JUST-- WELL, REI, YOU KNOW.
YEAH, SHE'S DOWN TO THIRD.
WELL, SHE *IS* WORKING THE SAME ROUTINE, DAY AFTER DAY.
I WONDER IF THERE'S ANYTHING WE COULD DO TO GIVE HER A SHOT IN THE ARM, YOU KNOW?
HMM...
...
I THINK I'LL MAKE A SUGGES-TION TO THE DIREC-TOR.

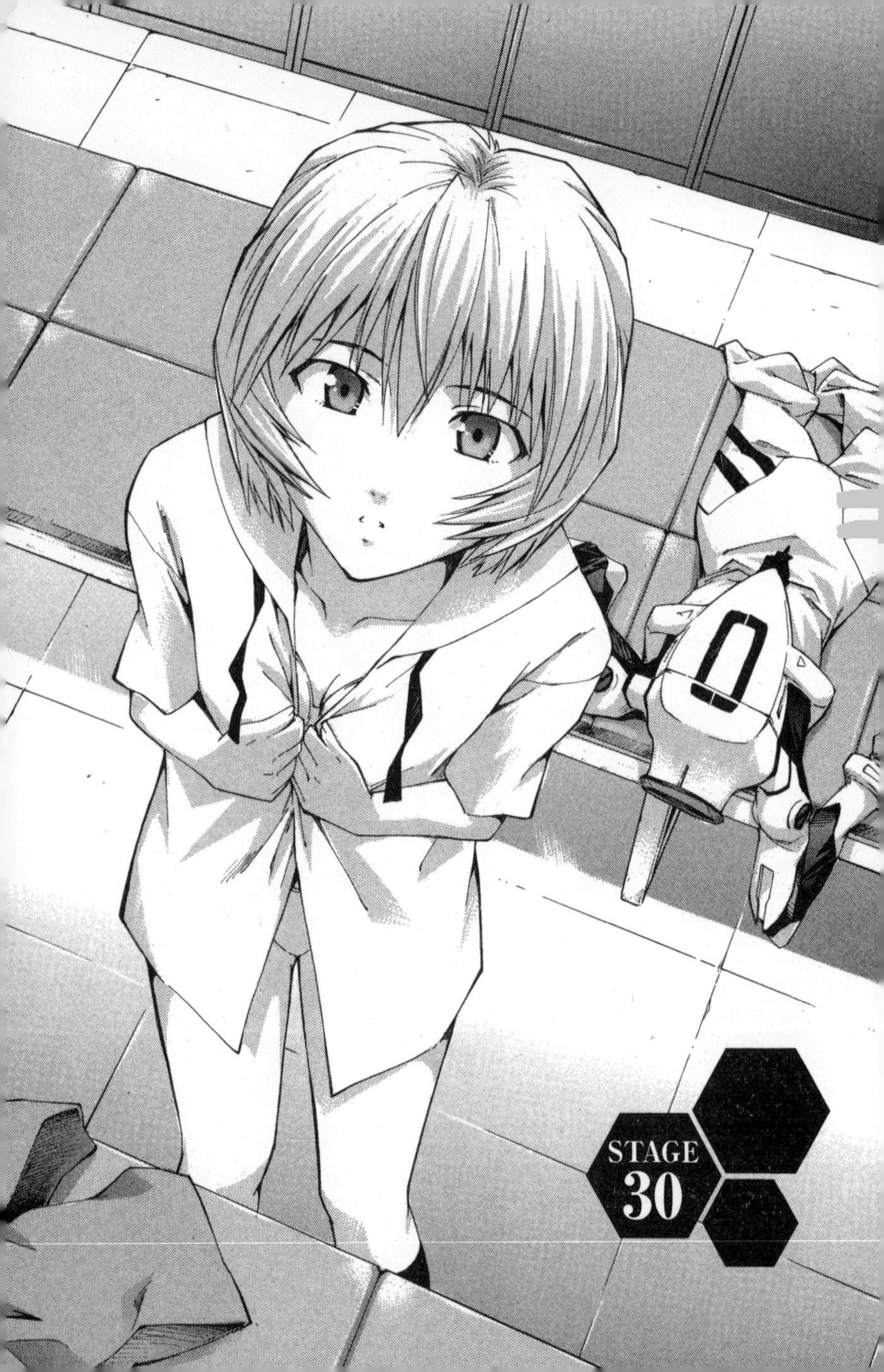
STAGE
30

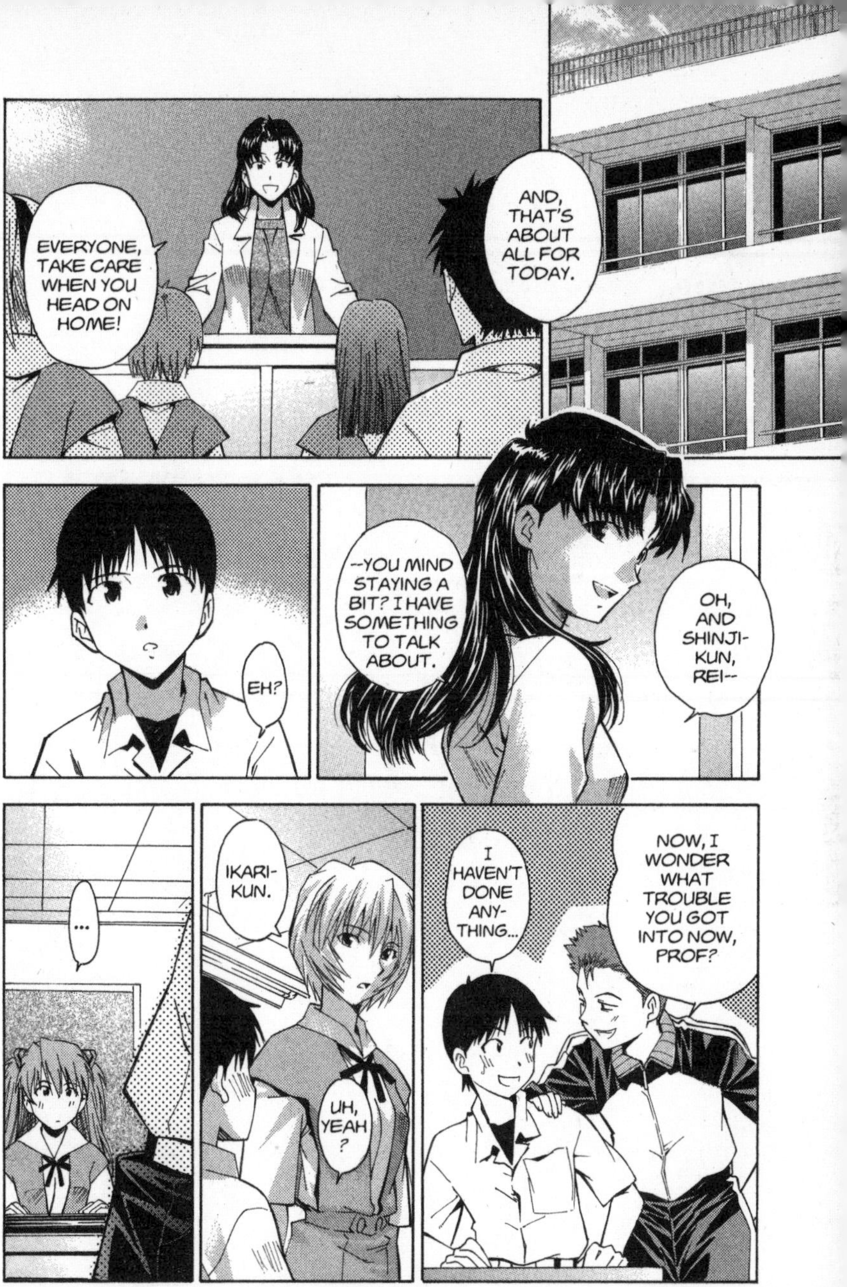
AND, THAT'S ABOUT ALL FOR TODAY.
EVERYONE, TAKE CARE WHEN YOU HEAD ON HOME!
OH, AND SHINJI-KUN, REI--
--YOU MIND STAYING A BIT? I HAVE SOMETHING TO TALK ABOUT.
EH?
NOW, I WONDER WHAT TROUBLE YOU GOT INTO NOW, PROF?
I HAVEN'T DONE ANY-THING...
IKARI-KUN.
UH, YEAH?
...

AH, THERE YOU TWO ARE.
MISATO-SAN, WHAT'S THIS ALL ABOUT...?
THERE'S A CERTAIN EXPERIMENT I'D LIKE YOU TWO TO PARTICIPATE IN TODAY.
WOULD YOU MIND WAITING BY MY CAR? I'LL DRIVE YOU OVER.
...BUT THERE WAS NOTHING ON THE SCHEDULE TODAY.
YEAH, YOU'RE RIGHT. THIS WAS SOMETHING WE DECIDED LAST MINUTE.
I FEEL PRETTY BAD, BUT CAN YOU HELP ME OUT?
TRUTHFULLY, DO YOU FEEL ANYTHING AT ALL?
JUST SHUT UP AND GET IN THE CAR.
OH, HEY. MORE WORK DOWN AT THE LAB?
A-ASUKA...
I'M SURE IT'S JUST SOME REVIEW AND REDO, SHINJI.
WHY DON'T YOU JUST TRY TO KEEP UP?
CAN IT, ASUKA.

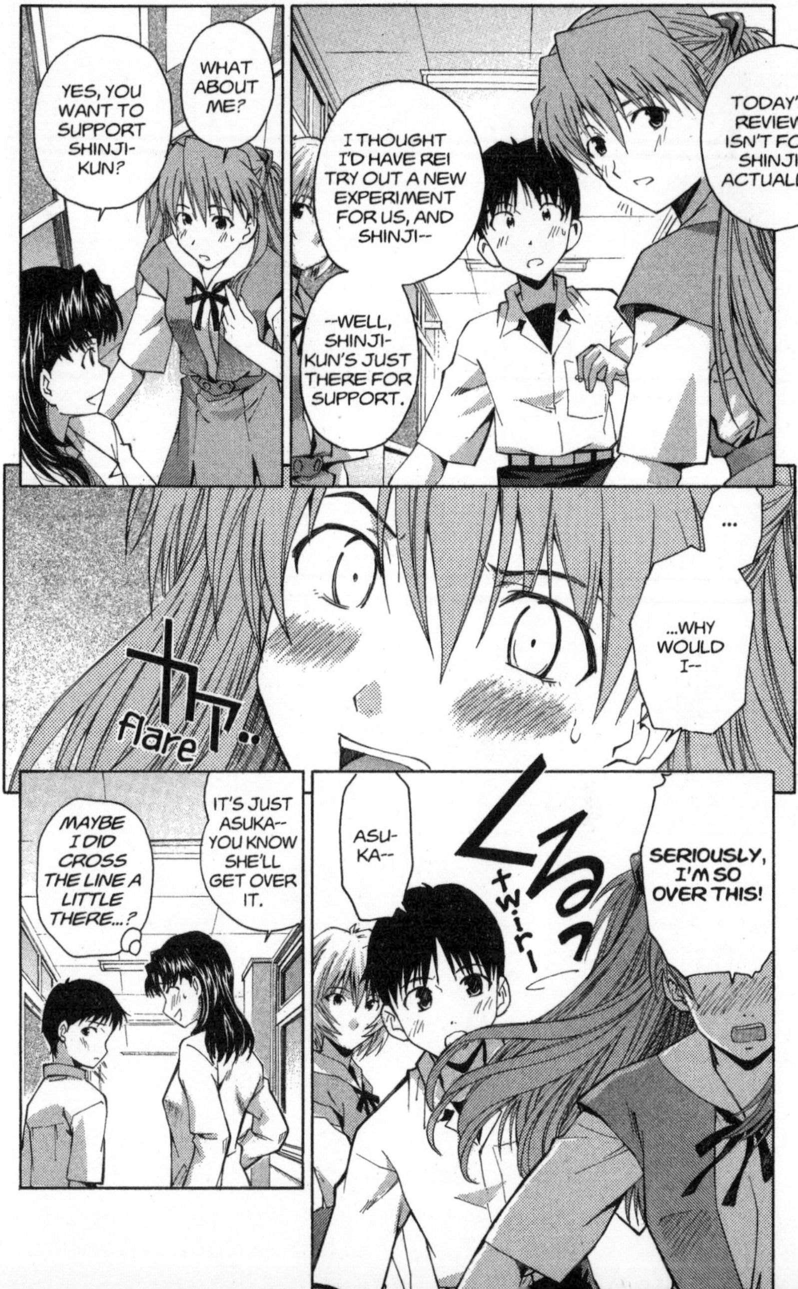
TODAY'S REVIEW ISN'T FOR SHINJI, ACTUALLY.
I THOUGHT I'D HAVE REI TRY OUT A NEW EXPERIMENT FOR US, AND SHINJI--
--WELL, SHINJI-KUN'S JUST THERE FOR SUPPORT.
WHAT ABOUT ME?
YES, YOU WANT TO SUPPORT SHINJI-KUN?
...
...WHY WOULD I--
flare
SERIOUSLY, I'M SO OVER THIS!
twirl
ASU-KA--
IT'S JUST ASUKA-- YOU KNOW SHE'LL GET OVER IT.
MAYBE I DID CROSS THE LINE A LITTLE THERE...?

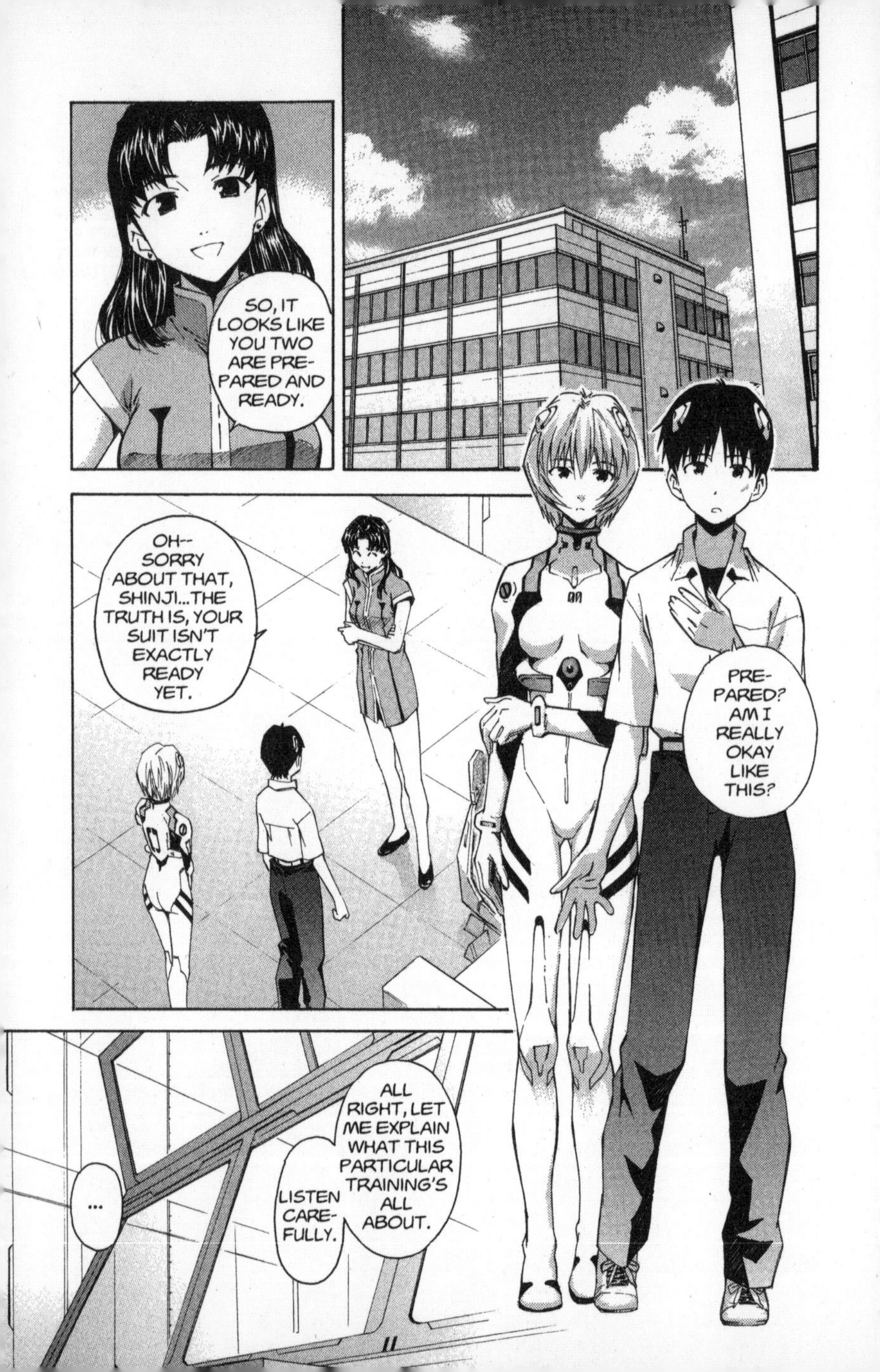
SO, IT LOOKS LIKE YOU TWO ARE PRE-PARED AND READY.
PRE-PARED? AM I REALLY OKAY LIKE THIS?
OH-- SORRY ABOUT THAT, SHINJI...THE TRUTH IS, YOUR SUIT ISN'T EXACTLY READY YET.
ALL RIGHT, LET ME EXPLAIN WHAT THIS PARTICULAR TRAINING'S ALL ABOUT.
LISTEN CARE-FULLY.
...

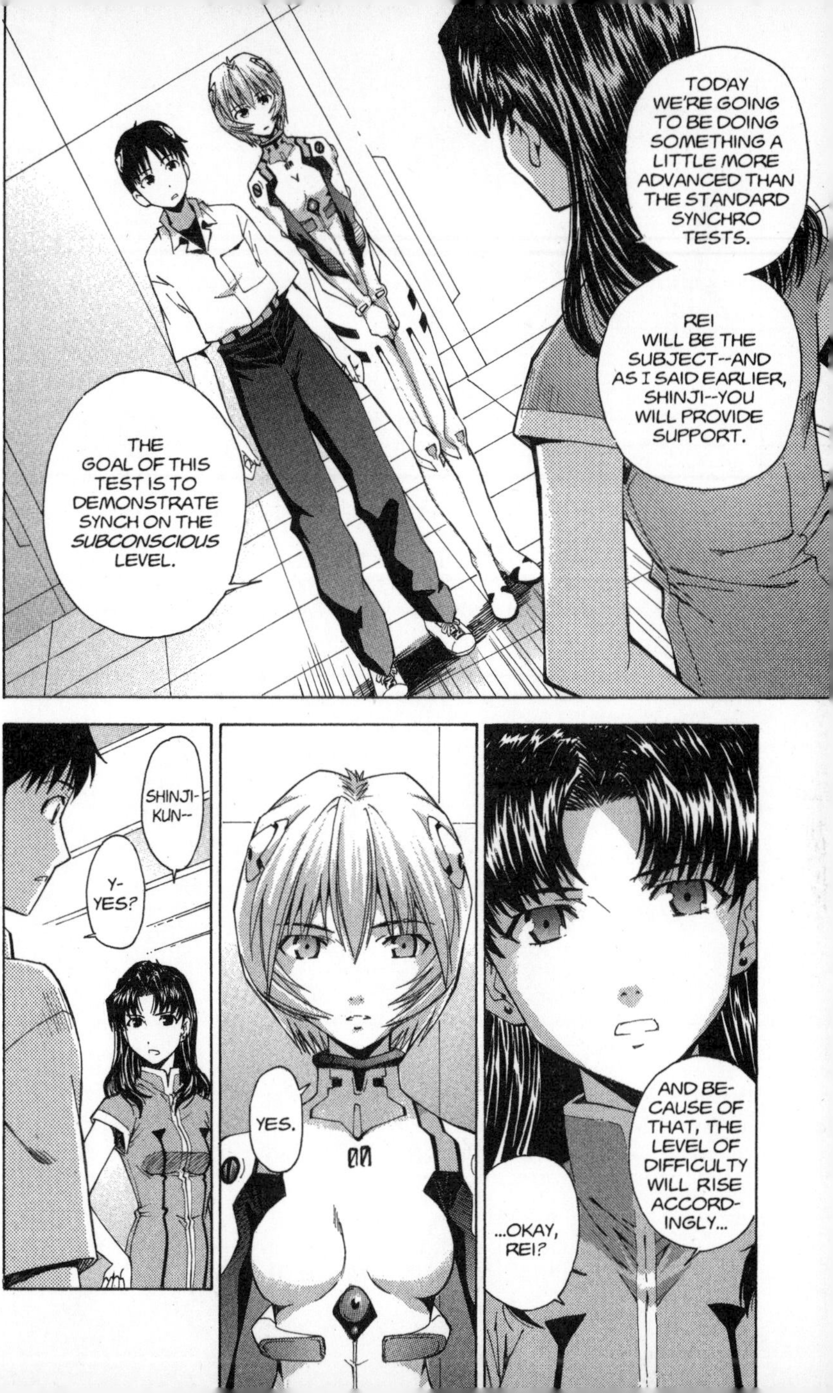
TODAY WE'RE GOING TO BE DOING SOMETHING A LITTLE MORE ADVANCED THAN THE STANDARD SYNCHRO TESTS.
REI WILL BE THE SUBJECT--AND AS I SAID EARLIER, SHINJI--YOU WILL PROVIDE SUPPORT.
THE GOAL OF THIS TEST IS TO DEMONSTRATE SYNCH ON THE *SUBCONSCIOUS* LEVEL.
AND BE-CAUSE OF THAT, THE LEVEL OF DIFFICULTY WILL RISE ACCORD-INGLY...
...OKAY, REI?
YES.
SHINJI-KUN--
Y-YES?

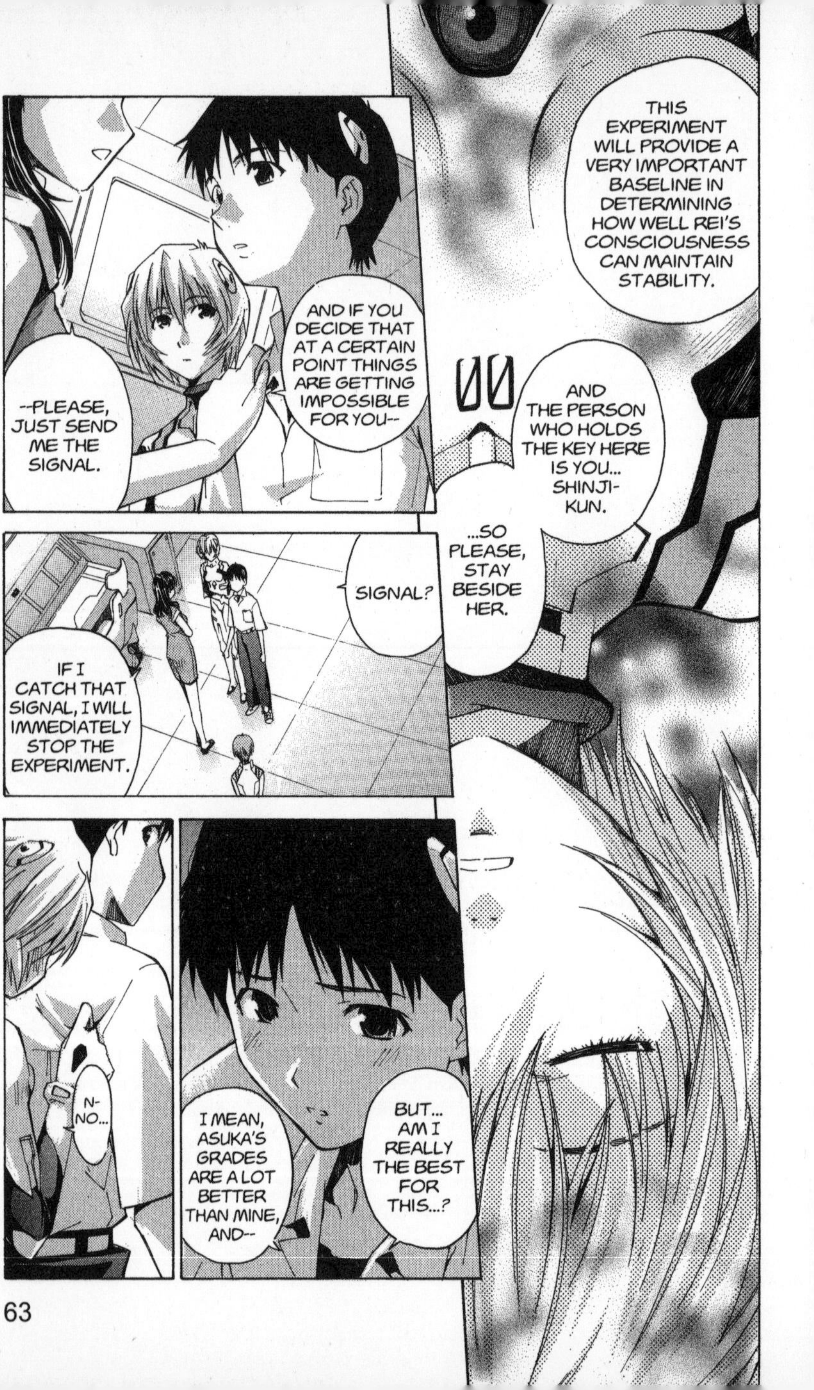
THIS EXPERIMENT WILL PROVIDE A VERY IMPORTANT BASELINE IN DETERMINING HOW WELL REI'S CONSCIOUSNESS CAN MAINTAIN STABILITY.
00
AND THE PERSON WHO HOLDS THE KEY HERE IS YOU... SHINJI-KUN.
...SO PLEASE, STAY BESIDE HER.
AND IF YOU DECIDE THAT AT A CERTAIN POINT THINGS ARE GETTING IMPOSSIBLE FOR YOU--
--PLEASE, JUST SEND ME THE SIGNAL.
SIGNAL?
IF I CATCH THAT SIGNAL, I WILL IMMEDIATELY STOP THE EXPERIMENT.
BUT... AM I REALLY THE BEST FOR THIS...?
I MEAN, ASUKA'S GRADES ARE A LOT BETTER THAN MINE, AND--
N-NO...

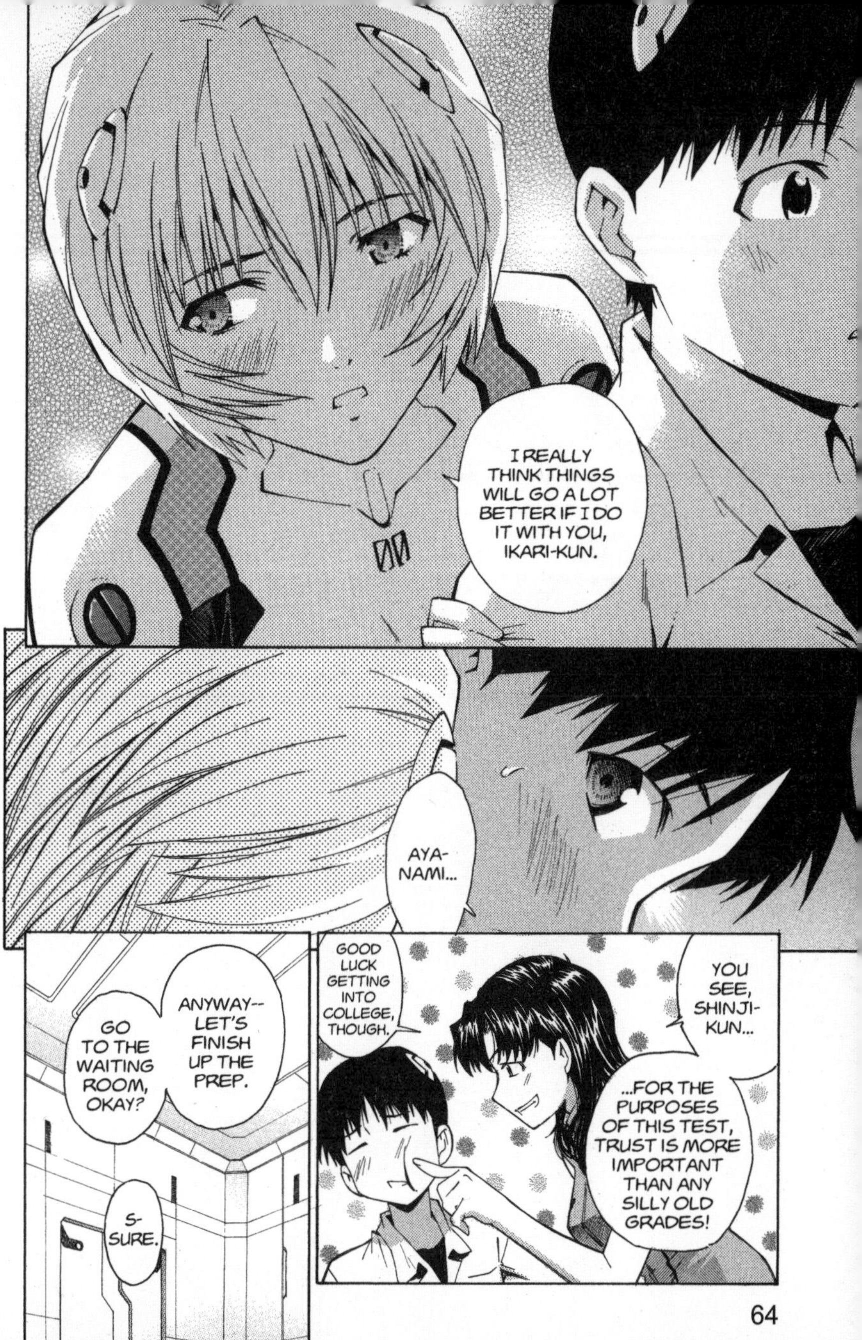
I REALLY THINK THINGS WILL GO A LOT BETTER IF I DO IT WITH YOU, IKARI-KUN.
AYA-NAMI...
YOU SEE, SHINJI-KUN...
...FOR THE PURPOSES OF THIS TEST, TRUST IS MORE IMPORTANT THAN ANY SILLY OLD GRADES!
GOOD LUCK GETTING INTO COLLEGE, THOUGH.
ANYWAY--LET'S FINISH UP THE PREP.
GO TO THE WAITING ROOM, OKAY?
S-SURE.

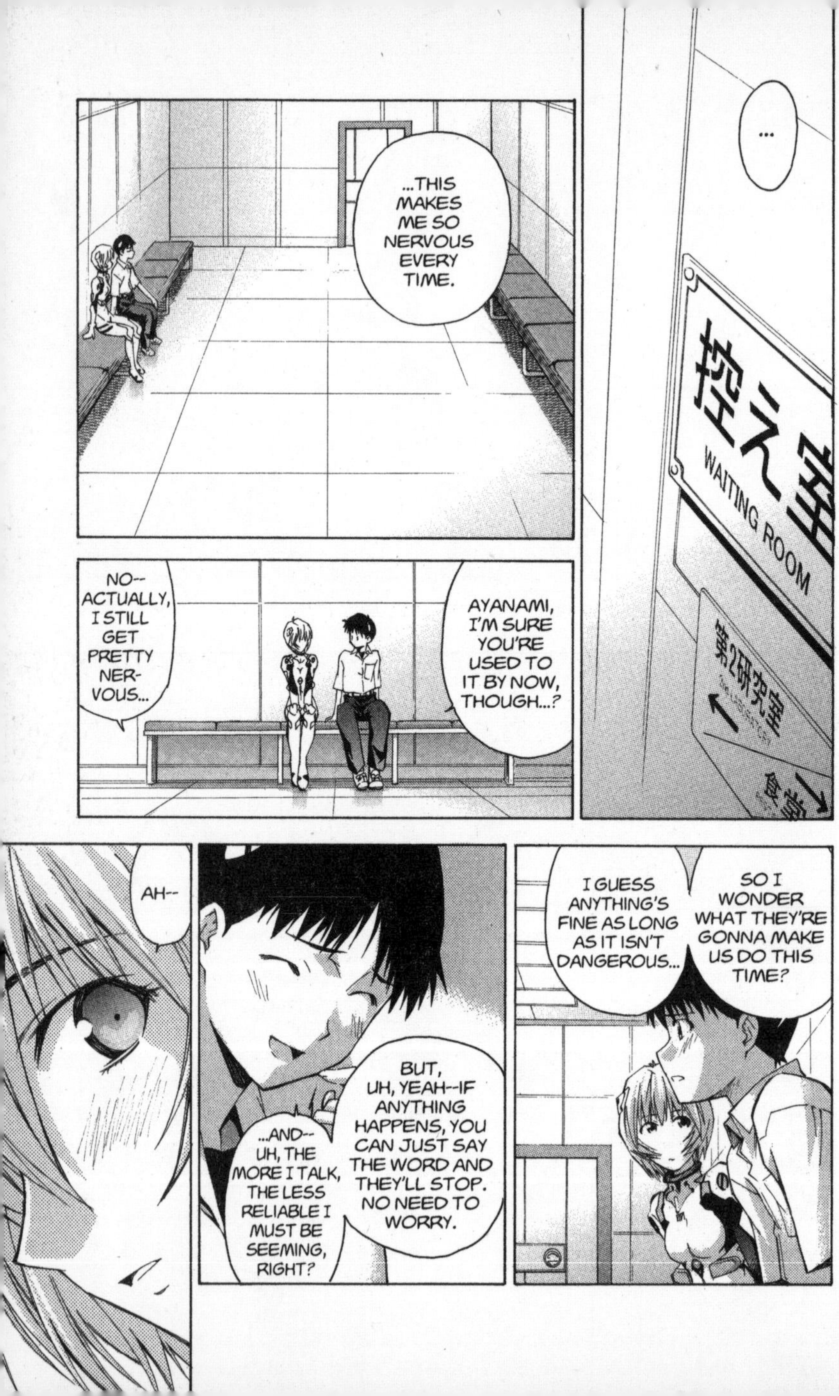
...
控え室
WAITING ROOM
第2研究室
...THIS MAKES ME SO NERVOUS EVERY TIME.
AYANAMI, I'M SURE YOU'RE USED TO IT BY NOW, THOUGH...?
NO-- ACTUALLY, I STILL GET PRETTY NER-VOUS...
SO I WONDER WHAT THEY'RE GONNA MAKE US DO THIS TIME?
I GUESS ANYTHING'S FINE AS LONG AS IT ISN'T DANGEROUS...
BUT, UH, YEAH--IF ANYTHING HAPPENS, YOU CAN JUST SAY THE WORD AND THEY'LL STOP. NO NEED TO WORRY.
...AND-- UH, THE MORE I TALK, THE LESS RELIABLE I MUST BE SEEMING, RIGHT?
AH--

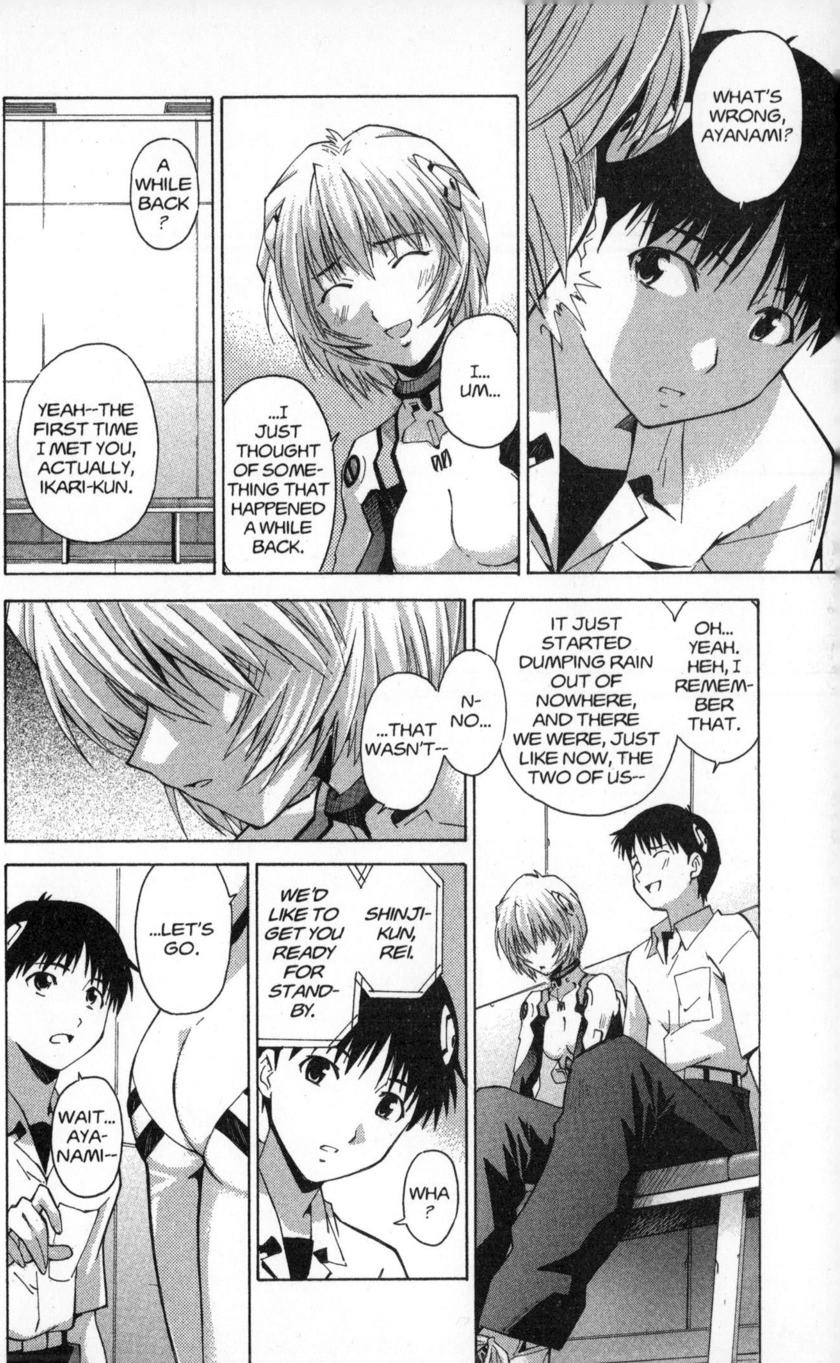
WHAT'S WRONG, AYANAMI?
I... UM...
...I JUST THOUGHT OF SOME-THING THAT HAPPENED A WHILE BACK.
A WHILE BACK?
YEAH--THE FIRST TIME I MET YOU, ACTUALLY, IKARI-KUN.
OH... YEAH. HEH, I REMEM-BER THAT.
IT JUST STARTED DUMPING RAIN OUT OF NOWHERE, AND THERE WE WERE, JUST LIKE NOW, THE TWO OF US--
N-NO...
...THAT WASN'T--
SHINJI-KUN, REI.
WE'D LIKE TO GET YOU READY FOR STAND-BY.
WHA?
...LET'S GO.
WAIT... AYA-NAMI--

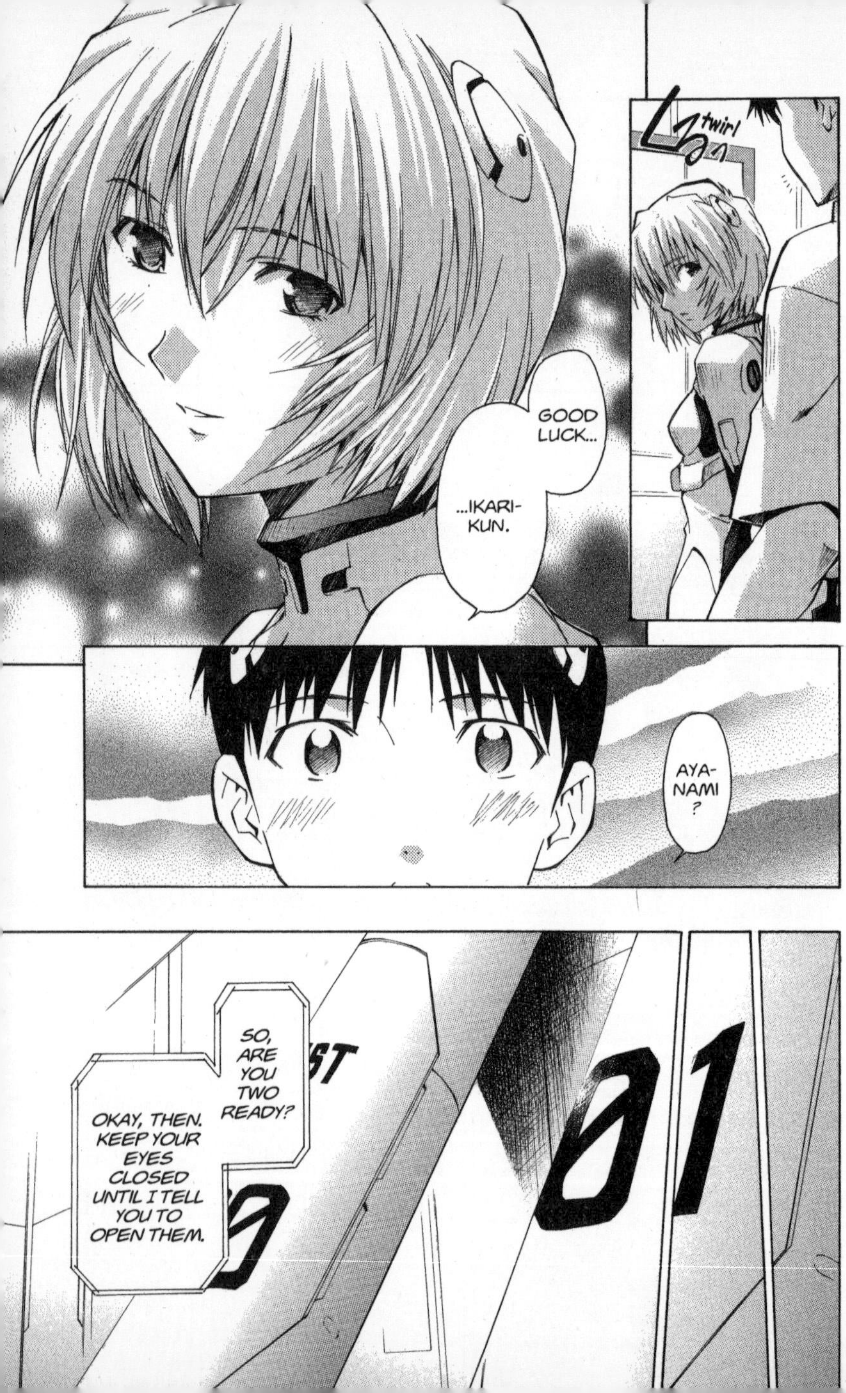
twirl
GOOD LUCK...
...IKARI-KUN.
AYA-NAMI?
SO, ARE YOU TWO READY?
OKAY, THEN. KEEP YOUR EYES CLOSED UNTIL I TELL YOU TO OPEN THEM.
01

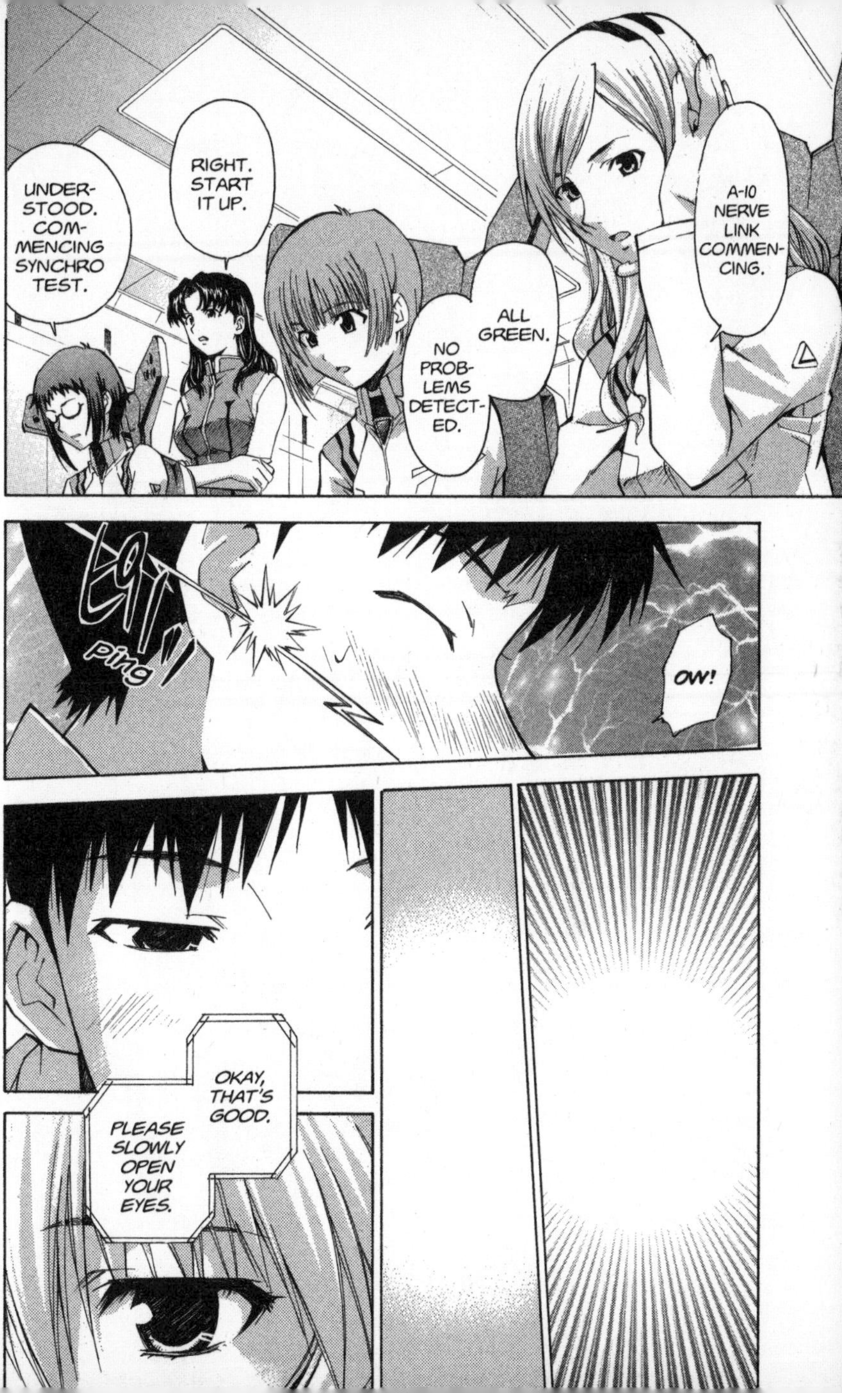
A-10 NERVE LINK COMMENCING.
ALL GREEN.
NO PROBLEMS DETECTED.
RIGHT. START IT UP.
UNDERSTOOD. COMMENCING SYNCHRO TEST.
OW!
ping
OKAY, THAT'S GOOD.
PLEASE SLOWLY OPEN YOUR EYES.

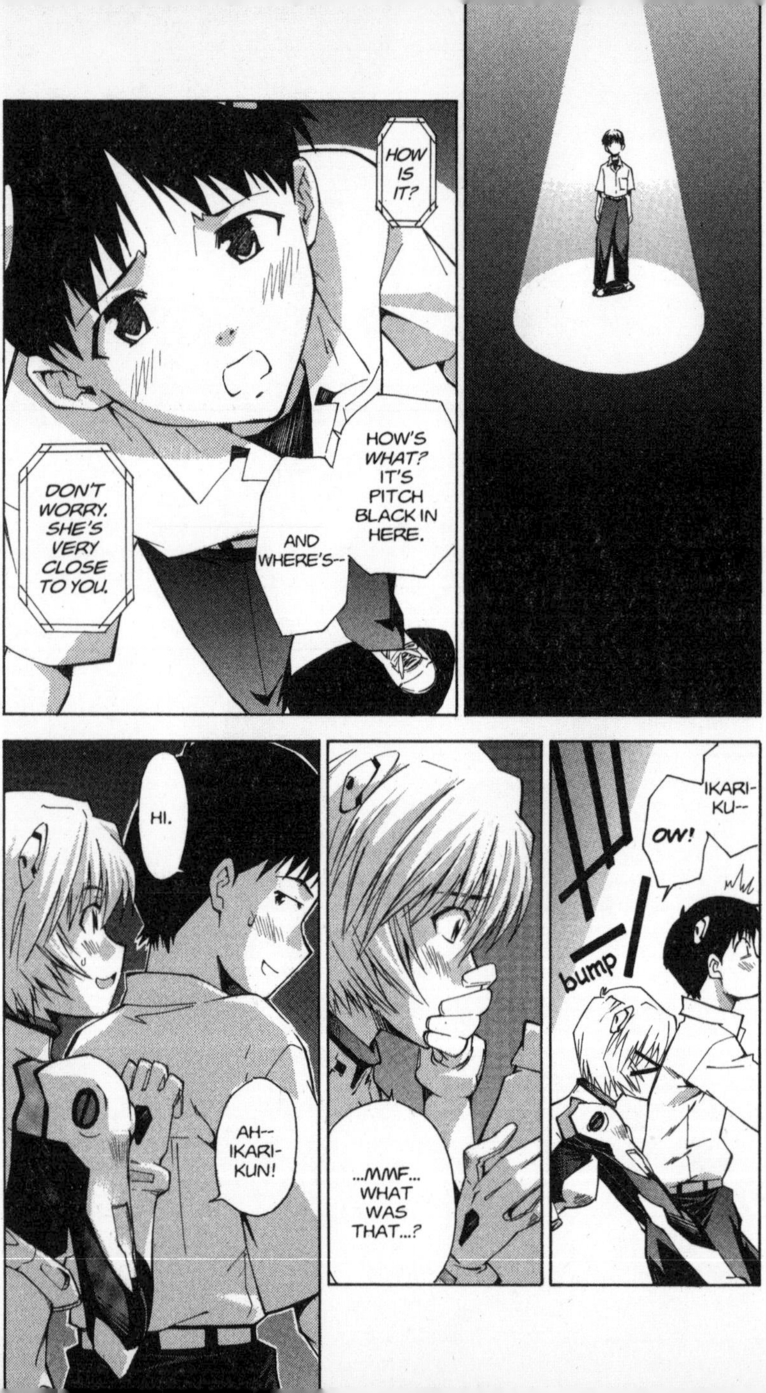
HOW IS IT?
HOW'S WHAT? IT'S PITCH BLACK IN HERE.
AND WHERE'S--
DON'T WORRY. SHE'S VERY CLOSE TO YOU.
IKARI-KU--
OW!
bump
...MMF... WHAT WAS THAT...?
HI.
AH-- IKARI-KUN!

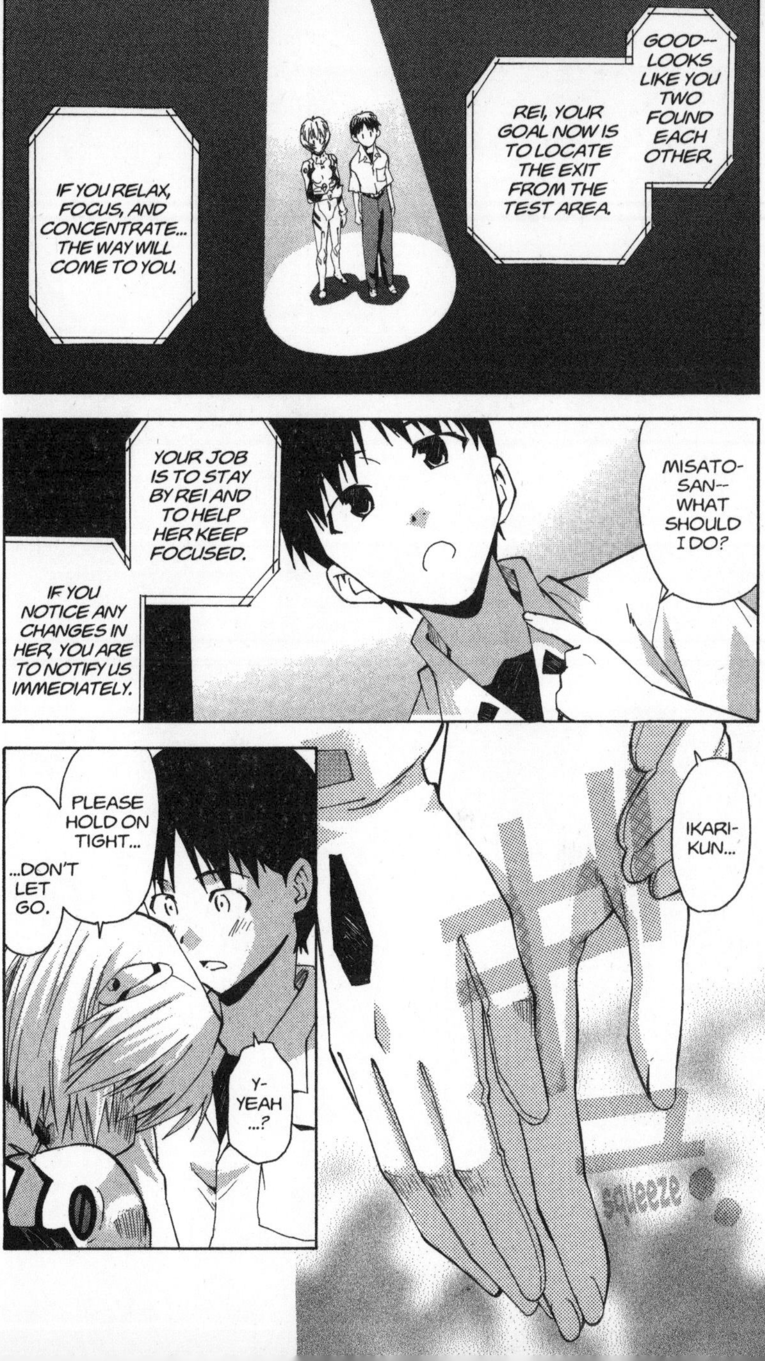
GOOD-- LOOKS LIKE YOU TWO FOUND EACH OTHER.
REI, YOUR GOAL NOW IS TO LOCATE THE EXIT FROM THE TEST AREA.
IF YOU RELAX, FOCUS, AND CONCENTRATE... THE WAY WILL COME TO YOU.
MISATO-SAN-- WHAT SHOULD I DO?
YOUR JOB IS TO STAY BY REI AND TO HELP HER KEEP FOCUSED.
IF YOU NOTICE ANY CHANGES IN HER, YOU ARE TO NOTIFY US IMMEDIATELY.
IKARI-KUN...
PLEASE HOLD ON TIGHT...
...DON'T LET GO.
Y-YEAH ...?
squeeze

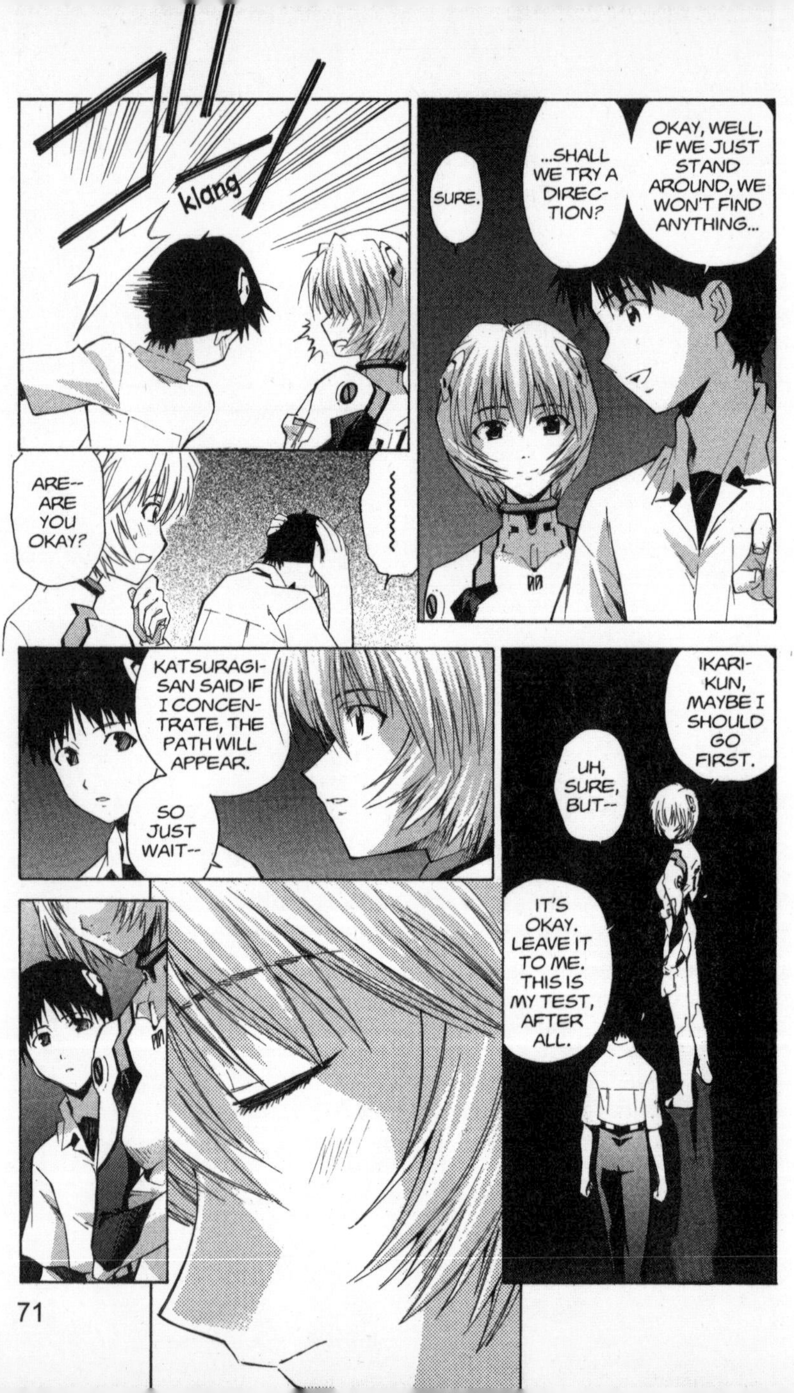
OKAY, WELL, IF WE JUST STAND AROUND, WE WON'T FIND ANYTHING...
...SHALL WE TRY A DIREC-TION?
SURE.
klang
ARE-- ARE YOU OKAY?
IKARI-KUN, MAYBE I SHOULD GO FIRST.
UH, SURE, BUT--
IT'S OKAY. LEAVE IT TO ME. THIS IS MY TEST, AFTER ALL.
KATSURAGI-SAN SAID IF I CONCEN-TRATE, THE PATH WILL APPEAR.
SO JUST WAIT--

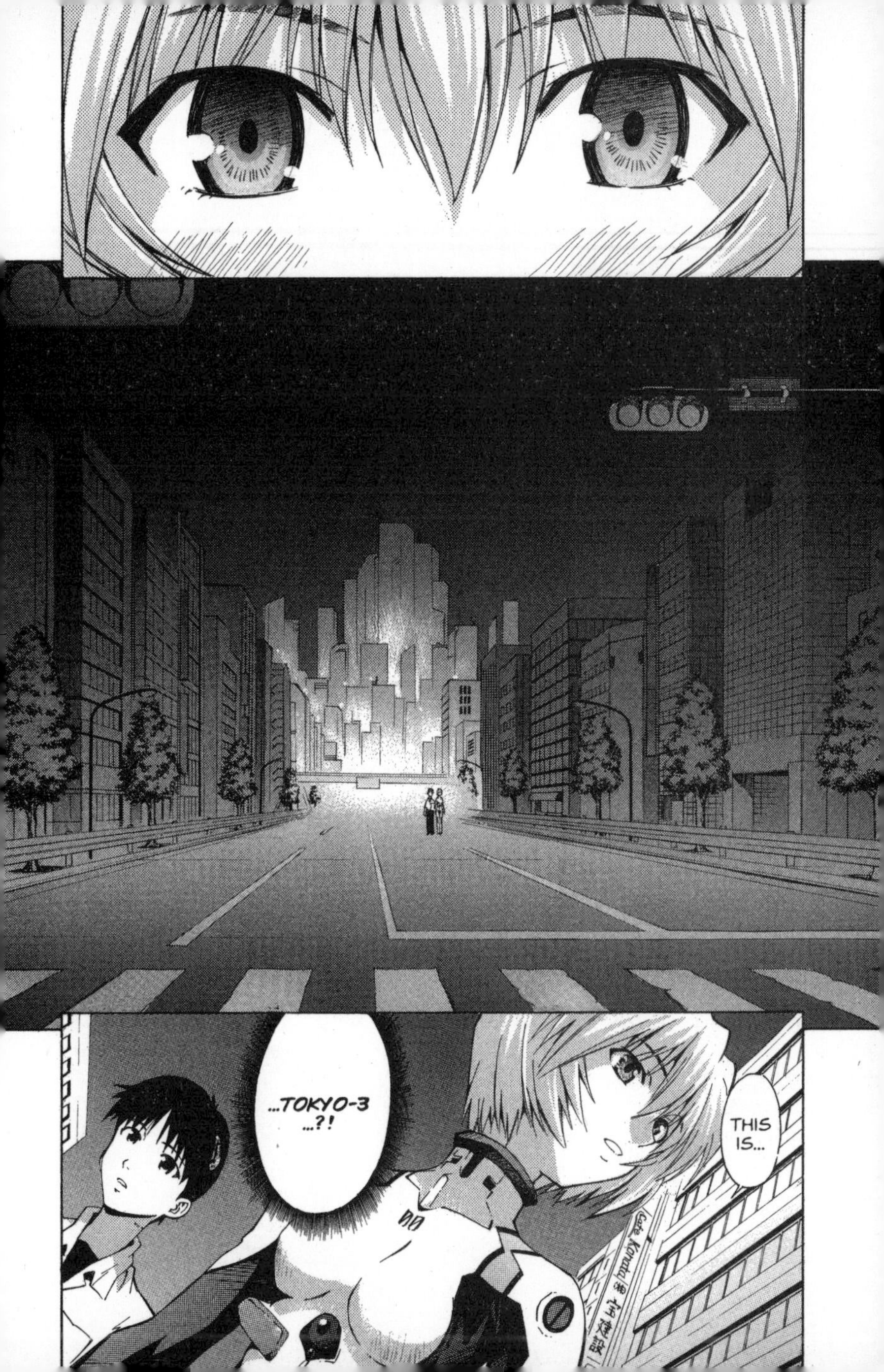
THIS IS...
...TOKYO-3 ...?!

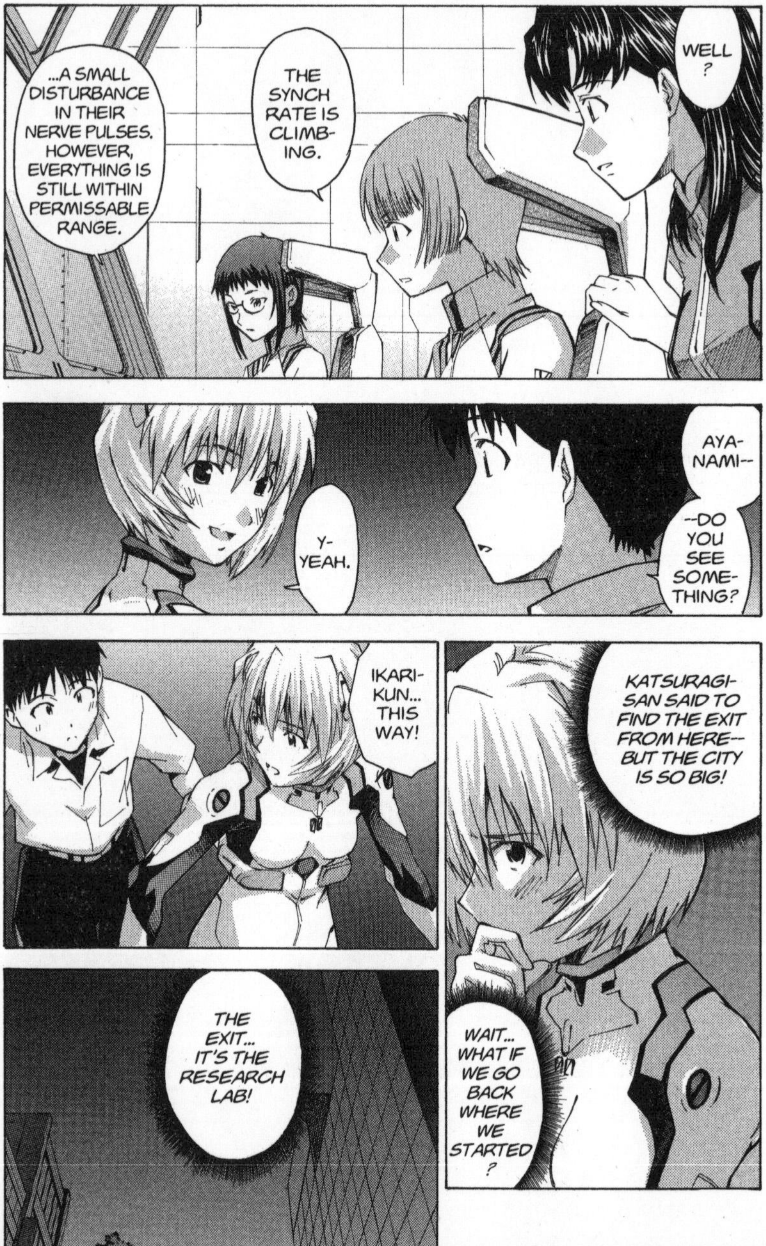
WELL?
THE SYNCH RATE IS CLIMB-ING.
...A SMALL DISTURBANCE IN THEIR NERVE PULSES. HOWEVER, EVERYTHING IS STILL WITHIN PERMISSABLE RANGE.
AYA-NAMI--
--DO YOU SEE SOME-THING?
Y-YEAH.
KATSURAGI-SAN SAID TO FIND THE EXIT FROM HERE-- BUT THE CITY IS SO BIG!
WAIT... WHAT IF WE GO BACK WHERE WE STARTED?
IKARI-KUN... THIS WAY!
THE EXIT... IT'S THE RESEARCH LAB!

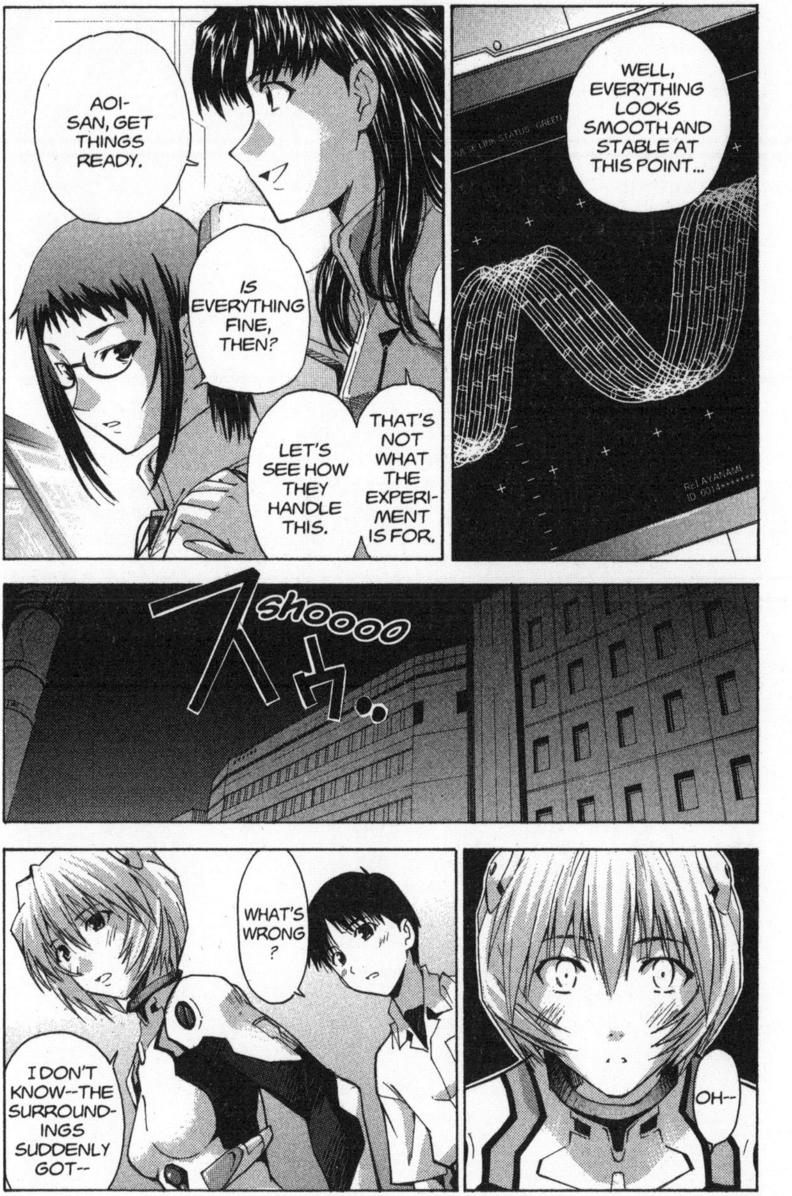
WELL, EVERYTHING LOOKS SMOOTH AND STABLE AT THIS POINT...
AOI-SAN, GET THINGS READY.
IS EVERYTHING FINE, THEN?
THAT'S NOT WHAT THE EXPERIMENT IS FOR.
LET'S SEE HOW THEY HANDLE THIS.
スゥ..
shoooo
OH--
WHAT'S WRONG?
I DON'T KNOW--THE SURROUNDINGS SUDDENLY GOT--

WHERE'D THEY GO? I DON'T SEE THEM--

A-AYA-NAMI, WAIT!

...ALL OF A SUDDEN, I CAN'T SEE ANYTHING!

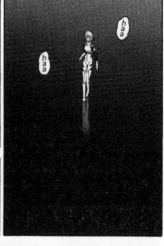

haa

haa

AYA-NAMI--

huh?

reach

..

IKARI-KUN...?!

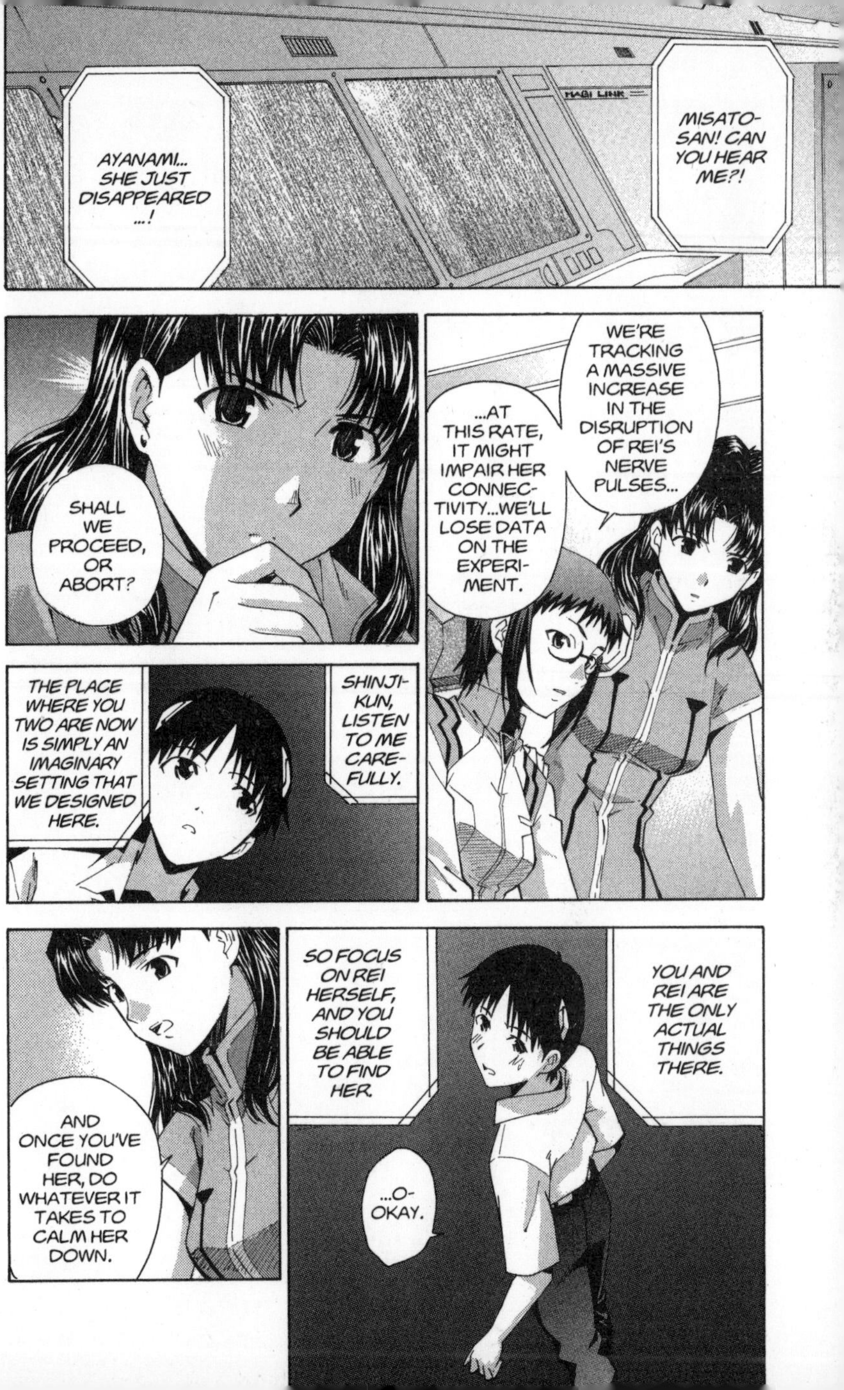
MAGI LINK
MISATO-SAN! CAN YOU HEAR ME?!
AYANAMI... SHE JUST DISAPPEARED ...!
WE'RE TRACKING A MASSIVE INCREASE IN THE DISRUPTION OF REI'S NERVE PULSES...
...AT THIS RATE, IT MIGHT IMPAIR HER CONNECTIVITY...WE'LL LOSE DATA ON THE EXPERIMENT.
SHALL WE PROCEED, OR ABORT?
SHINJI-KUN, LISTEN TO ME CAREFULLY.
THE PLACE WHERE YOU TWO ARE NOW IS SIMPLY AN IMAGINARY SETTING THAT WE DESIGNED HERE.
YOU AND REI ARE THE ONLY ACTUAL THINGS THERE.
SO FOCUS ON REI HERSELF, AND YOU SHOULD BE ABLE TO FIND HER.
...O-OKAY.
AND ONCE YOU'VE FOUND HER, DO WHATEVER IT TAKES TO CALM HER DOWN.

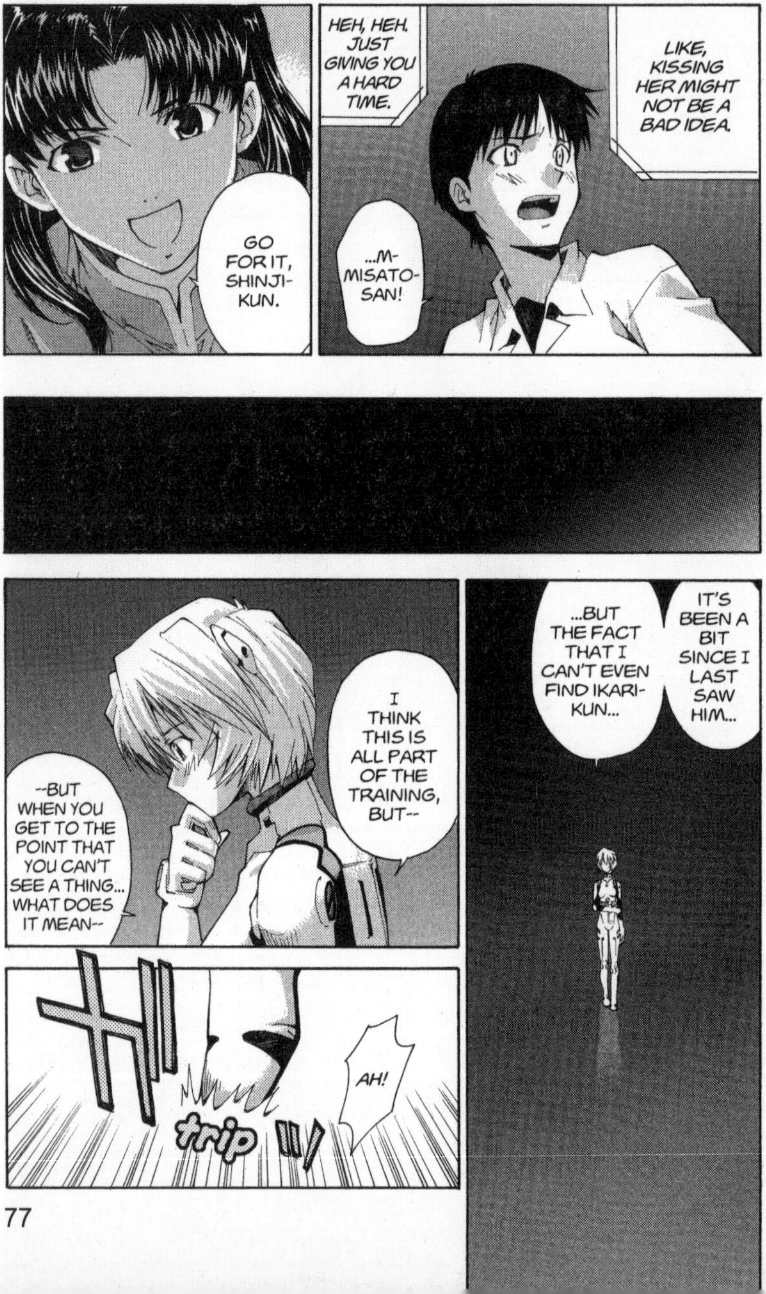
LIKE, KISSING HER MIGHT NOT BE A BAD IDEA.
HEH, HEH. JUST GIVING YOU A HARD TIME.
...M-MISATO-SAN!
GO FOR IT, SHINJI-KUN.
IT'S BEEN A BIT SINCE I LAST SAW HIM...
...BUT THE FACT THAT I CAN'T EVEN FIND IKARI-KUN...
I THINK THIS IS ALL PART OF THE TRAINING, BUT--
--BUT WHEN YOU GET TO THE POINT THAT YOU CAN'T SEE A THING... WHAT DOES IT MEAN--
AH!
trip

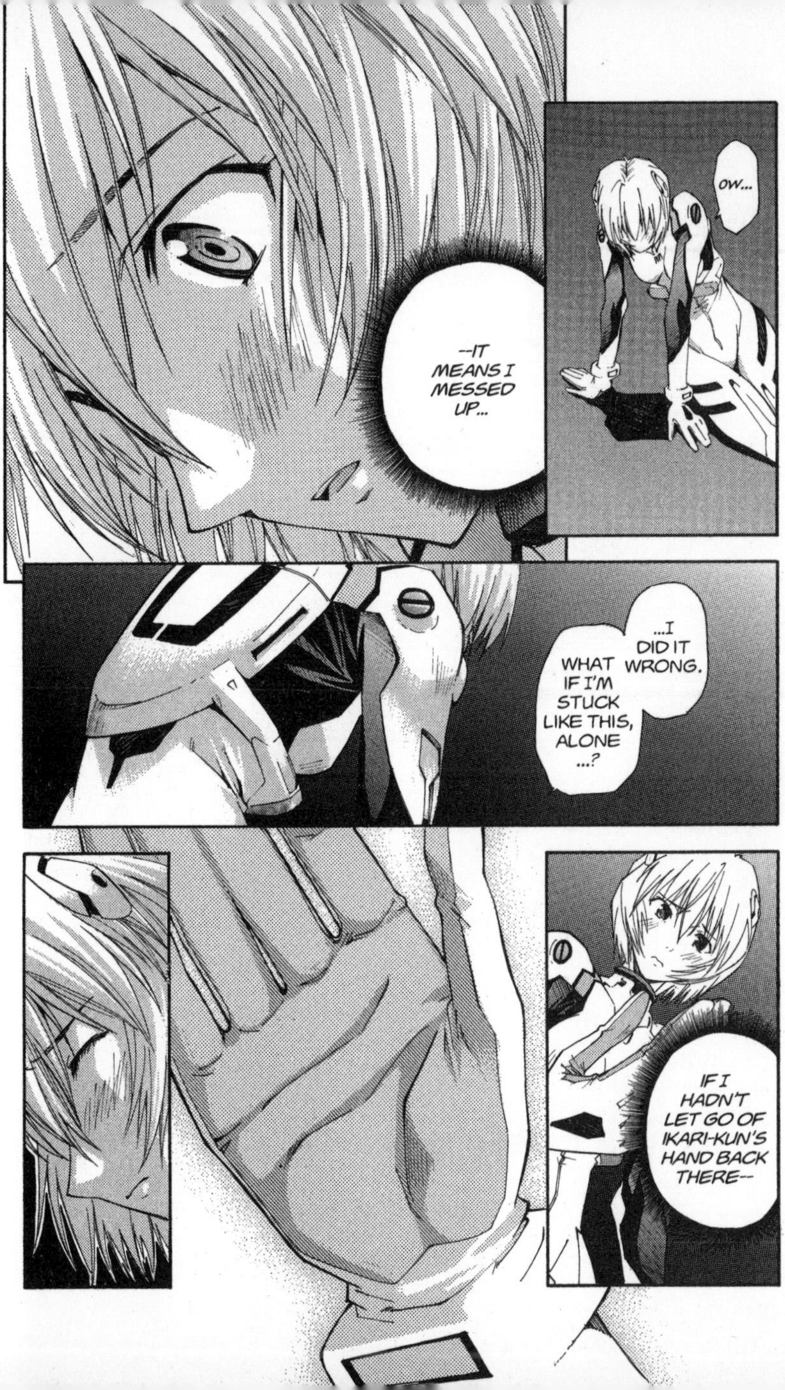
OW...
--IT MEANS I MESSED UP...
...I DID IT WRONG.
WHAT IF I'M STUCK LIKE THIS, ALONE ...?
IF I HADN'T LET GO OF IKARI-KUN'S HAND BACK THERE--

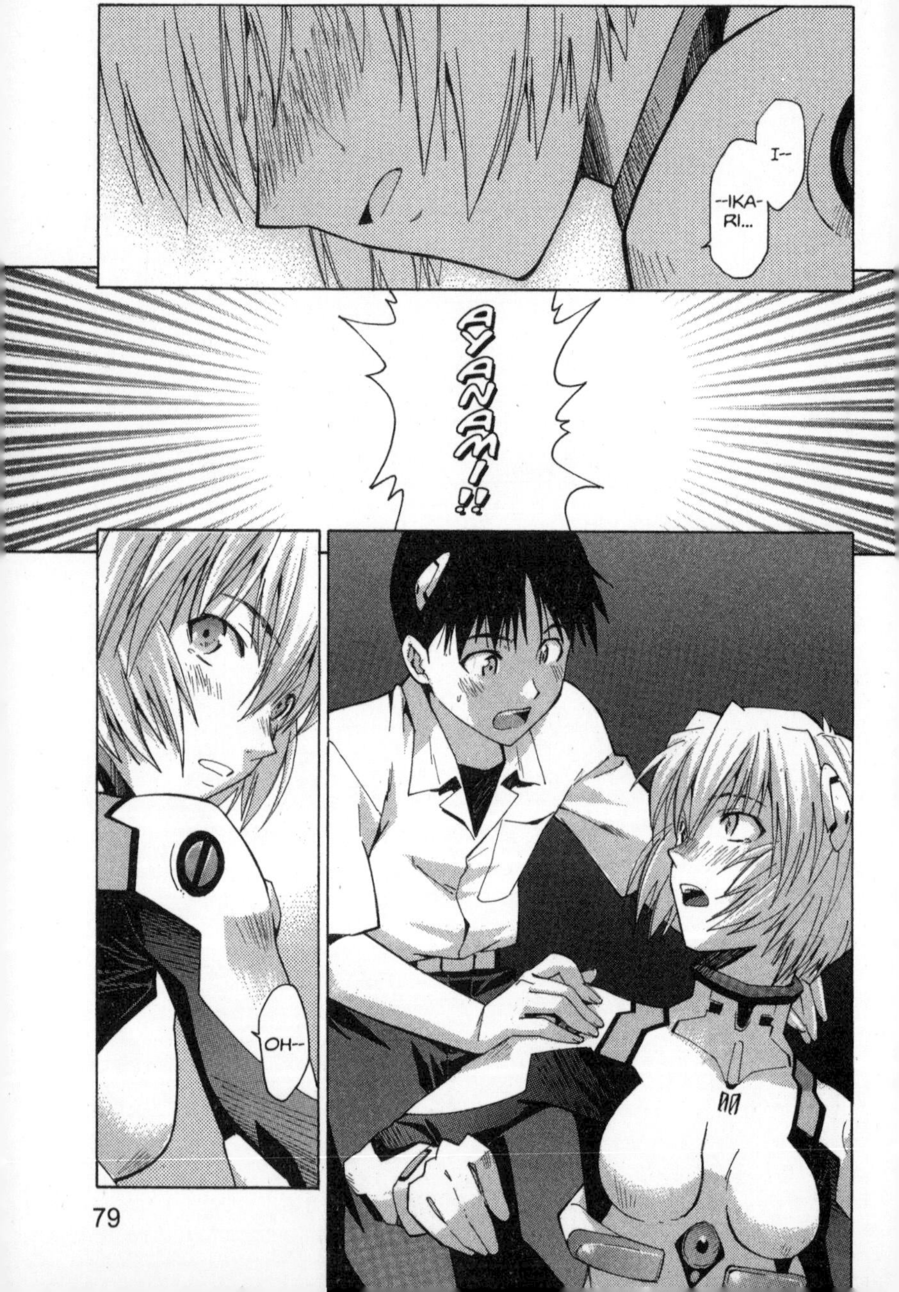
I--
--IKARI...
AYANAMI!!
OH--

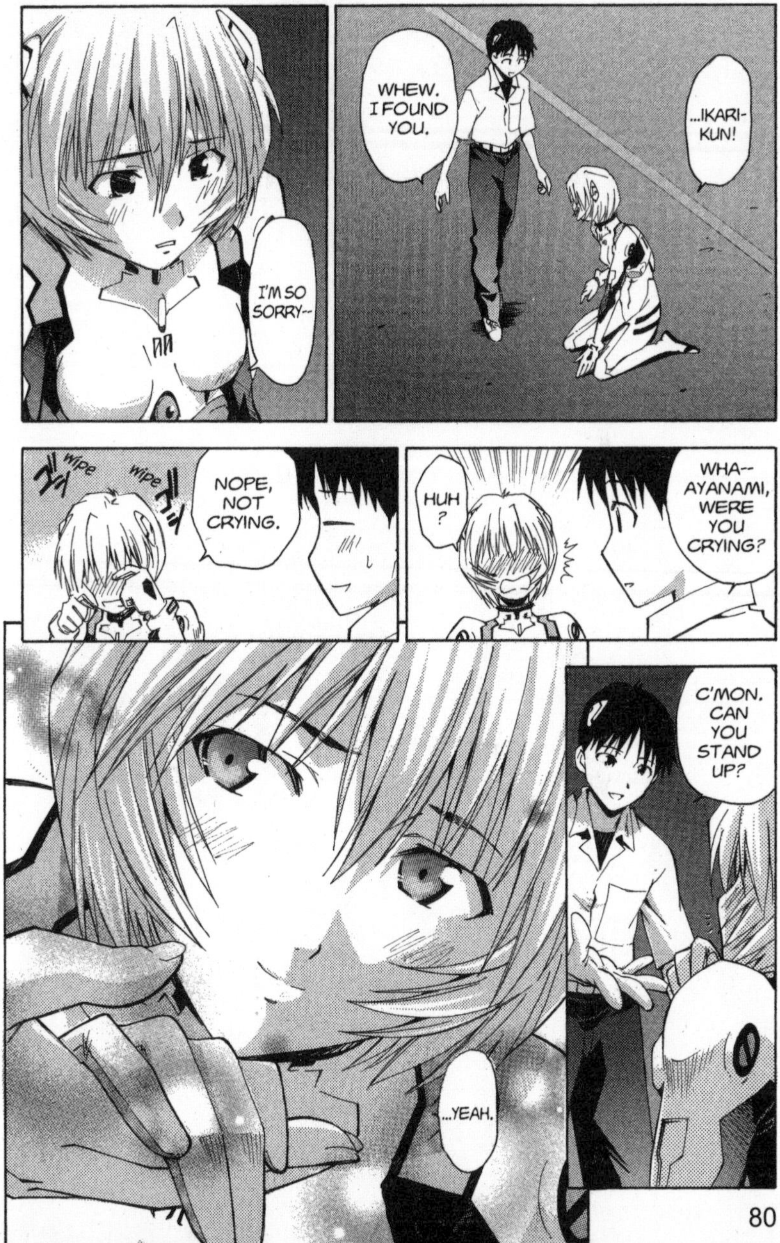
WHEW. I FOUND YOU.
...IKARI-KUN!
I'M SO SORRY--
WHA-- AYANAMI, WERE YOU CRYING?
HUH?
wipe
wipe
NOPE, NOT CRYING.
C'MON. CAN YOU STAND UP?
...YEAH.

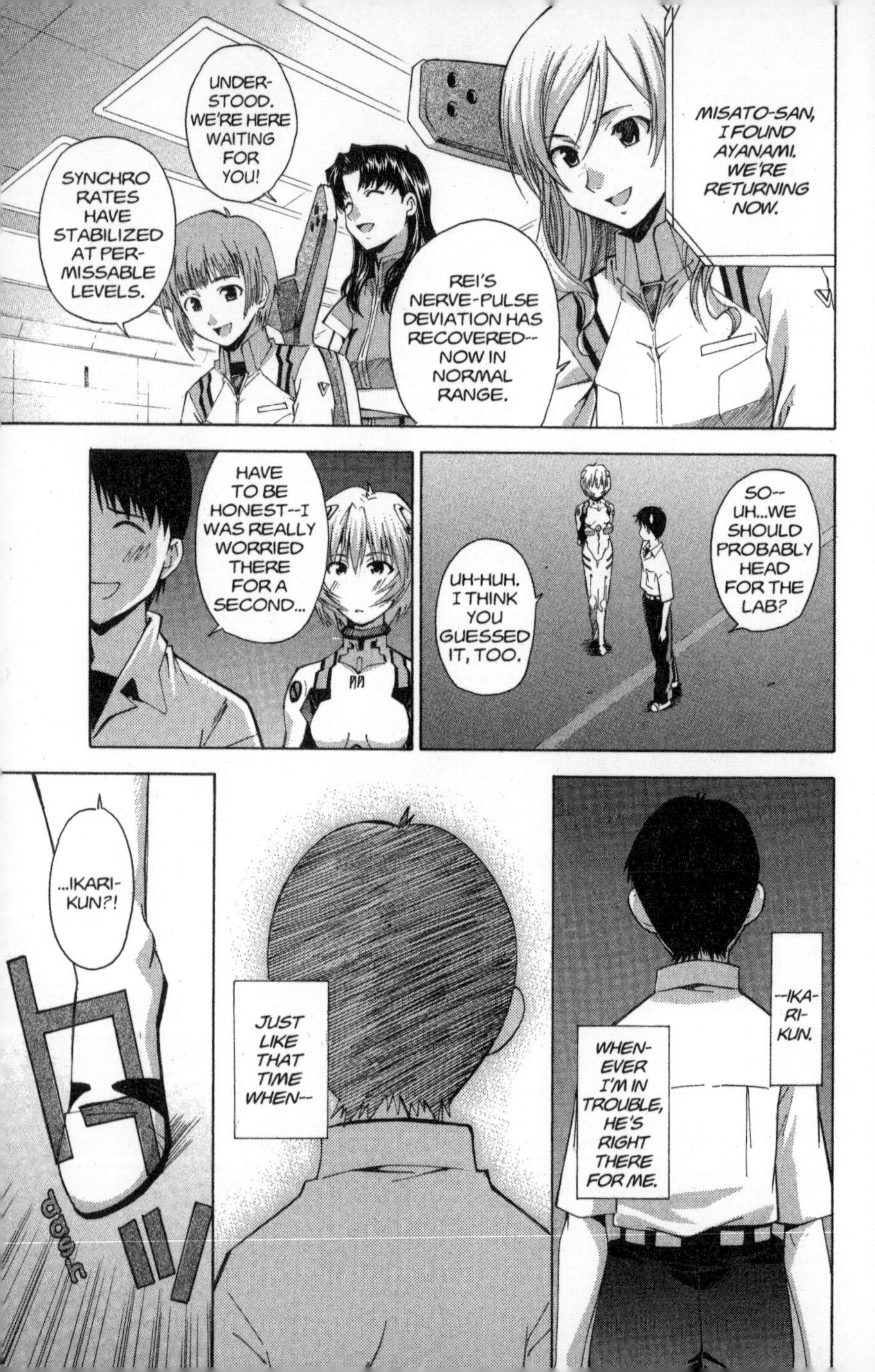
MISATO-SAN, I FOUND AYANAMI. WE'RE RETURNING NOW.
UNDER-STOOD. WE'RE HERE WAITING FOR YOU!
REI'S NERVE-PULSE DEVIATION HAS RECOVERED-- NOW IN NORMAL RANGE.
SYNCHRO RATES HAVE STABILIZED AT PER-MISSABLE LEVELS.
SO-- UH...WE SHOULD PROBABLY HEAD FOR THE LAB?
UH-HUH. I THINK YOU GUESSED IT, TOO.
HAVE TO BE HONEST--I WAS REALLY WORRIED THERE FOR A SECOND...
--IKA-RI-KUN.
WHEN-EVER I'M IN TROUBLE, HE'S RIGHT THERE FOR ME.
JUST LIKE THAT TIME WHEN--
...IKARI-KUN?!

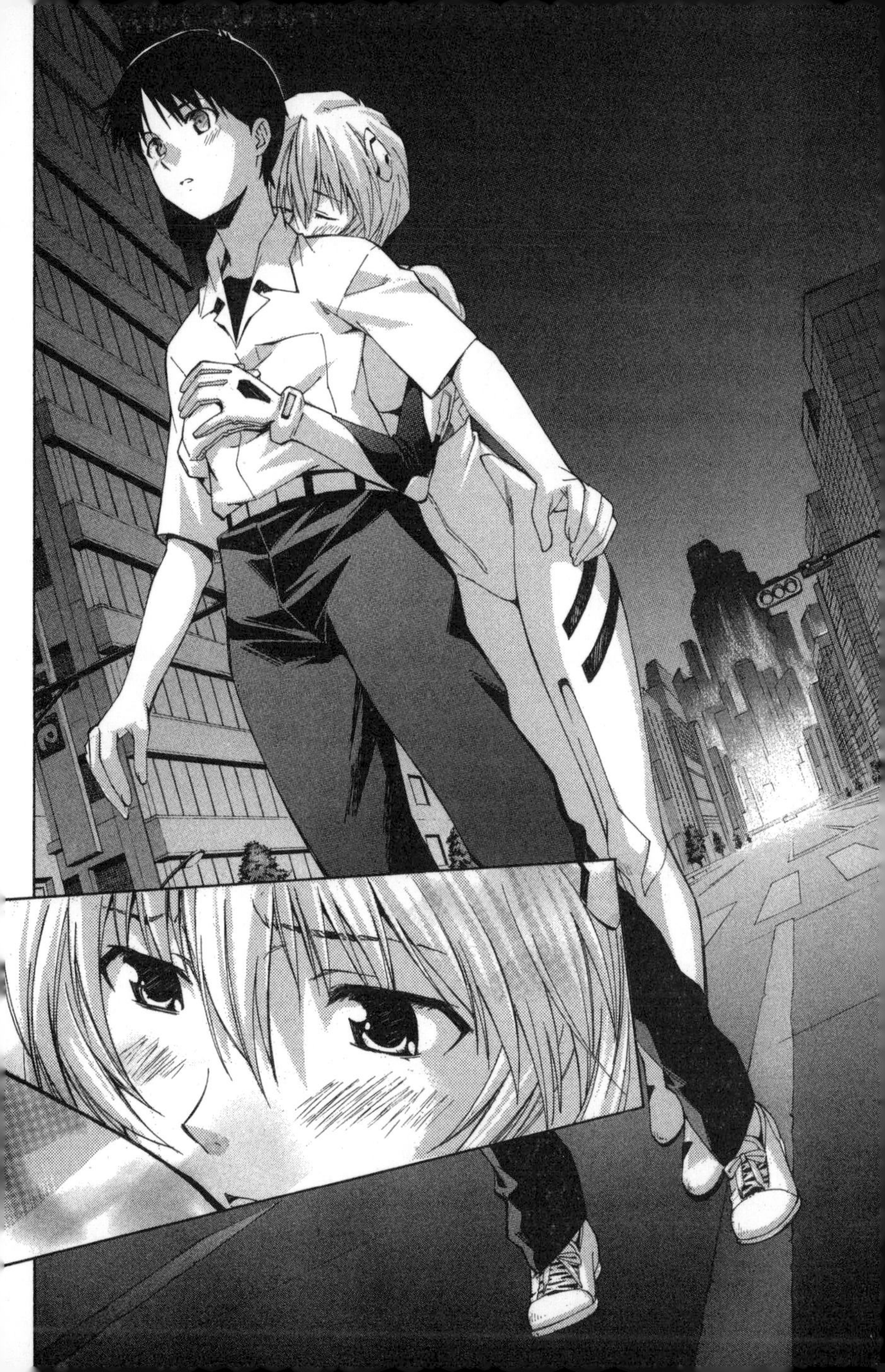

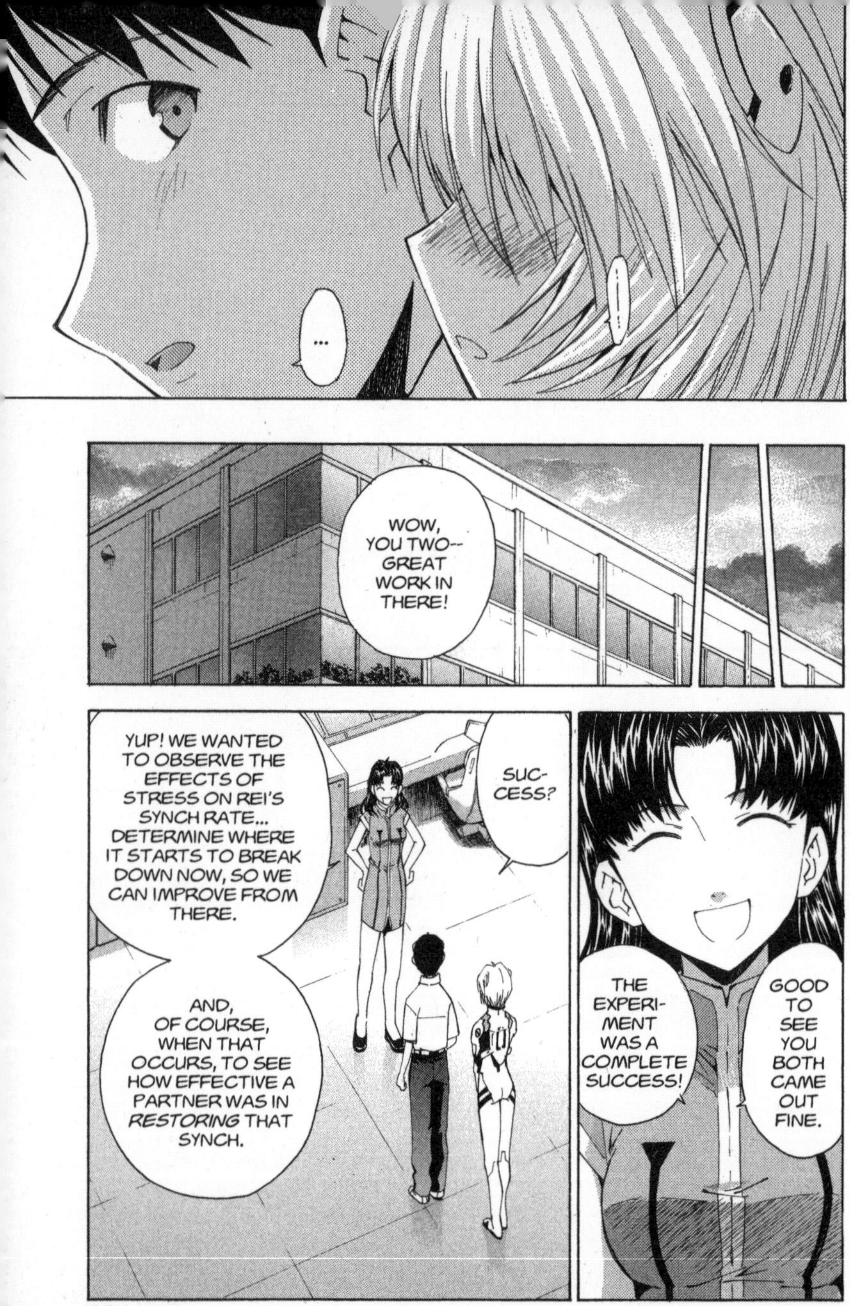
!
...
WOW, YOU TWO-- GREAT WORK IN THERE!
GOOD TO SEE YOU BOTH CAME OUT FINE.
THE EXPERIMENT WAS A COMPLETE SUCCESS!
SUCCESS?
YUP! WE WANTED TO OBSERVE THE EFFECTS OF STRESS ON REI'S SYNCH RATE... DETERMINE WHERE IT STARTS TO BREAK DOWN NOW, SO WE CAN IMPROVE FROM THERE.
AND, OF COURSE, WHEN THAT OCCURS, TO SEE HOW EFFECTIVE A PARTNER WAS IN *RESTORING* THAT SYNCH.

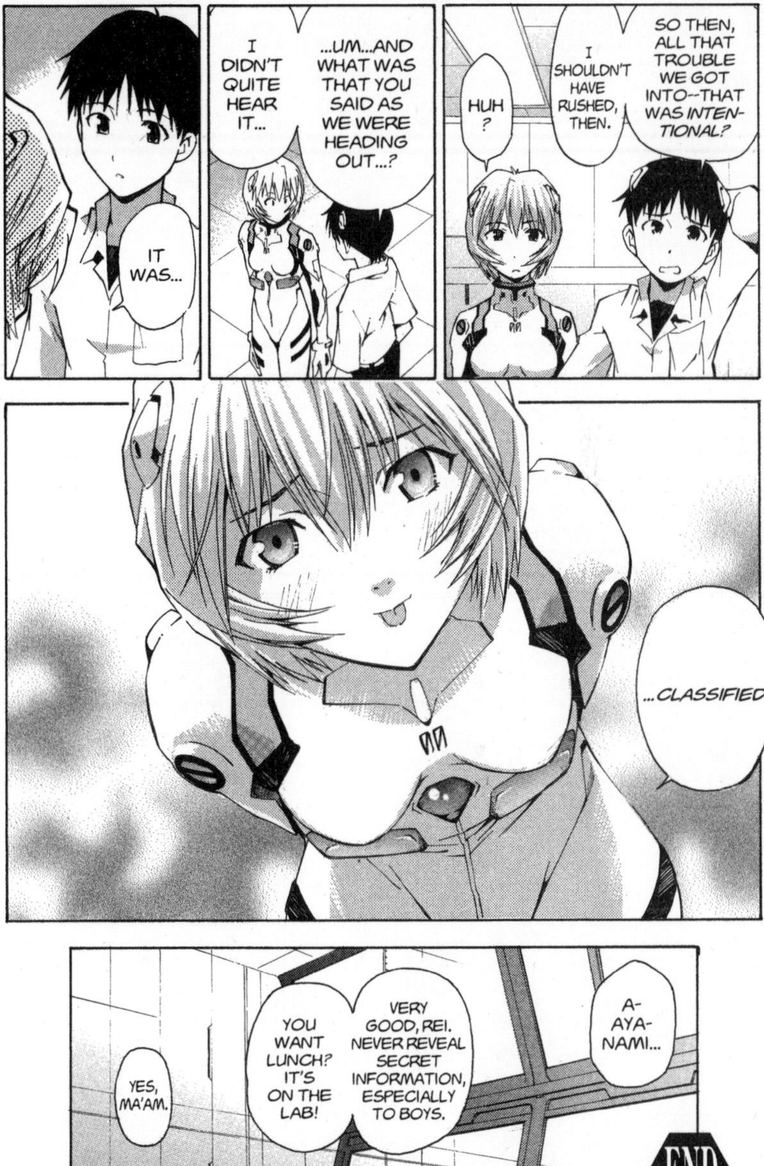
SO THEN, ALL THAT TROUBLE WE GOT INTO--THAT WAS INTENTIONAL?
I SHOULDN'T HAVE RUSHED, THEN.
HUH ?
...UM...AND WHAT WAS THAT YOU SAID AS WE WERE HEADING OUT...?
I DIDN'T QUITE HEAR IT...
IT WAS...
...CLASSIFIED.
A-AYA-NAMI...
VERY GOOD, REI. NEVER REVEAL SECRET INFORMATION, ESPECIALLY TO BOYS.
YOU WANT LUNCH? IT'S ON THE LAB!
YES, MA'AM.
END

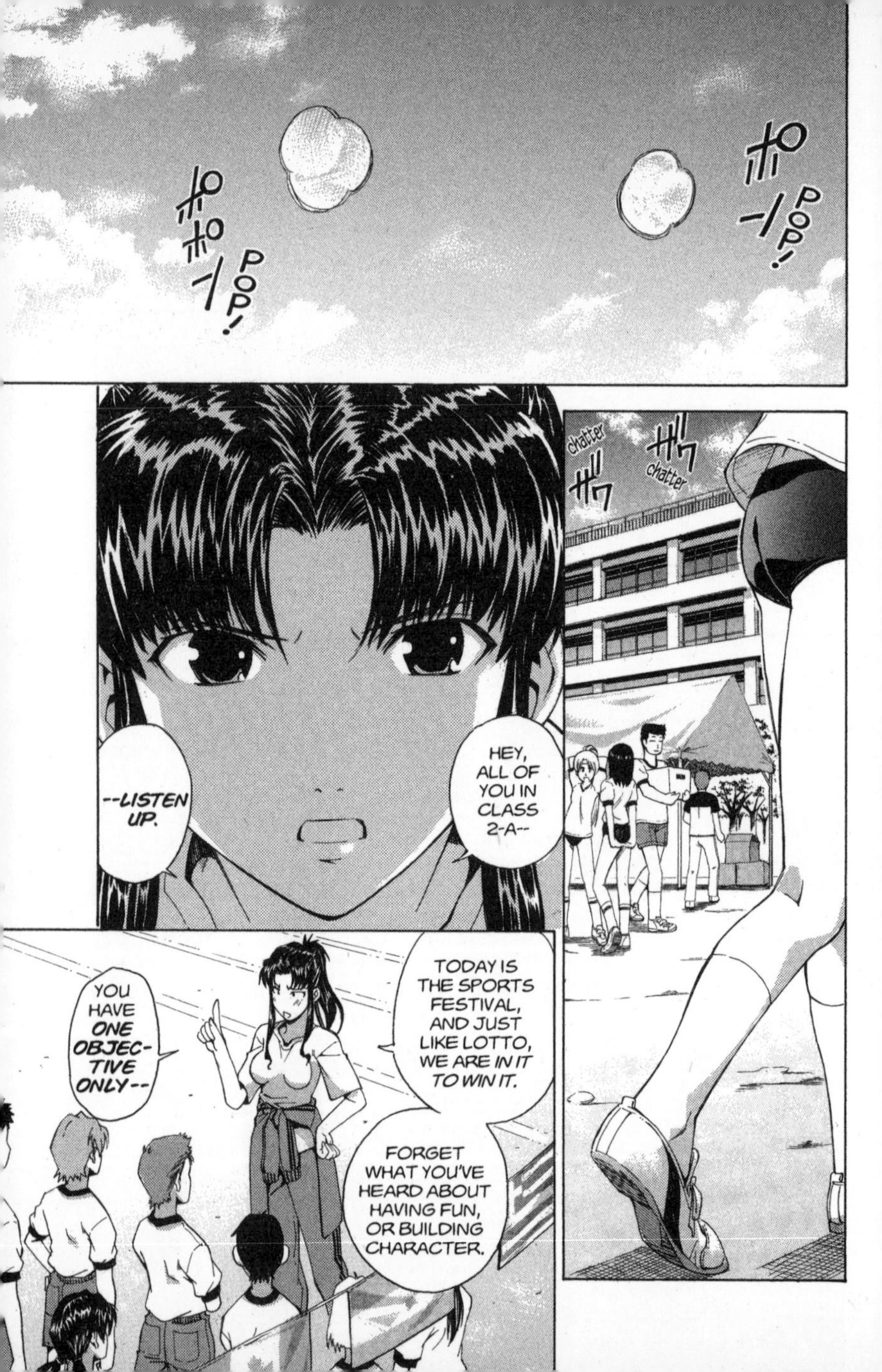
POP!
POP!
chatter
chatter
HEY, ALL OF YOU IN CLASS 2-A--
--LISTEN UP.
TODAY IS THE SPORTS FESTIVAL, AND JUST LIKE LOTTO, WE ARE *IN IT TO WIN IT.*
YOU HAVE *ONE OBJECTIVE ONLY*--
FORGET WHAT YOU'VE HEARD ABOUT HAVING FUN, OR BUILDING CHARACTER.

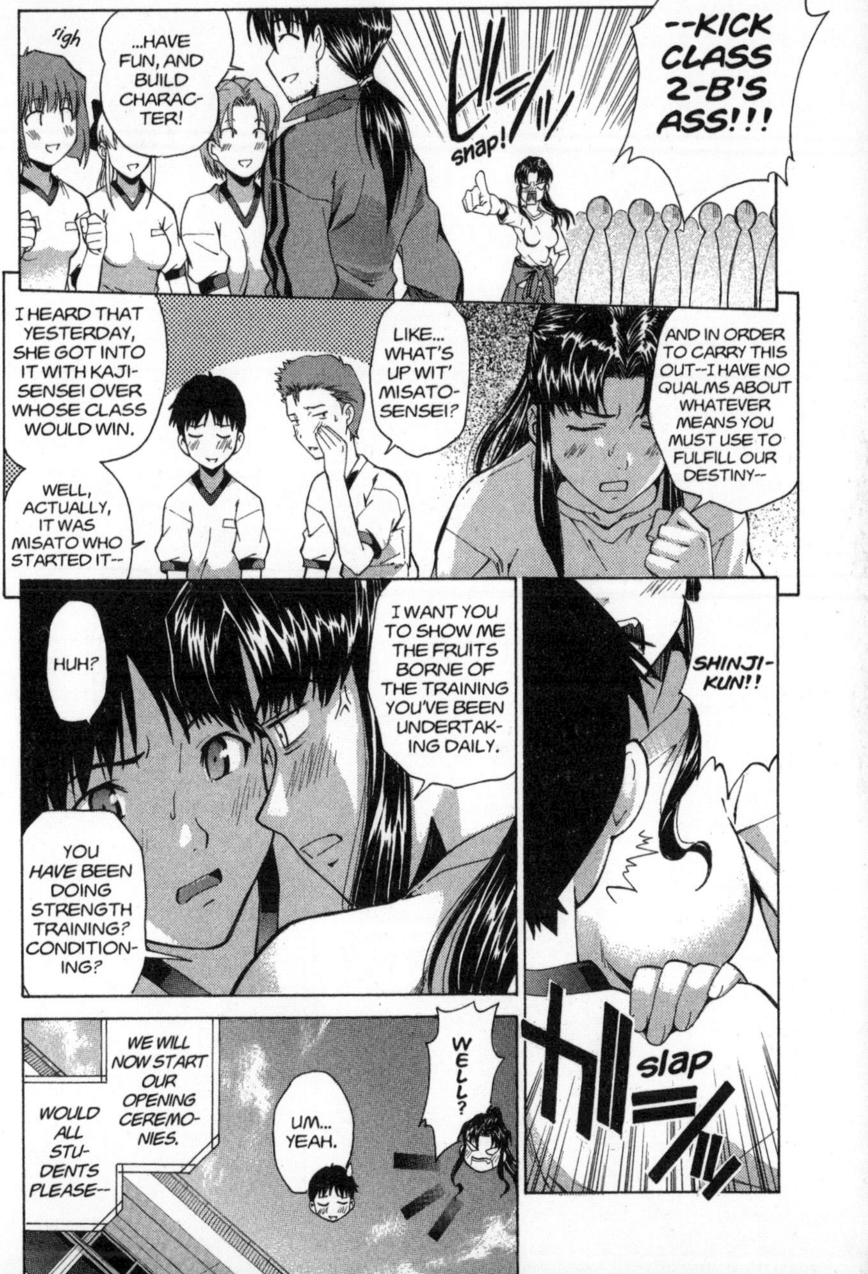
--KICK CLASS 2-B'S ASS!!!
snap!
...HAVE FUN, AND BUILD CHARACTER!
sigh
AND IN ORDER TO CARRY THIS OUT--I HAVE NO QUALMS ABOUT WHATEVER MEANS YOU MUST USE TO FULFILL OUR DESTINY--
LIKE... WHAT'S UP WIT' MISATO-SENSEI?
I HEARD THAT YESTERDAY, SHE GOT INTO IT WITH KAJI-SENSEI OVER WHOSE CLASS WOULD WIN.
WELL, ACTUALLY, IT WAS MISATO WHO STARTED IT--
SHINJI-KUN!!
slap
I WANT YOU TO SHOW ME THE FRUITS BORNE OF THE TRAINING YOU'VE BEEN UNDERTAKING DAILY.
HUH?
YOU HAVE BEEN DOING STRENGTH TRAINING? CONDITIONING?
WELL?
UM... YEAH.
WE WILL NOW START OUR OPENING CEREMONIES.
WOULD ALL STUDENTS PLEASE--

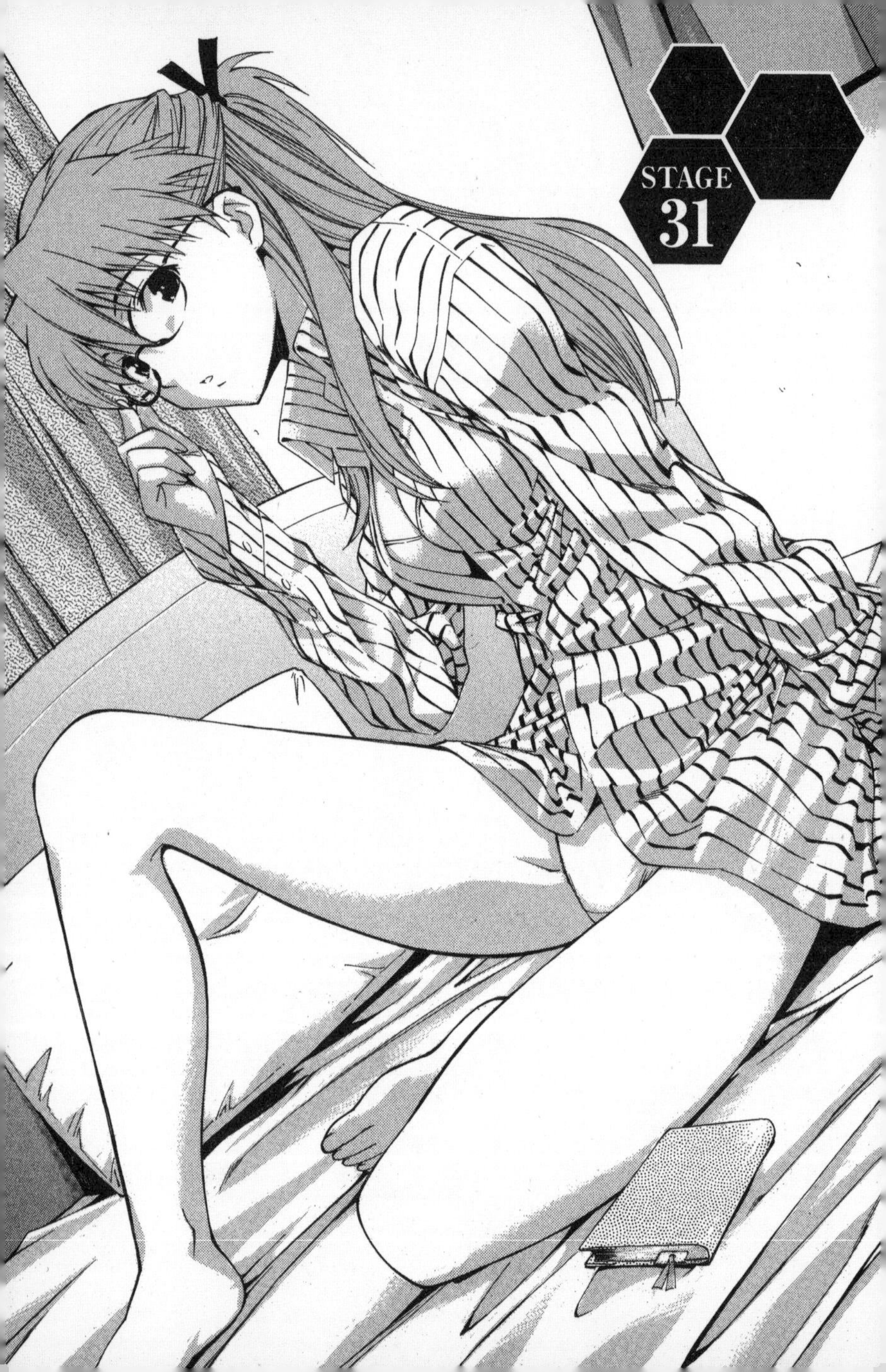
STAGE
31

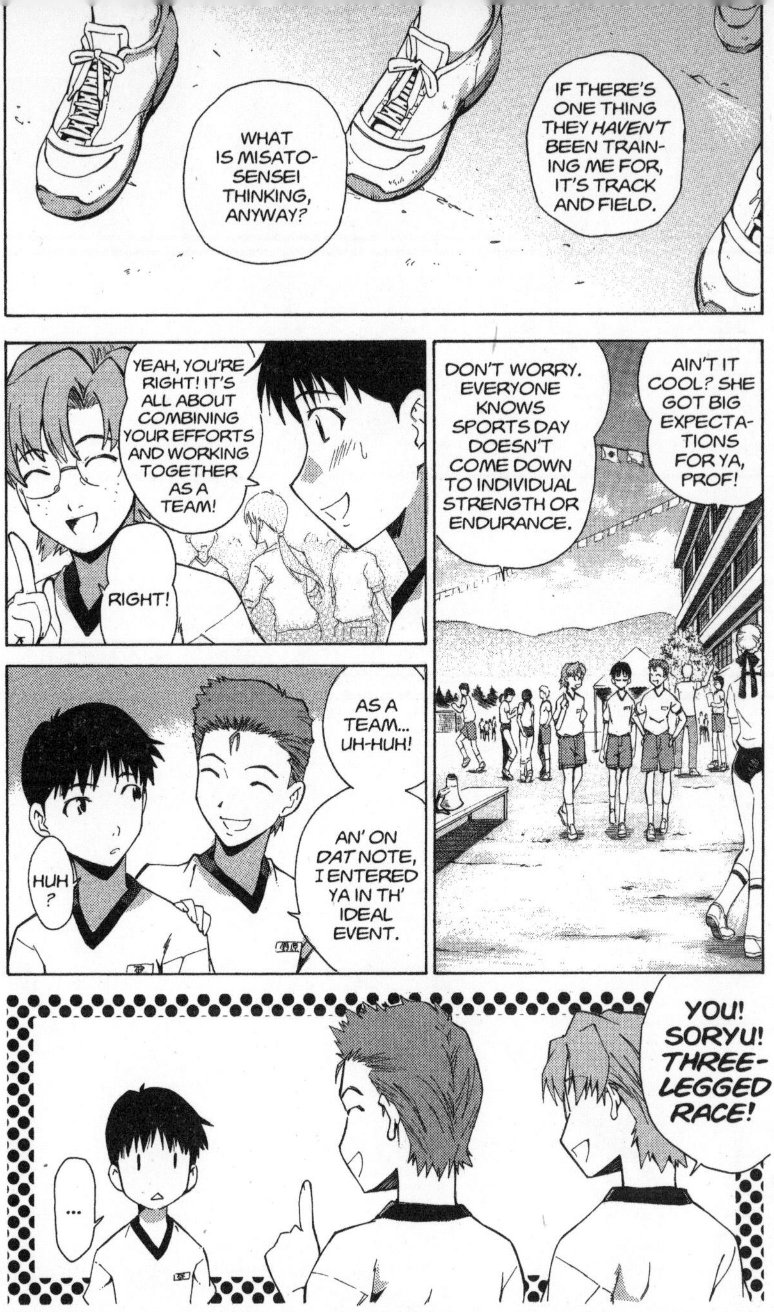
IF THERE'S ONE THING THEY *HAVEN'T* BEEN TRAINING ME FOR, IT'S TRACK AND FIELD.
WHAT IS MISATO-SENSEI THINKING, ANYWAY?
AIN'T IT COOL? SHE GOT BIG EXPECTATIONS FOR YA, PROF!
DON'T WORRY. EVERYONE KNOWS SPORTS DAY DOESN'T COME DOWN TO INDIVIDUAL STRENGTH OR ENDURANCE.
YEAH, YOU'RE RIGHT! IT'S ALL ABOUT COMBINING YOUR EFFORTS AND WORKING TOGETHER AS A TEAM!
RIGHT!
AS A TEAM... UH-HUH!
AN' ON *DAT* NOTE, I ENTERED YA IN TH' IDEAL EVENT.
HUH?
YOU! SORYU! *THREE-LEGGED RACE!*
...

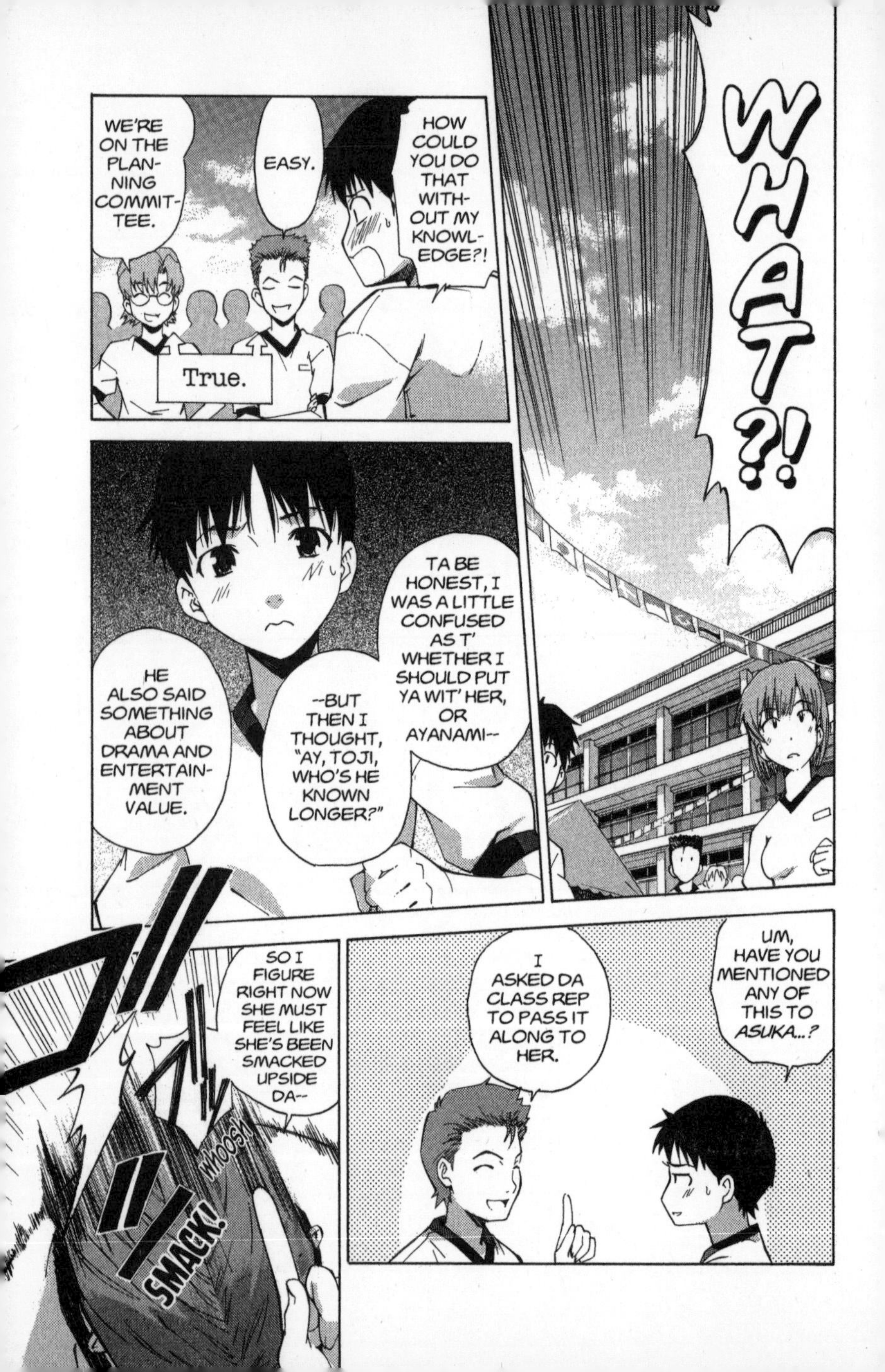
WHAT?!
HOW COULD YOU DO THAT WITH-OUT MY KNOWL-EDGE?!
EASY.
WE'RE ON THE PLAN-NING COMMIT-TEE.
True.
TA BE HONEST, I WAS A LITTLE CONFUSED AS T' WHETHER I SHOULD PUT YA WIT' HER, OR AYANAMI--
--BUT THEN I THOUGHT, "AY, TOJI, WHO'S HE KNOWN LONGER?"
HE ALSO SAID SOMETHING ABOUT DRAMA AND ENTERTAIN-MENT VALUE.
UM, HAVE YOU MENTIONED ANY OF THIS TO ASUKA...?
I ASKED DA CLASS REP TO PASS IT ALONG TO HER.
SO I FIGURE RIGHT NOW SHE MUST FEEL LIKE SHE'S BEEN SMACKED UPSIDE DA--
WHOOSH
SMACK!

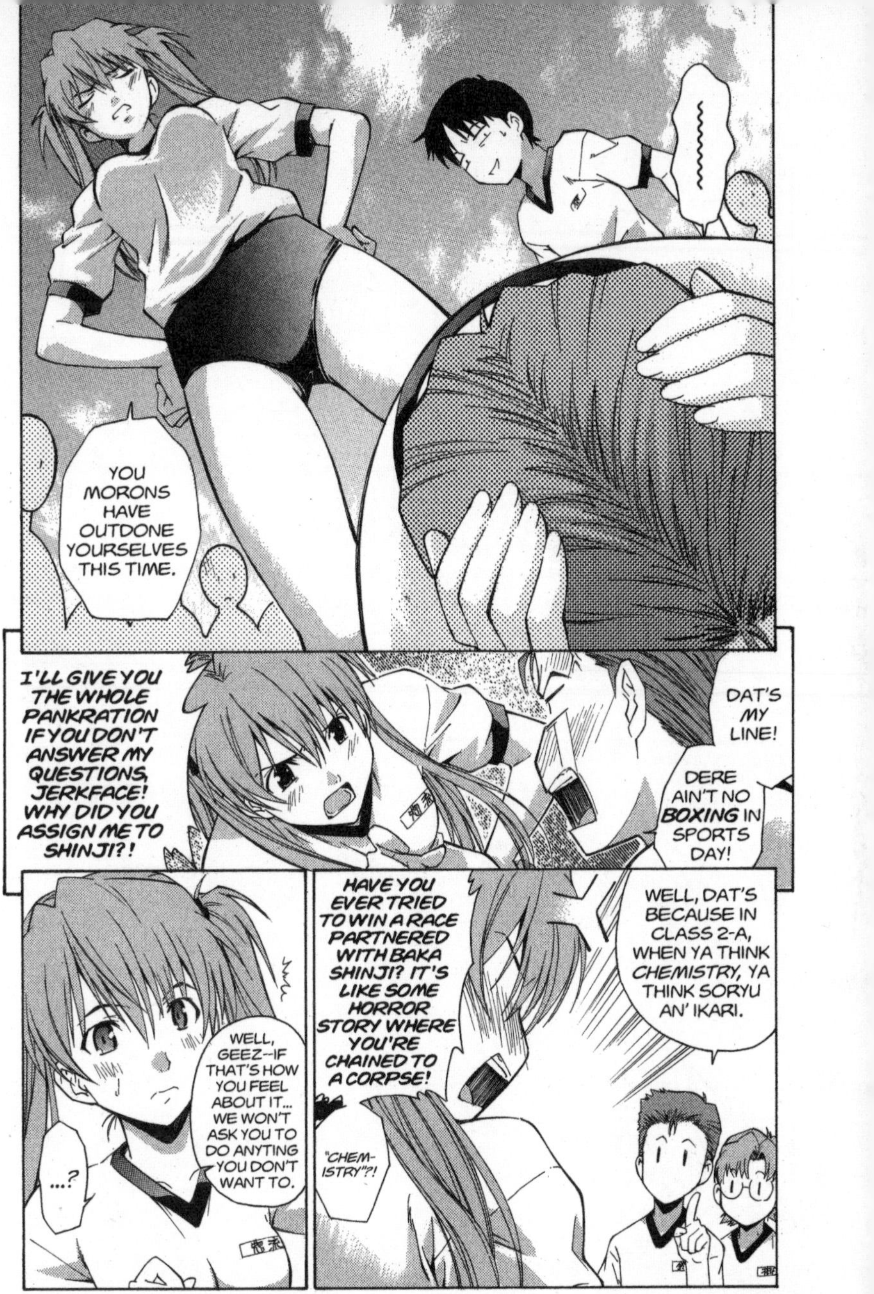
YOU MORONS HAVE OUTDONE YOURSELVES THIS TIME.
I'LL GIVE YOU THE WHOLE PANKRATION IF YOU DON'T ANSWER MY QUESTIONS, JERKFACE! WHY DID YOU ASSIGN ME TO SHINJI?!
DAT'S MY LINE!
DERE AIN'T NO BOXING IN SPORTS DAY!
WELL, DAT'S BECAUSE IN CLASS 2-A, WHEN YA THINK CHEMISTRY, YA THINK SORYU AN' IKARI.
"CHEM-ISTRY"?!
HAVE YOU EVER TRIED TO WIN A RACE PARTNERED WITH BAKA SHINJI? IT'S LIKE SOME HORROR STORY WHERE YOU'RE CHAINED TO A CORPSE!
WELL, GEEZ--IF THAT'S HOW YOU FEEL ABOUT IT... WE WON'T ASK YOU TO DO ANYTING YOU DON'T WANT TO.
...?

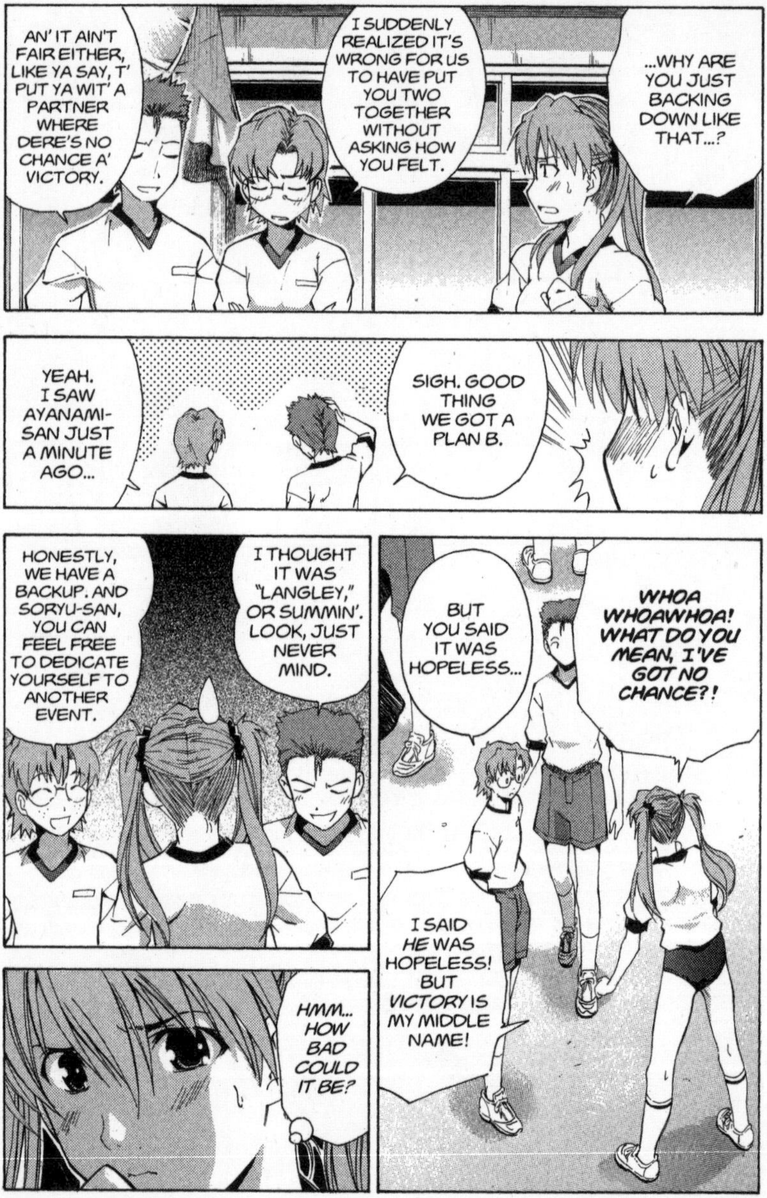
...WHY ARE YOU JUST BACKING DOWN LIKE THAT...?
I SUDDENLY REALIZED IT'S WRONG FOR US TO HAVE PUT YOU TWO TOGETHER WITHOUT ASKING HOW YOU FELT.
AN' IT AIN'T FAIR EITHER, LIKE YA SAY, T' PUT YA WIT' A PARTNER WHERE DERE'S NO CHANCE A' VICTORY.
SIGH. GOOD THING WE GOT A PLAN B.
YEAH. I SAW AYANAMI-SAN JUST A MINUTE AGO...
WHOA WHOAWHOA! WHAT DO YOU MEAN, I'VE GOT NO CHANCE?!
BUT YOU SAID IT WAS HOPELESS...
I SAID *HE* WAS HOPELESS! BUT *VICTORY* IS MY MIDDLE NAME!
I THOUGHT IT WAS "LANGLEY," OR SUMMIN'. LOOK, JUST NEVER MIND.
HONESTLY, WE HAVE A BACKUP. AND SORYU-SAN, YOU CAN FEEL FREE TO DEDICATE YOURSELF TO ANOTHER EVENT.
HMM... HOW BAD COULD IT BE?

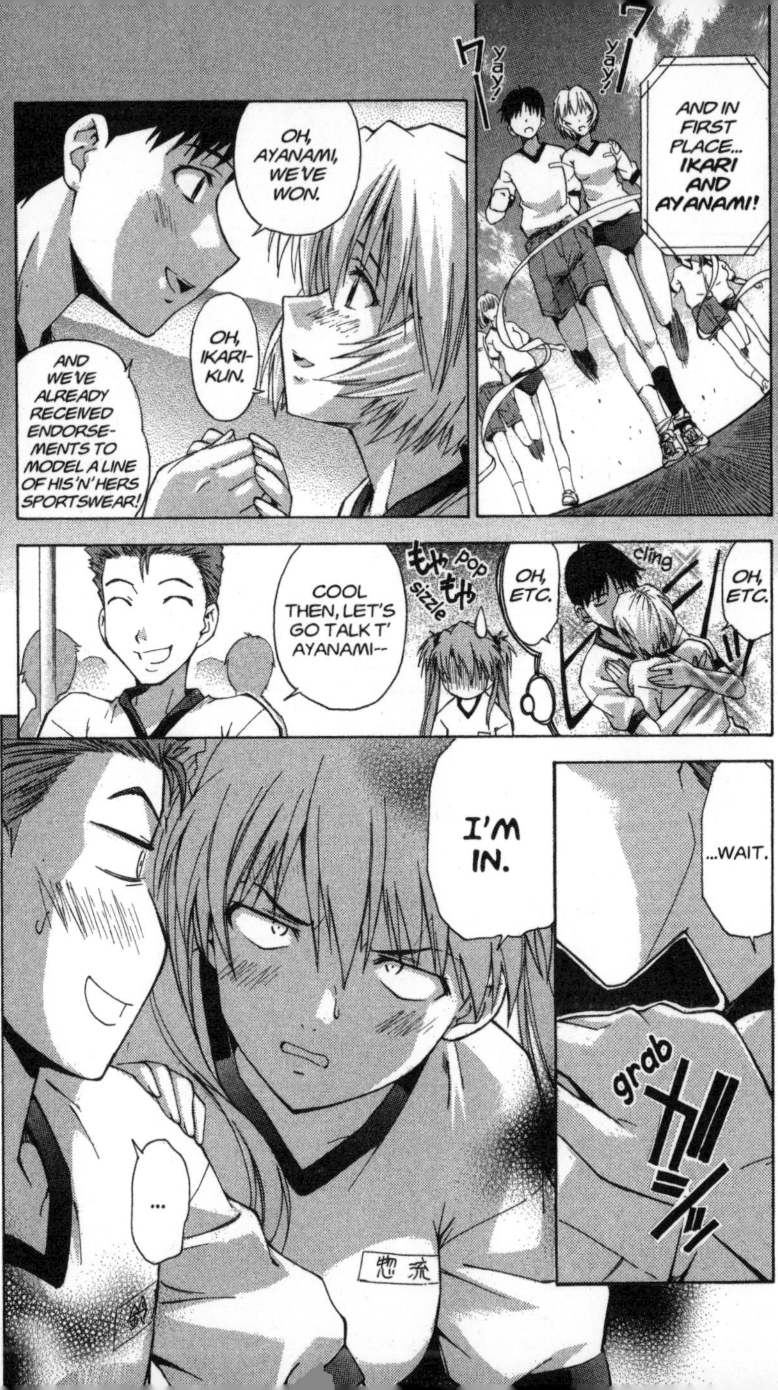
ワー
yay!
ワー
yay!
AND IN FIRST PLACE... IKARI AND AYANAMI!
OH, AYANAMI, WE'VE WON.
OH, IKARI-KUN.
AND WE'VE ALREADY RECEIVED ENDORSEMENTS TO MODEL A LINE OF HIS'N'HERS SPORTSWEAR!
OH, ETC.
cling
OH, ETC.
もやもや
pop
sizzle
COOL THEN, LET'S GO TALK T' AYANAMI--
...WAIT.
grab
ガッ
I'M IN.
...
惣流

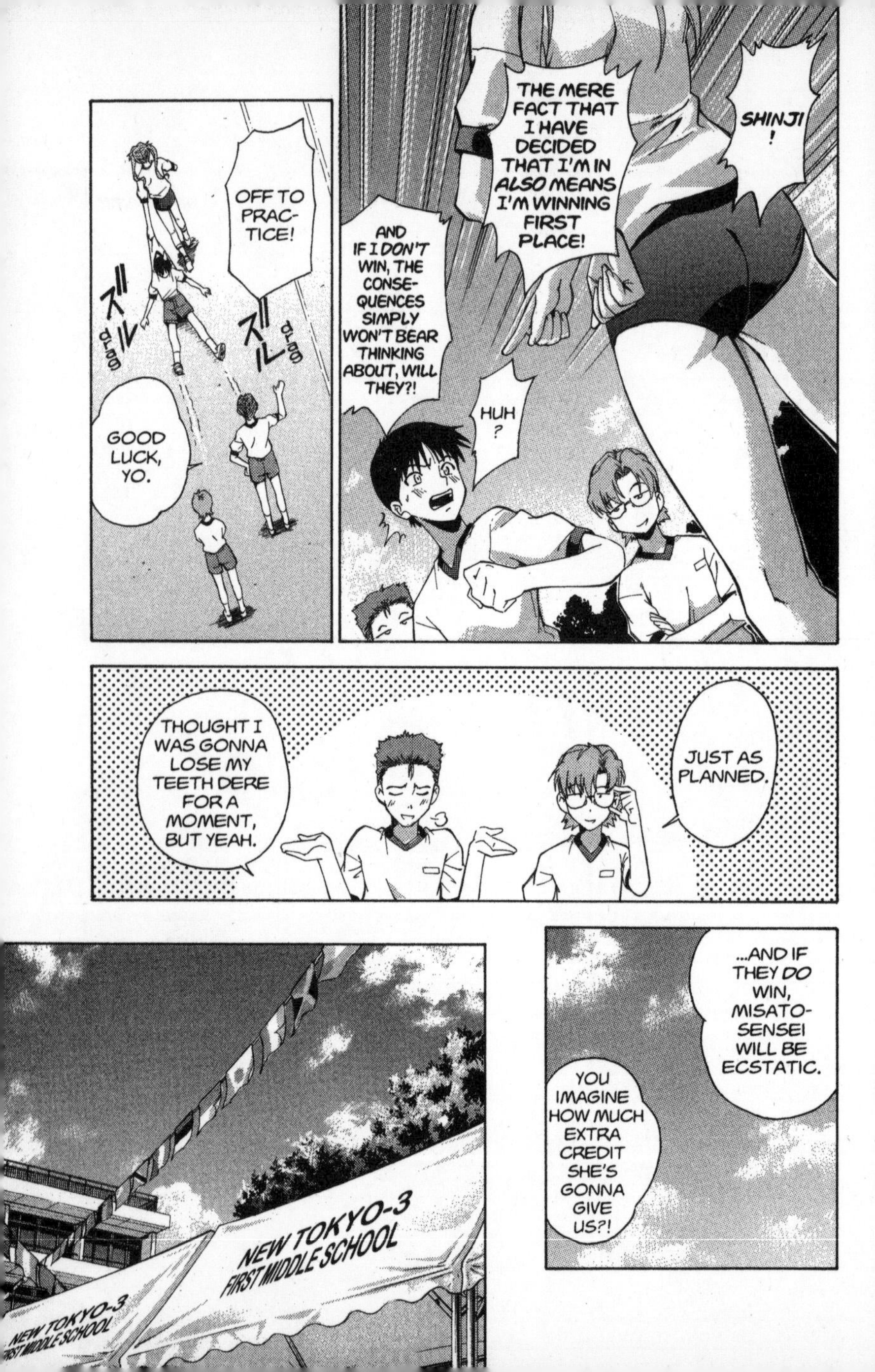
SHINJI!
THE MERE FACT THAT I HAVE DECIDED THAT I'M IN *ALSO* MEANS I'M WINNING FIRST PLACE!
AND IF I DON'T WIN, THE CONSEQUENCES SIMPLY WON'T BEAR THINKING ABOUT, WILL THEY?!
HUH?
OFF TO PRAC-TICE!
ズル drag
ズル drag
GOOD LUCK, YO.
JUST AS PLANNED.
THOUGHT I WAS GONNA LOSE MY TEETH DERE FOR A MOMENT, BUT YEAH.
...AND IF THEY *DO* WIN, MISATO-SENSEI WILL BE ECSTATIC.
YOU IMAGINE HOW MUCH EXTRA CREDIT SHE'S GONNA GIVE US?!
NEW TOKYO-3 FIRST MIDDLE SCHOOL
NEW TOKYO-3 FIRST MIDDLE SCHOOL

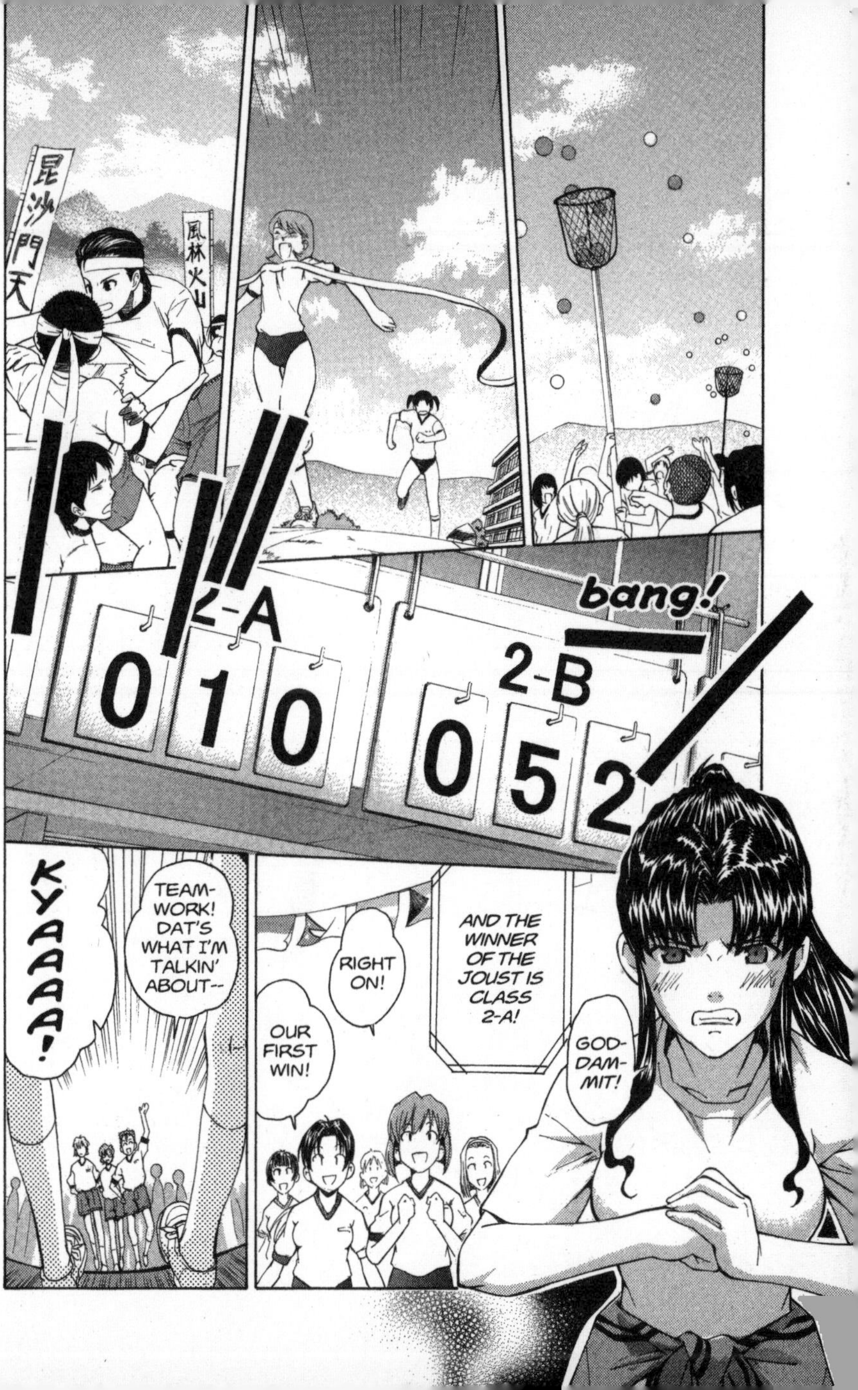

毘沙門天
風林火山
bang!
2-B
052
2-A
010
GOD-DAMMIT!
AND THE WINNER OF THE JOUST IS CLASS 2-A!
RIGHT ON!
OUR FIRST WIN!
TEAMWORK! DAT'S WHAT I'M TALKIN' ABOUT--
KYAAAAA!

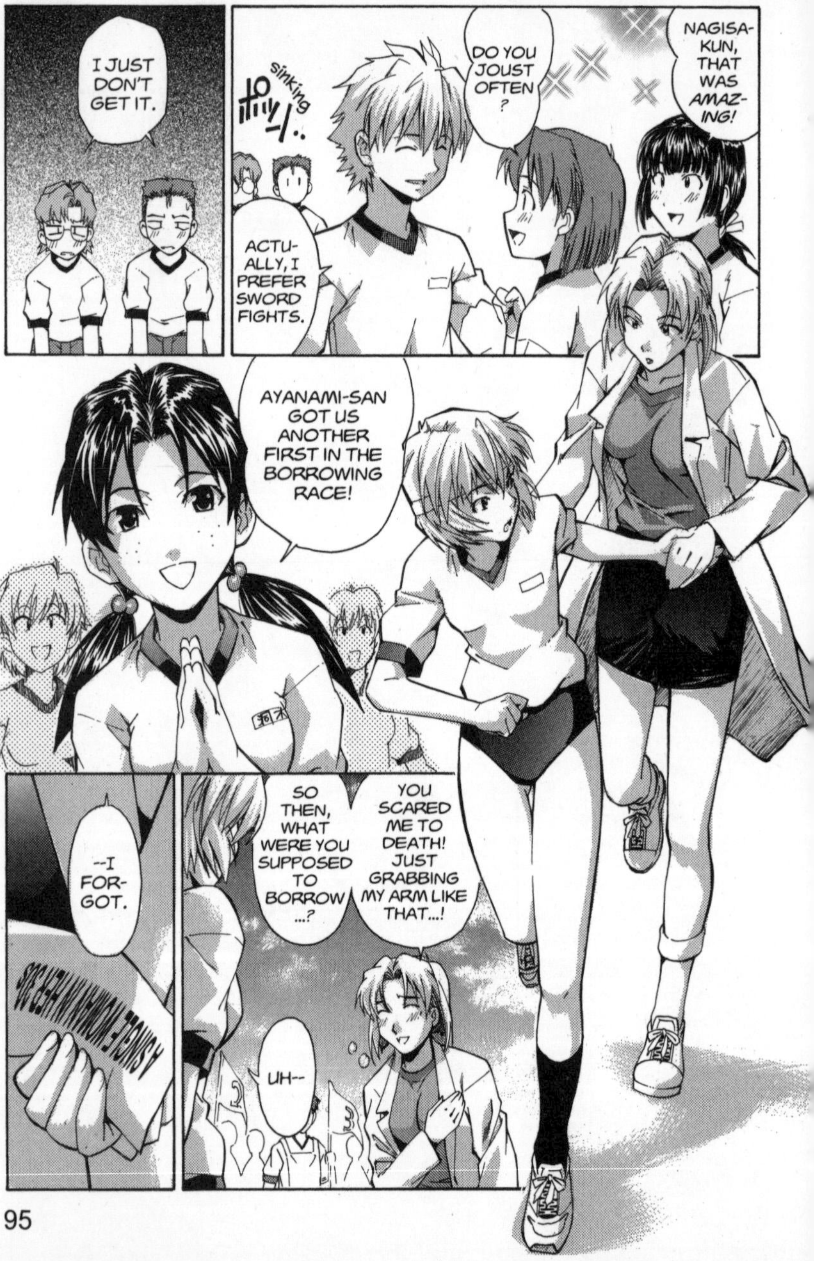
NAGISA-KUN, THAT WAS AMAZING!
DO YOU JOUST OFTEN?
sinking
ACTUALLY, I PREFER SWORD FIGHTS.
I JUST DON'T GET IT.
AYANAMI-SAN GOT US ANOTHER FIRST IN THE BORROWING RACE!
YOU SCARED ME TO DEATH! JUST GRABBING MY ARM LIKE THAT...!
SO THEN, WHAT WERE YOU SUPPOSED TO BORROW...?
UH--
--I FORGOT.
A SINGLE WOMAN IN HER 30S

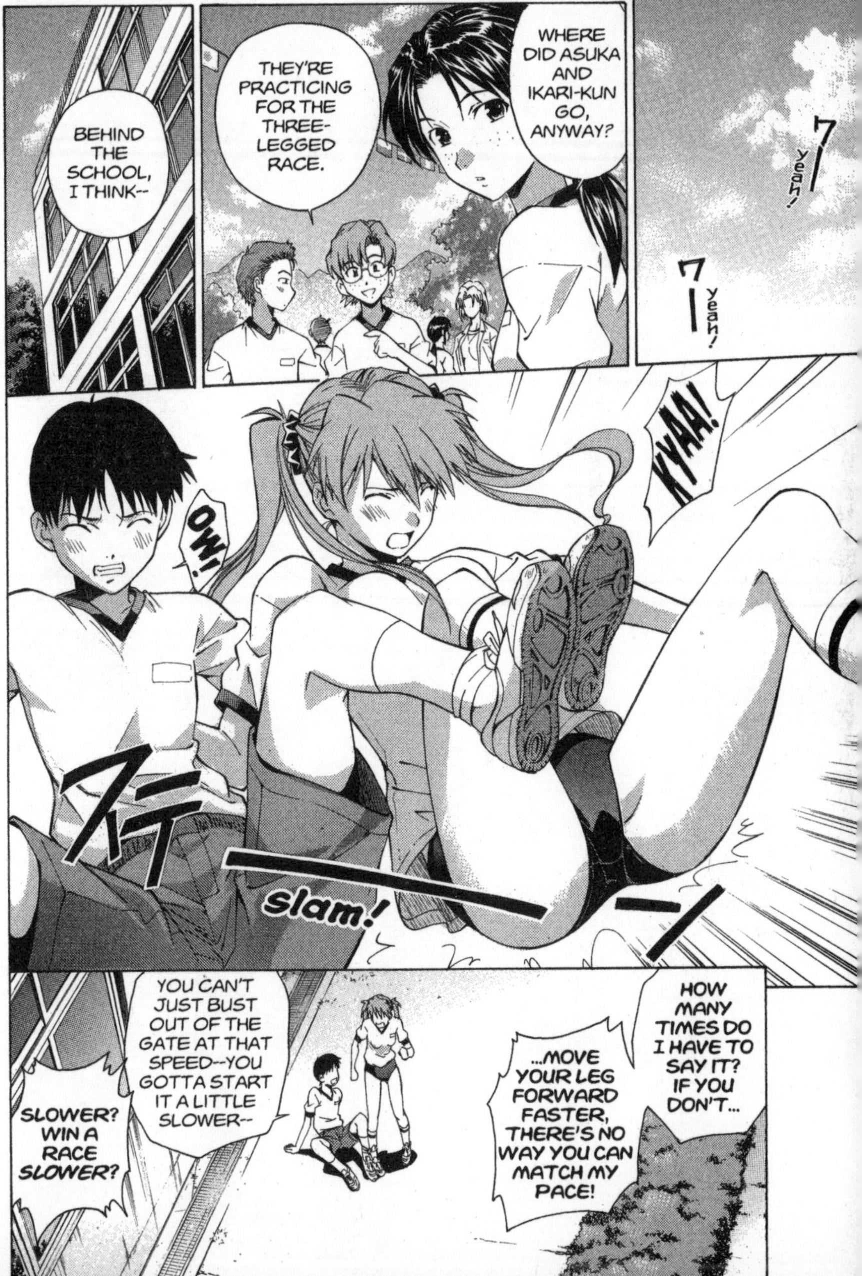
Yeah!
Yeah!
WHERE DID ASUKA AND IKARI-KUN GO, ANYWAY?
THEY'RE PRACTICING FOR THE THREE-LEGGED RACE.
BEHIND THE SCHOOL, I THINK--
KYAA!
OW!
slam!
HOW MANY TIMES DO I HAVE TO SAY IT? IF YOU DON'T...
...MOVE YOUR LEG FORWARD FASTER, THERE'S NO WAY YOU CAN MATCH MY PACE!
YOU CAN'T JUST BUST OUT OF THE GATE AT THAT SPEED--YOU GOTTA START IT A LITTLE SLOWER--
SLOWER? WIN A RACE SLOWER?

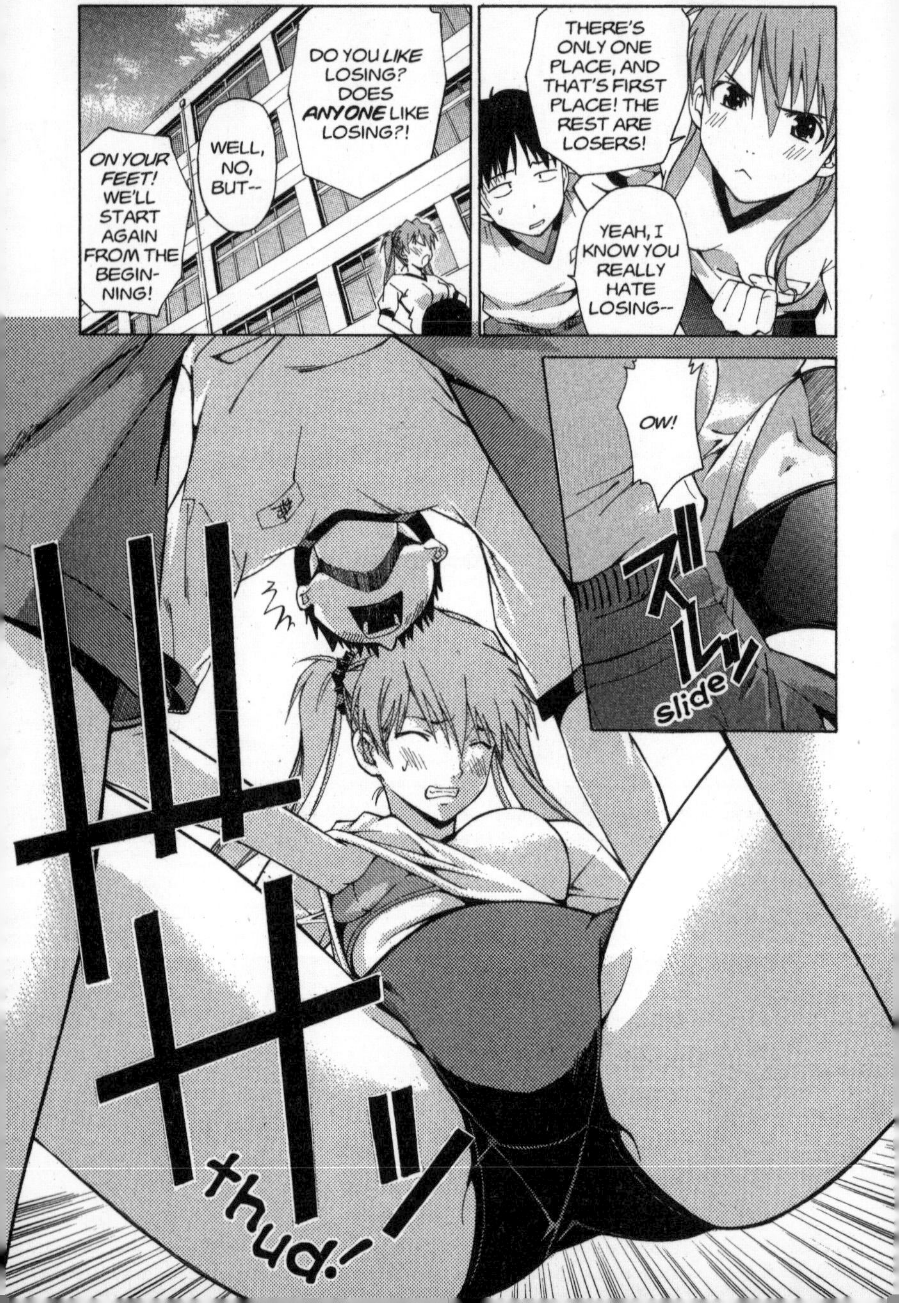
THERE'S ONLY ONE PLACE, AND THAT'S FIRST PLACE! THE REST ARE LOSERS!
YEAH, I KNOW YOU REALLY HATE LOSING--
DO YOU *LIKE* LOSING? DOES ***ANYONE*** LIKE LOSING?!
WELL, NO, BUT--
ON YOUR FEET! WE'LL START AGAIN FROM THE BEGIN-NING!
OW!
slide
thud!

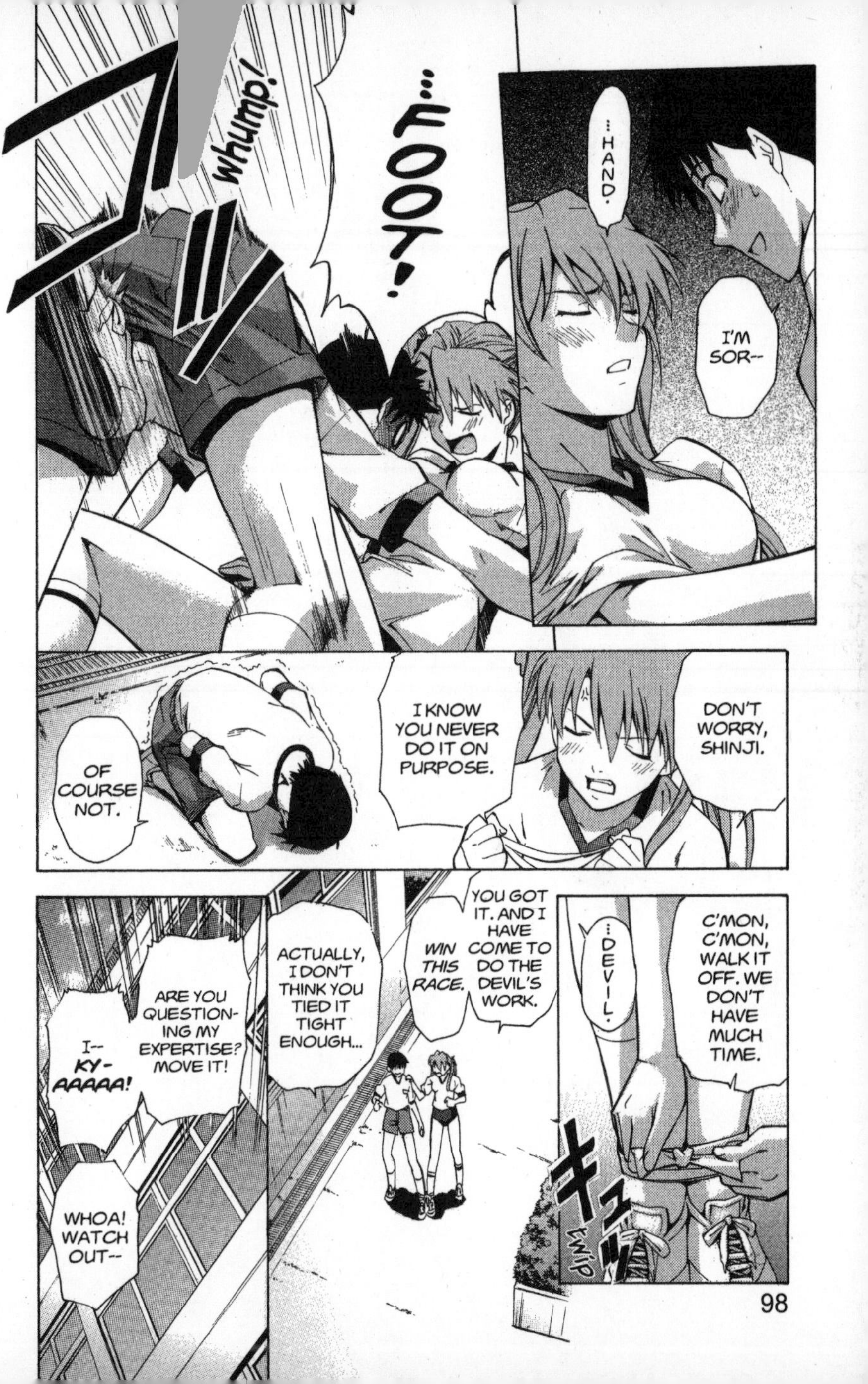
...HAND.
I'M SOR--
...FOOT!
whump!
DON'T WORRY, SHINJI.
I KNOW YOU NEVER DO IT ON PURPOSE.
OF COURSE NOT.
C'MON, C'MON, WALK IT OFF. WE DON'T HAVE MUCH TIME.
...DEVIL.
twip
YOU GOT IT. AND I HAVE COME TO DO THE DEVIL'S WORK.
WIN THIS RACE.
ACTUALLY, I DON'T THINK YOU TIED IT TIGHT ENOUGH...
ARE YOU QUESTIONING MY EXPERTISE? MOVE IT!
I-- KY-AAAAA!
WHOA! WATCH OUT--

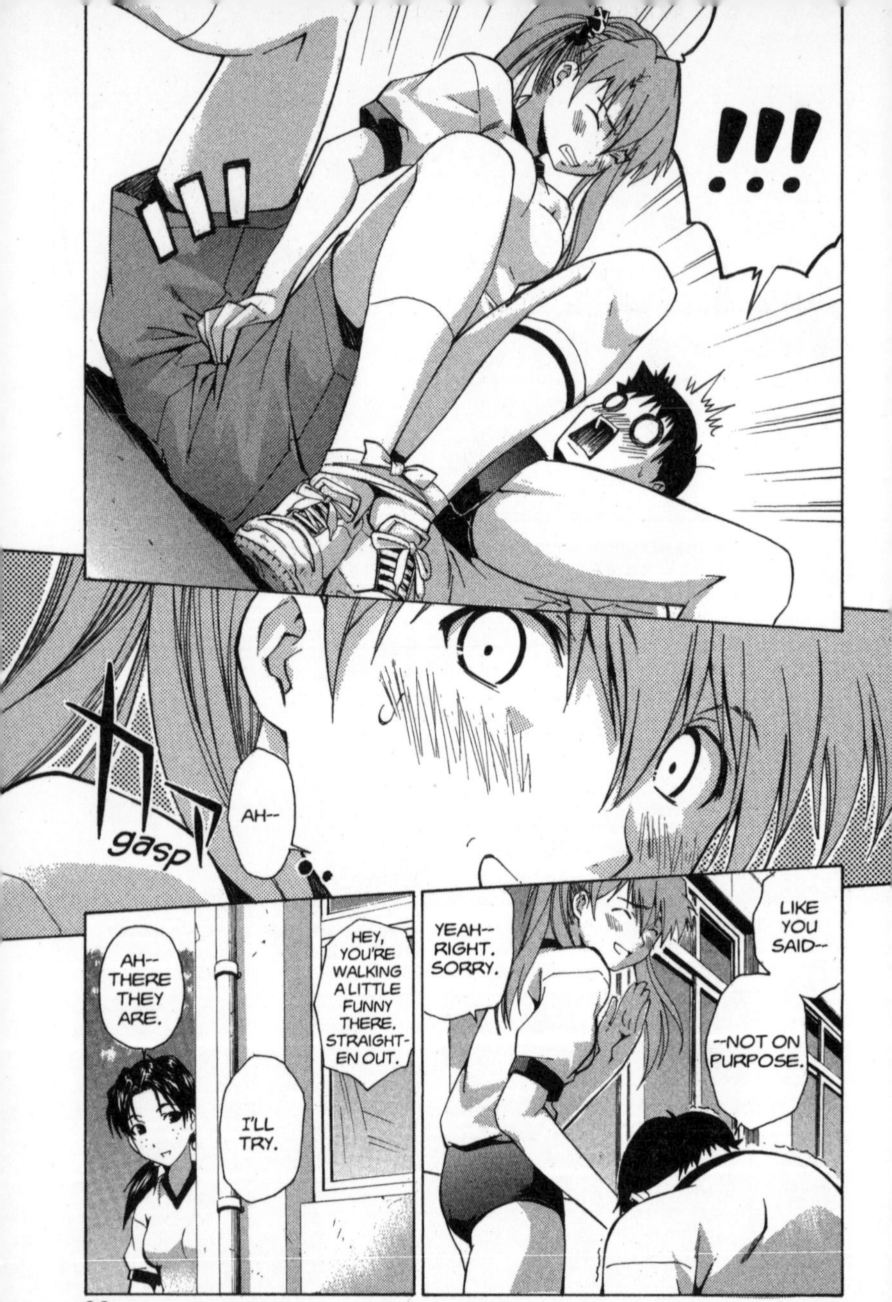
!!!
AH--
gasp
...
LIKE YOU SAID--
--NOT ON PURPOSE.
YEAH-- RIGHT. SORRY.
HEY, YOU'RE WALKING A LITTLE FUNNY THERE. STRAIGHT-EN OUT.
AH-- THERE THEY ARE.
I'LL TRY.

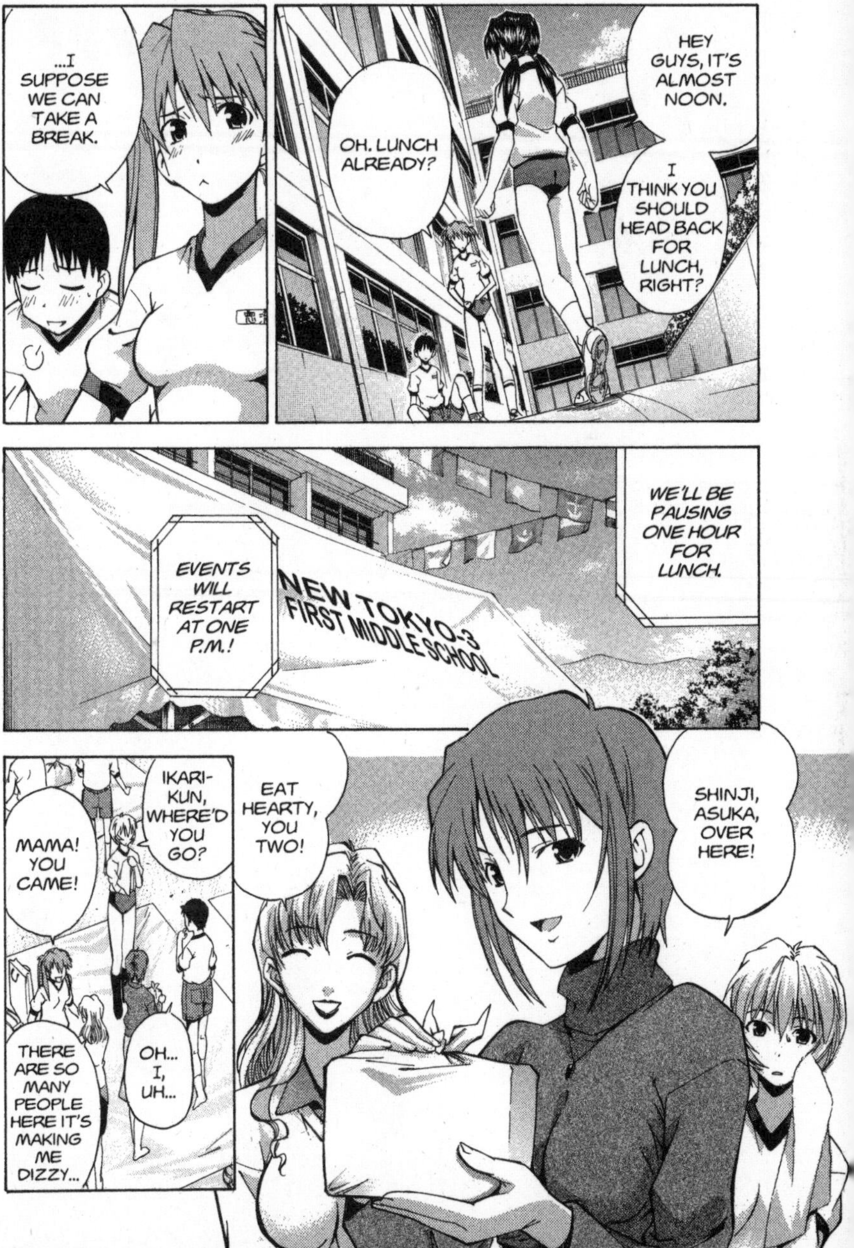
HEY GUYS, IT'S ALMOST NOON.
I THINK YOU SHOULD HEAD BACK FOR LUNCH, RIGHT?
OH. LUNCH ALREADY?
...I SUPPOSE WE CAN TAKE A BREAK.
WE'LL BE PAUSING ONE HOUR FOR LUNCH.
NEW TOKYO-3 FIRST MIDDLE SCHOOL
EVENTS WILL RESTART AT ONE P.M.!
SHINJI, ASUKA, OVER HERE!
EAT HEARTY, YOU TWO!
IKARI-KUN, WHERE'D YOU GO?
MAMA! YOU CAME!
OH... I, UH...
THERE ARE SO MANY PEOPLE HERE IT'S MAKING ME DIZZY...

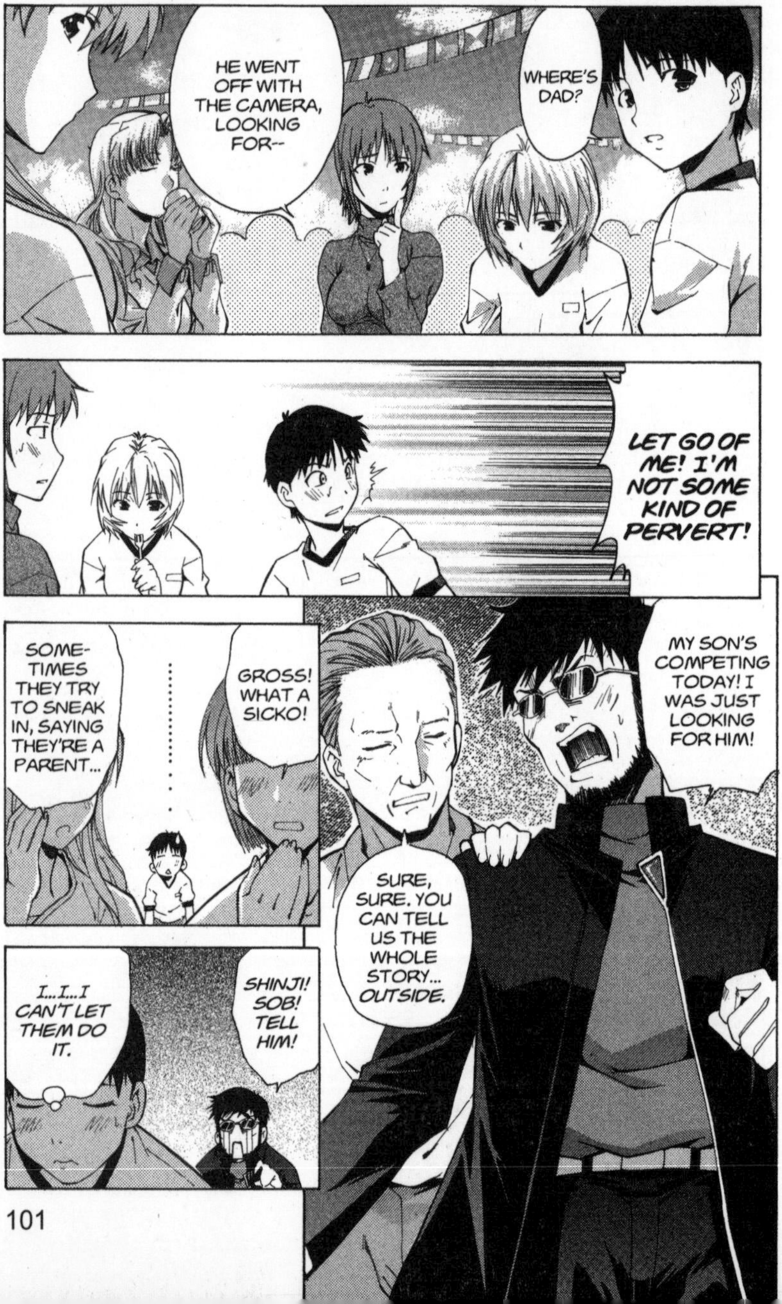

WHERE'S DAD?
HE WENT OFF WITH THE CAMERA, LOOKING FOR--
LET GO OF ME! I'M NOT SOME KIND OF PERVERT!
MY SON'S COMPETING TODAY! I WAS JUST LOOKING FOR HIM!
SURE, SURE. YOU CAN TELL US THE WHOLE STORY... OUTSIDE.
GROSS! WHAT A SICKO!
......
SOME-TIMES THEY TRY TO SNEAK IN, SAYING THEY'RE A PARENT...
SHINJI! SOB! TELL HIM!
I...I...I CAN'T LET THEM DO IT.

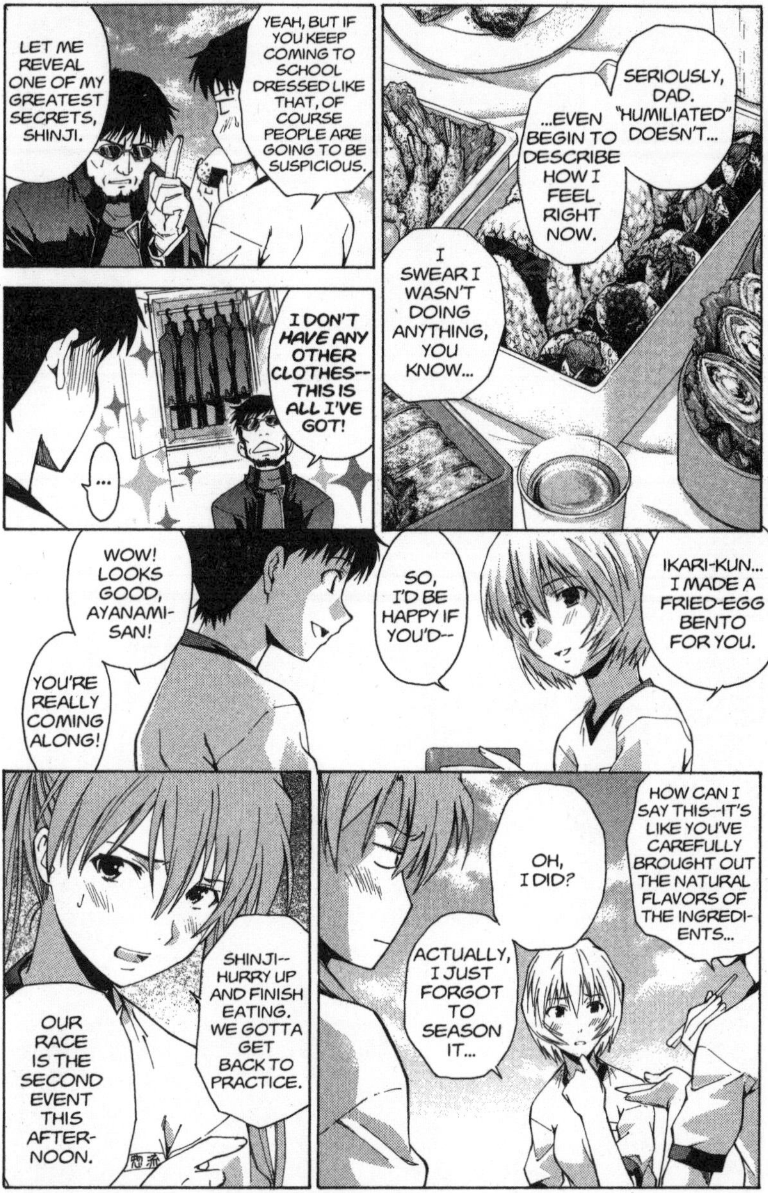
SERIOUSLY, DAD. "HUMILIATED" DOESN'T...
...EVEN BEGIN TO DESCRIBE HOW I FEEL RIGHT NOW.
I SWEAR I WASN'T DOING ANYTHING, YOU KNOW...
YEAH, BUT IF YOU KEEP COMING TO SCHOOL DRESSED LIKE THAT, OF COURSE PEOPLE ARE GOING TO BE SUSPICIOUS.
LET ME REVEAL ONE OF MY GREATEST SECRETS, SHINJI.
I DON'T *HAVE* ANY OTHER CLOTHES-- THIS IS ALL I'VE GOT!
...
IKARI-KUN... I MADE A FRIED-EGG BENTO FOR YOU.
SO, I'D BE HAPPY IF YOU'D--
WOW! LOOKS GOOD, AYANAMI-SAN!
YOU'RE REALLY COMING ALONG!
HOW CAN I SAY THIS--IT'S LIKE YOU'VE CAREFULLY BROUGHT OUT THE NATURAL FLAVORS OF THE INGREDI-ENTS...
OH, I DID?
ACTUALLY, I JUST FORGOT TO SEASON IT...
SHINJI-- HURRY UP AND FINISH EATING. WE GOTTA GET BACK TO PRACTICE.
OUR RACE IS THE SECOND EVENT THIS AFTER-NOON.

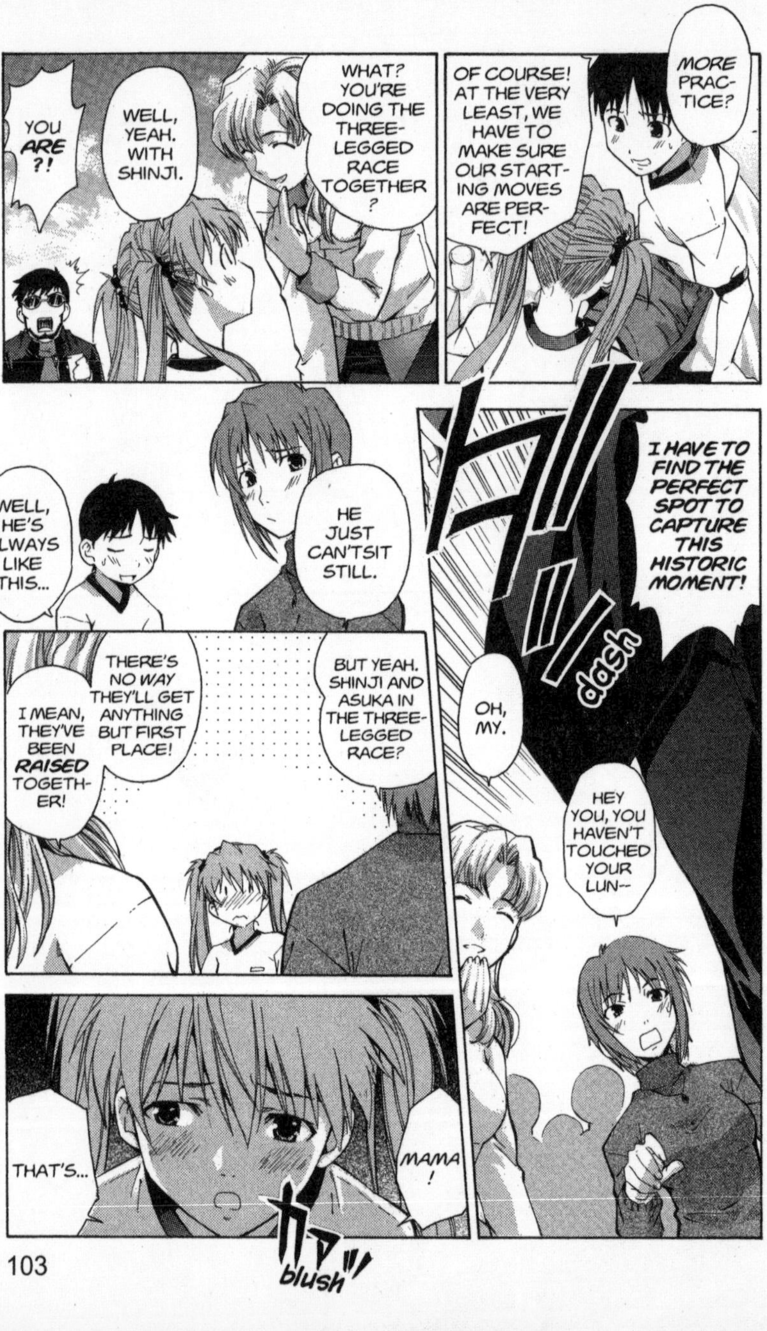
MORE PRAC-TICE?
OF COURSE! AT THE VERY LEAST, WE HAVE TO MAKE SURE OUR START-ING MOVES ARE PER-FECT!
WHAT? YOU'RE DOING THE THREE-LEGGED RACE TOGETHER ?
WELL, YEAH. WITH SHINJI.
YOU ARE ?!
dash
I HAVE TO FIND THE PERFECT SPOT TO CAPTURE THIS HISTORIC MOMENT!
OH, MY.
HEY YOU, YOU HAVEN'T TOUCHED YOUR LUN--
MAMA !
HE JUST CAN'TSIT STILL.
WELL, HE'S ALWAYS LIKE THIS...
BUT YEAH. SHINJI AND ASUKA IN THE THREE-LEGGED RACE?
THERE'S NO WAY THEY'LL GET ANYTHING BUT FIRST PLACE!
I MEAN, THEY'VE BEEN RAISED TOGETH-ER!
THAT'S...
blush

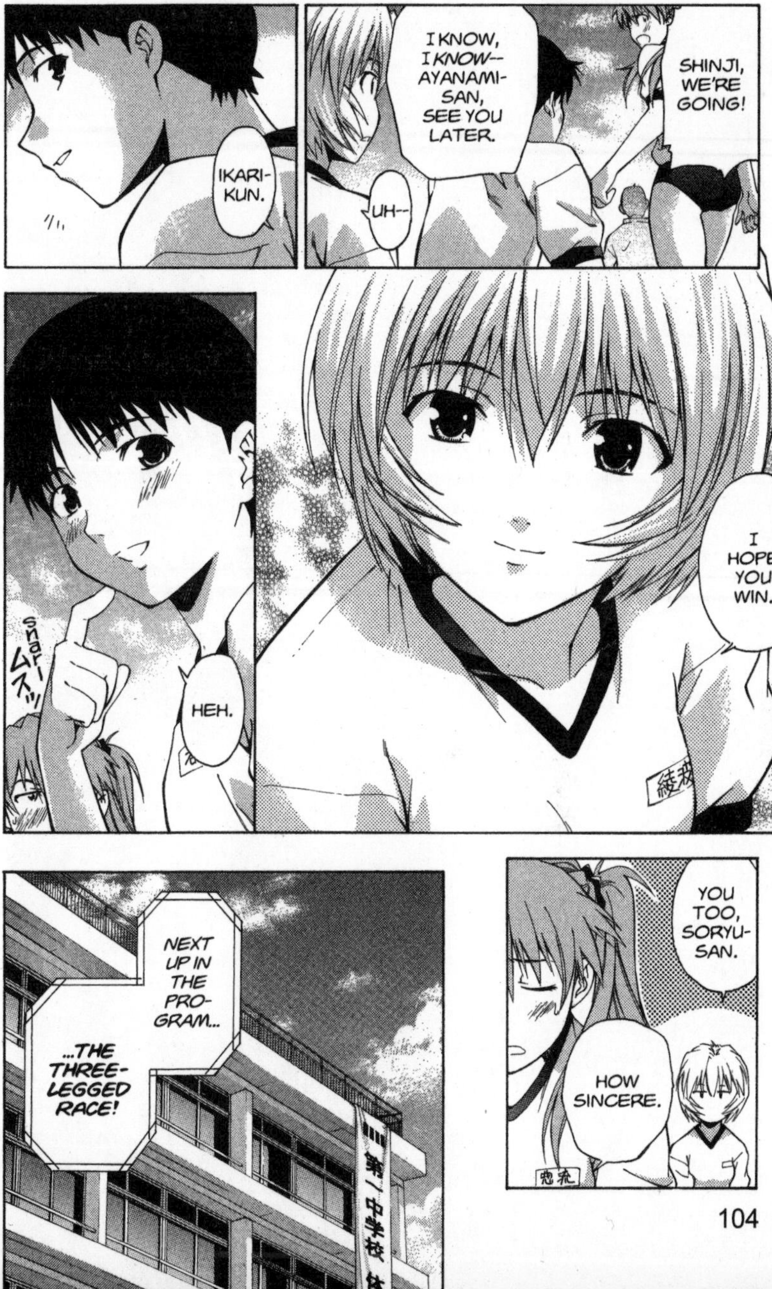
SHINJI, WE'RE GOING!
I KNOW, I KNOW--AYANAMI-SAN, SEE YOU LATER.
UH--
IKARI-KUN.
I HOPE YOU WIN.
綾波
HEH.
snar-
ムスッ
YOU TOO, SORYU-SAN.
HOW SINCERE.
惣流
NEXT UP IN THE PROGRAM...
...THE THREE-LEGGED RACE!
第一中学校

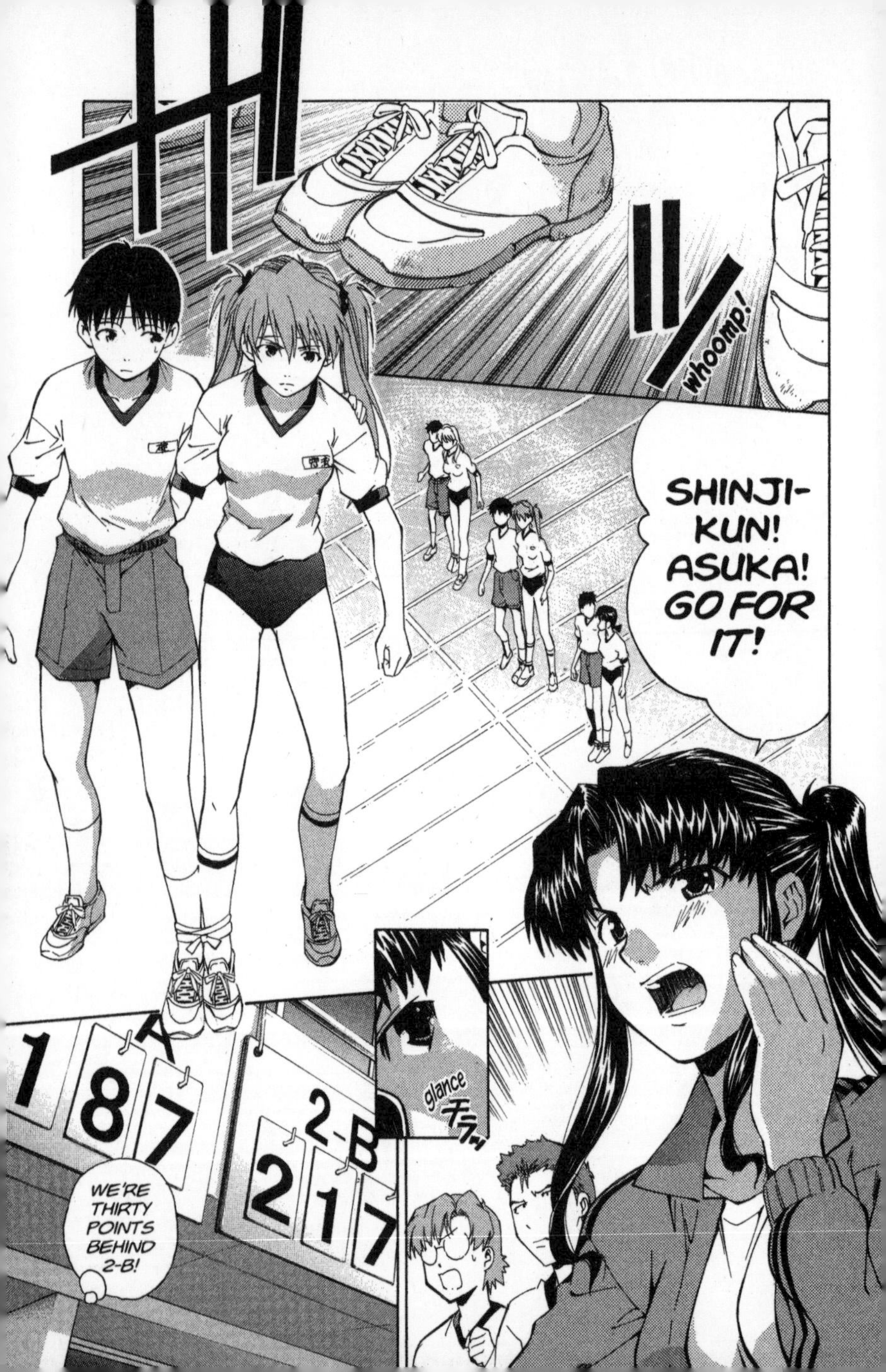
whoomp!
SHINJI-KUN! ASUKA! GO FOR IT!
glance
チラッ
A
187
2-B
217
WE'RE THIRTY POINTS BEHIND 2-B!

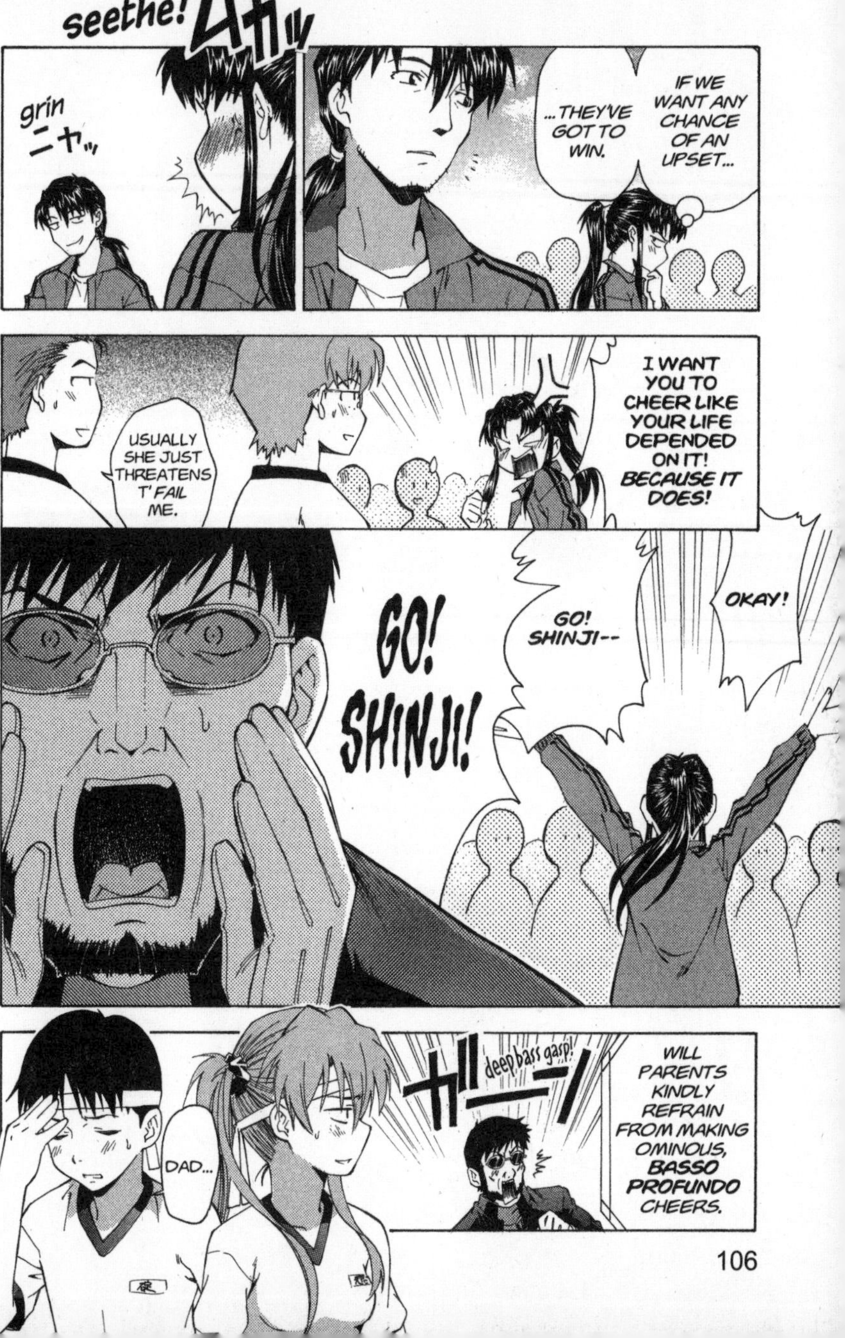
IF WE WANT ANY CHANCE OF AN UPSET...
...THEY'VE GOT TO WIN.
seethe! ムカッ
grin ニヤッ
I WANT YOU TO CHEER LIKE YOUR LIFE DEPENDED ON IT! BECAUSE IT DOES!
USUALLY SHE JUST THREATENS T' FAIL ME.
OKAY!
GO! SHINJI--
GO! SHINJI!
WILL PARENTS KINDLY REFRAIN FROM MAKING OMINOUS, BASSO PROFUNDO CHEERS.
ガーーー! deep bass gasp!
DAD...

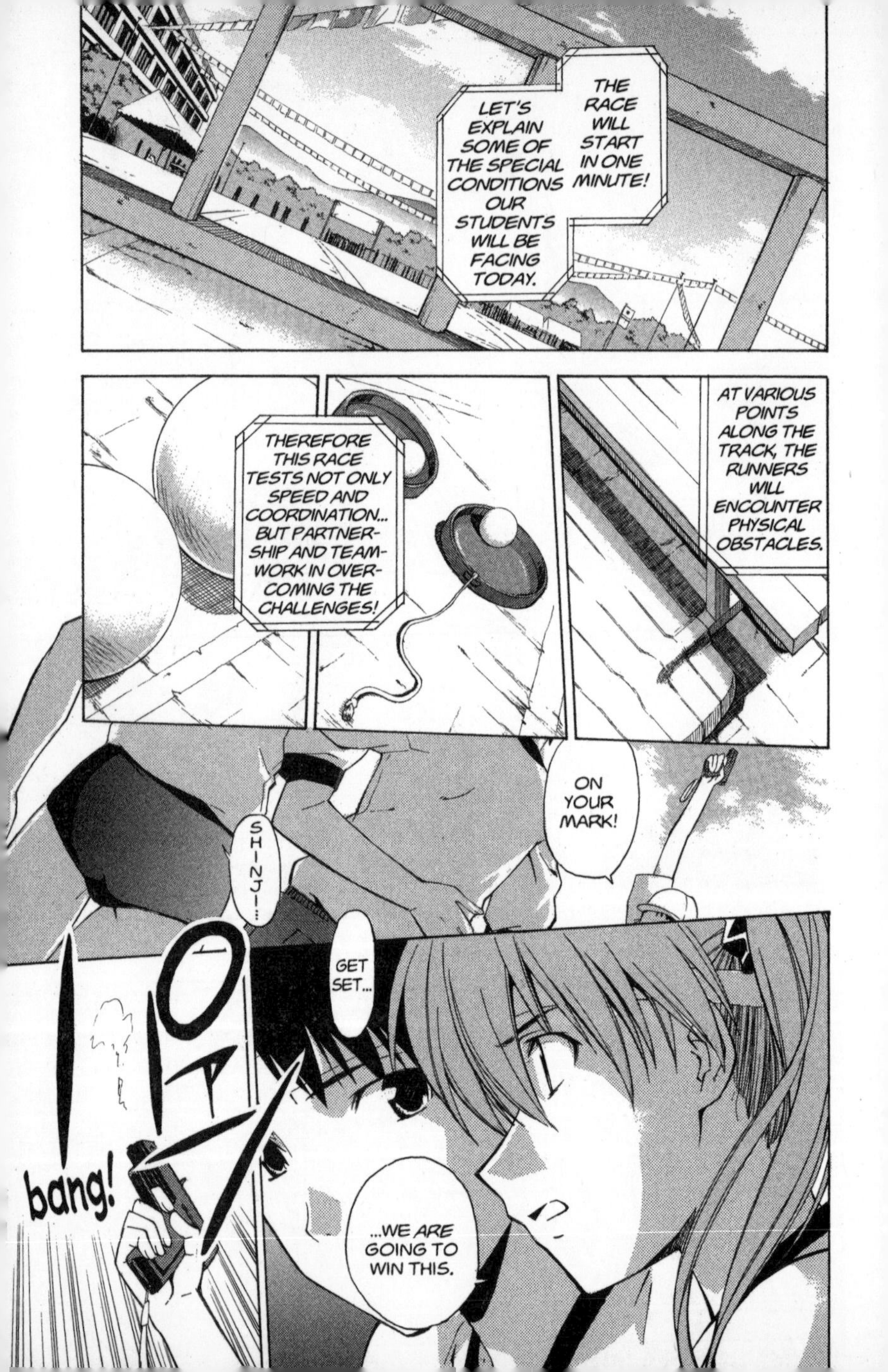
THE RACE WILL START IN ONE MINUTE!
LET'S EXPLAIN SOME OF THE SPECIAL CONDITIONS OUR STUDENTS WILL BE FACING TODAY.
AT VARIOUS POINTS ALONG THE TRACK, THE RUNNERS WILL ENCOUNTER PHYSICAL OBSTACLES.
THEREFORE THIS RACE TESTS NOT ONLY SPEED AND COORDINATION... BUT PARTNERSHIP AND TEAMWORK IN OVERCOMING THE CHALLENGES!
ON YOUR MARK!
SHINJI...
GET SET...
...WE ARE GOING TO WIN THIS.
bang!

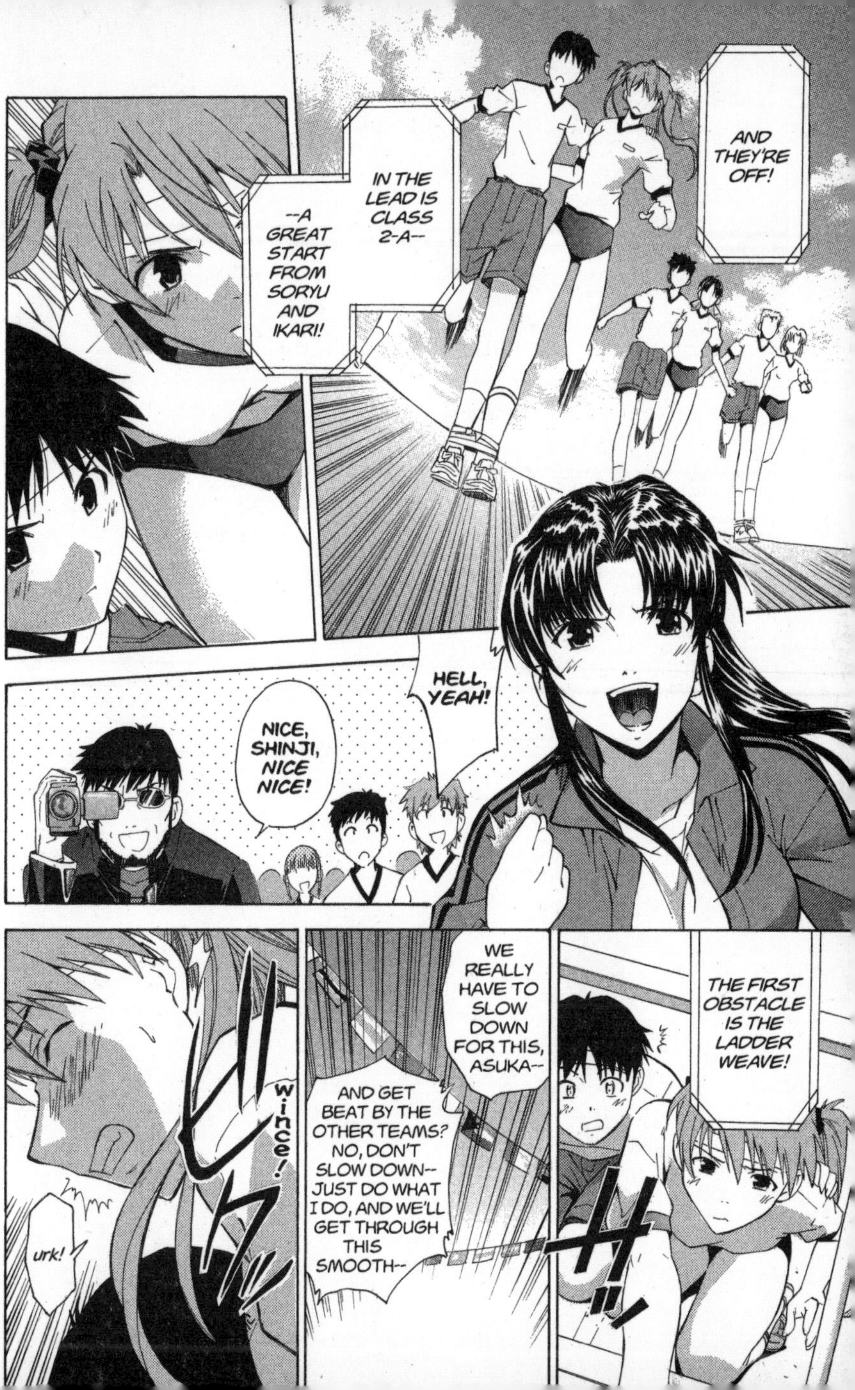
AND THEY'RE OFF!
IN THE LEAD IS CLASS 2-A--
--A GREAT START FROM SORYU AND IKARI!
HELL, YEAH!
NICE, SHINJI, NICE NICE!
THE FIRST OBSTACLE IS THE LADDER WEAVE!
WE REALLY HAVE TO SLOW DOWN FOR THIS, ASUKA--
AND GET BEAT BY THE OTHER TEAMS? NO, DON'T SLOW DOWN-- JUST DO WHAT I DO, AND WE'LL GET THROUGH THIS SMOOTH--
wince!
urk!

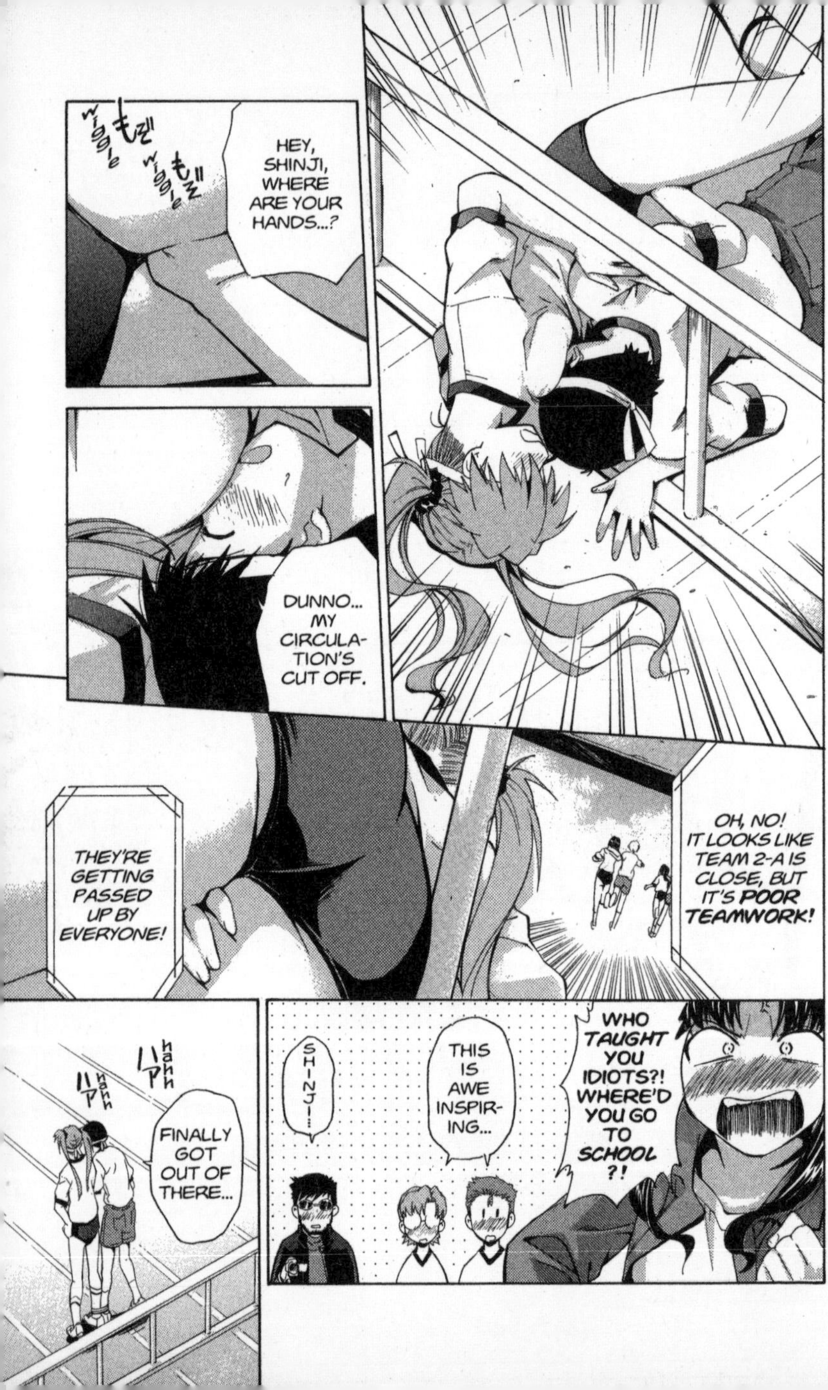
wiggle もぞ
wiggle もぞ
HEY, SHINJI, WHERE ARE YOUR HANDS...?
DUNNO... MY CIRCULATION'S CUT OFF.
OH, NO! IT LOOKS LIKE TEAM 2-A IS CLOSE, BUT IT'S **POOR TEAMWORK!**
THEY'RE GETTING PASSED UP BY EVERYONE!
WHO **TAUGHT** YOU IDIOTS?! WHERE'D YOU GO TO **SCHOOL**?!
THIS IS AWE INSPIRING...
SHINJI...!
hahh ハァ
hahh ハァ
FINALLY GOT OUT OF THERE...

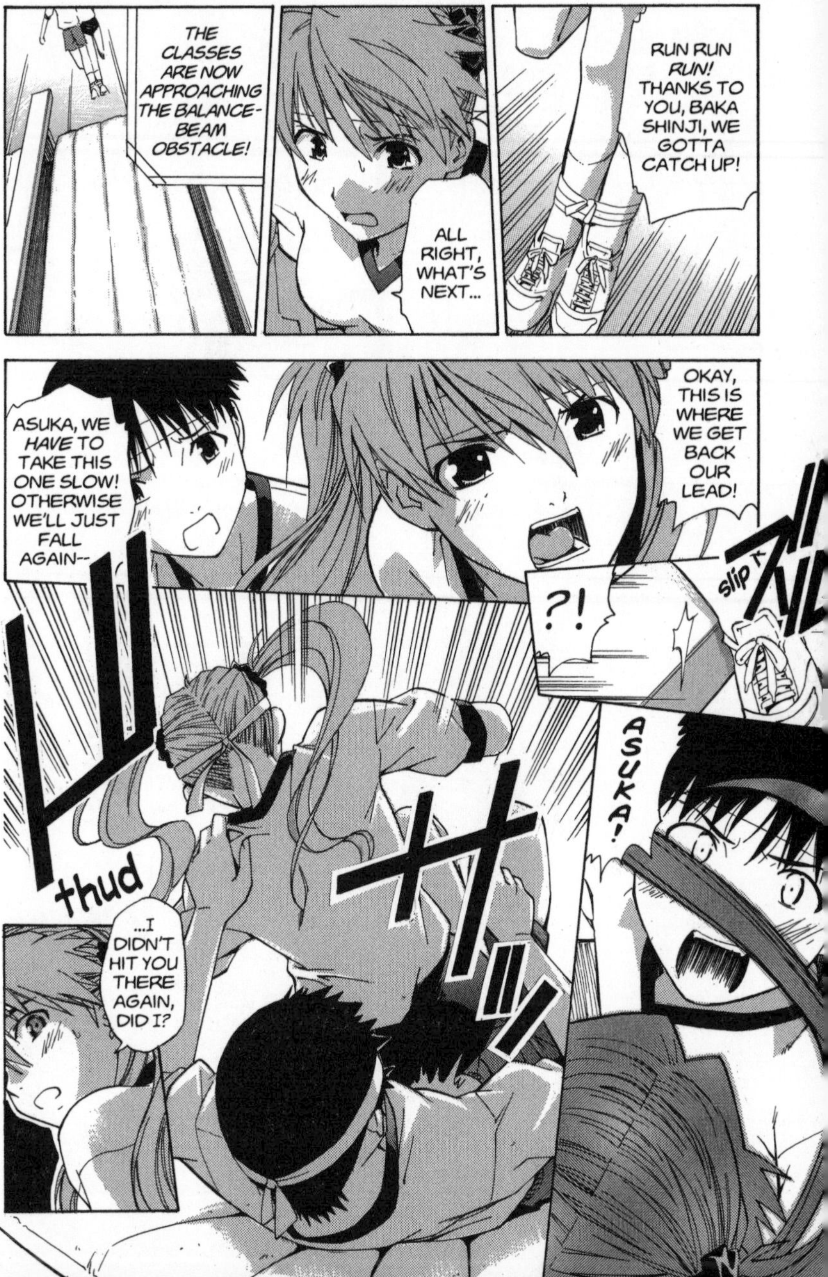
RUN RUN RUN! THANKS TO YOU, BAKA SHINJI, WE GOTTA CATCH UP!
ALL RIGHT, WHAT'S NEXT...
THE CLASSES ARE NOW APPROACHING THE BALANCE-BEAM OBSTACLE!
OKAY, THIS IS WHERE WE GET BACK OUR LEAD!
ASUKA, WE HAVE TO TAKE THIS ONE SLOW! OTHERWISE WE'LL JUST FALL AGAIN--
slip
?!
ASUKA!
thud
...I DIDN'T HIT YOU THERE AGAIN, DID I?

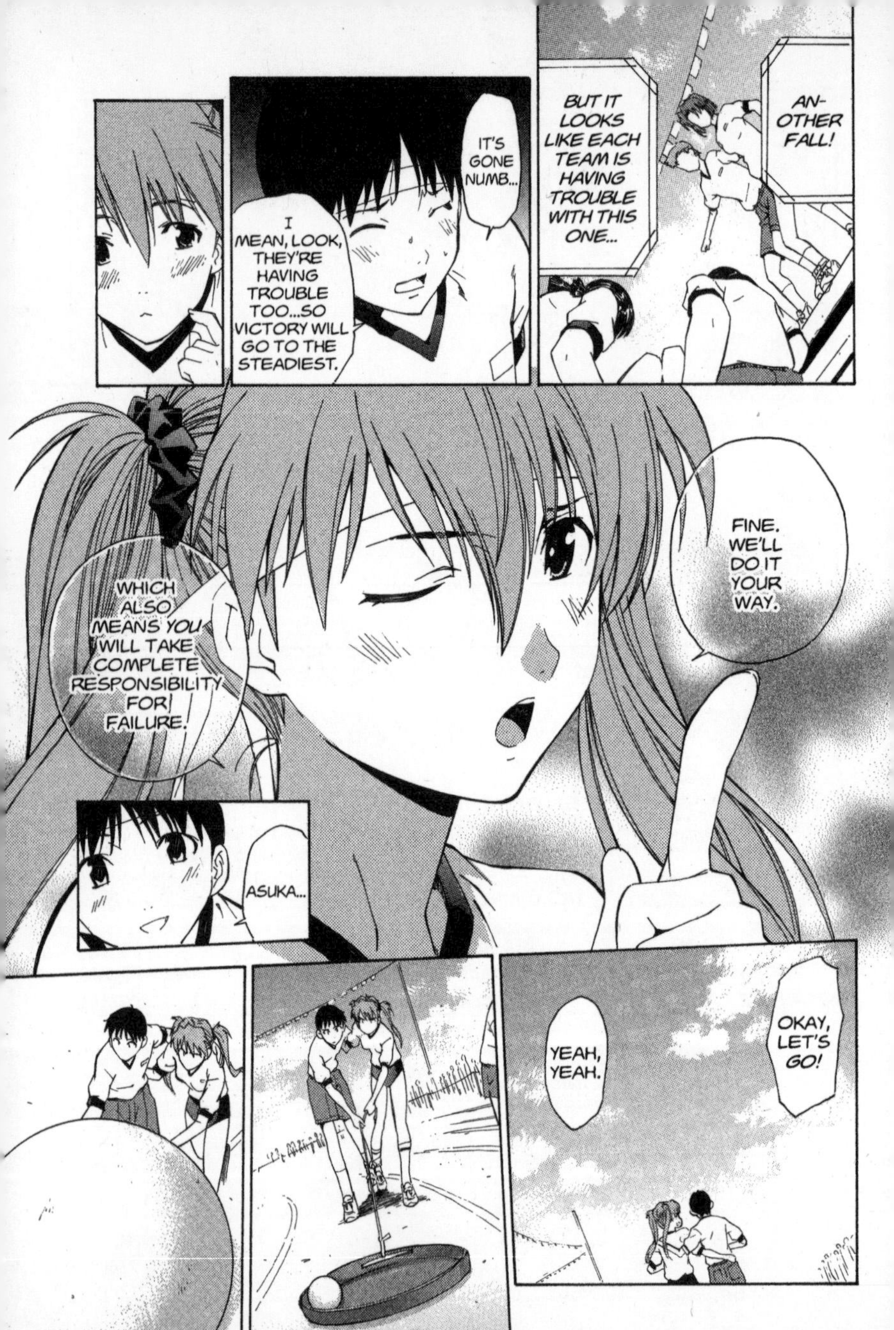
AN-OTHER FALL!
BUT IT LOOKS LIKE EACH TEAM IS HAVING TROUBLE WITH THIS ONE...
IT'S GONE NUMB...
I MEAN, LOOK, THEY'RE HAVING TROUBLE TOO...SO VICTORY WILL GO TO THE STEADIEST.
FINE. WE'LL DO IT YOUR WAY.
WHICH ALSO MEANS *YOU* WILL TAKE COMPLETE RESPONSIBILITY FOR FAILURE.
ASUKA...
OKAY, LET'S GO!
YEAH, YEAH.

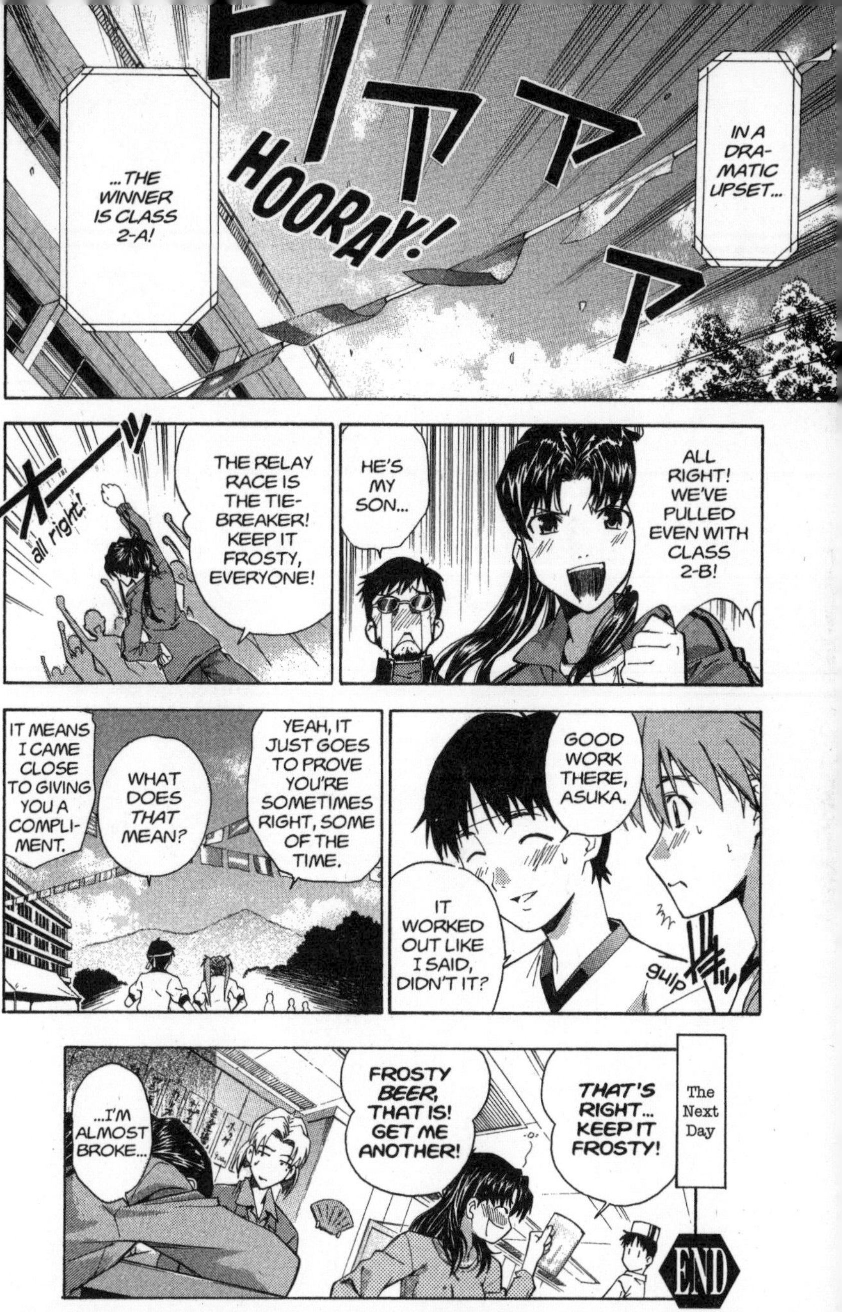
IN A DRA-MATIC UPSET...
HOORAY!
...THE WINNER IS CLASS 2-A!
ALL RIGHT! WE'VE PULLED EVEN WITH CLASS 2-B!
HE'S MY SON...
THE RELAY RACE IS THE TIE-BREAKER! KEEP IT FROSTY, EVERYONE!
all right!
GOOD WORK THERE, ASUKA.
IT WORKED OUT LIKE I SAID, DIDN'T IT?
gulp
YEAH, IT JUST GOES TO PROVE YOU'RE SOMETIMES RIGHT, SOME OF THE TIME.
WHAT DOES THAT MEAN?
IT MEANS I CAME CLOSE TO GIVING YOU A COMPLIMENT.
The Next Day
THAT'S RIGHT... KEEP IT FROSTY!
FROSTY BEER, THAT IS! GET ME ANOTHER!
...I'M ALMOST BROKE...
END

ALL NERVE LINKS COMPLETE.

CNS HUB ELEMENTS SHOW NO ABNORMALITIES.

PASSING THROUGH THRESHOLD TO THE PNR.

IN 1.0...

...0.8...

...0.5...

beeeeep

SUBJECT REI

SUBJECT KA

SUBJECT INJI

BORDER-LINE CLEAR!!

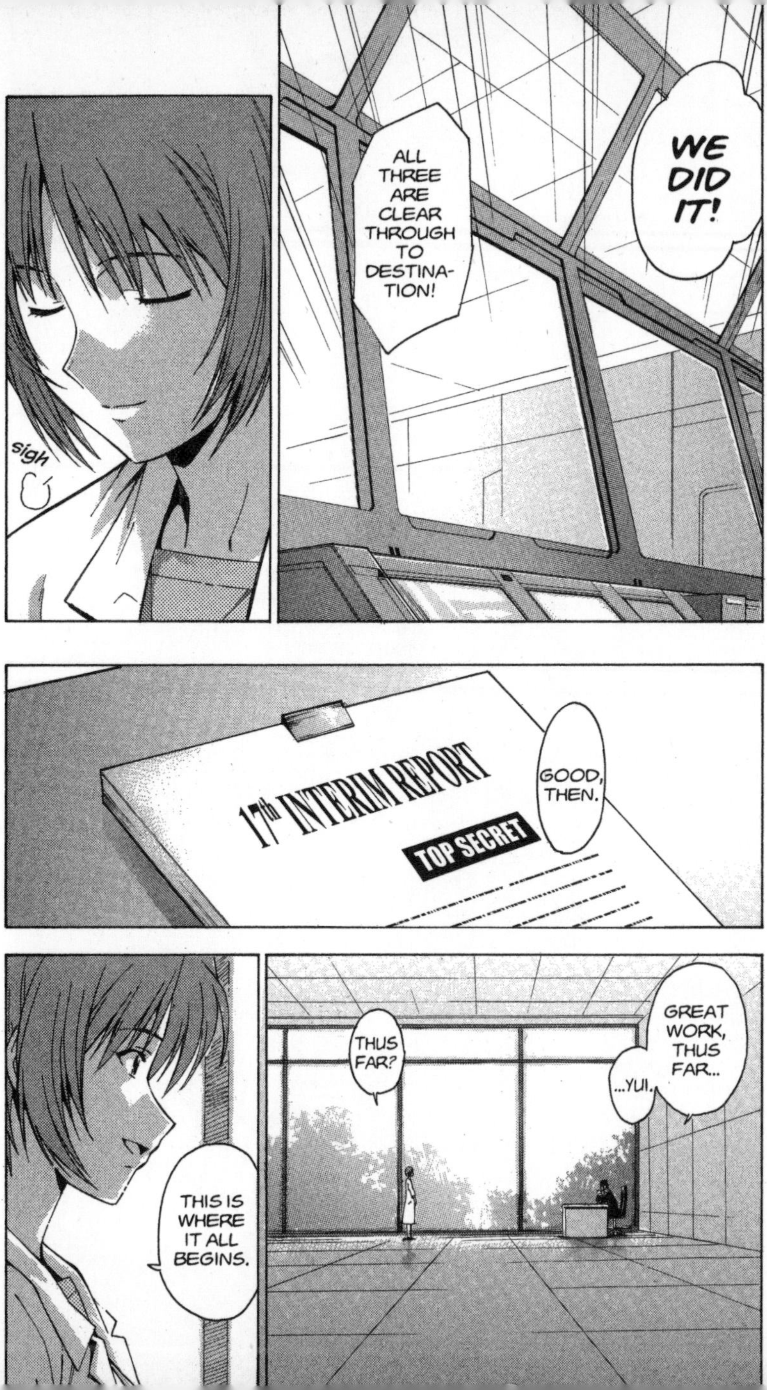
WE DID IT!
ALL THREE ARE CLEAR THROUGH TO DESTINA-TION!
sigh
17th INTERIM REPORT
TOP SECRET
GOOD, THEN.
GREAT WORK, THUS FAR...
...YUI.
THUS FAR?
THIS IS WHERE IT ALL BEGINS.

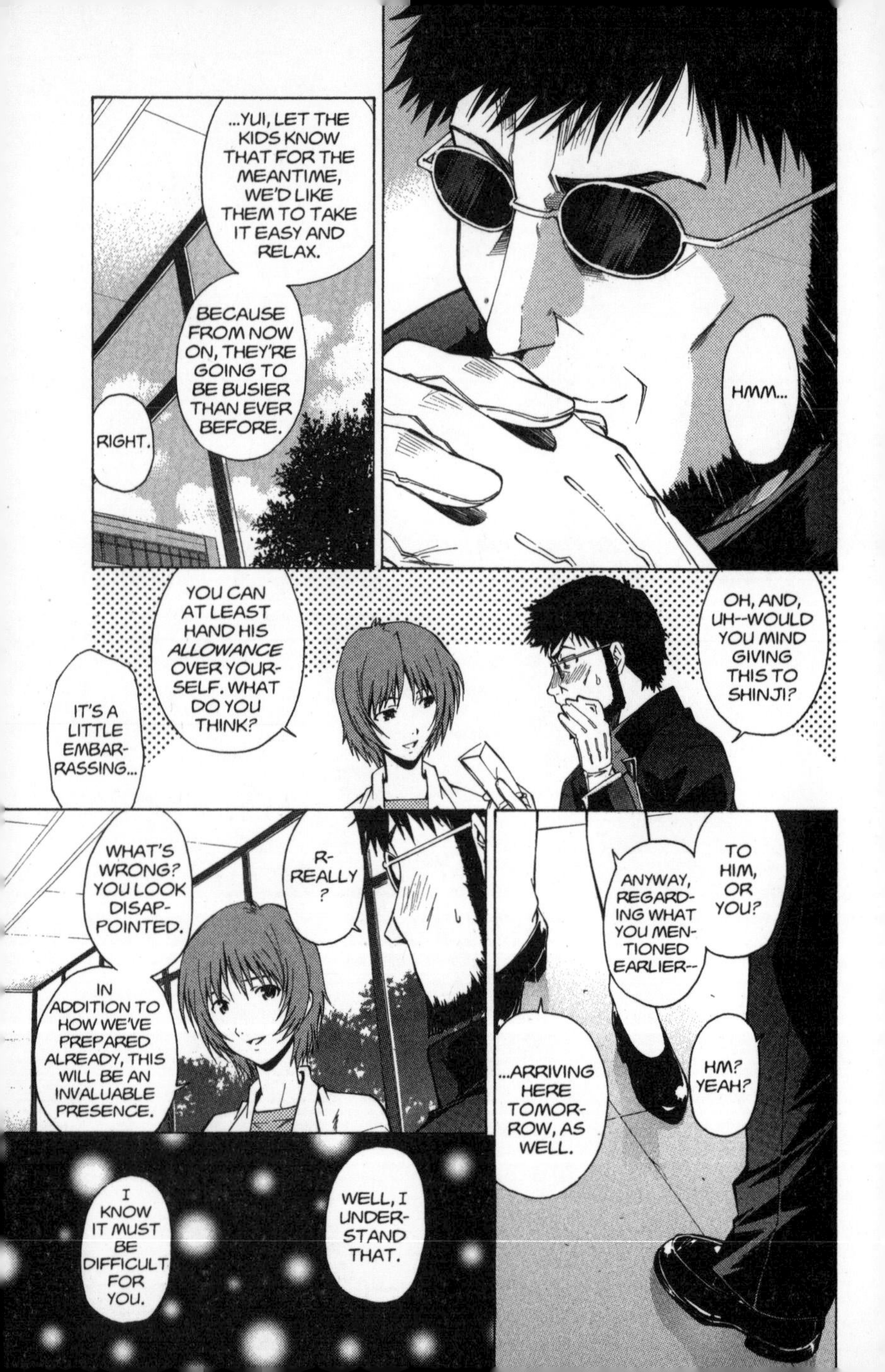
HMM...
...YUI, LET THE KIDS KNOW THAT FOR THE MEANTIME, WE'D LIKE THEM TO TAKE IT EASY AND RELAX.
BECAUSE FROM NOW ON, THEY'RE GOING TO BE BUSIER THAN EVER BEFORE.
RIGHT.
OH, AND, UH--WOULD YOU MIND GIVING THIS TO SHINJI?
YOU CAN AT LEAST HAND HIS *ALLOWANCE* OVER YOURSELF. WHAT DO YOU THINK?
IT'S A LITTLE EMBARRASSING...
TO HIM, OR YOU?
ANYWAY, REGARDING WHAT YOU MENTIONED EARLIER--
HM? YEAH?
...ARRIVING HERE TOMORROW, AS WELL.
R-REALLY?
WHAT'S WRONG? YOU LOOK DISAPPOINTED.
IN ADDITION TO HOW WE'VE PREPARED ALREADY, THIS WILL BE AN INVALUABLE PRESENCE.
WELL, I UNDERSTAND THAT.
I KNOW IT MUST BE DIFFICULT FOR YOU.

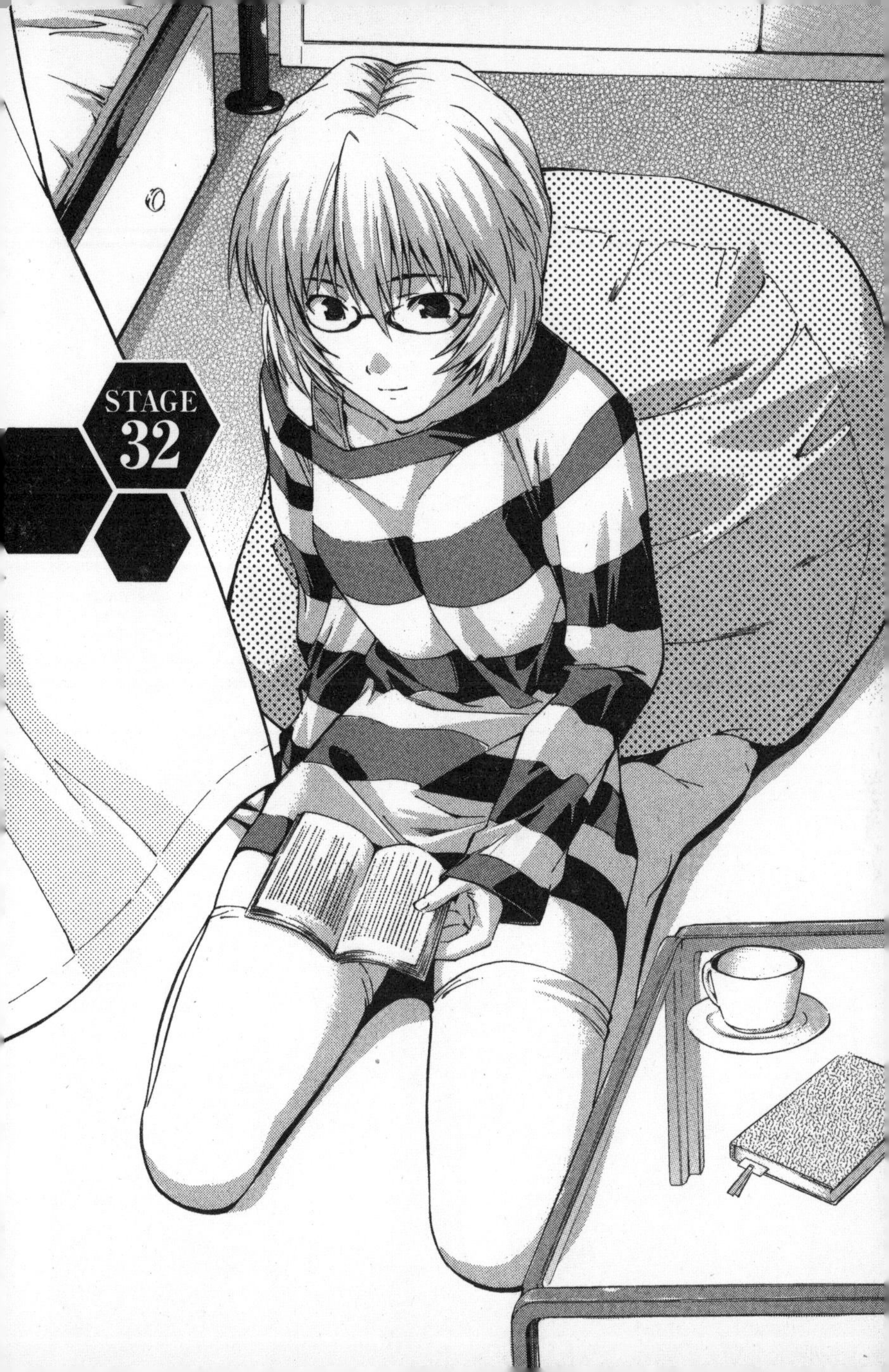
STAGE
32

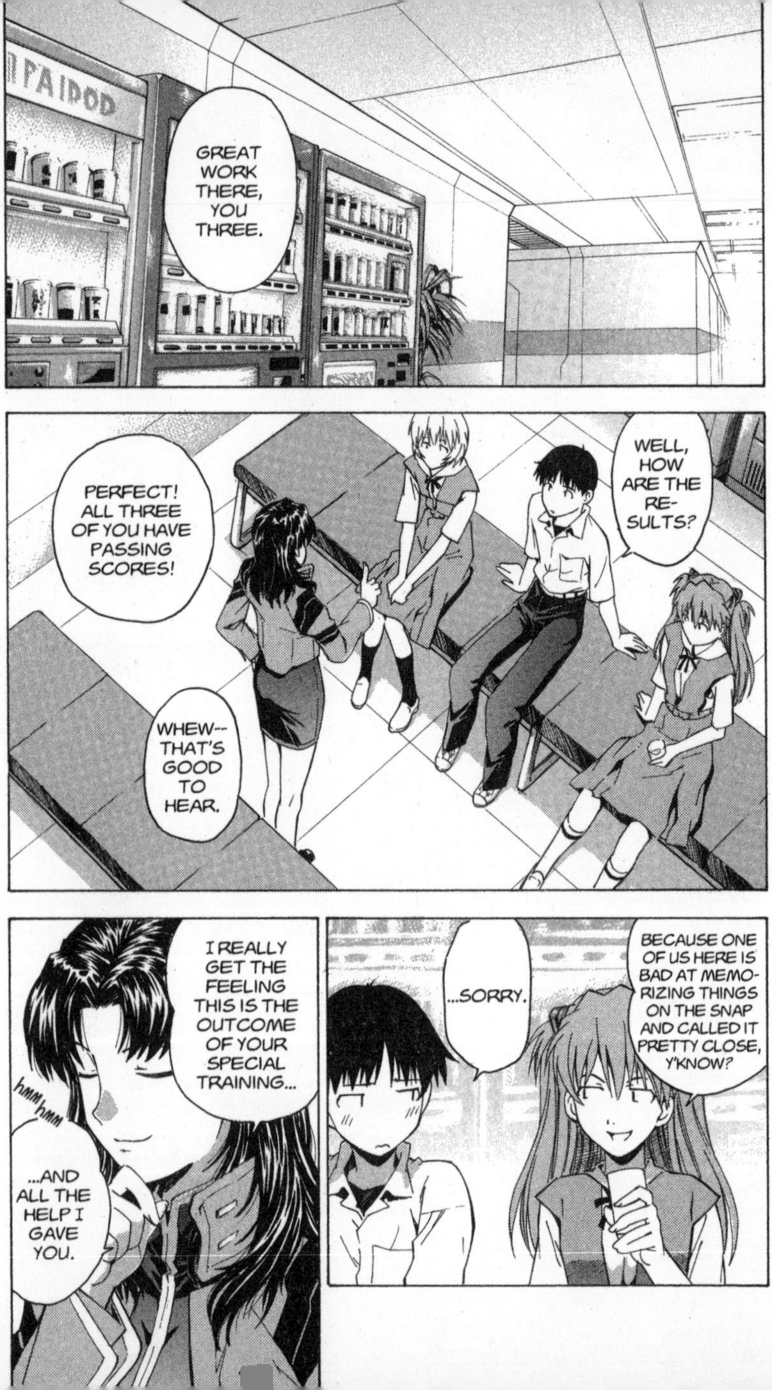
GREAT WORK THERE, YOU THREE.
WELL, HOW ARE THE RE-SULTS?
PERFECT! ALL THREE OF YOU HAVE PASSING SCORES!
WHEW-- THAT'S GOOD TO HEAR.
BECAUSE ONE OF US HERE IS BAD AT MEMO-RIZING THINGS ON THE SNAP AND CALLED IT PRETTY CLOSE, Y'KNOW?
...SORRY.
I REALLY GET THE FEELING THIS IS THE OUTCOME OF YOUR SPECIAL TRAINING...
hmm hmm
...AND ALL THE HELP I GAVE YOU.

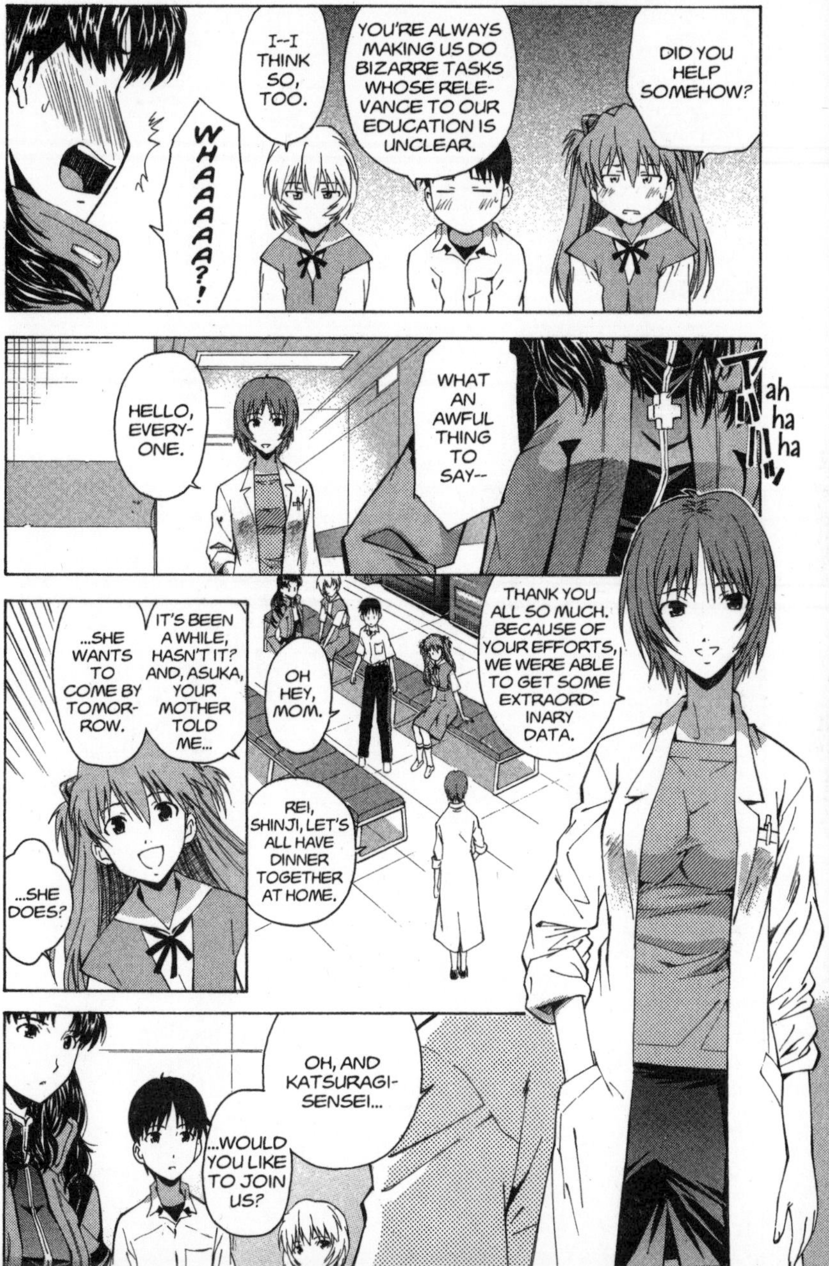
DID YOU HELP SOMEHOW?
YOU'RE ALWAYS MAKING US DO BIZARRE TASKS WHOSE RELE-VANCE TO OUR EDUCATION IS UNCLEAR.
I--I THINK SO, TOO.
WHAAAAAA?!
ah ha ha
WHAT AN AWFUL THING TO SAY--
HELLO, EVERY-ONE.
THANK YOU ALL SO MUCH. BECAUSE OF YOUR EFFORTS, WE WERE ABLE TO GET SOME EXTRAORD-INARY DATA.
OH HEY, MOM.
REI, SHINJI, LET'S ALL HAVE DINNER TOGETHER AT HOME.
IT'S BEEN A WHILE, HASN'T IT? AND, ASUKA, YOUR MOTHER TOLD ME...
...SHE WANTS TO COME BY TOMOR-ROW.
...SHE DOES?
OH, AND KATSURAGI-SENSEI...
...WOULD YOU LIKE TO JOIN US?

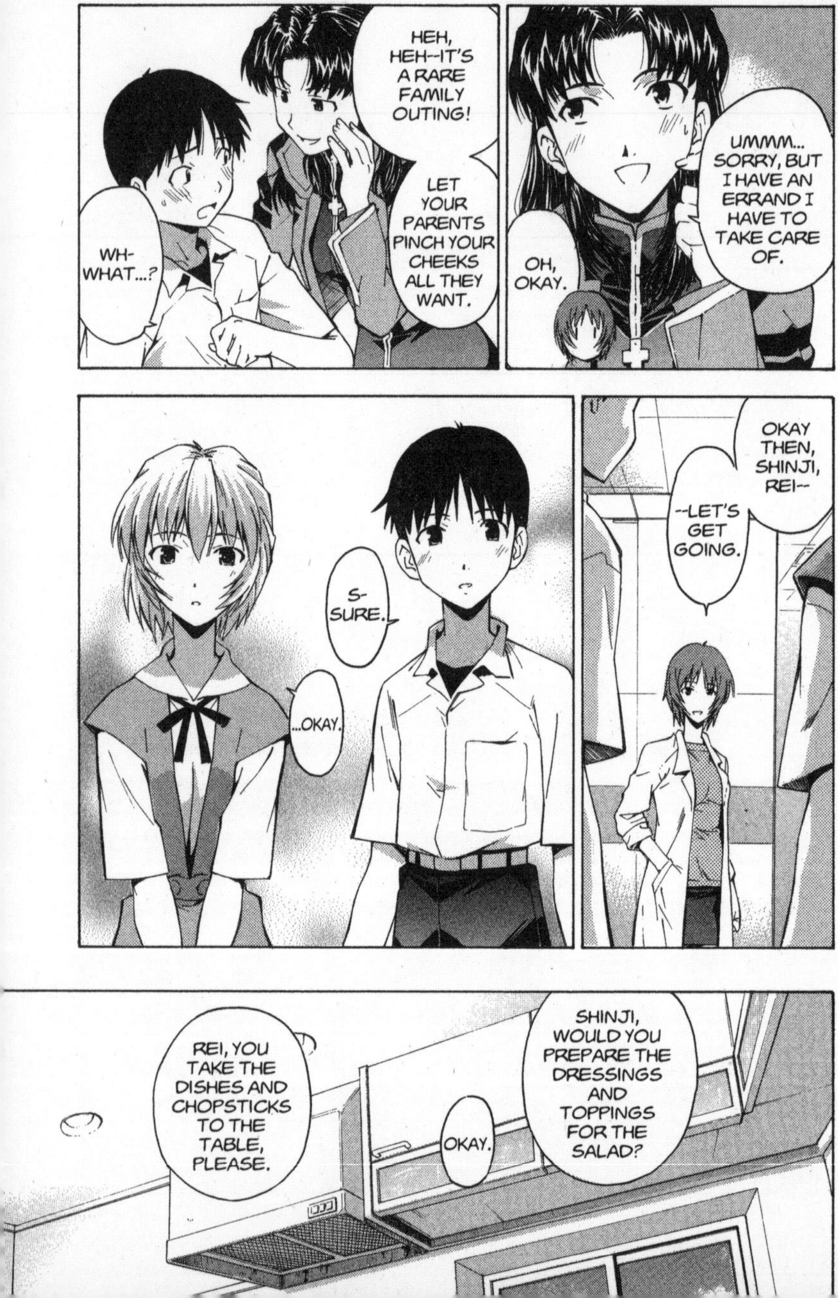
UMMM... SORRY, BUT I HAVE AN ERRAND I HAVE TO TAKE CARE OF.
OH, OKAY.
HEH, HEH--IT'S A RARE FAMILY OUTING!
LET YOUR PARENTS PINCH YOUR CHEEKS ALL THEY WANT.
WH-WHAT...?
OKAY THEN, SHINJI, REI--
--LET'S GET GOING.
S-SURE.
...OKAY.
SHINJI, WOULD YOU PREPARE THE DRESSINGS AND TOPPINGS FOR THE SALAD?
OKAY.
REI, YOU TAKE THE DISHES AND CHOPSTICKS TO THE TABLE, PLEASE.

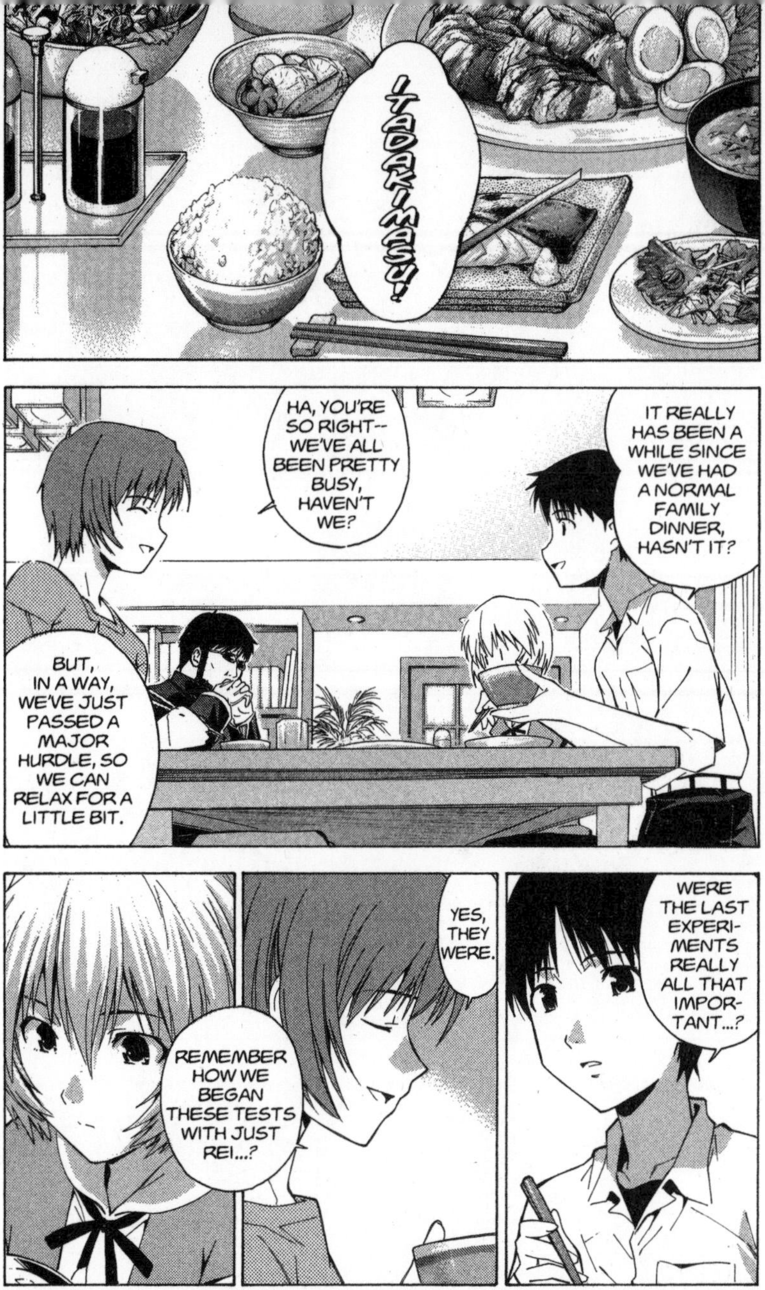
ITADAKIMASU!
IT REALLY HAS BEEN A WHILE SINCE WE'VE HAD A NORMAL FAMILY DINNER, HASN'T IT?
HA, YOU'RE SO RIGHT-- WE'VE ALL BEEN PRETTY BUSY, HAVEN'T WE?
BUT, IN A WAY, WE'VE JUST PASSED A MAJOR HURDLE, SO WE CAN RELAX FOR A LITTLE BIT.
WERE THE LAST EXPERI-MENTS REALLY ALL THAT IMPOR-TANT...?
YES, THEY WERE.
REMEMBER HOW WE BEGAN THESE TESTS WITH JUST REI...?

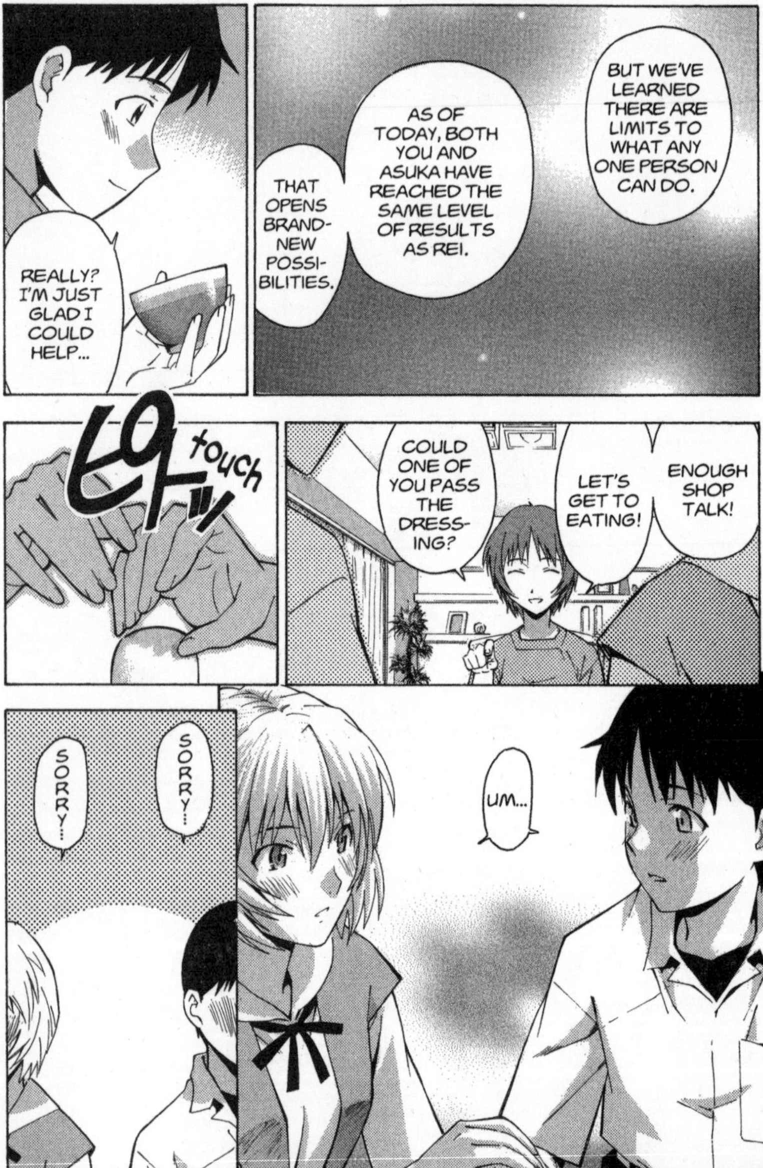
BUT WE'VE LEARNED THERE ARE LIMITS TO WHAT ANY ONE PERSON CAN DO.
AS OF TODAY, BOTH YOU AND ASUKA HAVE REACHED THE SAME LEVEL OF RESULTS AS REI.
THAT OPENS BRAND-NEW POSSIBILITIES.
REALLY? I'M JUST GLAD I COULD HELP...
ENOUGH SHOP TALK!
LET'S GET TO EATING!
COULD ONE OF YOU PASS THE DRESSING?
touch
UM...
SORRY...
SORRY...

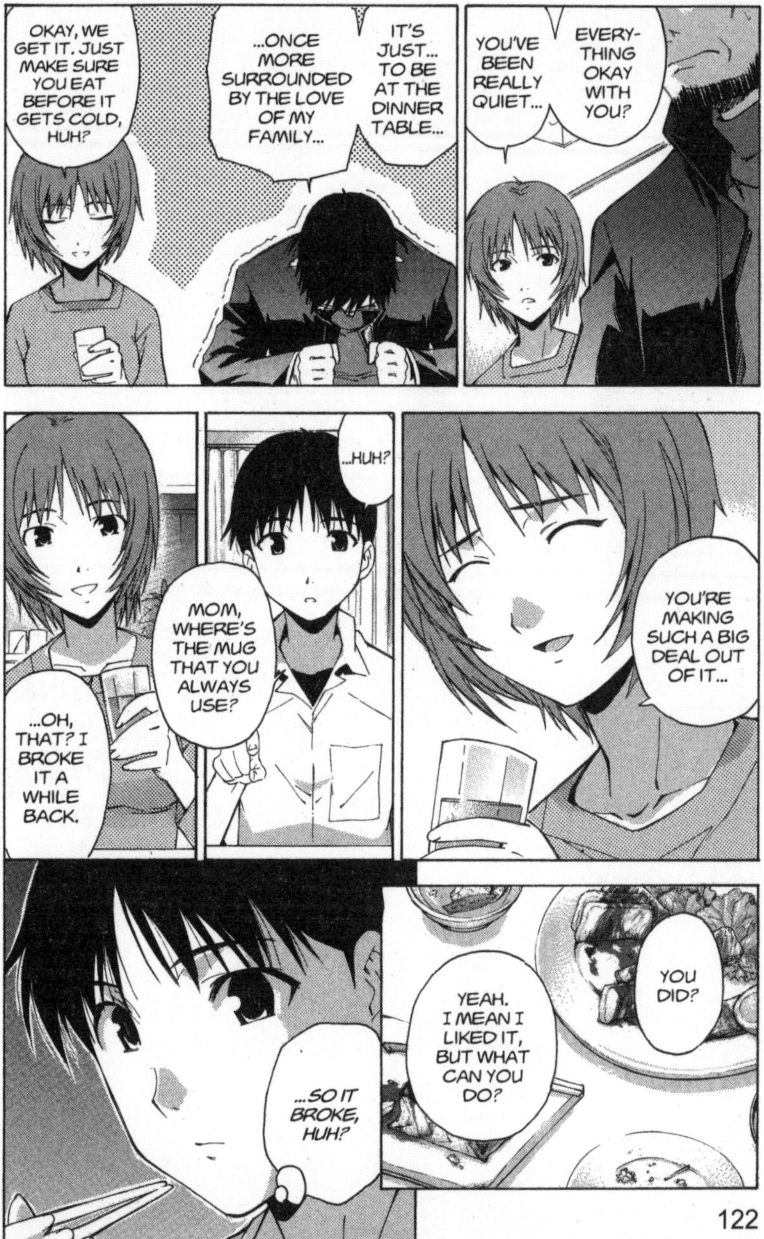
EVERY-THING OKAY WITH YOU?
YOU'VE BEEN REALLY QUIET...
IT'S JUST... TO BE AT THE DINNER TABLE...
...ONCE MORE SURROUNDED BY THE LOVE OF MY FAMILY...
OKAY, WE GET IT. JUST MAKE SURE YOU EAT BEFORE IT GETS COLD, HUH?
YOU'RE MAKING SUCH A BIG DEAL OUT OF IT...
...HUH?
MOM, WHERE'S THE MUG THAT YOU ALWAYS USE?
...OH, THAT? I BROKE IT A WHILE BACK.
YOU DID?
YEAH. I MEAN I LIKED IT, BUT WHAT CAN YOU DO?
...SO IT BROKE, HUH?

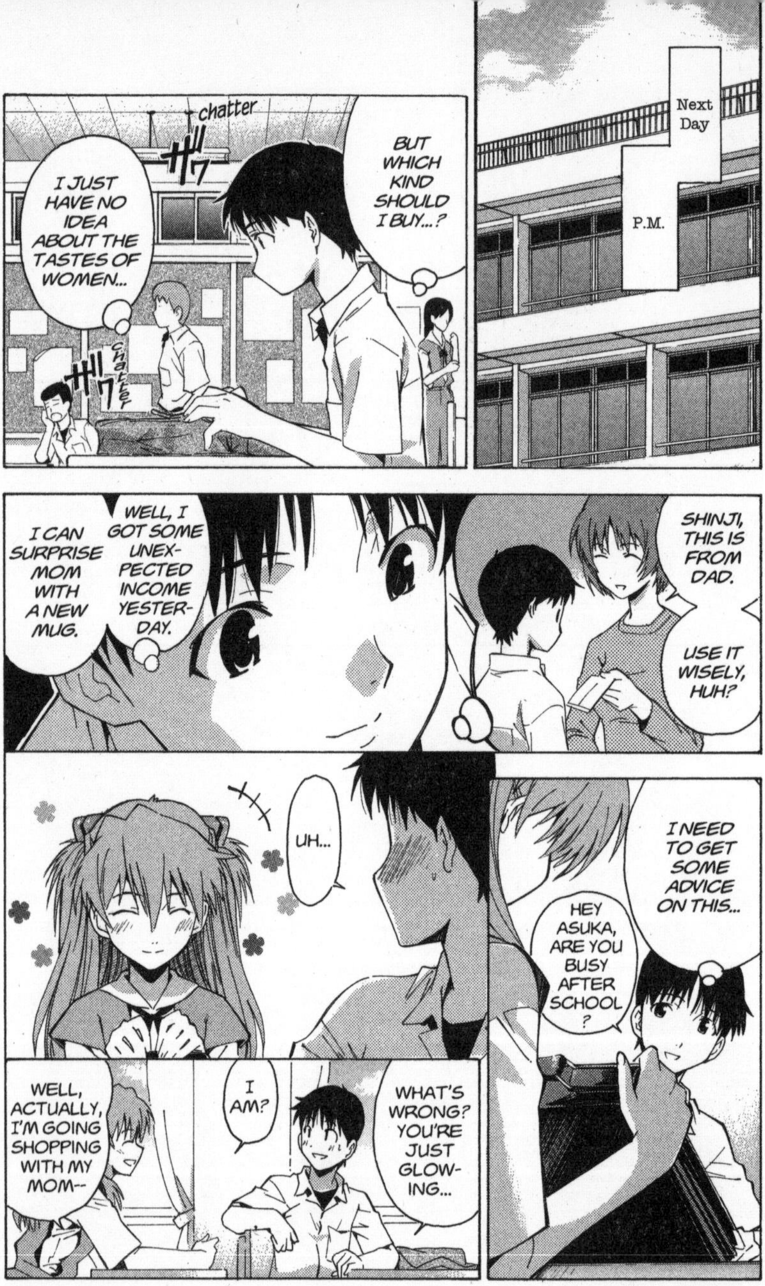
Next Day
P.M.
BUT WHICH KIND SHOULD I BUY...?
ザワ
chatter
I JUST HAVE NO IDEA ABOUT THE TASTES OF WOMEN...
ザワ
chatter
SHINJI, THIS IS FROM DAD.
USE IT WISELY, HUH?
WELL, I GOT SOME UNEXPECTED INCOME YESTERDAY.
I CAN SURPRISE MOM WITH A NEW MUG.
I NEED TO GET SOME ADVICE ON THIS...
HEY ASUKA, ARE YOU BUSY AFTER SCHOOL?
UH...
WHAT'S WRONG? YOU'RE JUST GLOWING...
I AM?
WELL, ACTUALLY, I'M GOING SHOPPING WITH MY MOM--

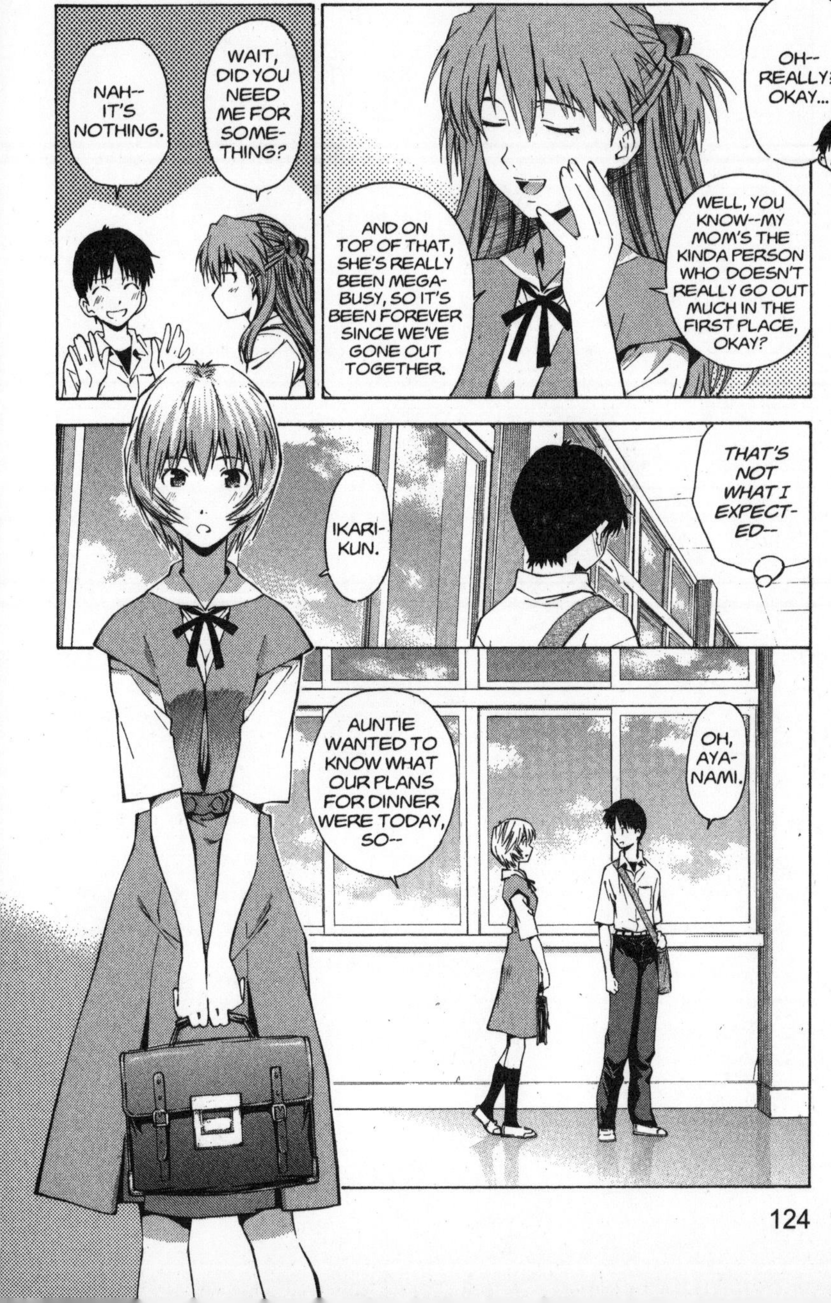
OH-- REALLY? OKAY...
WELL, YOU KNOW--MY MOM'S THE KINDA PERSON WHO DOESN'T REALLY GO OUT MUCH IN THE FIRST PLACE, OKAY?
AND ON TOP OF THAT, SHE'S REALLY BEEN MEGA-BUSY, SO IT'S BEEN FOREVER SINCE WE'VE GONE OUT TOGETHER.
WAIT, DID YOU NEED ME FOR SOME-THING?
NAH-- IT'S NOTHING.
THAT'S NOT WHAT I EXPECT-ED--
IKARI-KUN.
OH, AYA-NAMI.
AUNTIE WANTED TO KNOW WHAT OUR PLANS FOR DINNER WERE TODAY, SO--

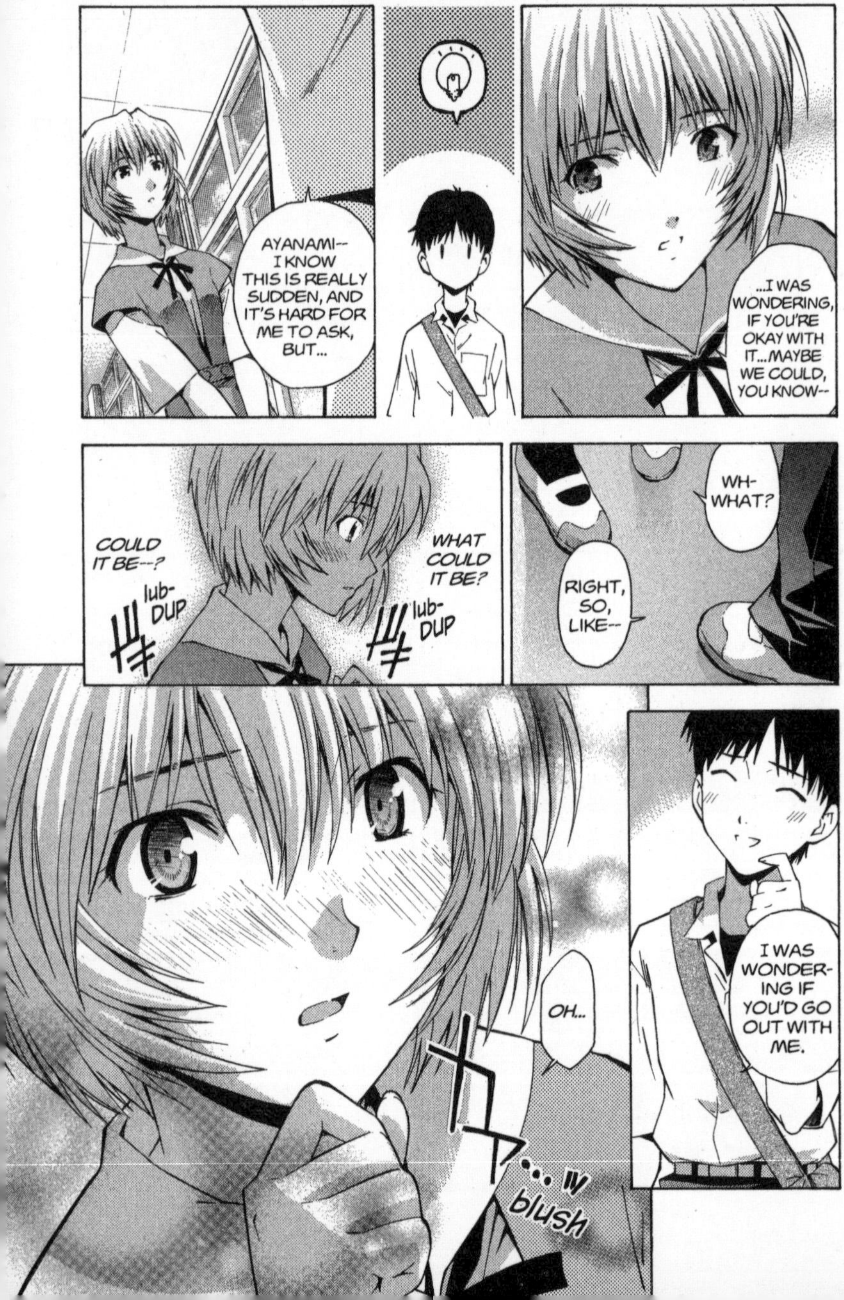
...I WAS WONDERING, IF YOU'RE OKAY WITH IT...MAYBE WE COULD, YOU KNOW--
AYANAMI-- I KNOW THIS IS REALLY SUDDEN, AND IT'S HARD FOR ME TO ASK, BUT...
WH- WHAT?
RIGHT, SO, LIKE--
WHAT COULD IT BE?
lub- DUP
COULD IT BE--?
lub- DUP
I WAS WONDER- ING IF YOU'D GO OUT WITH ME.
OH...
blush

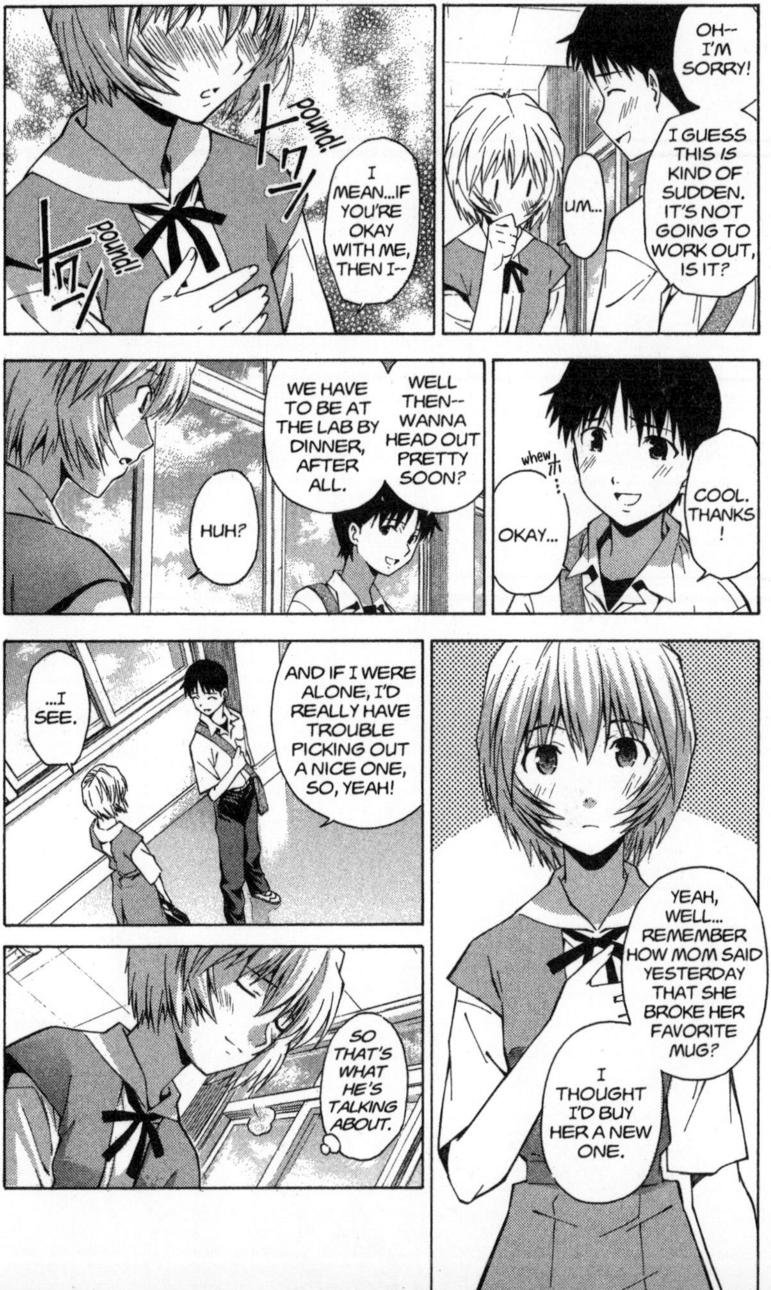
OH-- I'M SORRY!
I GUESS THIS IS KIND OF SUDDEN. IT'S NOT GOING TO WORK OUT, IS IT?
UM...
pound!
I MEAN...IF YOU'RE OKAY WITH ME, THEN I--
pound!
COOL. THANKS!
whew
OKAY...
WELL THEN-- WANNA HEAD OUT PRETTY SOON?
WE HAVE TO BE AT THE LAB BY DINNER, AFTER ALL.
HUH?
YEAH, WELL... REMEMBER HOW MOM SAID YESTERDAY THAT SHE BROKE HER FAVORITE MUG?
I THOUGHT I'D BUY HER A NEW ONE.
AND IF I WERE ALONE, I'D REALLY HAVE TROUBLE PICKING OUT A NICE ONE, SO, YEAH!
...I SEE.
SO THAT'S WHAT HE'S TALKING ABOUT.

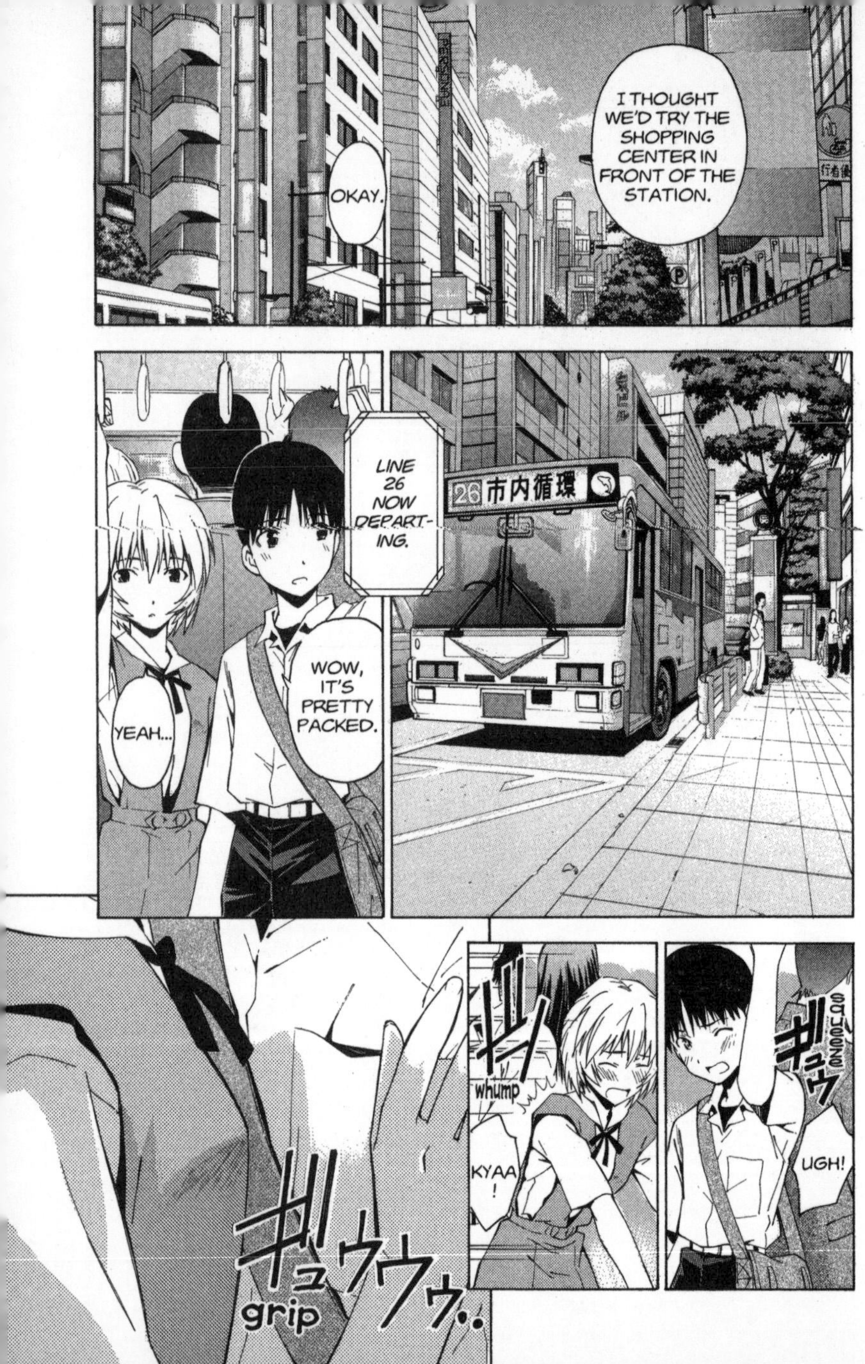
I THOUGHT WE'D TRY THE SHOPPING CENTER IN FRONT OF THE STATION.
OKAY.
26 市内循環
LINE 26 NOW DEPARTING.
WOW, IT'S PRETTY PACKED.
YEAH...
squeeze
UGH!
whump
KYAA!
grip

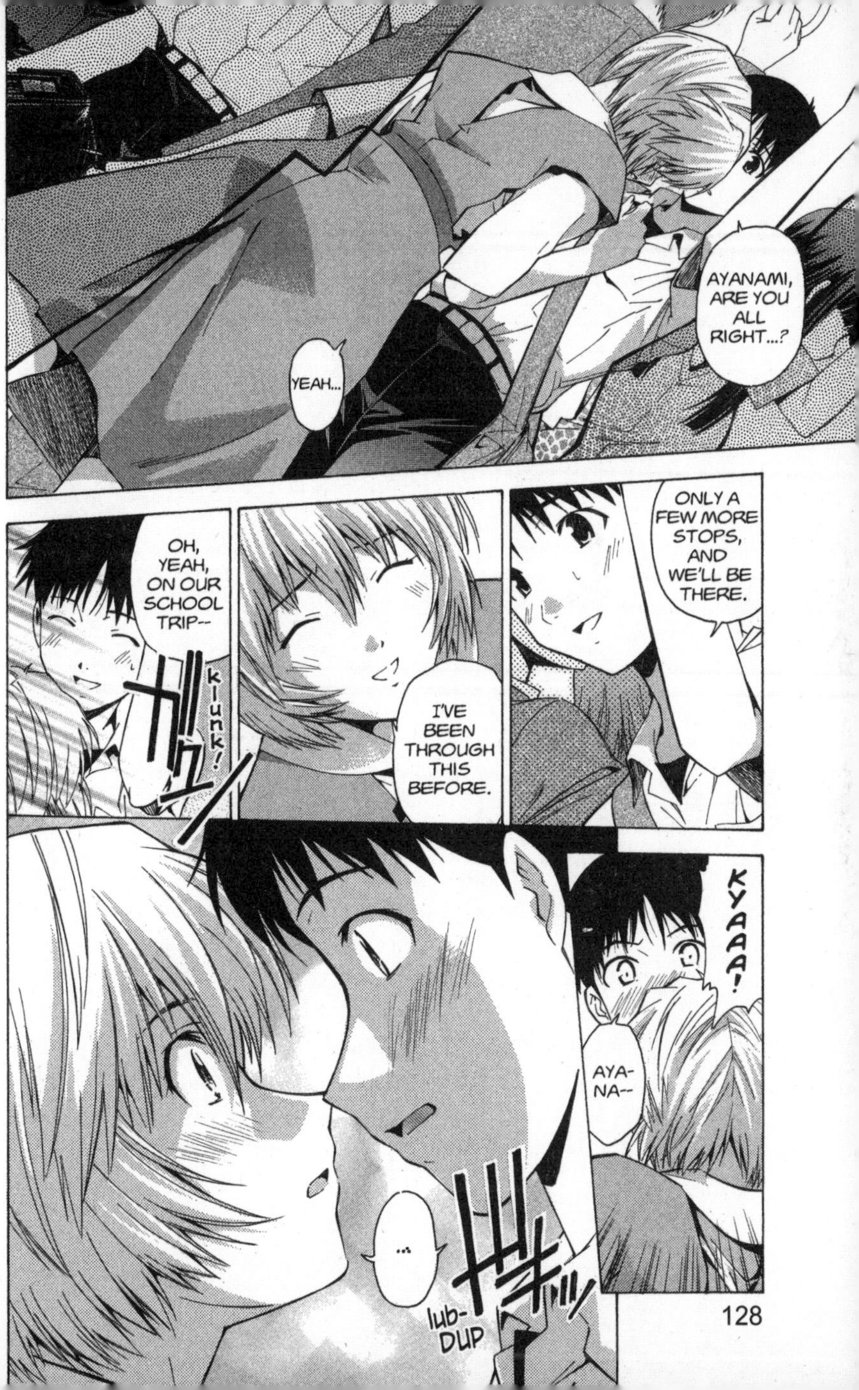
AYANAMI, ARE YOU ALL RIGHT...?
YEAH...
ONLY A FEW MORE STOPS, AND WE'LL BE THERE.
I'VE BEEN THROUGH THIS BEFORE.
OH, YEAH, ON OUR SCHOOL TRIP--
klunk!
KYAAAA!
AYA-NA--
...
lub-DUP

FOR WHAT ...?

I-I'M SORRY...

lub·DUP
lub·DUP
lub·DUP

...

SORYU-SAN AND HORAKI-SAN SAID THEY'VE SHOPPED HERE BEFORE.

HERE?

TOKYO DO Life Style Shop

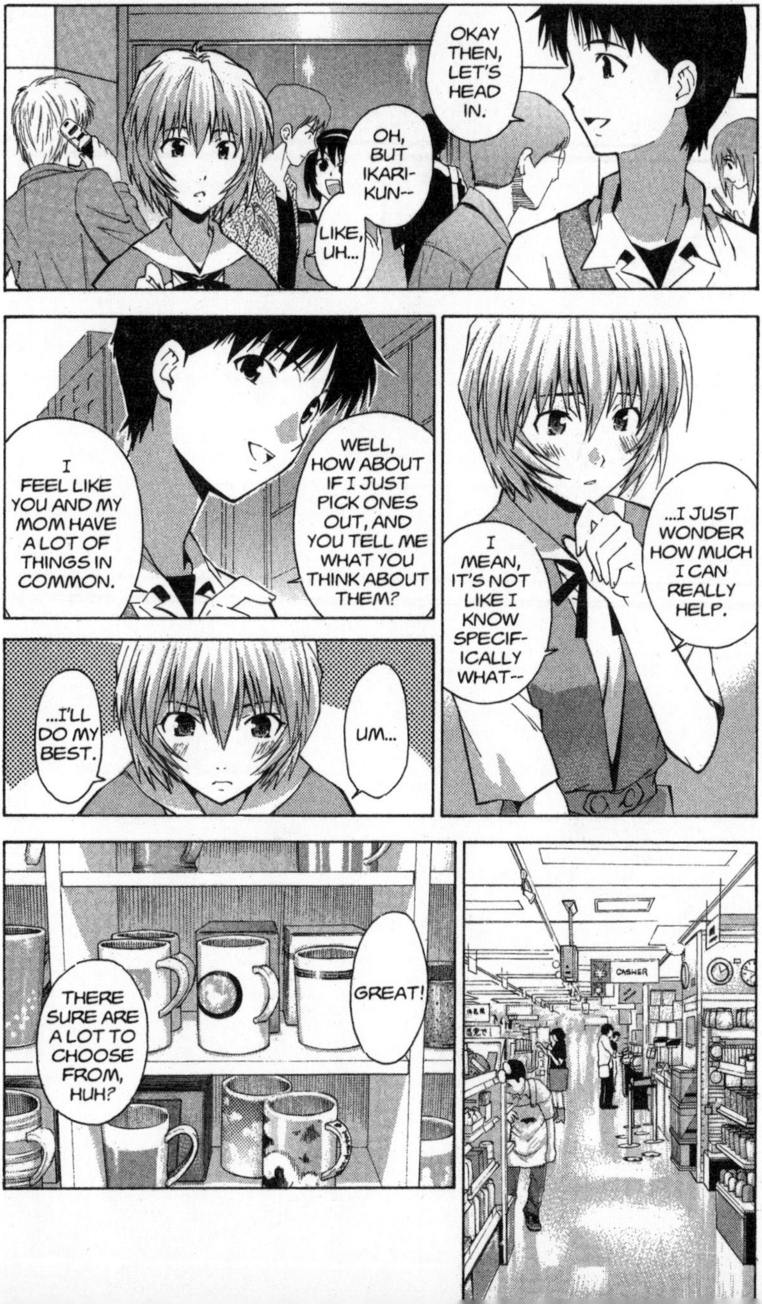
OKAY THEN, LET'S HEAD IN.
OH, BUT IKARI-KUN--
LIKE, UH...
...I JUST WONDER HOW MUCH I CAN REALLY HELP.
I MEAN, IT'S NOT LIKE I KNOW SPECIFICALLY WHAT--
WELL, HOW ABOUT IF I JUST PICK ONES OUT, AND YOU TELL ME WHAT YOU THINK ABOUT THEM?
I FEEL LIKE YOU AND MY MOM HAVE A LOT OF THINGS IN COMMON.
UM...
...I'LL DO MY BEST.
GREAT!
THERE SURE ARE A LOT TO CHOOSE FROM, HUH?

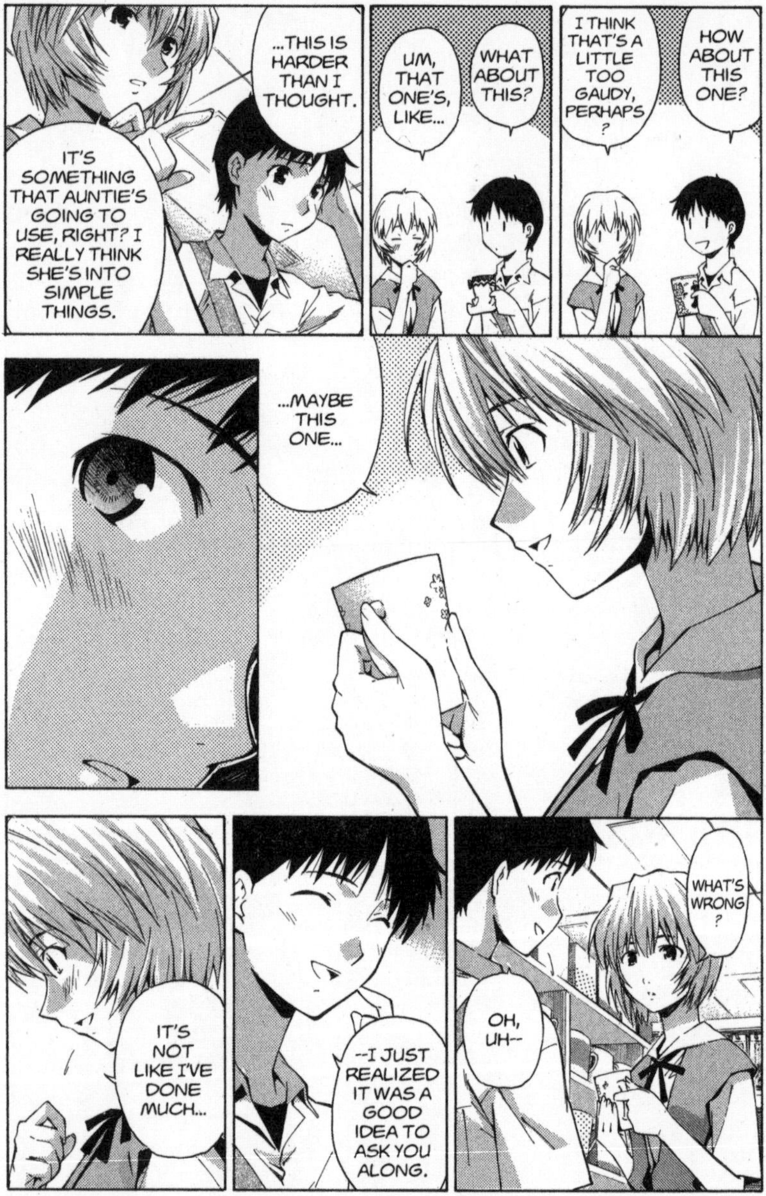
HOW ABOUT THIS ONE?
I THINK THAT'S A LITTLE TOO GAUDY, PERHAPS?
WHAT ABOUT THIS?
UM, THAT ONE'S, LIKE...
...THIS IS HARDER THAN I THOUGHT.
IT'S SOMETHING THAT AUNTIE'S GOING TO USE, RIGHT? I REALLY THINK SHE'S INTO SIMPLE THINGS.
...MAYBE THIS ONE...
WHAT'S WRONG?
OH, UH--
--I JUST REALIZED IT WAS A GOOD IDEA TO ASK YOU ALONG.
IT'S NOT LIKE I'VE DONE MUCH...

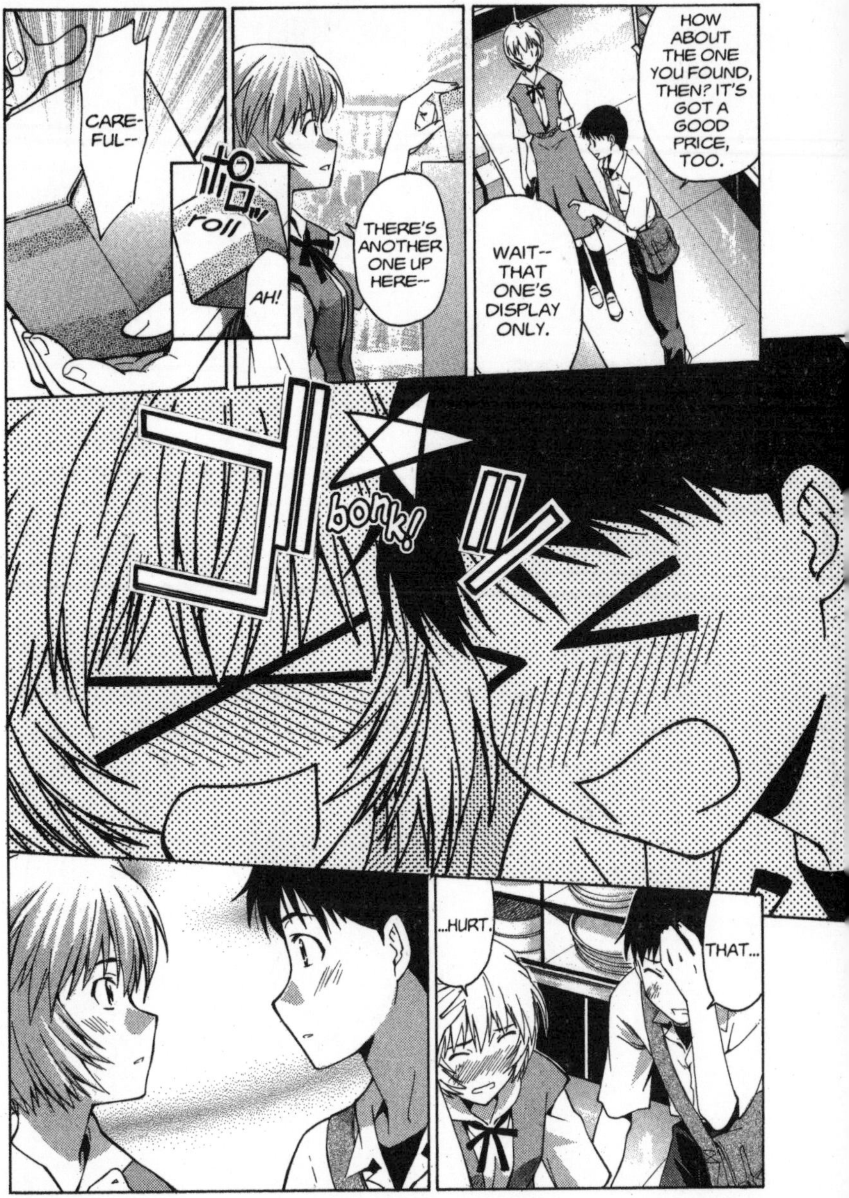
HOW ABOUT THE ONE YOU FOUND, THEN? IT'S GOT A GOOD PRICE, TOO.
WAIT-- THAT ONE'S DISPLAY ONLY.
THERE'S ANOTHER ONE UP HERE--
ポロッ
roll
AH!
CARE-FUL--
ゴッ
bonk!
THAT...
...HURT.

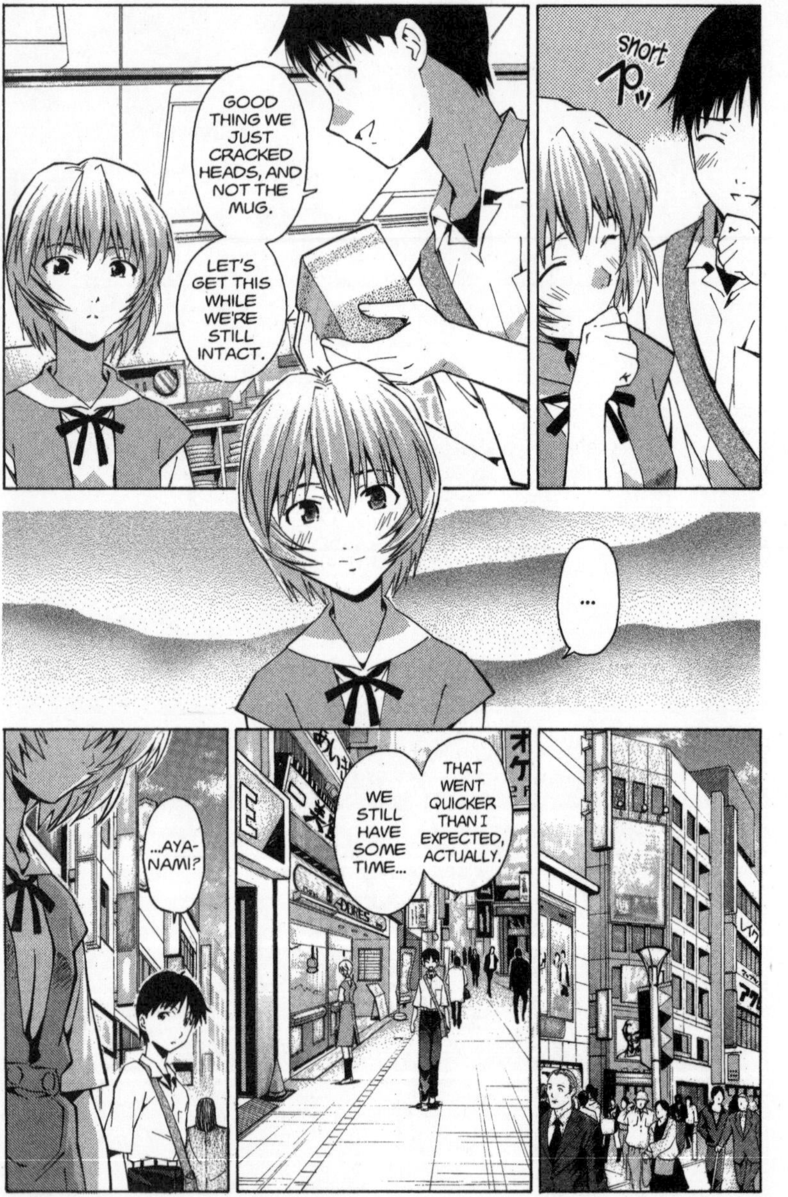
snort
プッ
GOOD THING WE JUST CRACKED HEADS, AND NOT THE MUG.
LET'S GET THIS WHILE WE'RE STILL INTACT.
...
THAT WENT QUICKER THAN I EXPECTED, ACTUALLY.
WE STILL HAVE SOME TIME...
...AYA-NAMI?

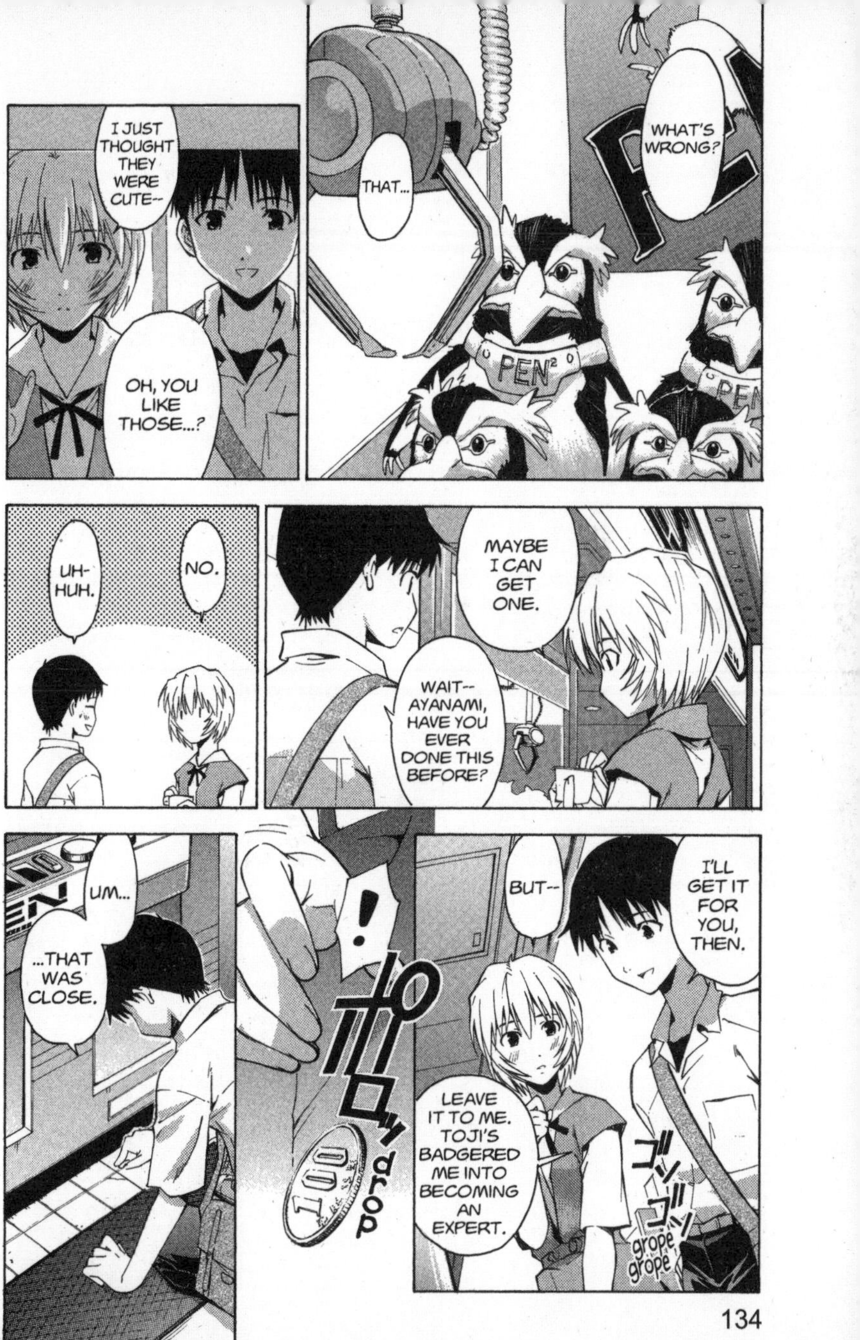
WHAT'S WRONG?
THAT...
I JUST THOUGHT THEY WERE CUTE--
OH, YOU LIKE THOSE...?
MAYBE I CAN GET ONE.
WAIT-- AYANAMI, HAVE YOU EVER DONE THIS BEFORE?
NO.
UH-HUH.
I'LL GET IT FOR YOU, THEN.
BUT--
LEAVE IT TO ME. TOJI'S BADGERED ME INTO BECOMING AN EXPERT.
ゴソゴソ
grope grope
!
ポロッ
drop
UM...
...THAT WAS CLOSE.

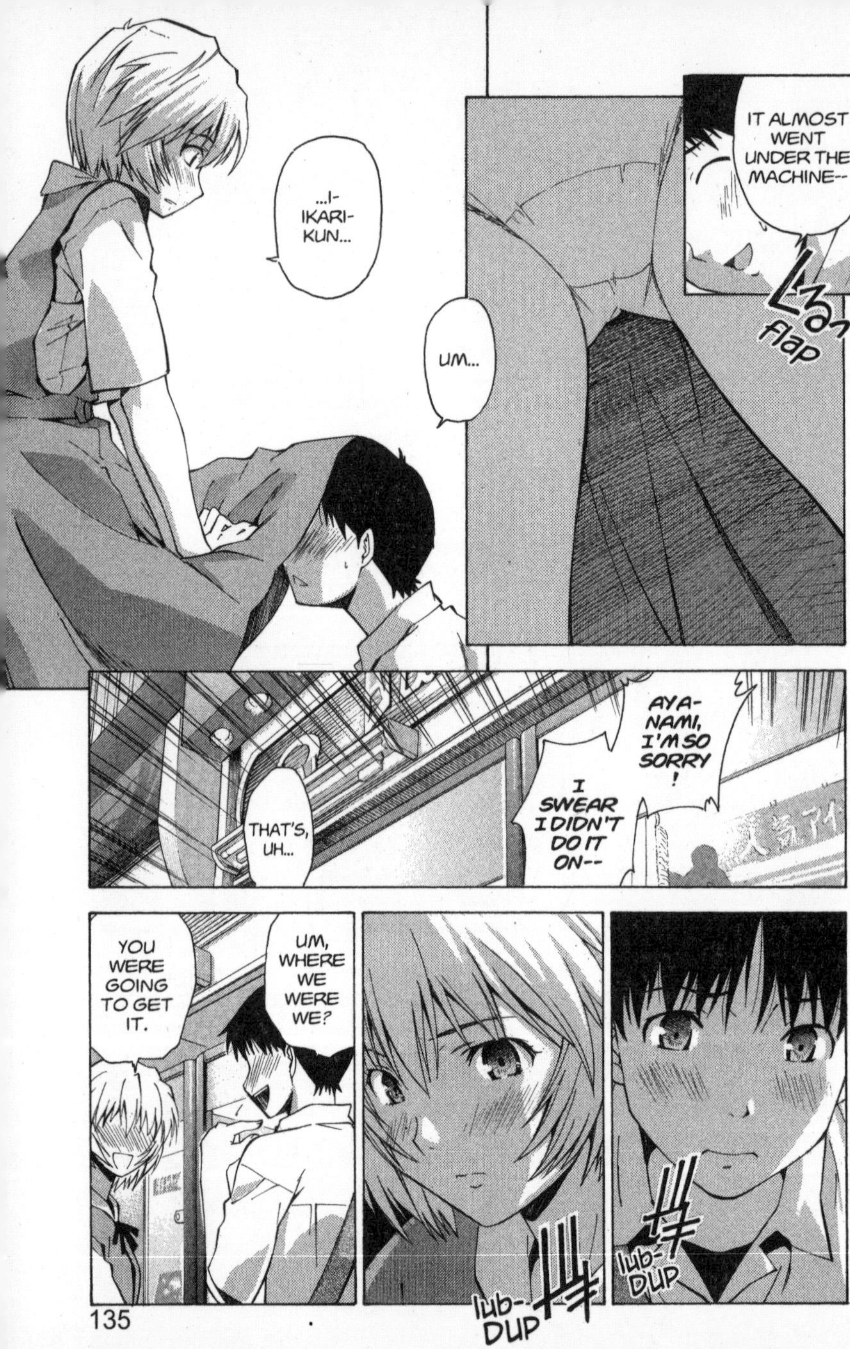
IT ALMOST WENT UNDER THE MACHINE--
くるっ
flap
...I-IKARI-KUN...
UM...
AYA-NAMI, I'M SO SORRY!
I SWEAR I DIDN'T DO IT ON--
THAT'S, UH...
lub-DUP
lub-DUP
UM, WHERE WE WERE WE?
YOU WERE GOING TO GET IT.

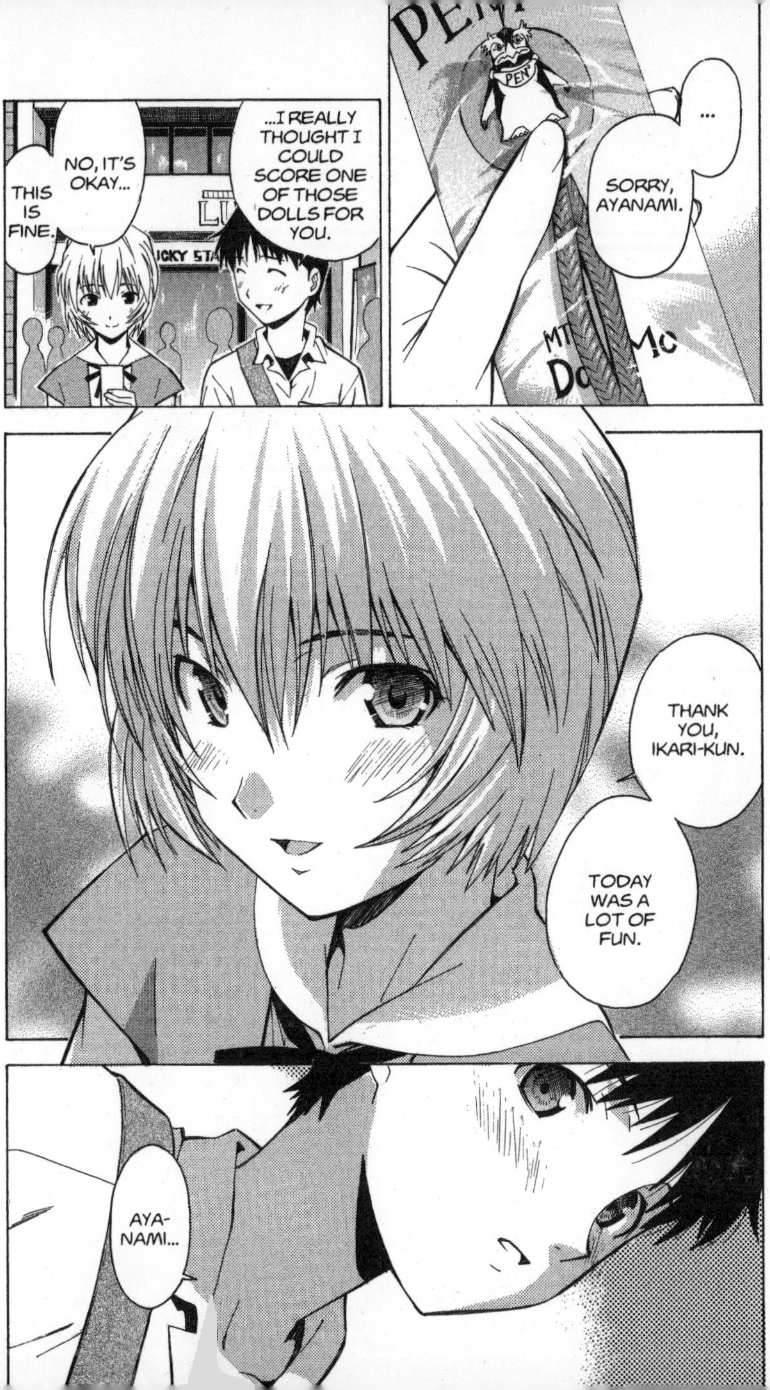
...
SORRY, AYANAMI.
...I REALLY THOUGHT I COULD SCORE ONE OF THOSE DOLLS FOR YOU.
NO, IT'S OKAY...
THIS IS FINE.
THANK YOU, IKARI-KUN.
TODAY WAS A LOT OF FUN.
AYA-NAMI...

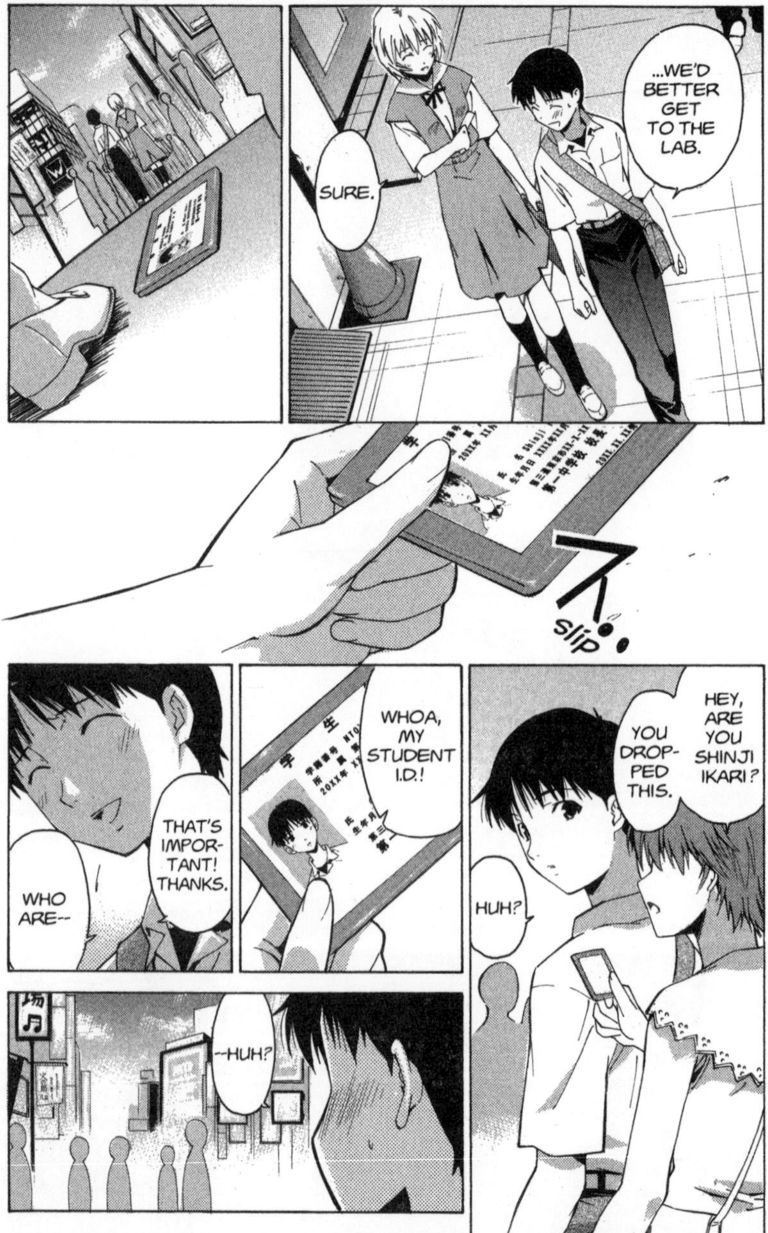
...WE'D BETTER GET TO THE LAB.
SURE.
slip
HEY, ARE YOU SHINJI IKARI?
YOU DROPPED THIS.
HUH?
WHOA, MY STUDENT I.D.!
THAT'S IMPORTANT! THANKS.
WHO ARE--
--HUH?

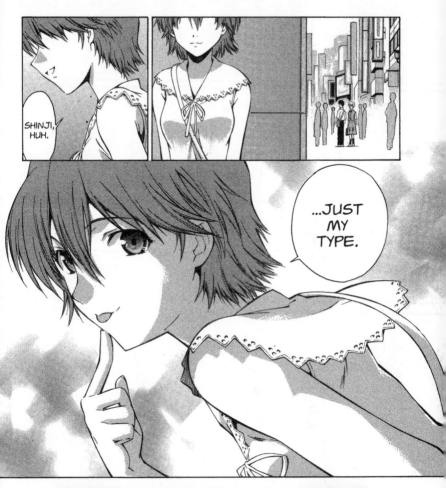

SHINJI, HUH.
...JUST MY TYPE.
OH, HOW NICE!
THANK YOU, SHINJI.
N-NO PRESENT FOR YOUR DAD...?!
END

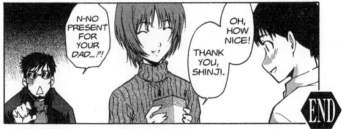

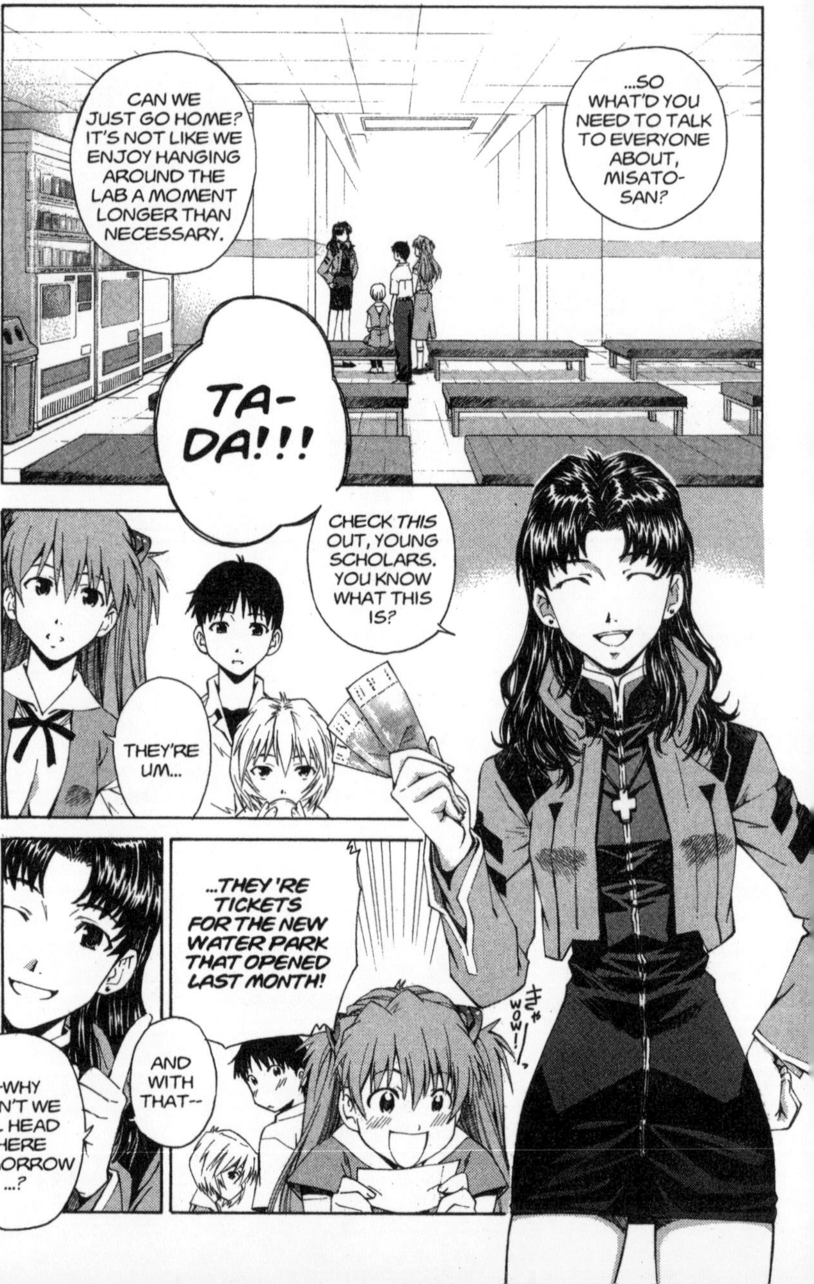
...SO WHAT'D YOU NEED TO TALK TO EVERYONE ABOUT, MISATO-SAN?
CAN WE JUST GO HOME? IT'S NOT LIKE WE ENJOY HANGING AROUND THE LAB A MOMENT LONGER THAN NECESSARY.
TA-DA!!!
CHECK THIS OUT, YOUNG SCHOLARS. YOU KNOW WHAT THIS IS?
THEY'RE UM...
...THEY'RE TICKETS FOR THE NEW WATER PARK THAT OPENED LAST MONTH!
WOW!!
AND WITH THAT--
--WHY DON'T WE ALL HEAD THERE TOMORROW ...?

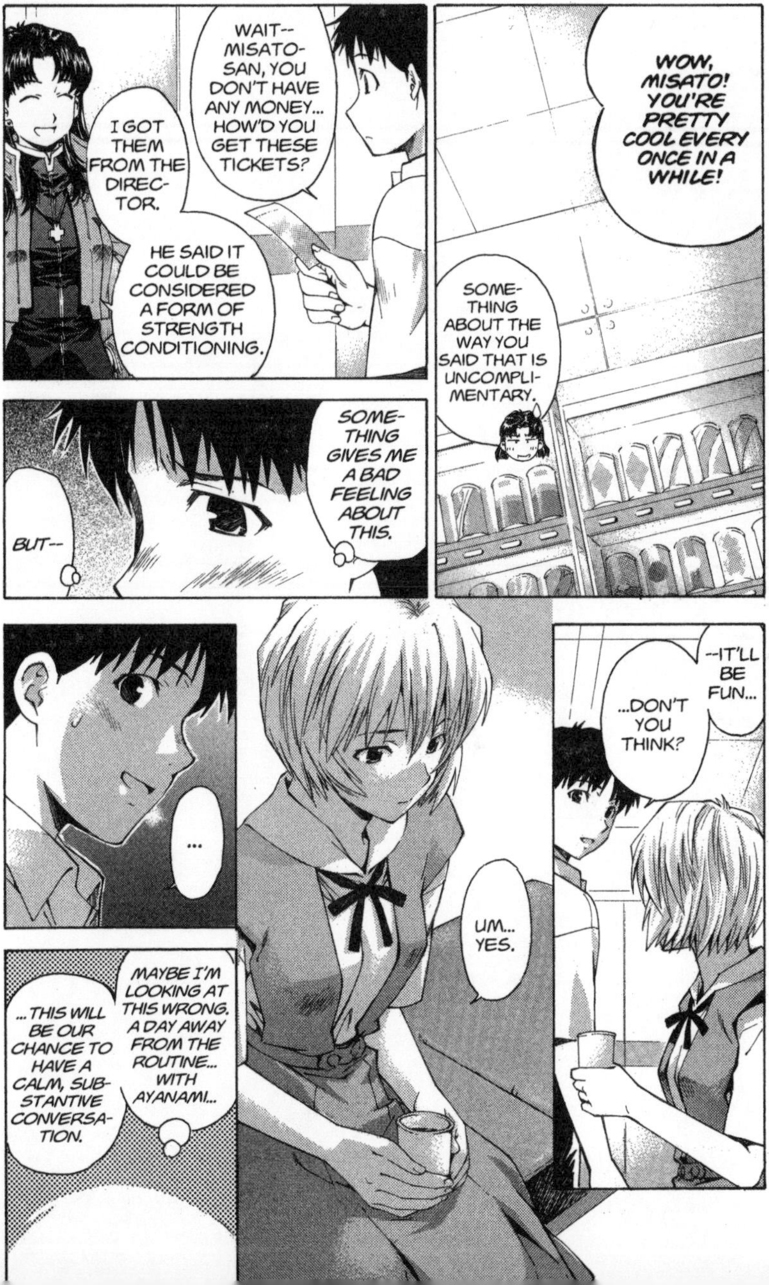
WOW, MISATO! YOU'RE PRETTY COOL EVERY ONCE IN A WHILE!
SOME-THING ABOUT THE WAY YOU SAID THAT IS UNCOMPLI-MENTARY.
WAIT-- MISATO-SAN, YOU DON'T HAVE ANY MONEY... HOW'D YOU GET THESE TICKETS?
I GOT THEM FROM THE DIREC-TOR.
HE SAID IT COULD BE CONSIDERED A FORM OF STRENGTH CONDITIONING.
SOME-THING GIVES ME A BAD FEELING ABOUT THIS.
BUT--
--IT'LL BE FUN...
...DON'T YOU THINK?
UM... YES.
...
MAYBE I'M LOOKING AT THIS WRONG. A DAY AWAY FROM THE ROUTINE... WITH AYANAMI...
...THIS WILL BE OUR CHANCE TO HAVE A CALM, SUB-STANTIVE CONVERSA-TION.

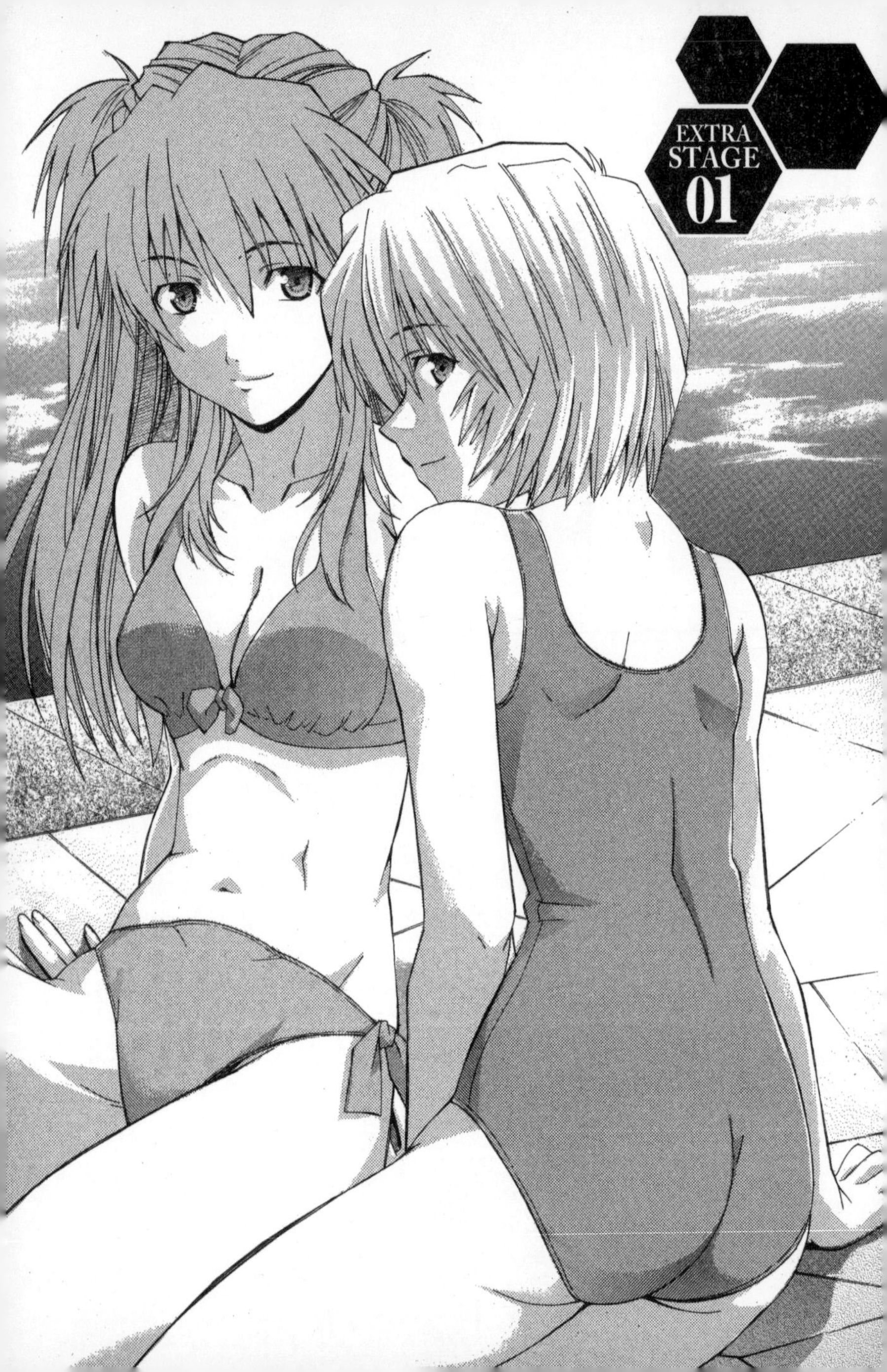
EXTRA
STAGE
01

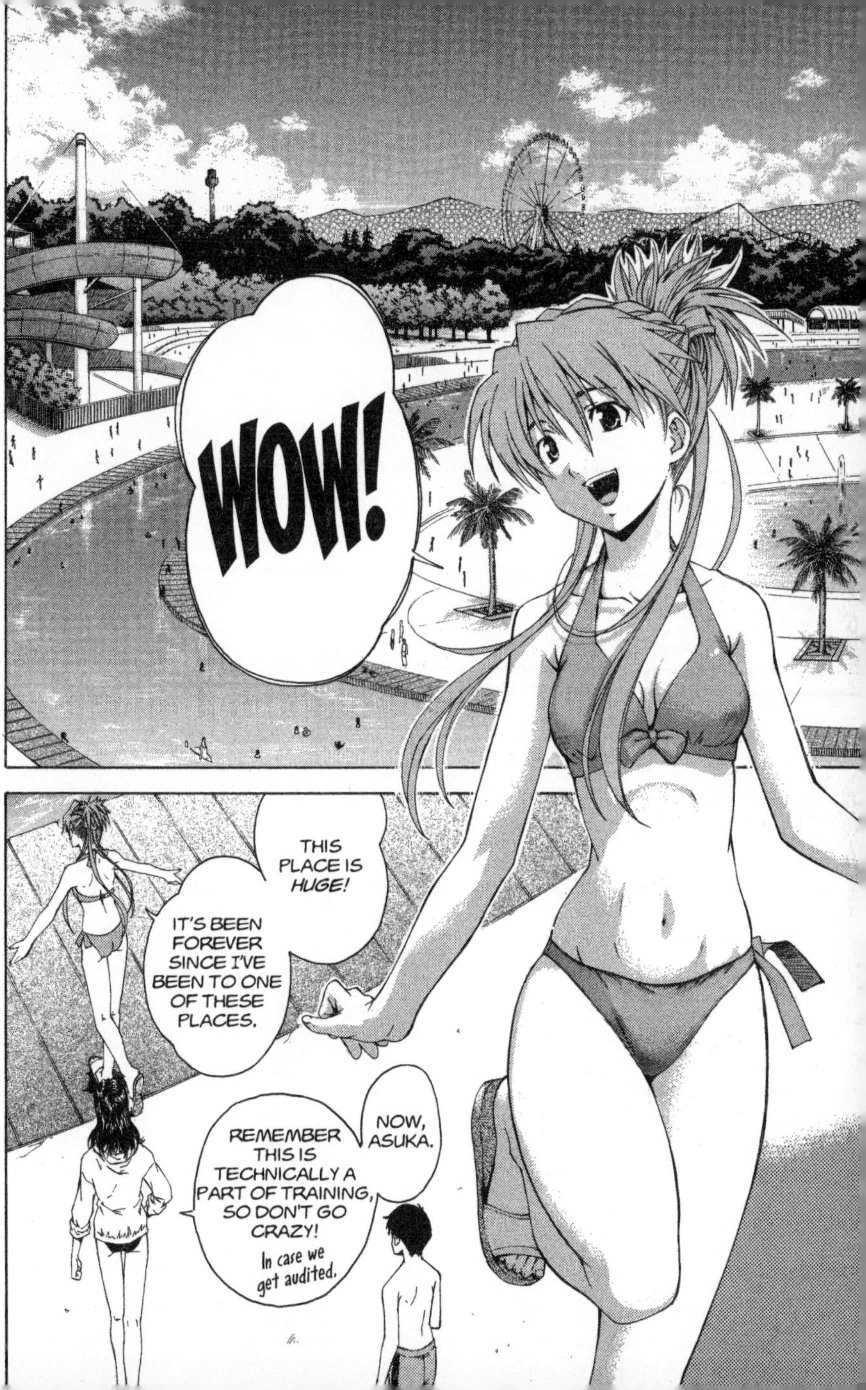
WOW!
THIS PLACE IS HUGE!
IT'S BEEN FOREVER SINCE I'VE BEEN TO ONE OF THESE PLACES.
NOW, ASUKA.
REMEMBER THIS IS TECHNICALLY A PART OF TRAINING, SO DON'T GO CRAZY!
In case we get audited.

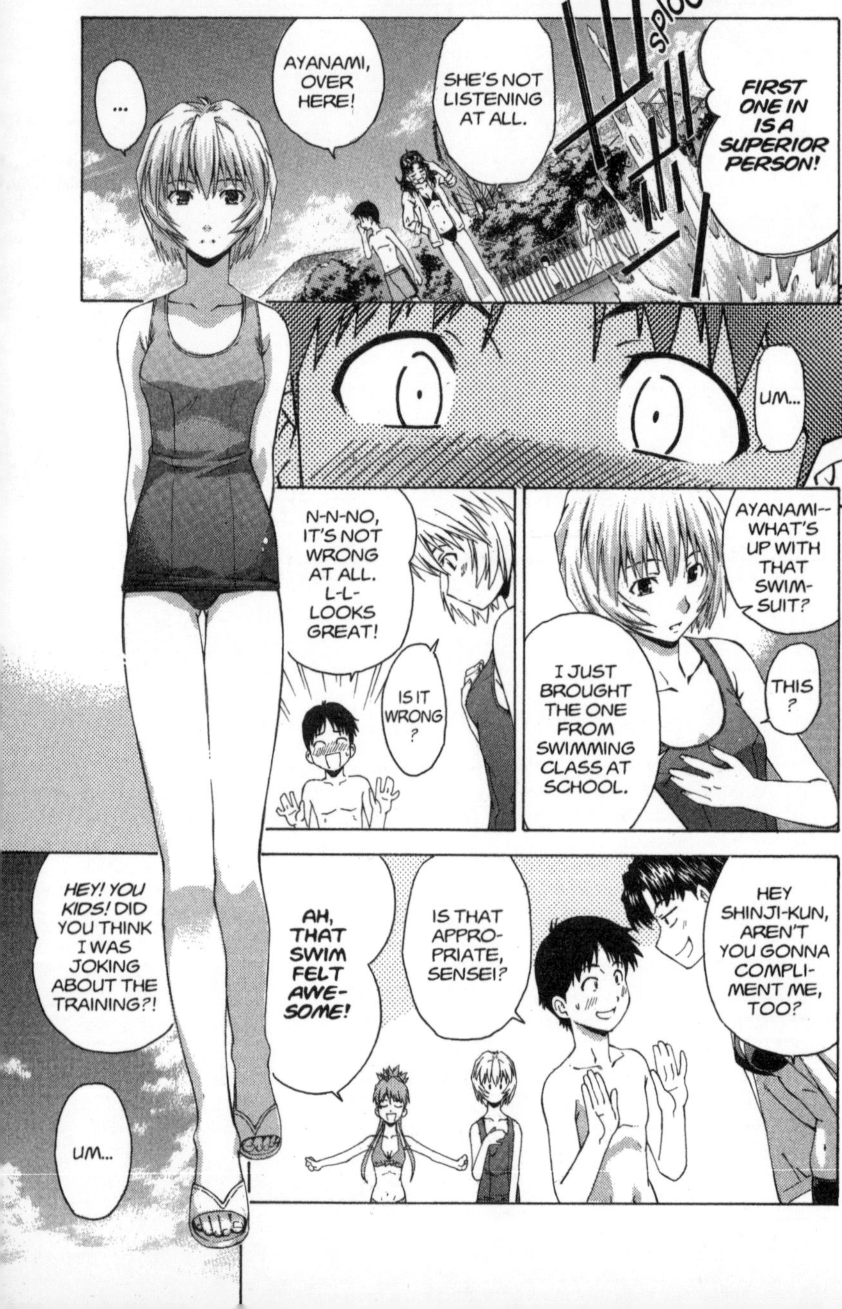
sploosh
FIRST ONE IN IS A SUPERIOR PERSON!
SHE'S NOT LISTENING AT ALL.
AYANAMI, OVER HERE!
...
UM...
AYANAMI--WHAT'S UP WITH THAT SWIM-SUIT?
THIS?
I JUST BROUGHT THE ONE FROM SWIMMING CLASS AT SCHOOL.
IS IT WRONG?
N-N-NO, IT'S NOT WRONG AT ALL. L-L-LOOKS GREAT!
HEY SHINJI-KUN, AREN'T YOU GONNA COMPLI-MENT ME, TOO?
IS THAT APPRO-PRIATE, SENSEI?
AH, THAT SWIM FELT AWE-SOME!
HEY! YOU KIDS! DID YOU THINK I WAS JOKING ABOUT THE TRAINING?!
UM...

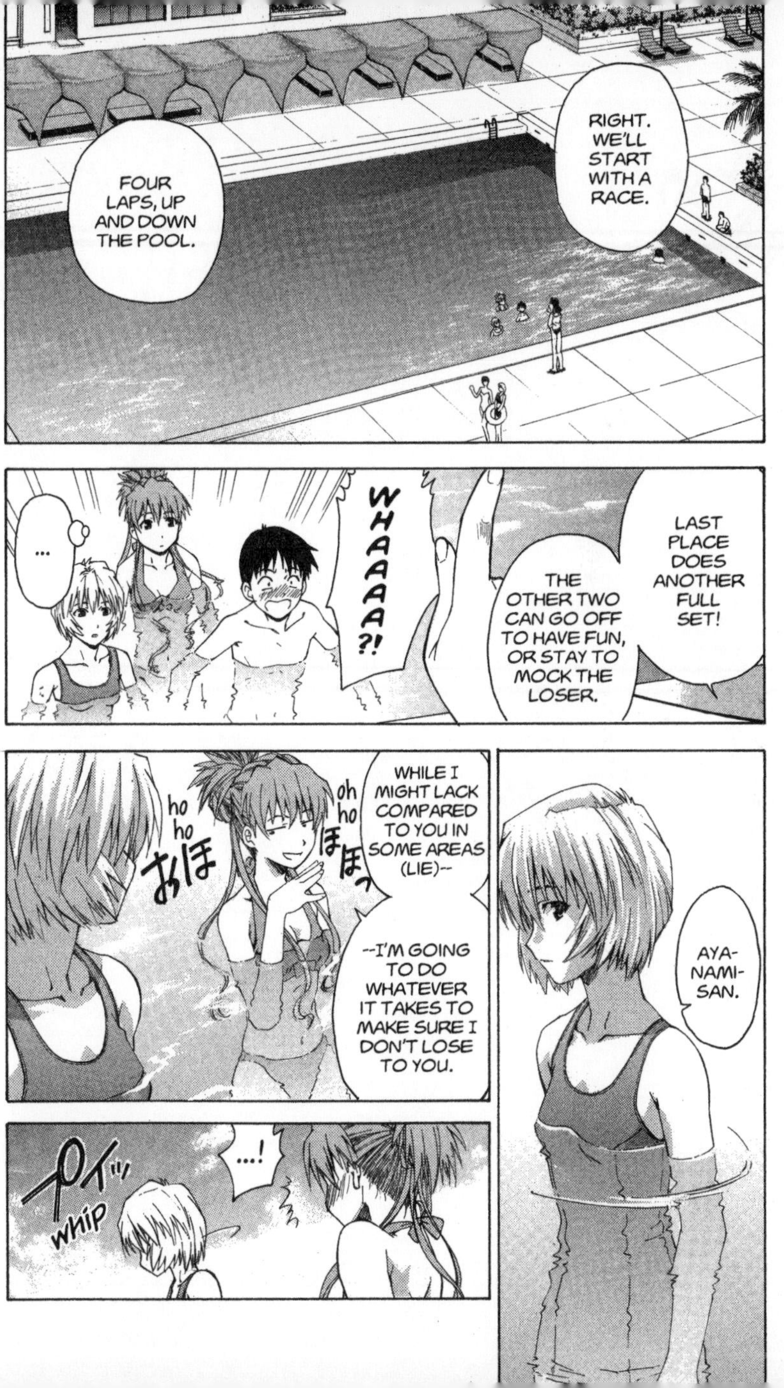
RIGHT. WE'LL START WITH A RACE.
FOUR LAPS, UP AND DOWN THE POOL.
LAST PLACE DOES ANOTHER FULL SET!
THE OTHER TWO CAN GO OFF TO HAVE FUN, OR STAY TO MOCK THE LOSER.
WHAAAAA?!
...
AYA-NAMI-SAN.
WHILE I MIGHT LACK COMPARED TO YOU IN SOME AREAS (LIE)--
ほほっ
oh ho
おほ
ho ho
--I'M GOING TO DO WHATEVER IT TAKES TO MAKE SURE I DON'T LOSE TO YOU.
...!
プイッ
whip

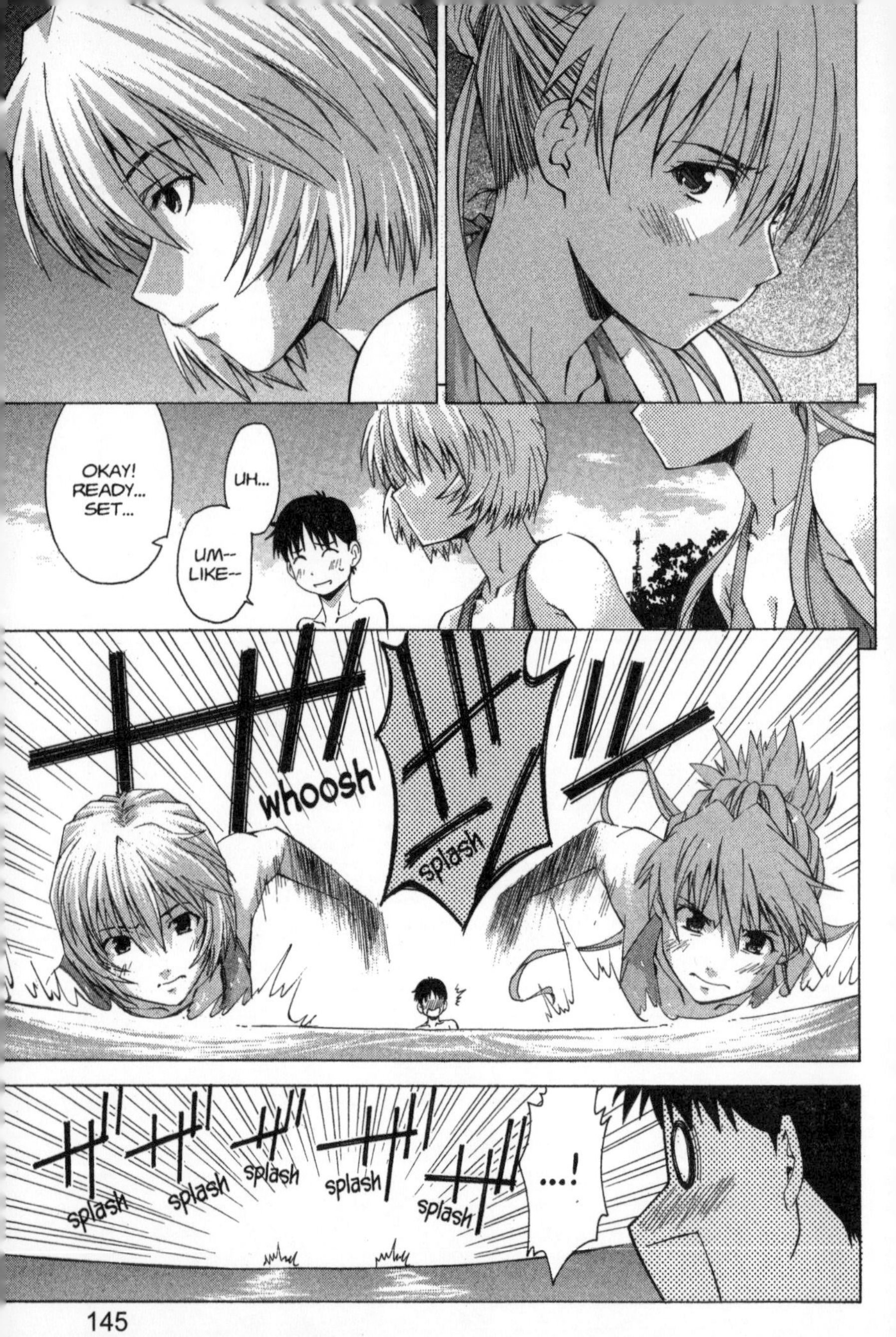
OKAY! READY... SET...
UH...
UM-- LIKE--
whoosh
splash
splash
splash
splash
splash
splash
...!

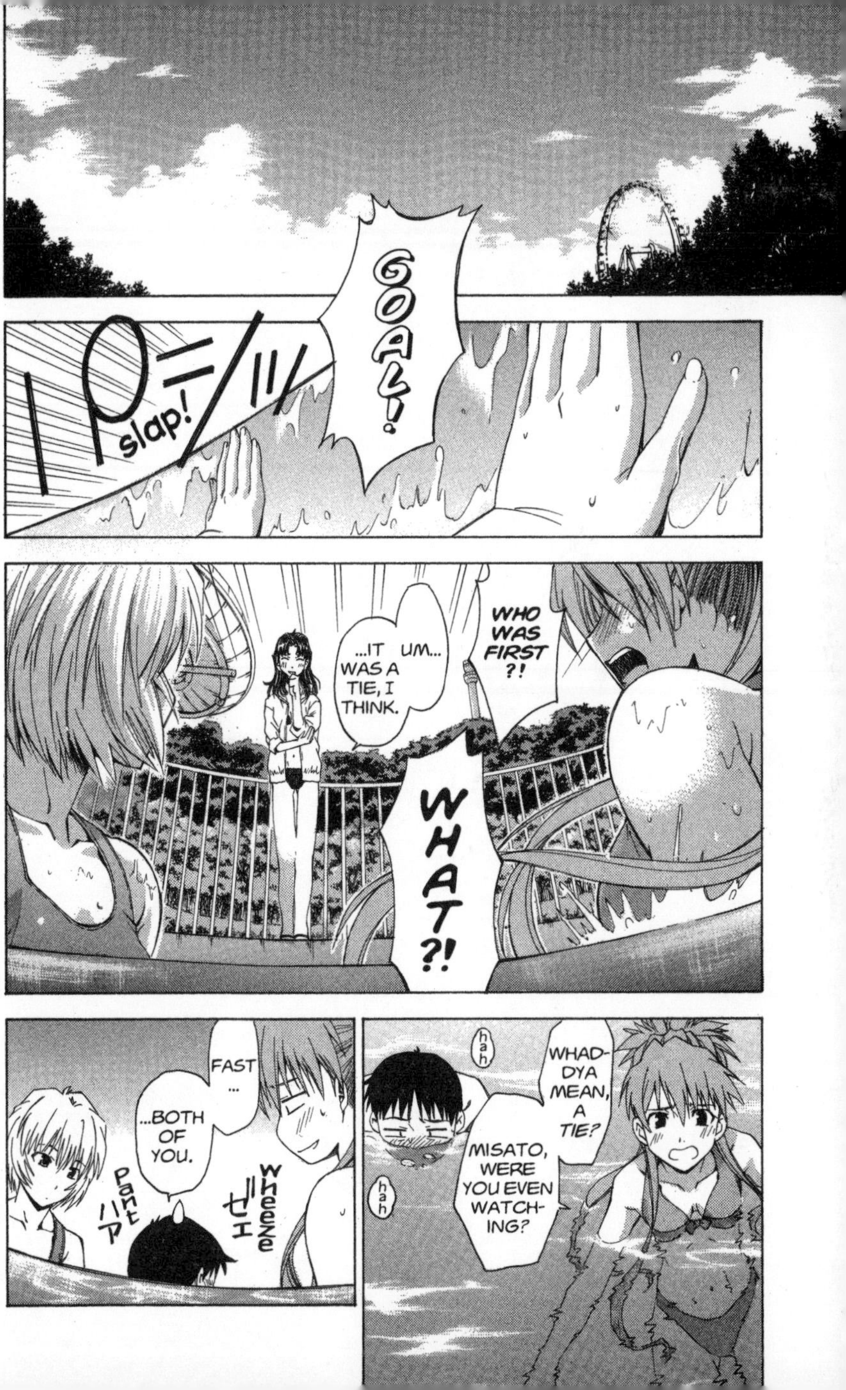
GOAL!
slap!
WHO WAS FIRST?!
UM...
...IT WAS A TIE, I THINK.
WHAT?!
hah
hah
WHAD-DYA MEAN, A TIE?
MISATO, WERE YOU EVEN WATCH-ING?
FAST...
...BOTH OF YOU.
wheeze
ゼイ
pant
ハア

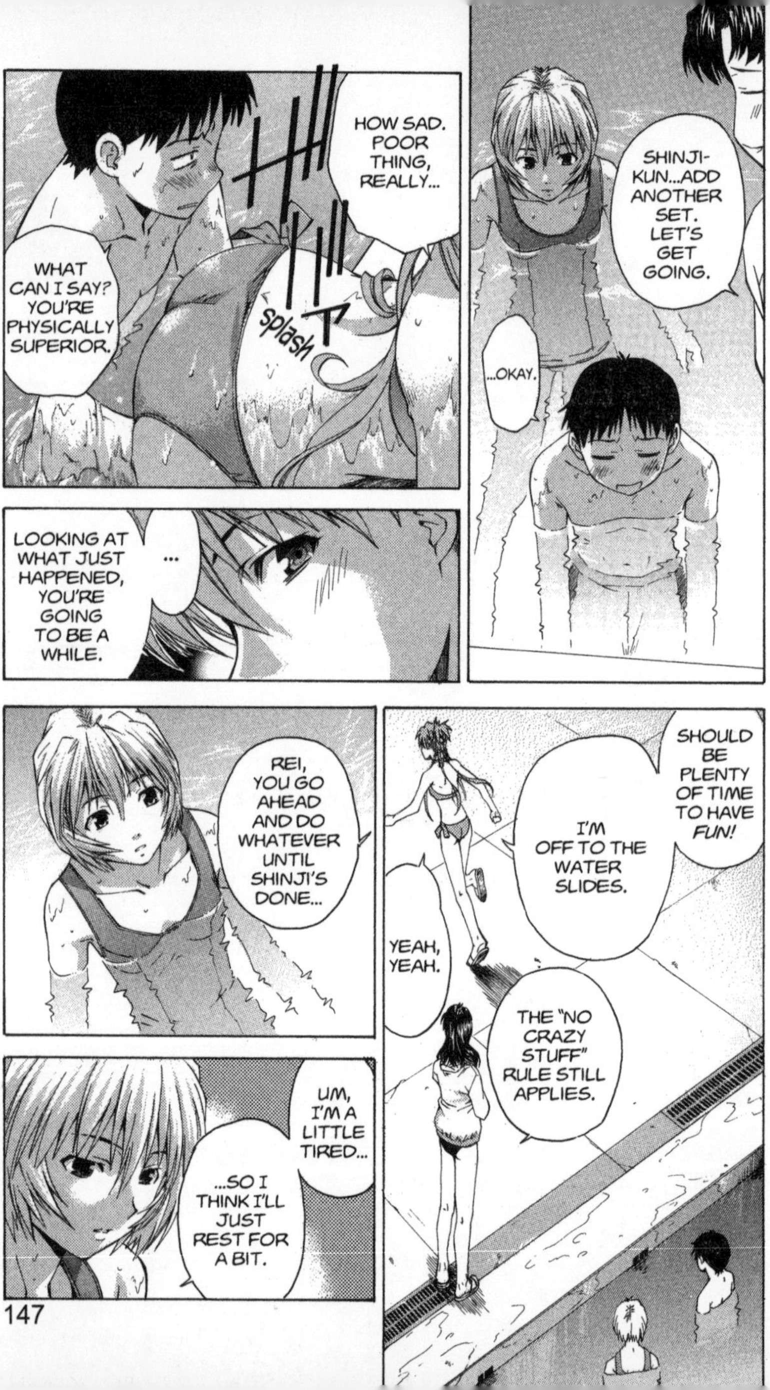
SHINJI-KUN...ADD ANOTHER SET. LET'S GET GOING.
...OKAY.
HOW SAD. POOR THING, REALLY...
splash
WHAT CAN I SAY? YOU'RE PHYSICALLY SUPERIOR.
...
LOOKING AT WHAT JUST HAPPENED, YOU'RE GOING TO BE A WHILE.
SHOULD BE PLENTY OF TIME TO HAVE *FUN!*
I'M OFF TO THE WATER SLIDES.
YEAH, YEAH.
THE "NO CRAZY STUFF" RULE STILL APPLIES.
REI, YOU GO AHEAD AND DO WHATEVER UNTIL SHINJI'S DONE...
UM, I'M A LITTLE TIRED...
...SO I THINK I'LL JUST REST FOR A BIT.

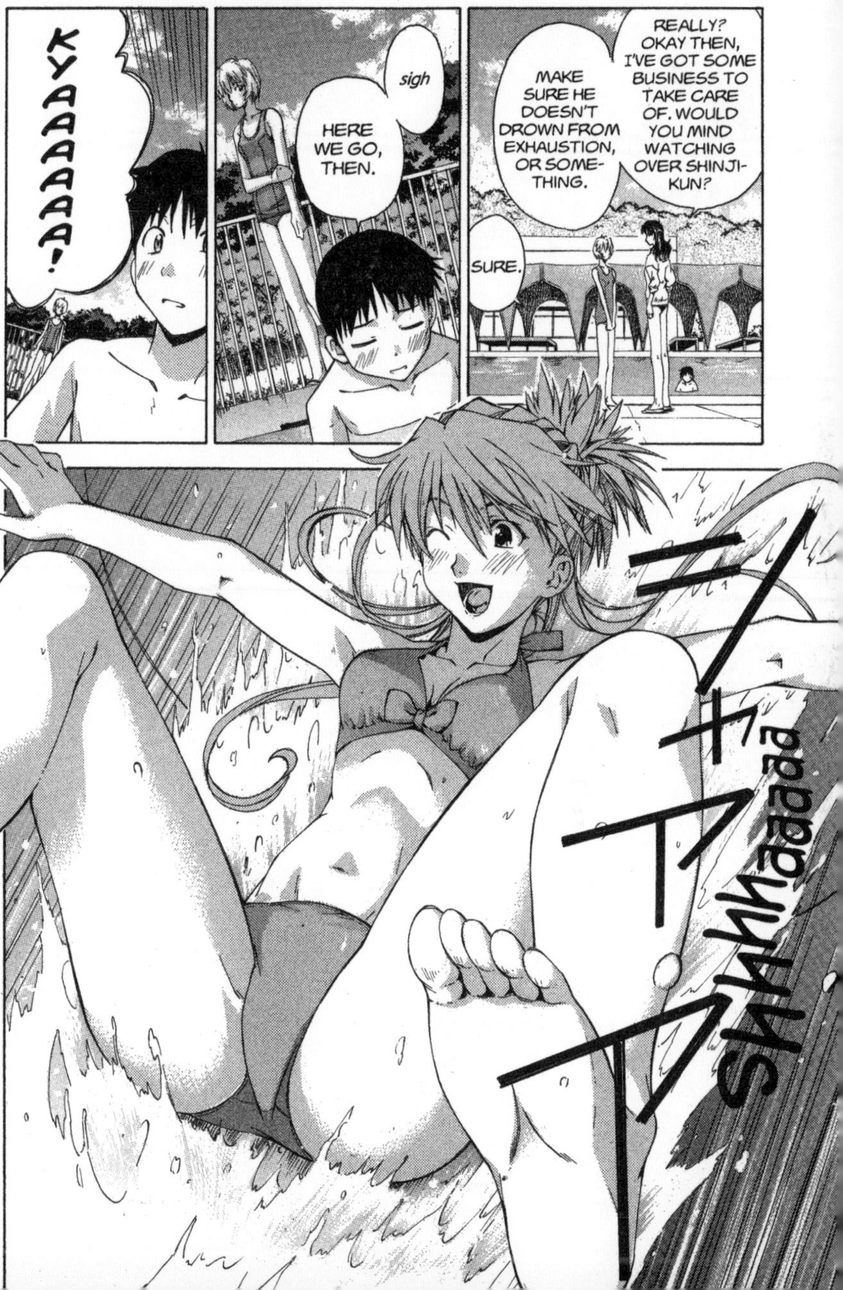
REALLY? OKAY THEN, I'VE GOT SOME BUSINESS TO TAKE CARE OF. WOULD YOU MIND WATCHING OVER SHINJI-KUN?
MAKE SURE HE DOESN'T DROWN FROM EXHAUSTION, OR SOMETHING.
SURE.
sigh
HERE WE GO, THEN.
KYAAAAAAAA!
SHHHaaaa

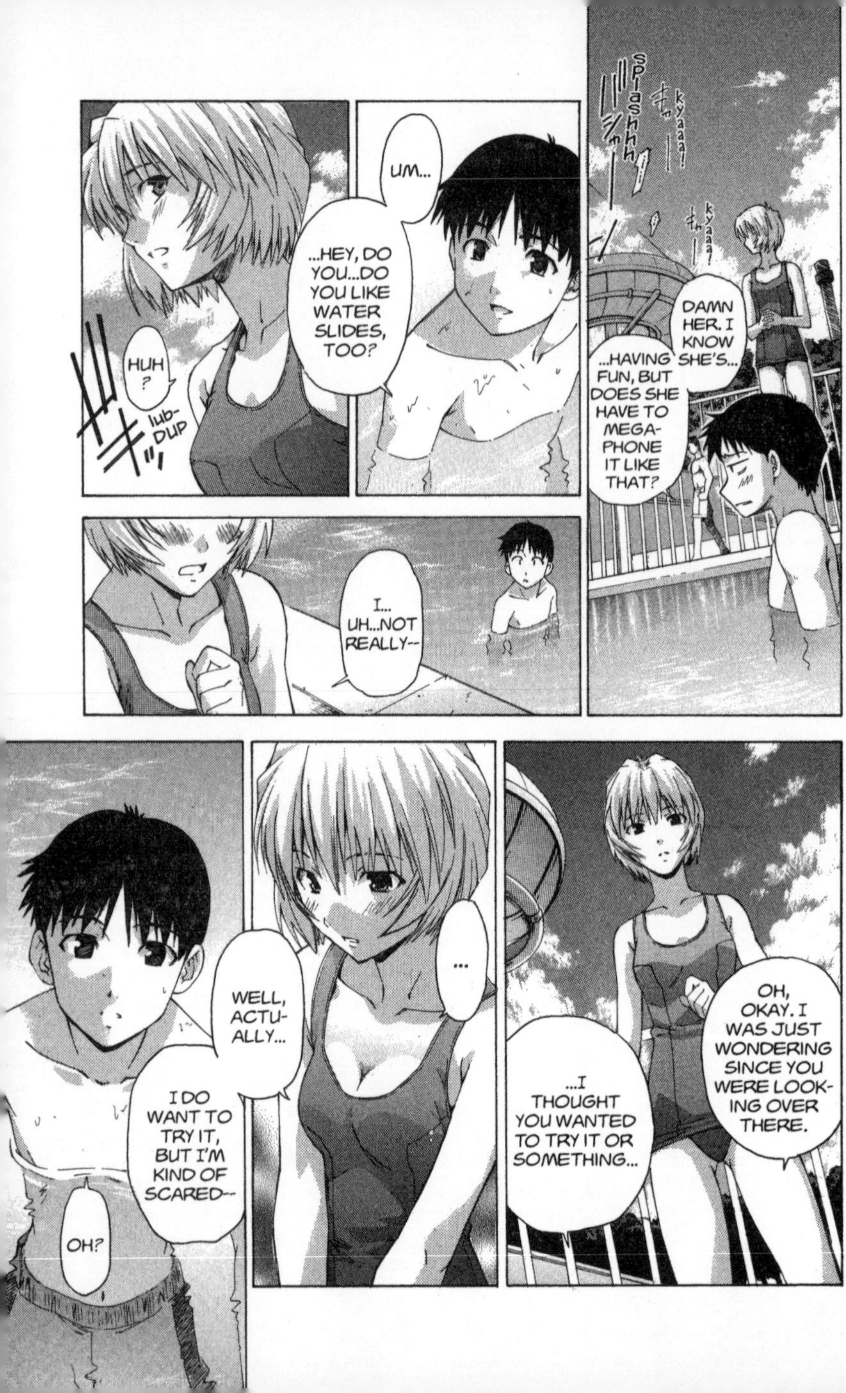
kyaaa!
splashhh
kyaaa!
DAMN HER. I KNOW SHE'S...
...HAVING FUN, BUT DOES SHE HAVE TO MEGA-PHONE IT LIKE THAT?
UM...
...HEY, DO YOU...DO YOU LIKE WATER SLIDES, TOO?
HUH?
lub-DUP
I... UH...NOT REALLY--
OH, OKAY. I WAS JUST WONDERING SINCE YOU WERE LOOK-ING OVER THERE.
...I THOUGHT YOU WANTED TO TRY IT OR SOMETHING...
...
WELL, ACTU-ALLY...
I DO WANT TO TRY IT, BUT I'M KIND OF SCARED--
OH?

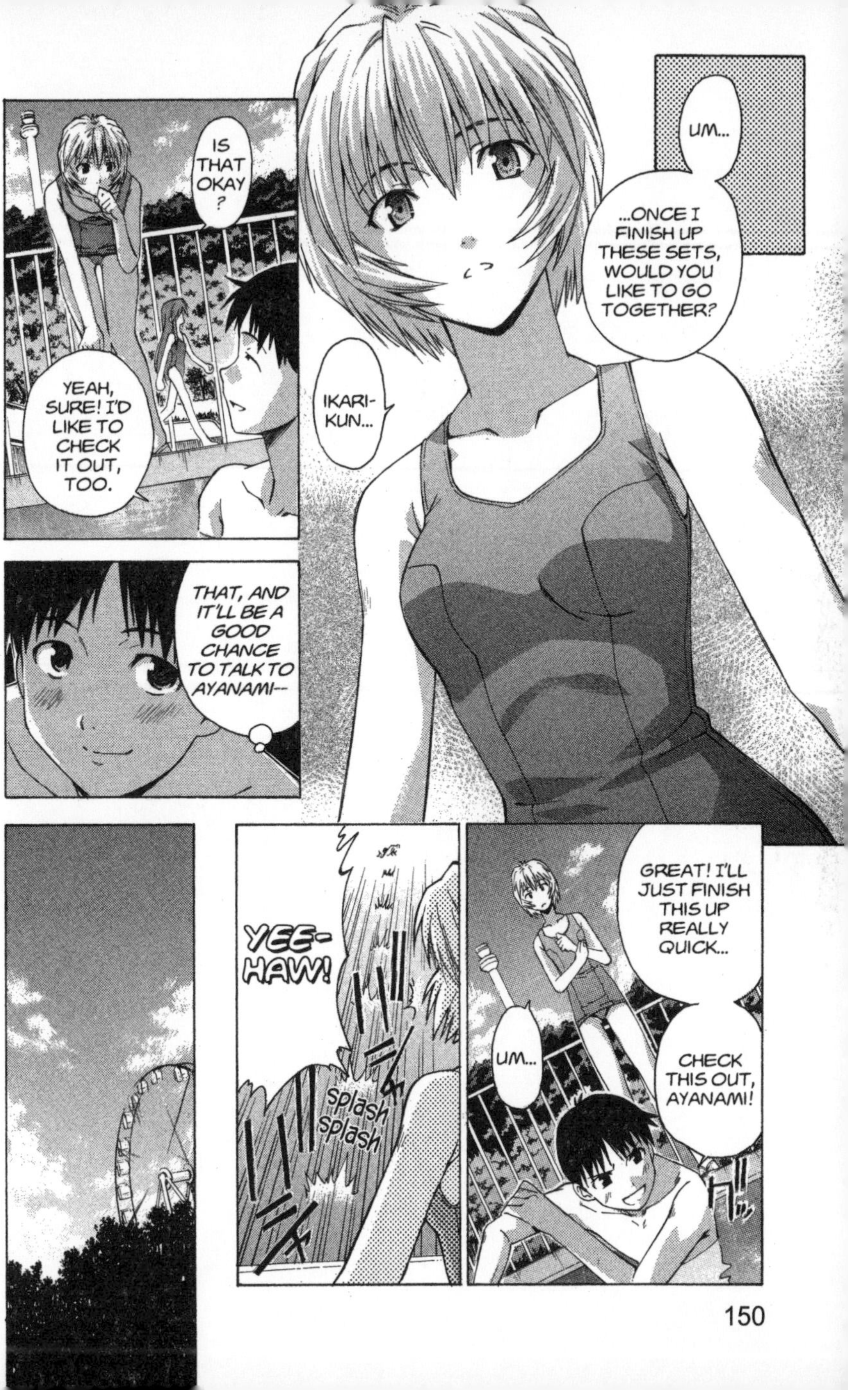
UM...
...ONCE I FINISH UP THESE SETS, WOULD YOU LIKE TO GO TOGETHER?
IKARI-KUN...
IS THAT OKAY?
YEAH, SURE! I'D LIKE TO CHECK IT OUT, TOO.
THAT, AND IT'LL BE A GOOD CHANCE TO TALK TO AYANAMI--
GREAT! I'LL JUST FINISH THIS UP REALLY QUICK...
CHECK THIS OUT, AYANAMI!
UM...
YEE-HAW!
splash splash

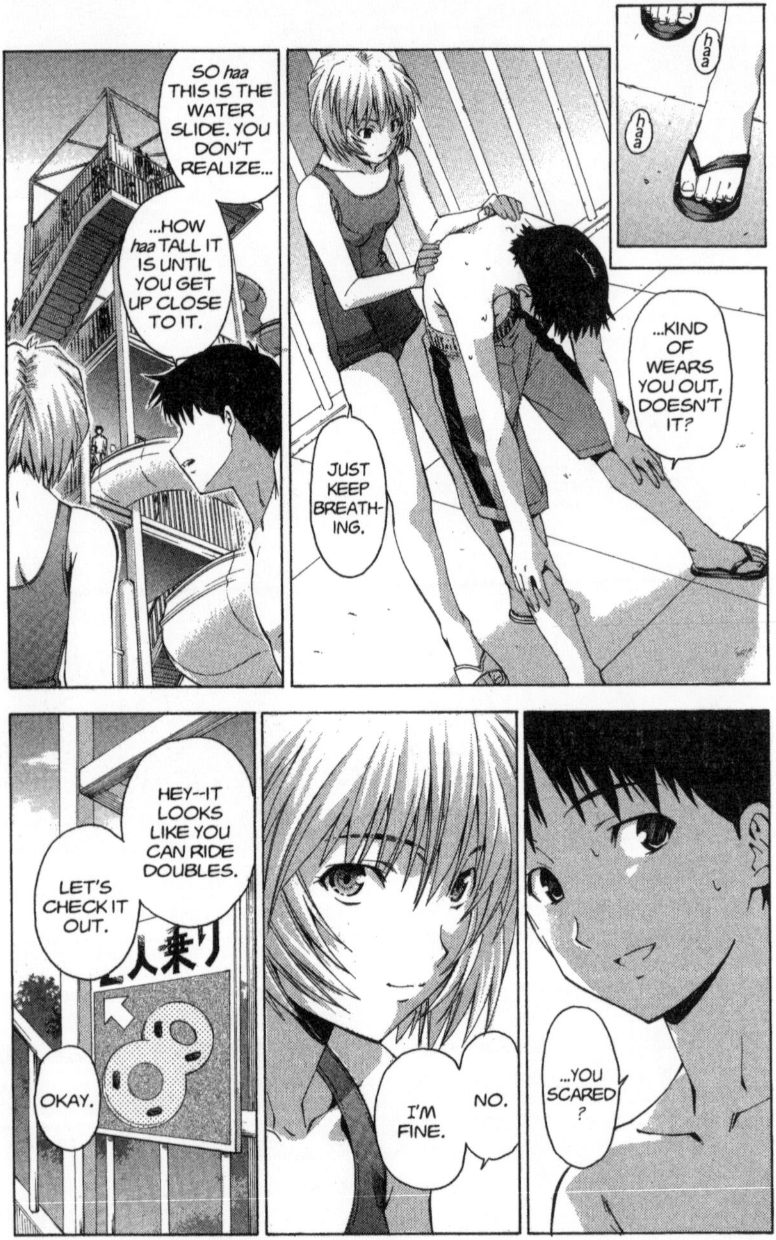
haa
haa
...KIND OF WEARS YOU OUT, DOESN'T IT?
JUST KEEP BREATHING.
SO haa THIS IS THE WATER SLIDE. YOU DON'T REALIZE...
...HOW haa TALL IT IS UNTIL YOU GET UP CLOSE TO IT.
...YOU SCARED?
NO.
I'M FINE.
HEY--IT LOOKS LIKE YOU CAN RIDE DOUBLES.
LET'S CHECK IT OUT.
人乗り
OKAY.

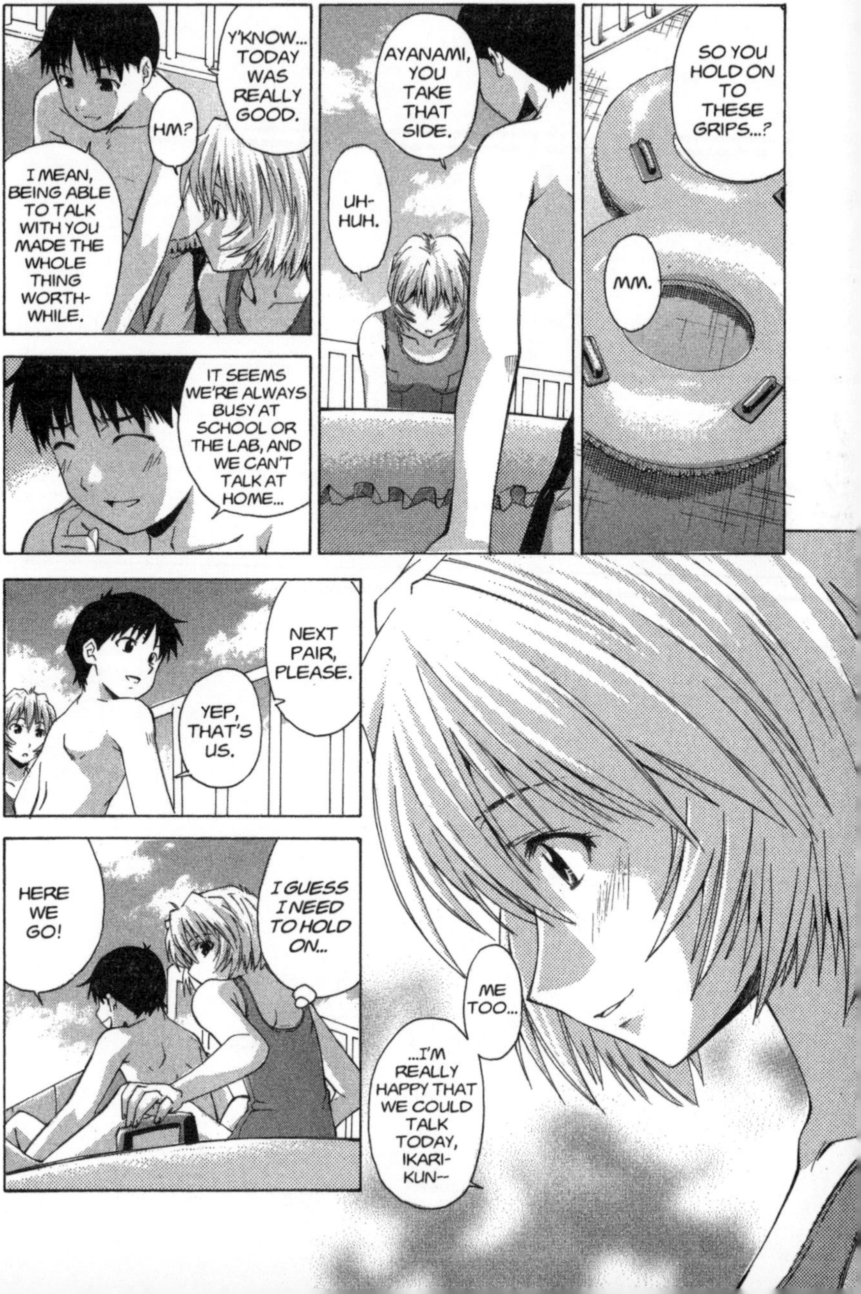
SO YOU HOLD ON TO THESE GRIPS...?
MM.
AYANAMI, YOU TAKE THAT SIDE.
UH-HUH.
Y'KNOW... TODAY WAS REALLY GOOD.
HM?
I MEAN, BEING ABLE TO TALK WITH YOU MADE THE WHOLE THING WORTH-WHILE.
IT SEEMS WE'RE ALWAYS BUSY AT SCHOOL OR THE LAB, AND WE CAN'T TALK AT HOME...
ME TOO...
...I'M REALLY HAPPY THAT WE COULD TALK TODAY, IKARI-KUN--
NEXT PAIR, PLEASE.
YEP, THAT'S US.
I GUESS I NEED TO HOLD ON...
HERE WE GO!

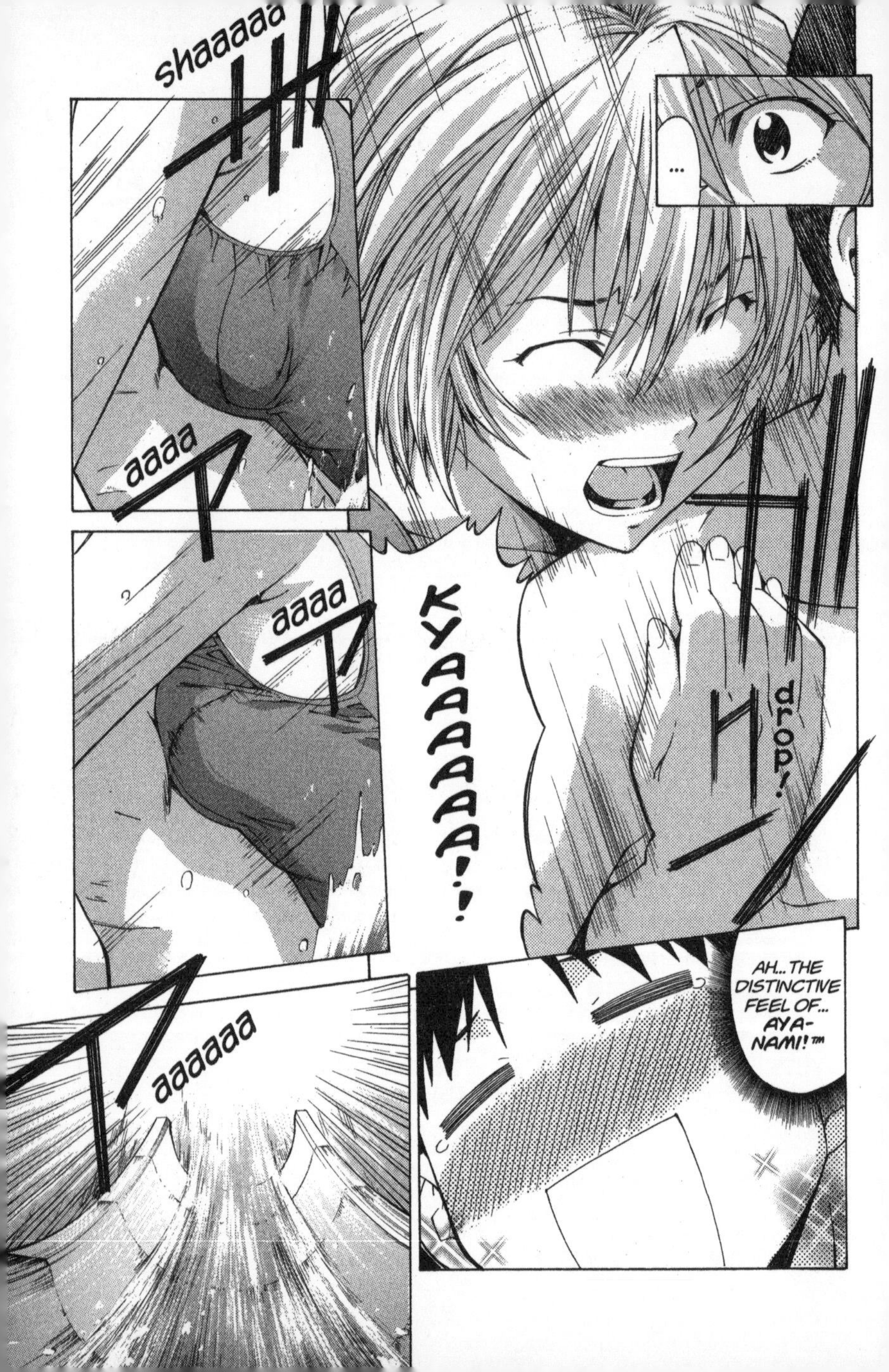
...
KYAAAAAAA!!
drop!
shaaaaa
aaaa
aaaa
AH... THE DISTINCTIVE FEEL OF... AYA-NAMI!™
aaaaaa

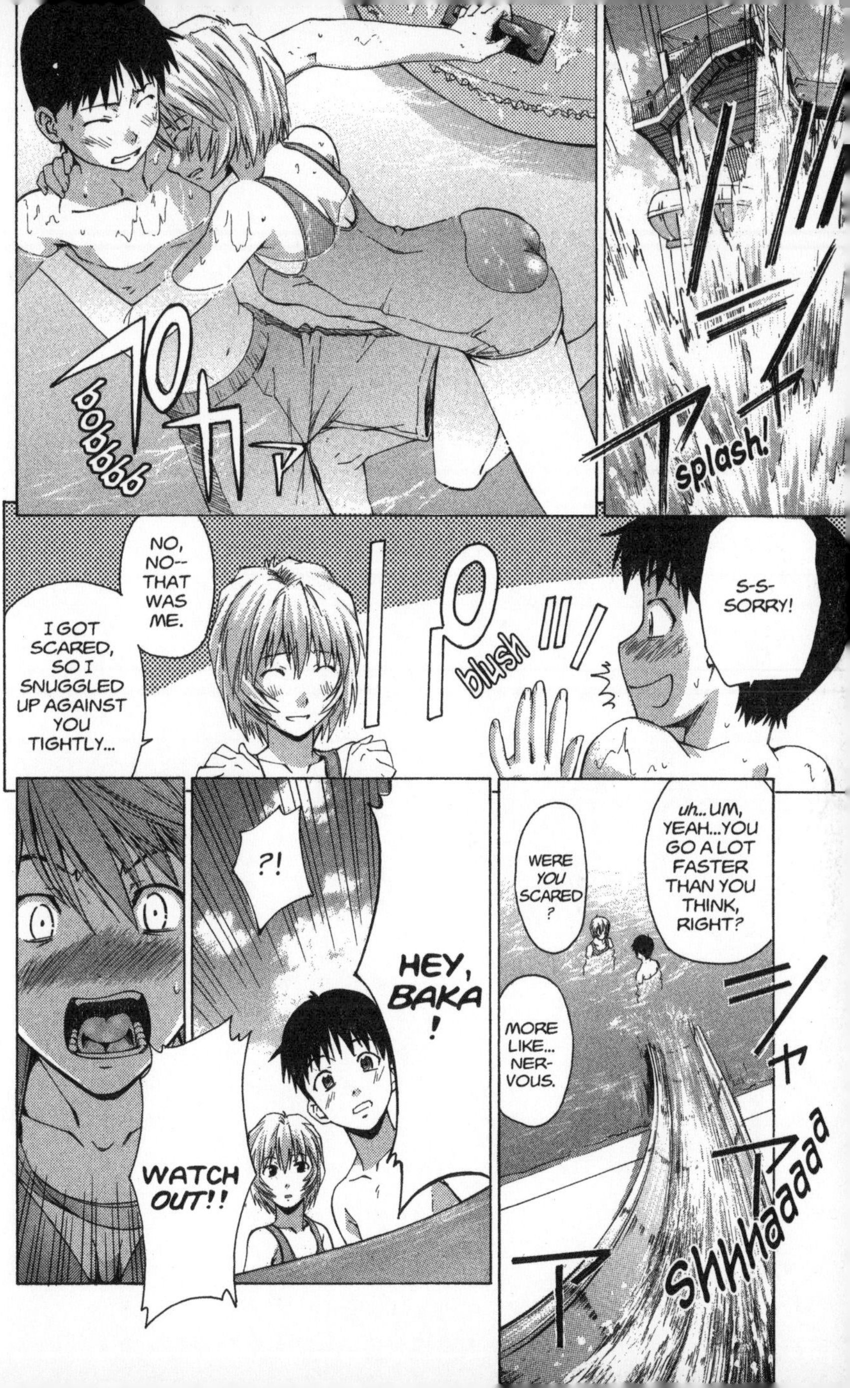
splash!
bobbbb
S-S-SORRY!
blush
NO, NO-- THAT WAS ME.
I GOT SCARED, SO I SNUGGLED UP AGAINST YOU TIGHTLY...
uh... UM, YEAH...YOU GO A LOT FASTER THAN YOU THINK, RIGHT?
WERE YOU SCARED?
MORE LIKE... NER-VOUS.
Shhhaaaaa
?!
HEY, BAKA!
WATCH OUT!!

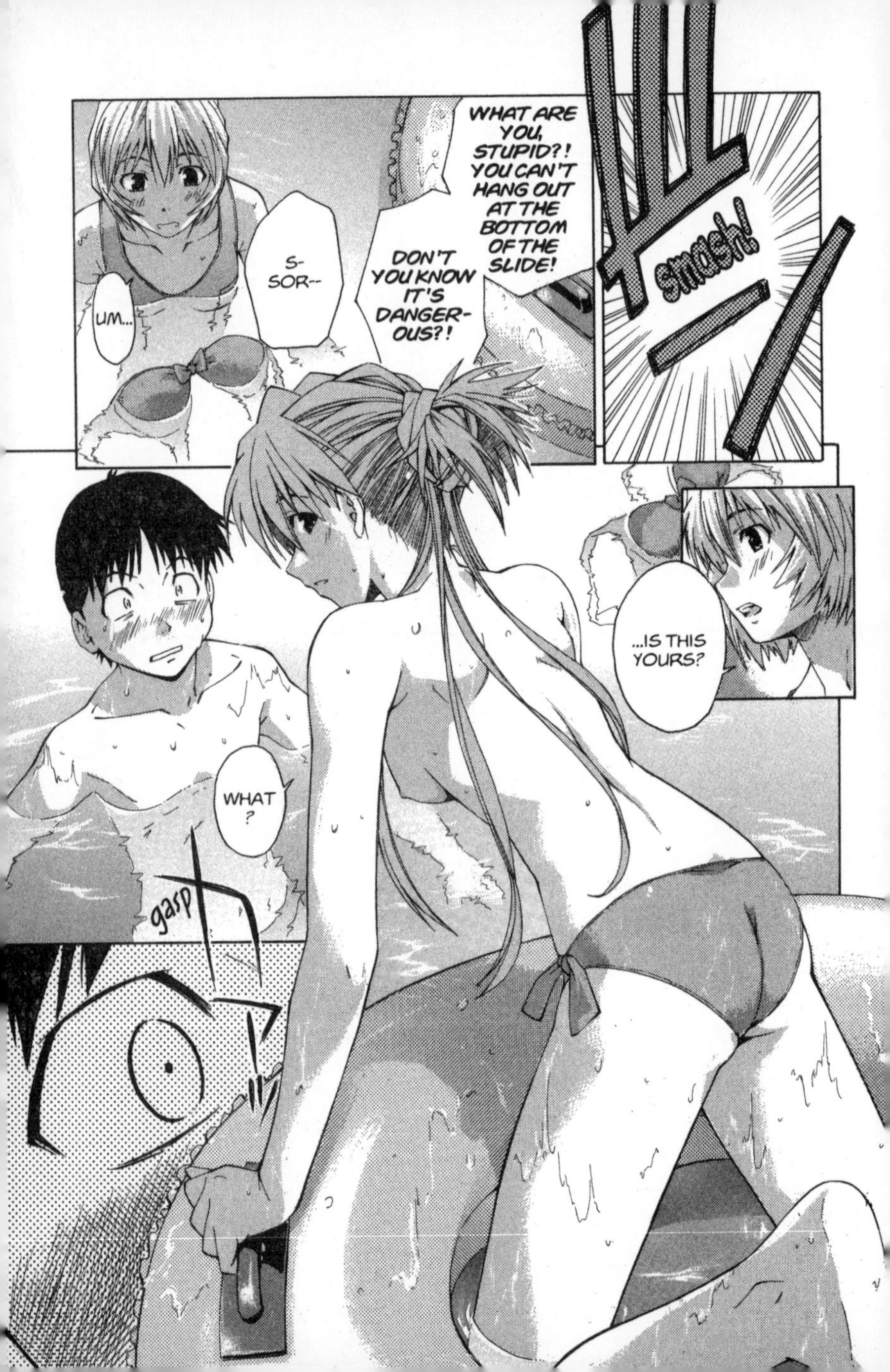
smash!
WHAT ARE YOU, STUPID?! YOU CAN'T HANG OUT AT THE BOTTOM OF THE SLIDE!
DON'T YOU KNOW IT'S DANGER-OUS?!
S- SOR--
UM...
...IS THIS YOURS?
WHAT ?
gasp

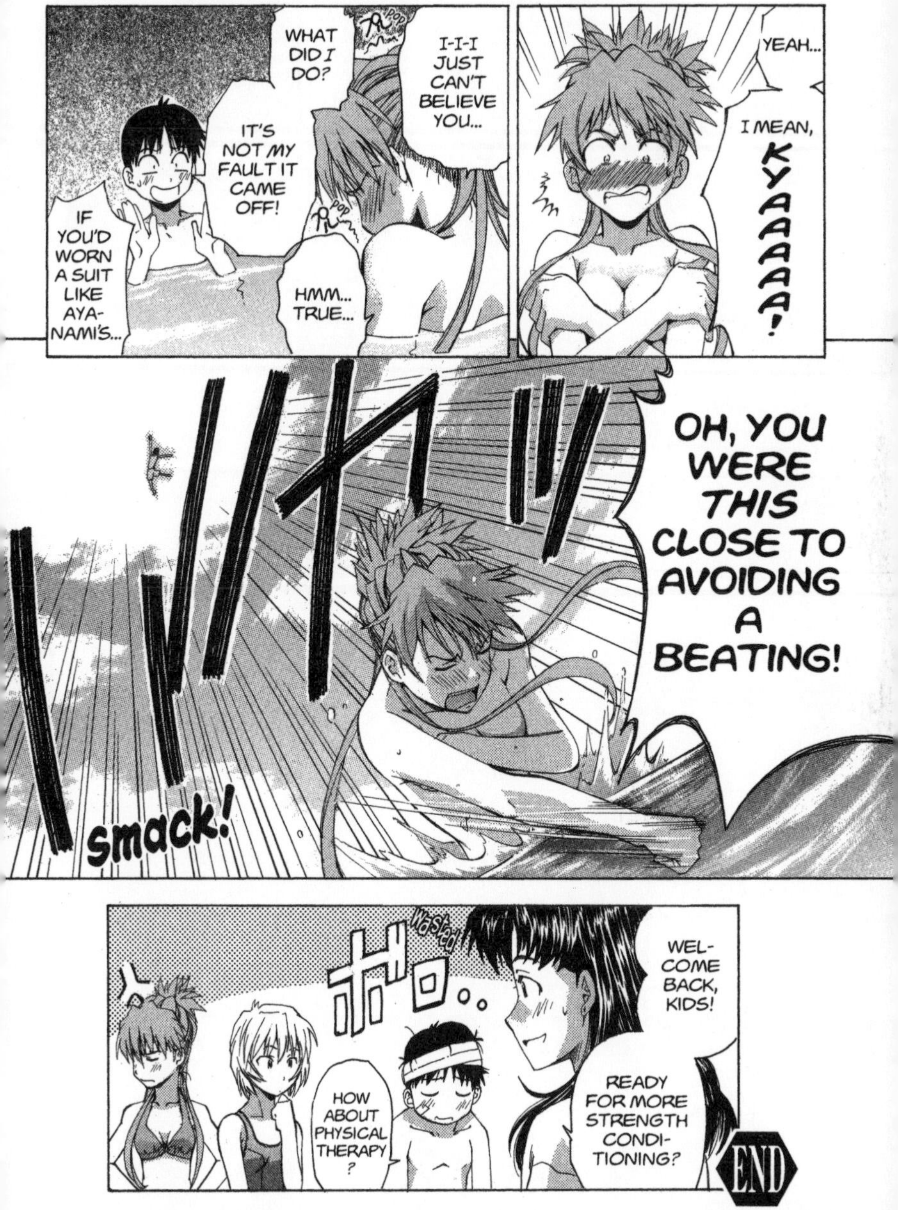
I-I-I JUST CAN'T BELIEVE YOU...
pop
WHAT DID I DO?
IT'S NOT MY FAULT IT CAME OFF!
IF YOU'D WORN A SUIT LIKE AYA-NAMI'S...
pop
HMM... TRUE...
YEAH...
I MEAN, KYAAAAAA!
OH, YOU WERE THIS CLOSE TO AVOIDING A BEATING!
smack!
wasted
WEL-COME BACK, KIDS!
READY FOR MORE STRENGTH CONDI-TIONING?
HOW ABOUT PHYSICAL THERAPY?
END

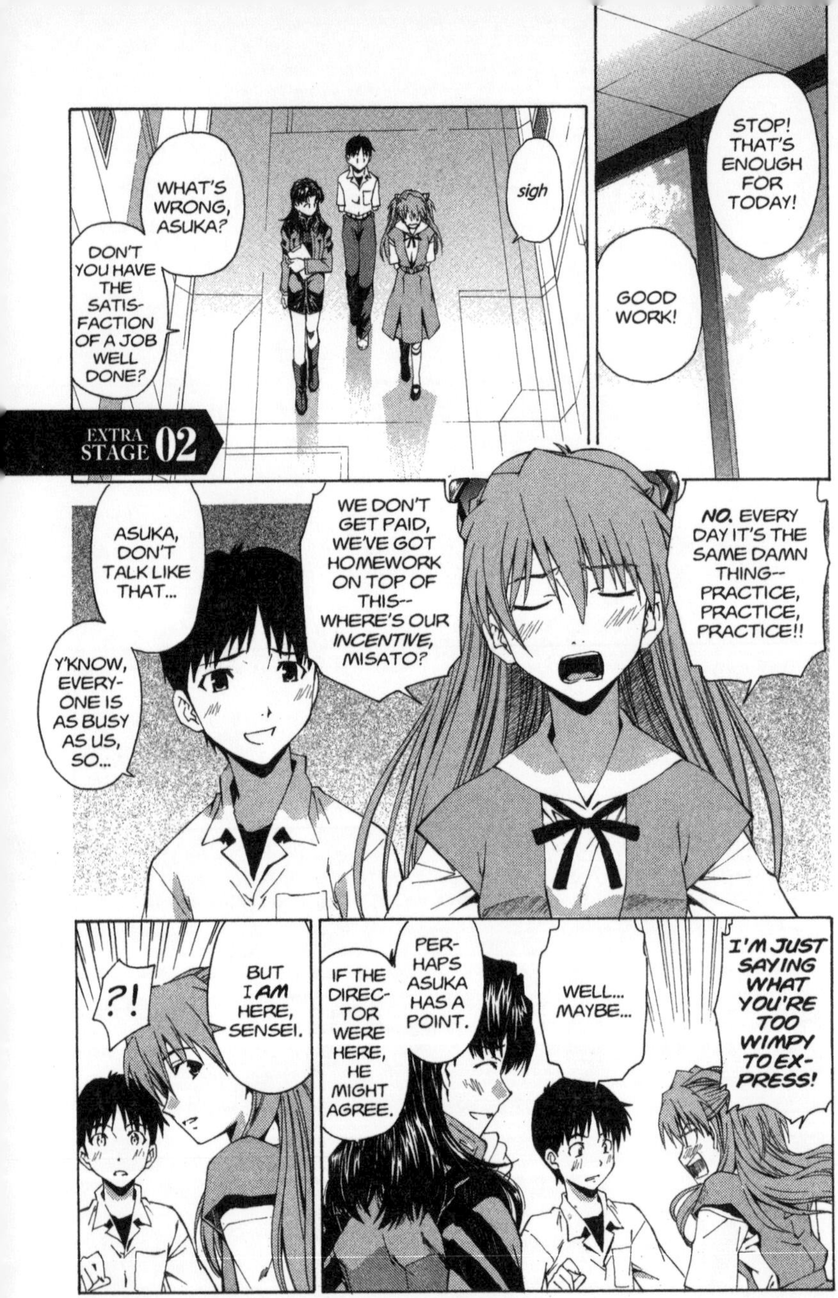
STOP! THAT'S ENOUGH FOR TODAY!
GOOD WORK!
sigh
WHAT'S WRONG, ASUKA?
DON'T YOU HAVE THE SATIS-FACTION OF A JOB WELL DONE?
EXTRA STAGE 02
NO. EVERY DAY IT'S THE SAME DAMN THING-- PRACTICE, PRACTICE, PRACTICE!!
WE DON'T GET PAID, WE'VE GOT HOMEWORK ON TOP OF THIS-- WHERE'S OUR *INCENTIVE,* MISATO?
ASUKA, DON'T TALK LIKE THAT...
Y'KNOW, EVERY-ONE IS AS BUSY AS US, SO...
I'M JUST SAYING WHAT YOU'RE TOO WIMPY TO EX-PRESS!
WELL... MAYBE...
PER-HAPS ASUKA HAS A POINT.
IF THE DIREC-TOR WERE HERE, HE MIGHT AGREE.
BUT I **AM** HERE, SENSEI.
?!

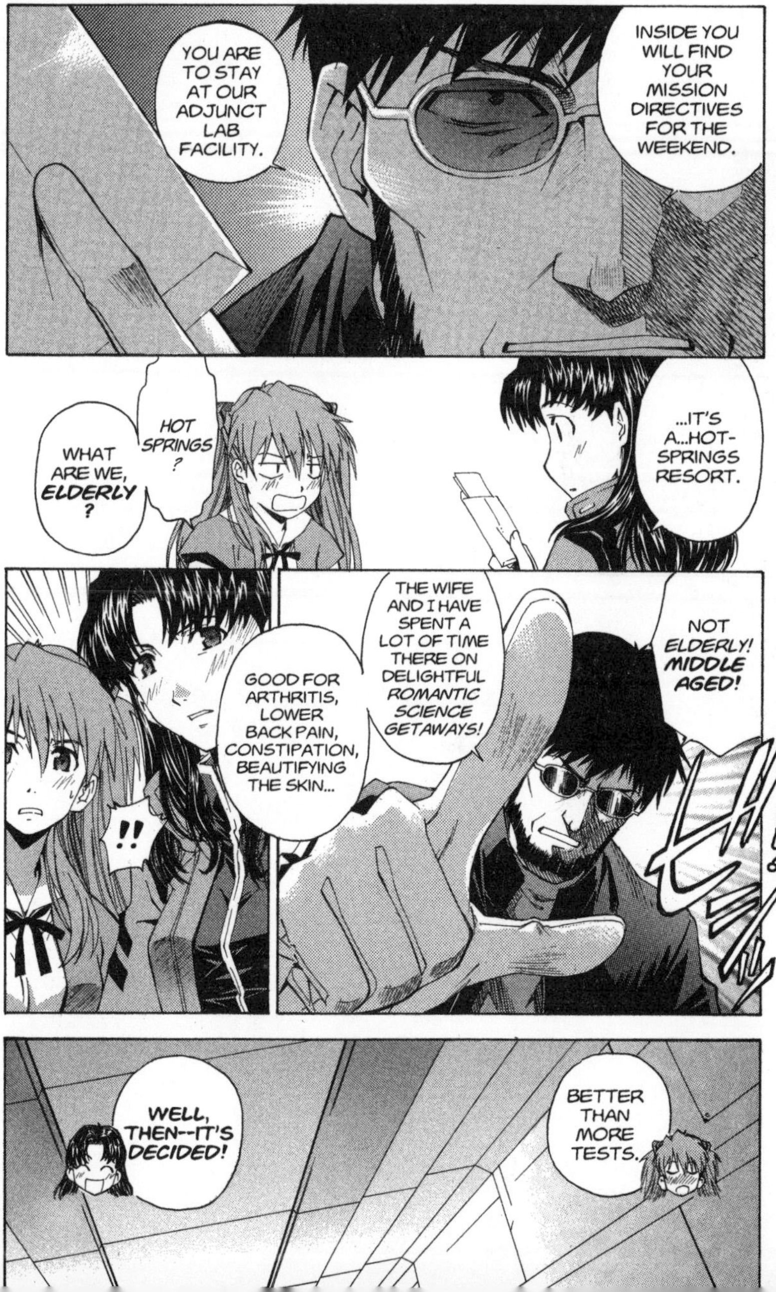
INSIDE YOU WILL FIND YOUR MISSION DIRECTIVES FOR THE WEEKEND.
YOU ARE TO STAY AT OUR ADJUNCT LAB FACILITY.
...IT'S A...HOT-SPRINGS RESORT.
HOT SPRINGS?
WHAT ARE WE, ELDERLY?
NOT ELDERLY! MIDDLE AGED!
WHOOSH!
THE WIFE AND I HAVE SPENT A LOT OF TIME THERE ON DELIGHTFUL ROMANTIC SCIENCE GETAWAYS!
GOOD FOR ARTHRITIS, LOWER BACK PAIN, CONSTIPATION, BEAUTIFYING THE SKIN...
!!
BETTER THAN MORE TESTS.
WELL, THEN--IT'S DECIDED!

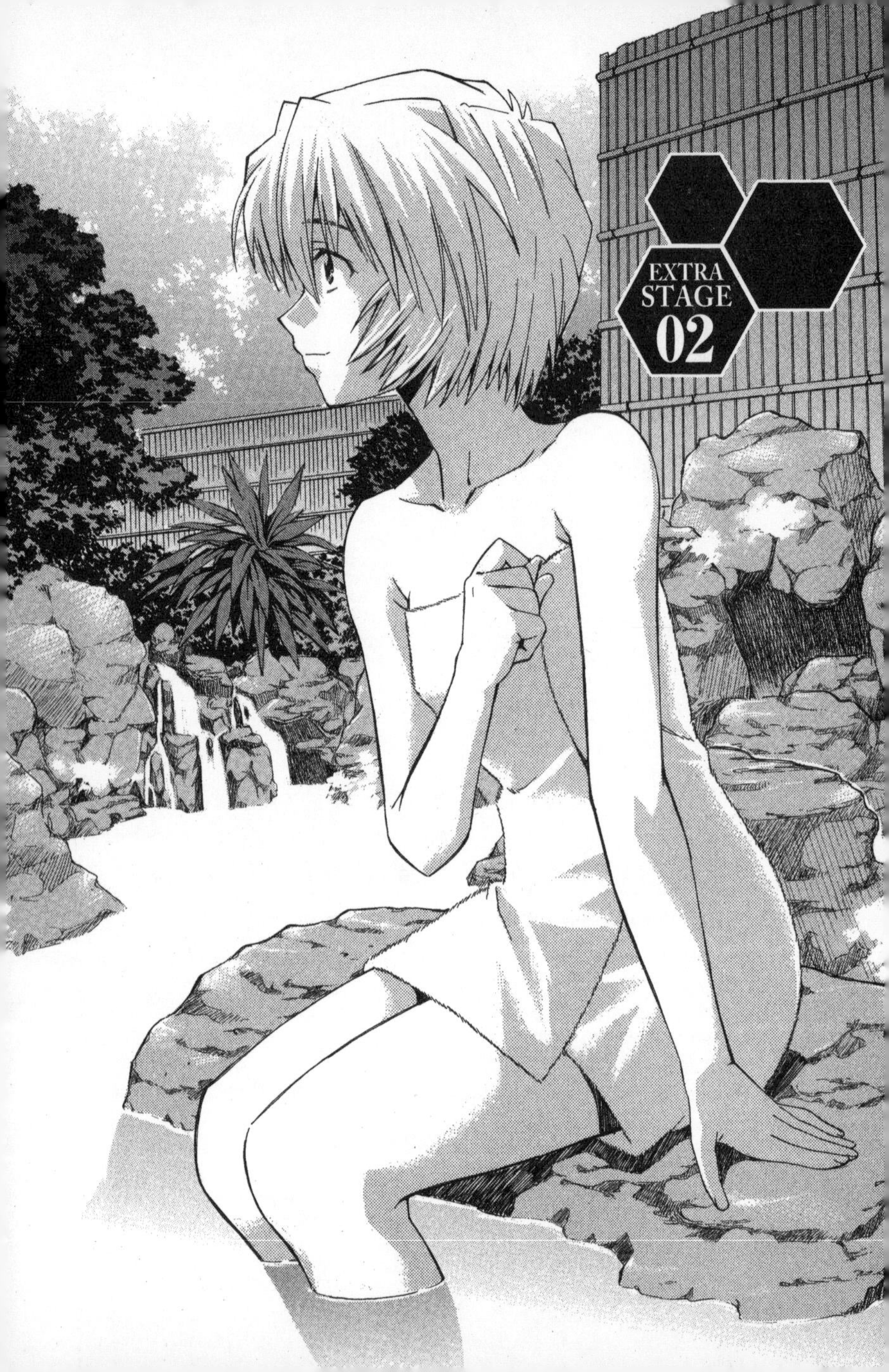
EXTRA
STAGE
02

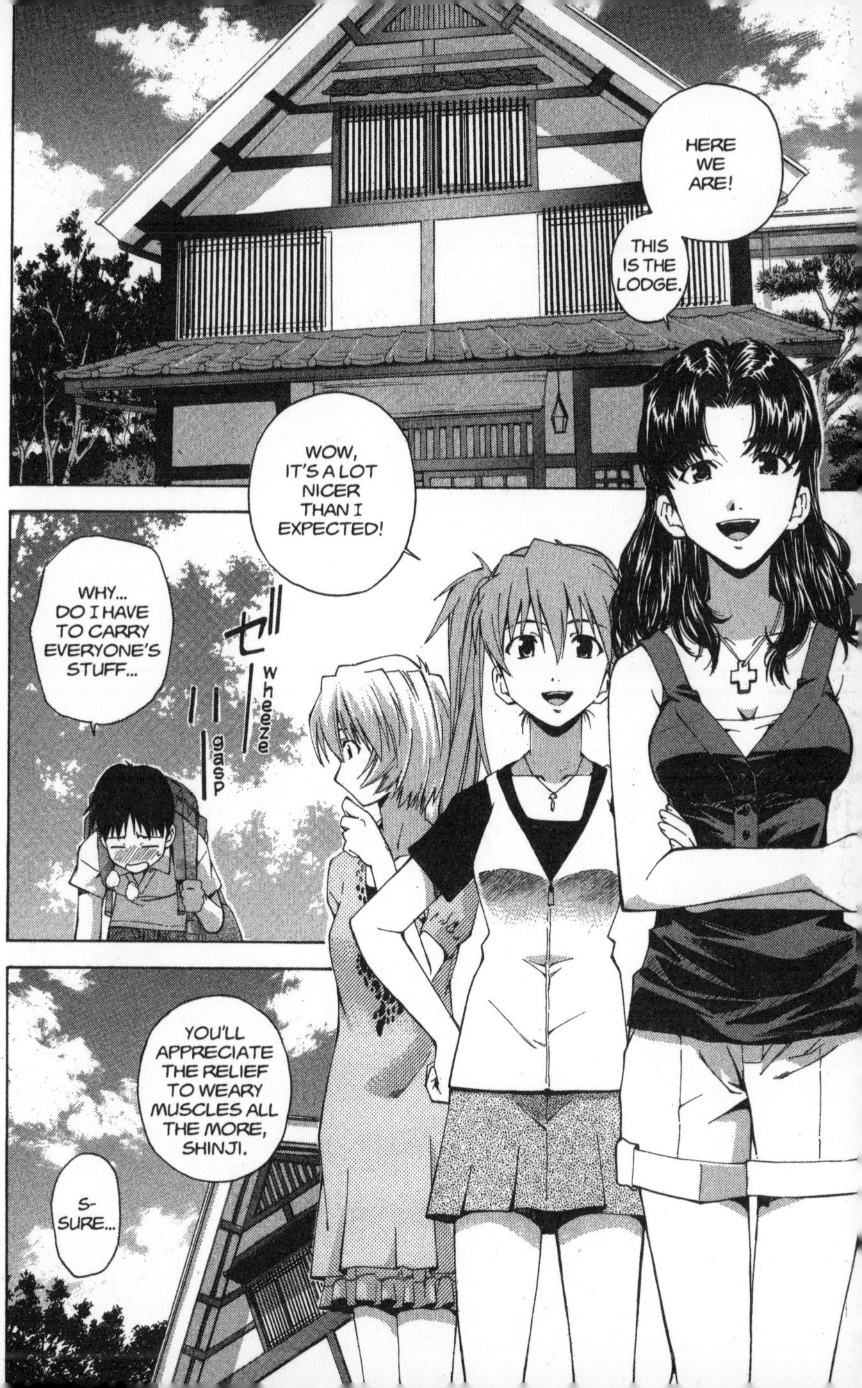
HERE WE ARE!
THIS IS THE LODGE.
WOW, IT'S A LOT NICER THAN I EXPECTED!
wheeze
gasp
WHY... DO I HAVE TO CARRY EVERYONE'S STUFF...
YOU'LL APPRECIATE THE RELIEF TO WEARY MUSCLES ALL THE MORE, SHINJI.
S-SURE...

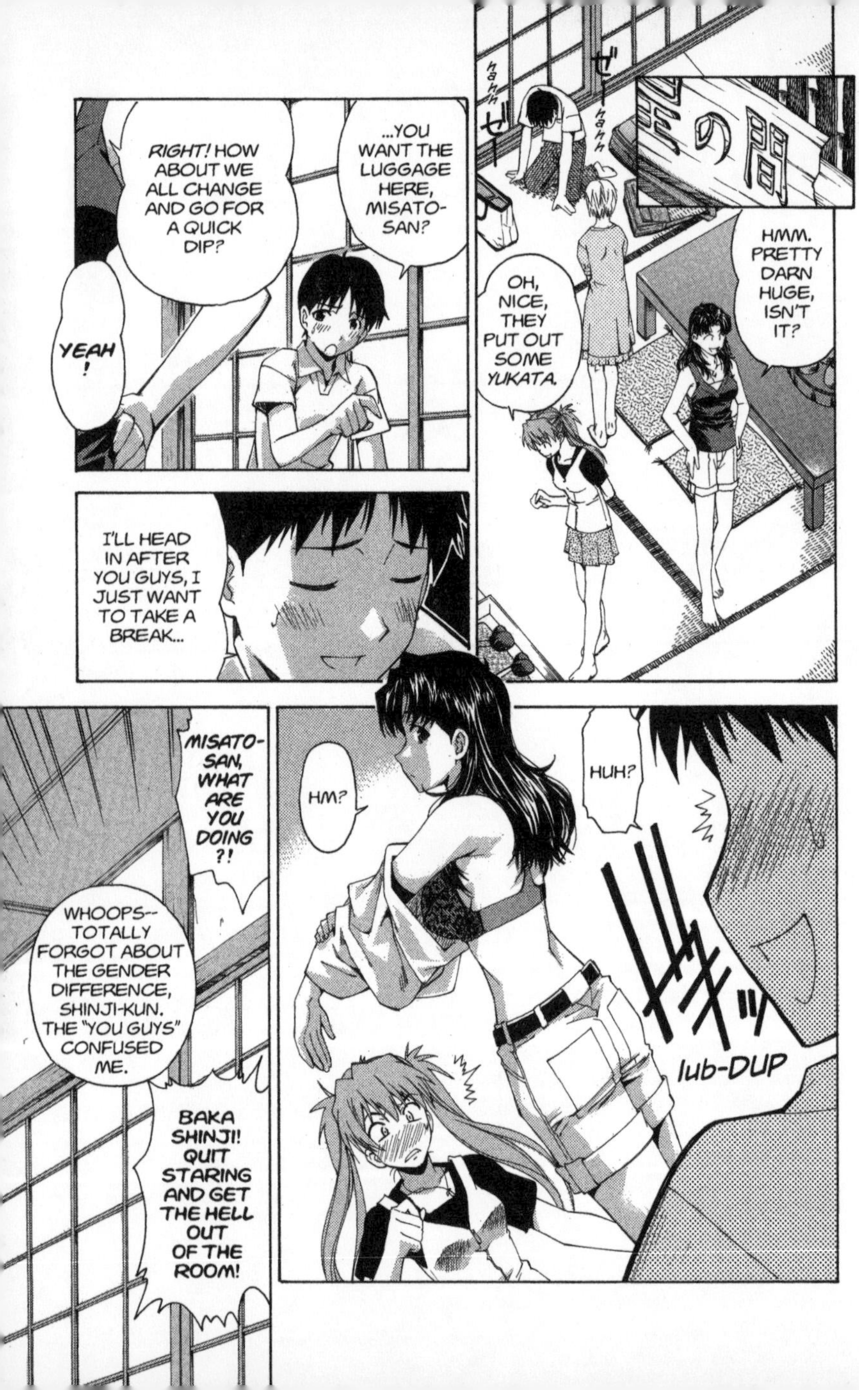
の間
HMM. PRETTY DARN HUGE, ISN'T IT?
OH, NICE, THEY PUT OUT SOME *YUKATA.*
...YOU WANT THE LUGGAGE HERE, MISATO-SAN?
RIGHT! HOW ABOUT WE ALL CHANGE AND GO FOR A QUICK DIP?
YEAH!
I'LL HEAD IN AFTER YOU GUYS, I JUST WANT TO TAKE A BREAK...
HUH?
HM?
lub-DUP
MISATO-SAN, WHAT ARE YOU DOING?!
WHOOPS-- TOTALLY FORGOT ABOUT THE GENDER DIFFERENCE, SHINJI-KUN. THE "YOU GUYS" CONFUSED ME.
BAKA SHINJI! QUIT STARING AND GET THE HELL OUT OF THE ROOM!

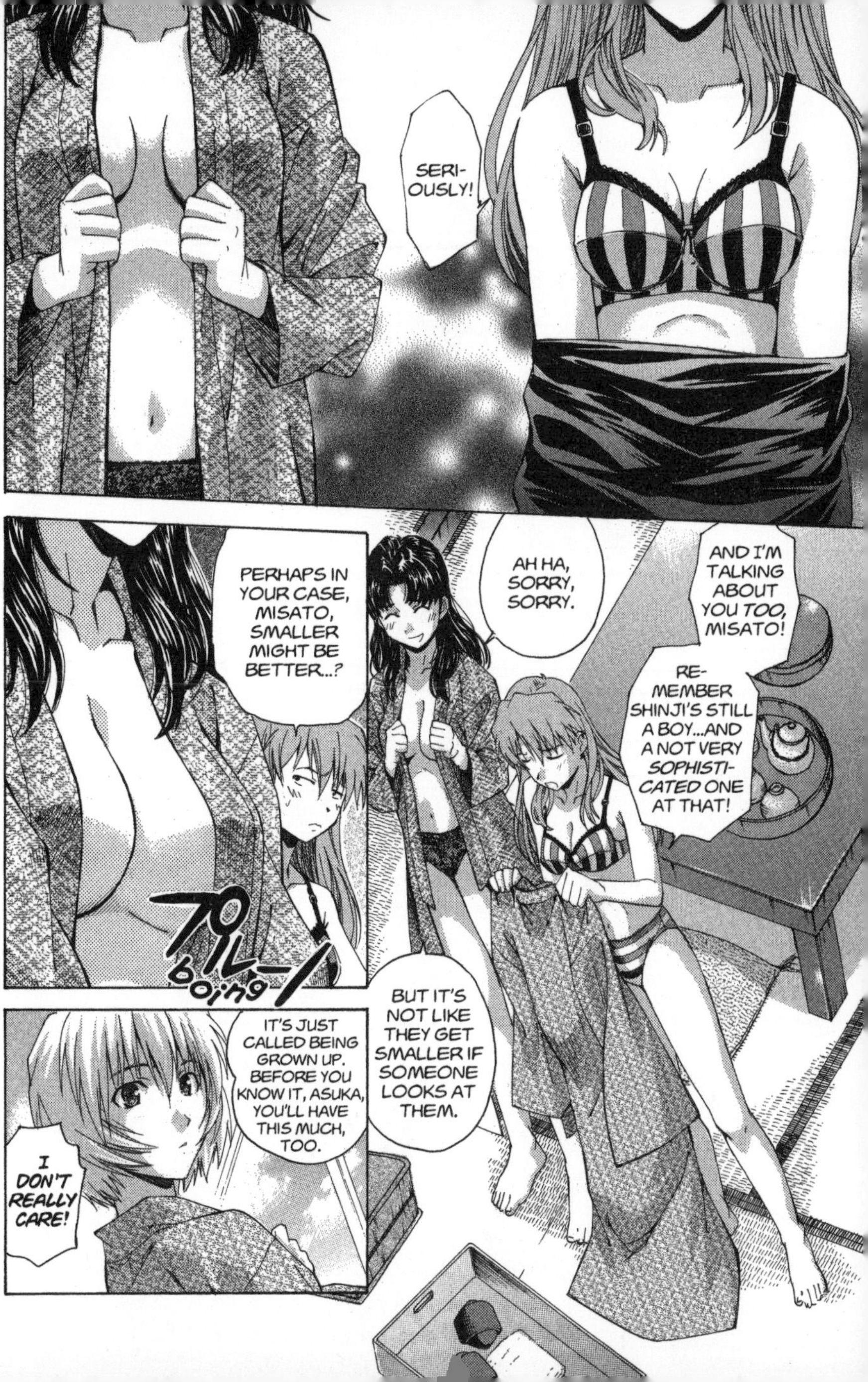
SERI-
OUSLY!
AND I'M TALKING ABOUT YOU *TOO*, MISATO!
AH HA, SORRY, SORRY.
RE-MEMBER SHINJI'S STILL A BOY...AND A NOT VERY *SOPHISTI-CATED* ONE AT THAT!
BUT IT'S NOT LIKE THEY GET SMALLER IF SOMEONE LOOKS AT THEM.
PERHAPS IN YOUR CASE, MISATO, SMALLER MIGHT BE BETTER...?
プルーン
boing
IT'S JUST CALLED BEING GROWN UP. BEFORE YOU KNOW IT, ASUKA, YOU'LL HAVE THIS MUCH, TOO.
I DON'T REALLY CARE!

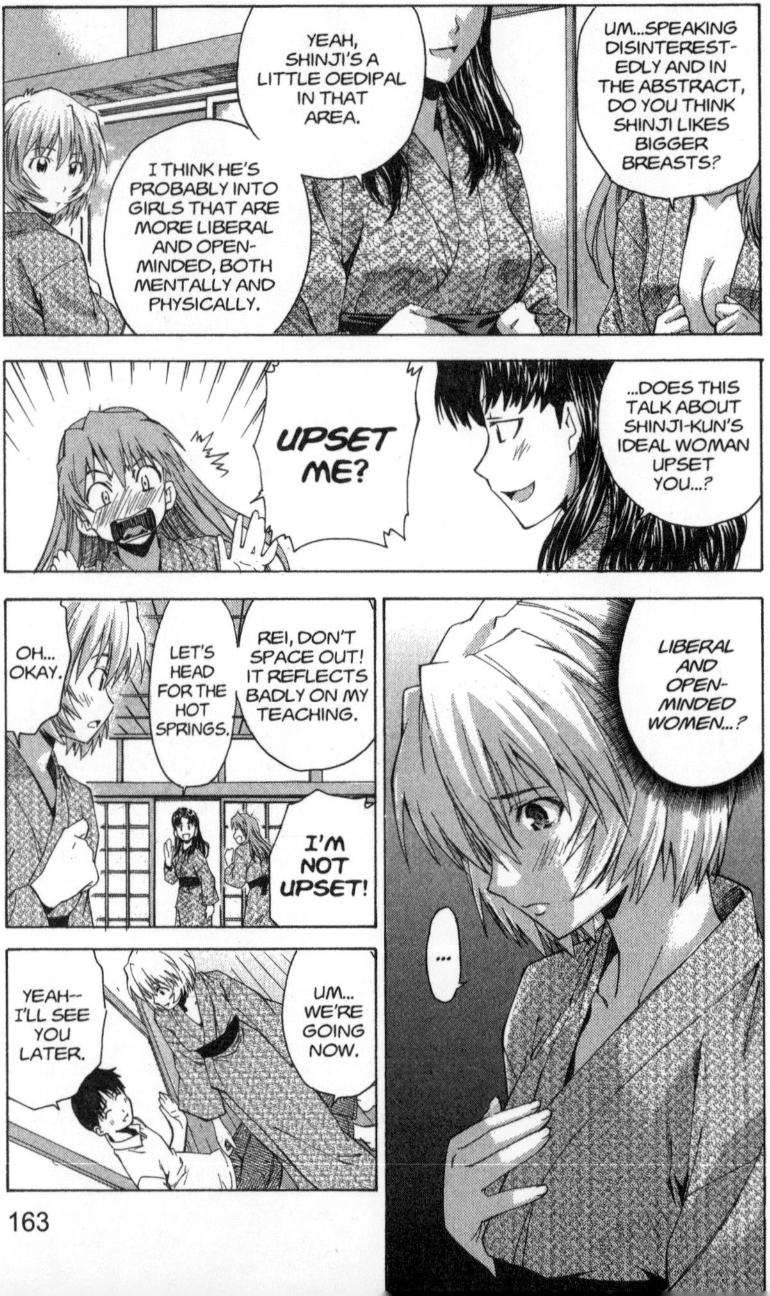
UM...SPEAKING DISINTEREST-EDLY AND IN THE ABSTRACT, DO YOU THINK SHINJI LIKES BIGGER BREASTS?
YEAH, SHINJI'S A LITTLE OEDIPAL IN THAT AREA.
I THINK HE'S PROBABLY INTO GIRLS THAT ARE MORE LIBERAL AND OPEN-MINDED, BOTH MENTALLY AND PHYSICALLY.
...DOES THIS TALK ABOUT SHINJI-KUN'S IDEAL WOMAN UPSET YOU...?
UPSET ME?
LIBERAL AND OPEN-MINDED WOMEN...?
...
REI, DON'T SPACE OUT! IT REFLECTS BADLY ON MY TEACHING.
LET'S HEAD FOR THE HOT SPRINGS.
I'M NOT UPSET!
OH... OKAY.
UM... WE'RE GOING NOW.
YEAH-- I'LL SEE YOU LATER.

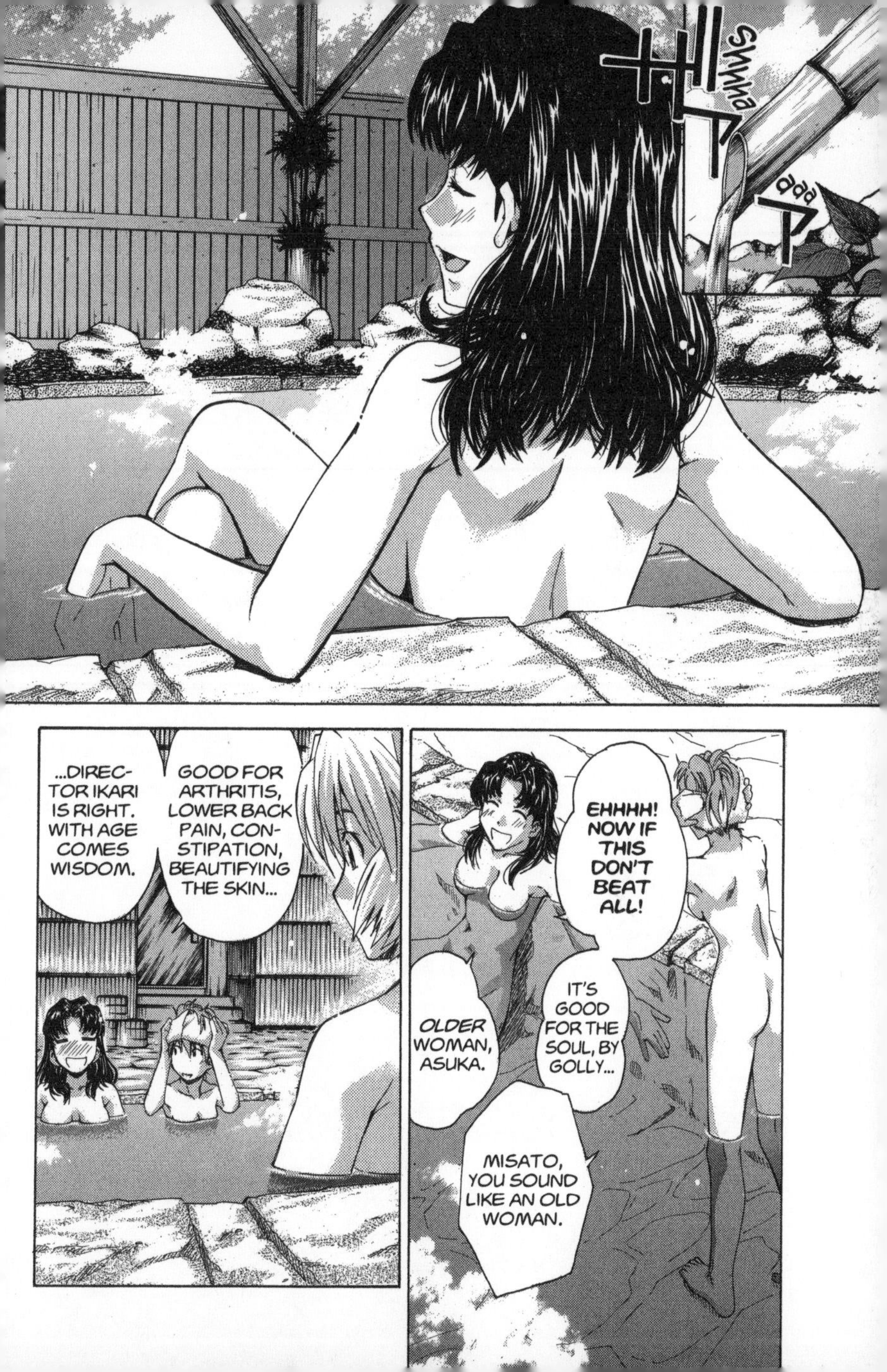
Shhha
aaa
EHHHH! NOW IF THIS DON'T BEAT ALL!
IT'S GOOD FOR THE SOUL, BY GOLLY...
MISATO, YOU SOUND LIKE AN OLD WOMAN.
OLDER WOMAN, ASUKA.
GOOD FOR ARTHRITIS, LOWER BACK PAIN, CONSTIPATION, BEAUTIFYING THE SKIN...
...DIRECTOR IKARI IS RIGHT. WITH AGE COMES WISDOM.

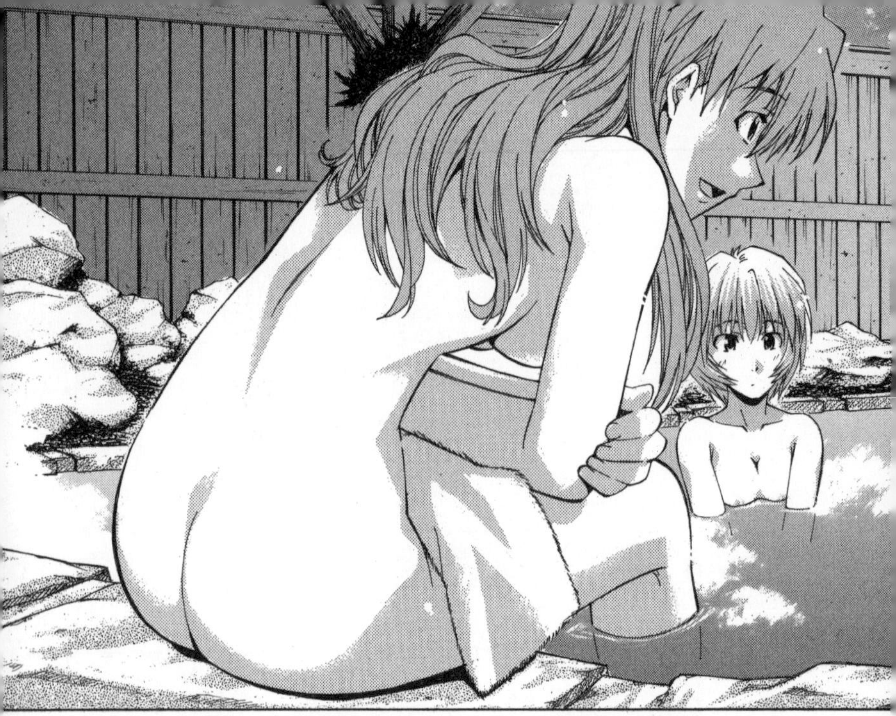

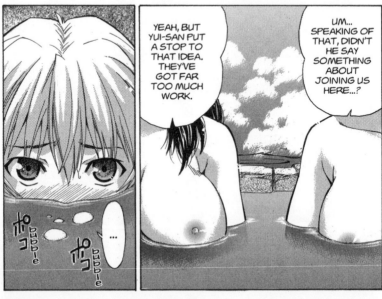

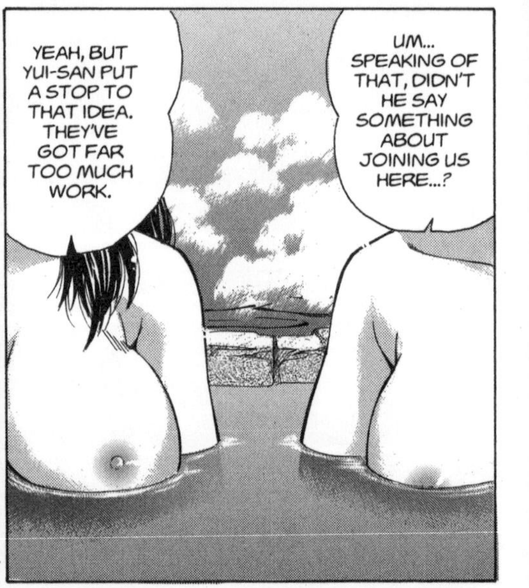
UM... SPEAKING OF THAT, DIDN'T HE SAY SOMETHING ABOUT JOINING US HERE...?
YEAH, BUT YUI-SAN PUT A STOP TO THAT IDEA. THEY'VE GOT FAR TOO MUCH WORK.

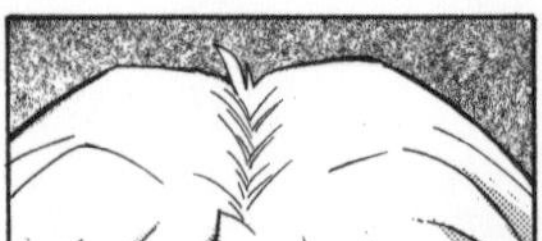
...
ポコ bubble
ポコ bubble

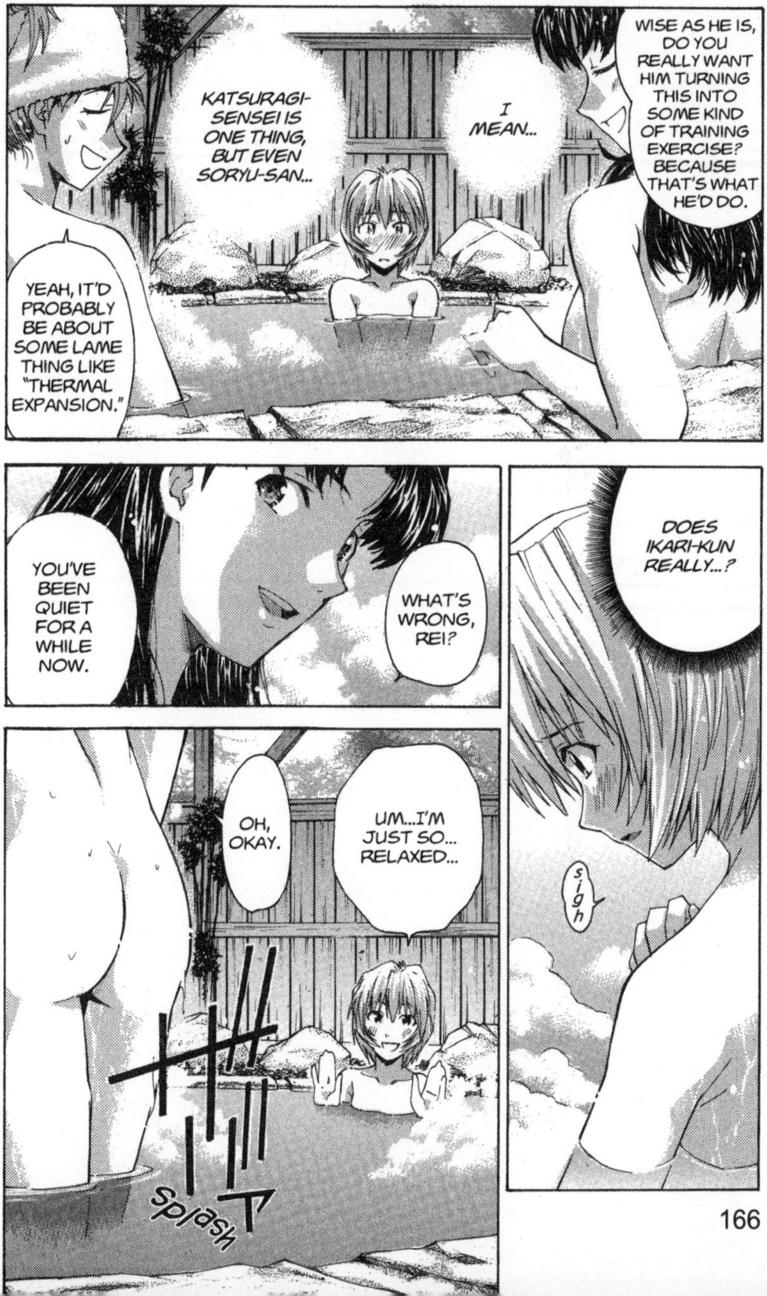
WISE AS HE IS, DO YOU REALLY WANT HIM TURNING THIS INTO SOME KIND OF TRAINING EXERCISE? BECAUSE THAT'S WHAT HE'D DO.
I MEAN...
KATSURAGI-SENSEI IS ONE THING, BUT EVEN SORYU-SAN...
YEAH, IT'D PROBABLY BE ABOUT SOME LAME THING LIKE "THERMAL EXPANSION."
DOES IKARI-KUN REALLY...?
sigh
WHAT'S WRONG, REI?
YOU'VE BEEN QUIET FOR A WHILE NOW.
UM...I'M JUST SO... RELAXED...
OH, OKAY.
Splash

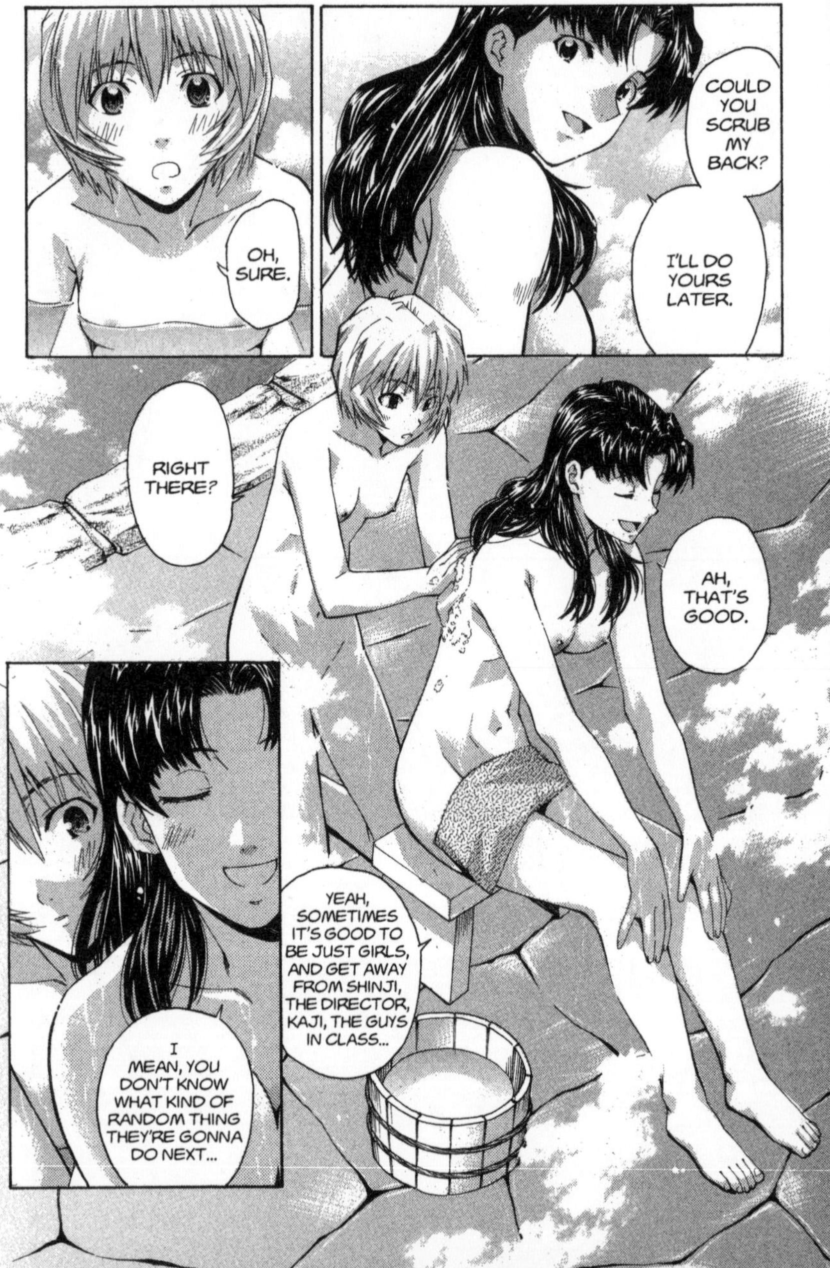
COULD YOU SCRUB MY BACK?
I'LL DO YOURS LATER.
OH, SURE.
AH, THAT'S GOOD.
RIGHT THERE?
YEAH, SOMETIMES IT'S GOOD TO BE JUST GIRLS, AND GET AWAY FROM SHINJI, THE DIRECTOR, KAJI, THE GUYS IN CLASS...
I MEAN, YOU DON'T KNOW WHAT KIND OF RANDOM THING THEY'RE GONNA DO NEXT...

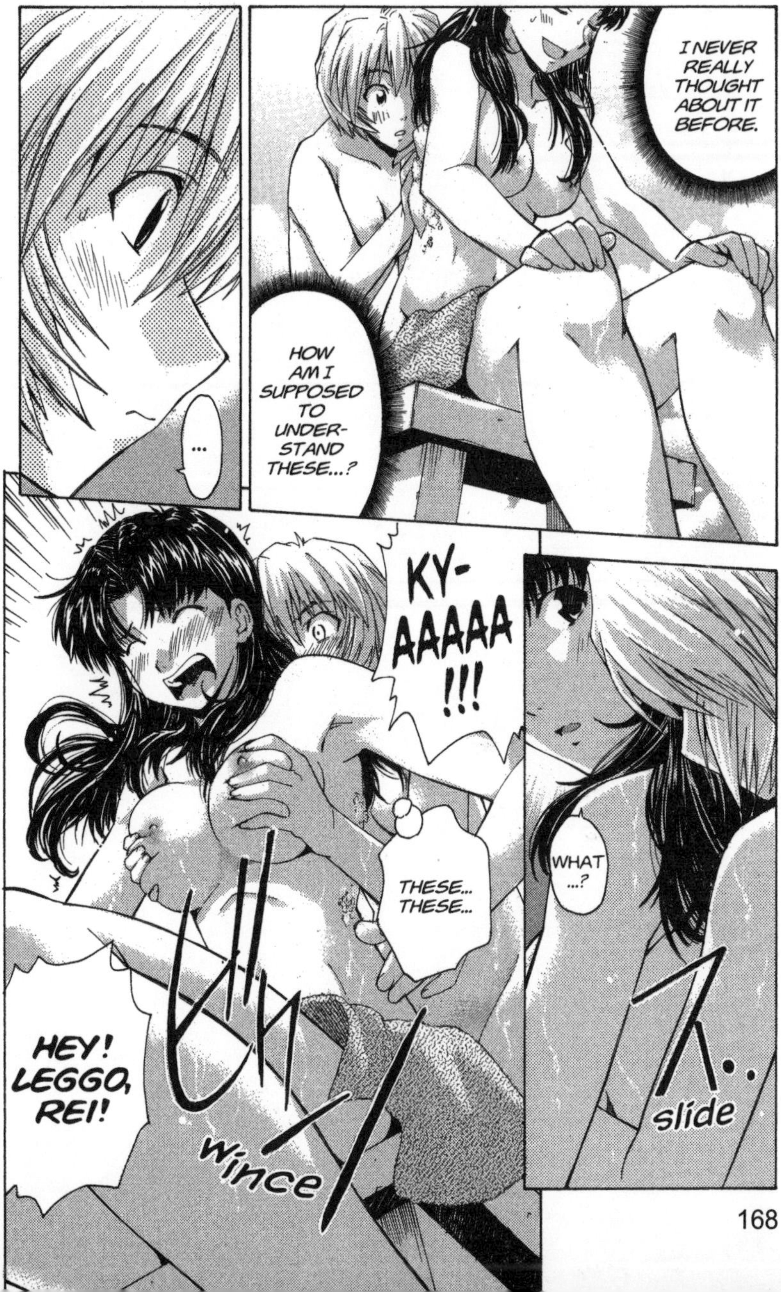
I NEVER REALLY THOUGHT ABOUT IT BEFORE.
HOW AM I SUPPOSED TO UNDER-STAND THESE...?
...
WHAT ...?
slide
KY-AAAAA !!!
THESE... THESE...
HEY! LEGGO, REI!
wince

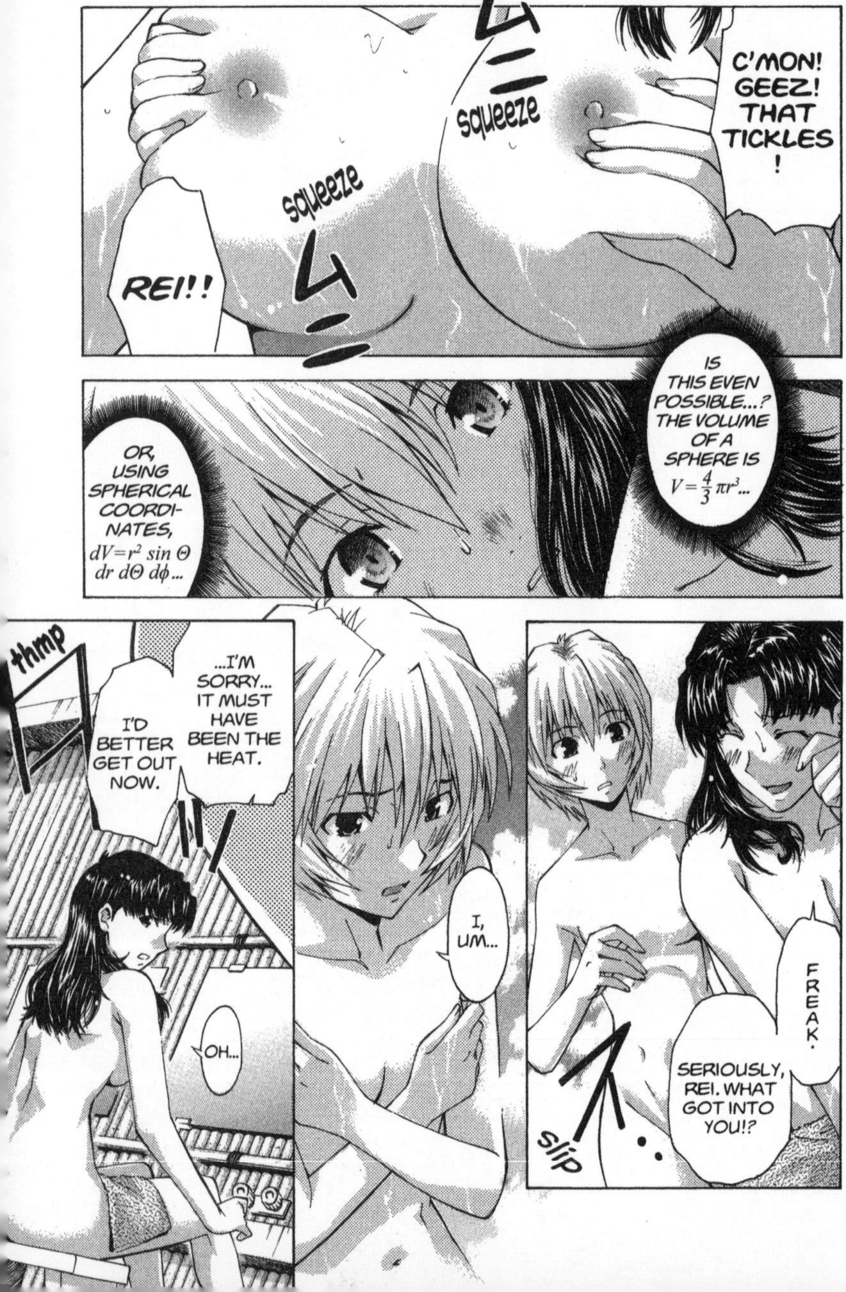
C'MON! GEEZ! THAT TICKLES!
squeeze
squeeze
REI!!
IS THIS EVEN POSSIBLE...? THE VOLUME OF A SPHERE IS $V=\frac{4}{3}\pi r^3$...
OR, USING SPHERICAL COORDINATES, $dV=r^2 \sin \Theta \, dr \, d\Theta \, d\phi$...
FREAK.
SERIOUSLY, REI. WHAT GOT INTO YOU!?
slip
I, UM...
...I'M SORRY... IT MUST HAVE BEEN THE HEAT.
I'D BETTER GET OUT NOW.
thmp
OH...

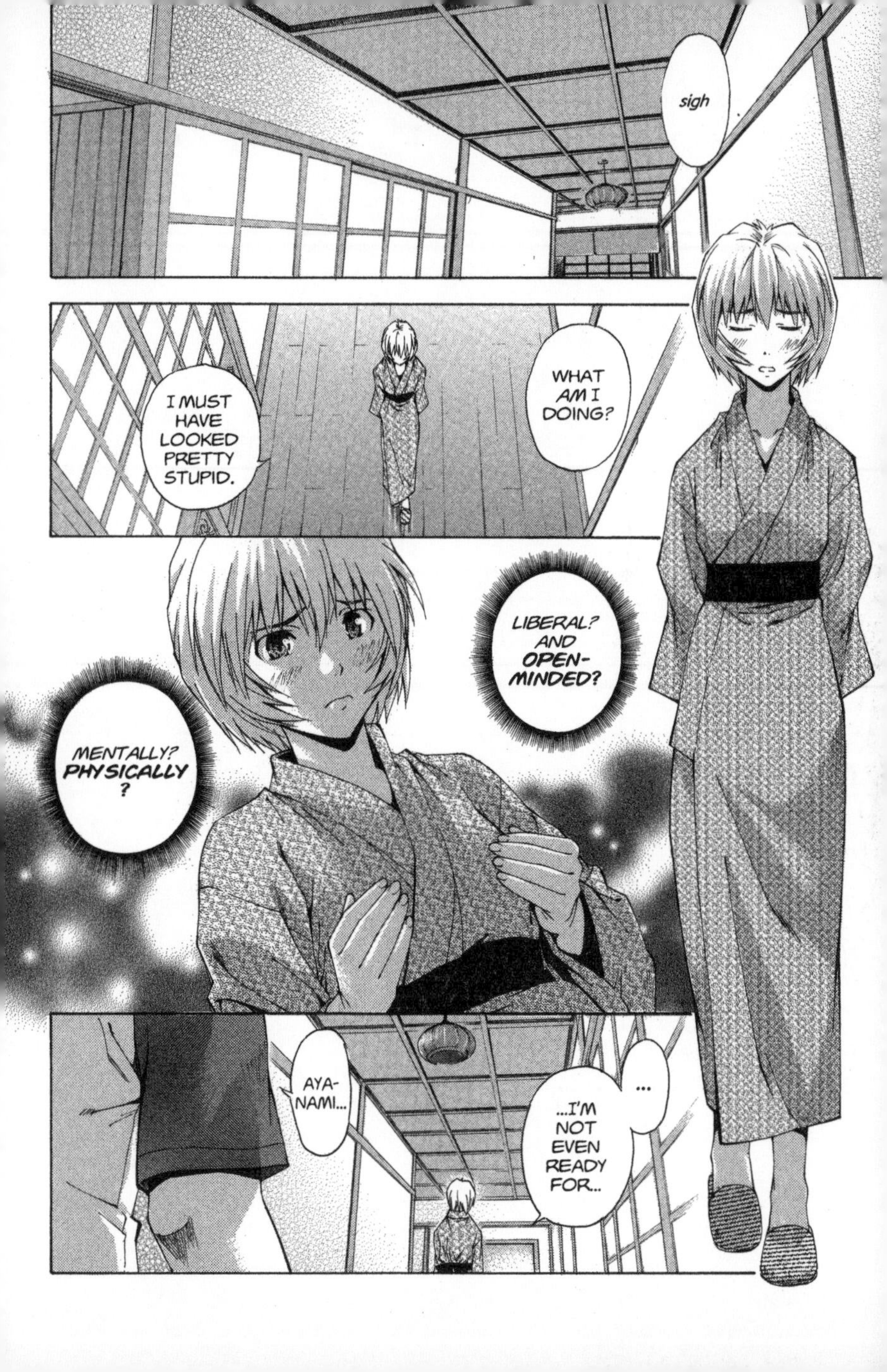
sigh
WHAT AM I DOING?
I MUST HAVE LOOKED PRETTY STUPID.
LIBERAL? AND OPEN-MINDED?
MENTALLY? PHYSICALLY?
...
...I'M NOT EVEN READY FOR..
AYA-NAMI...

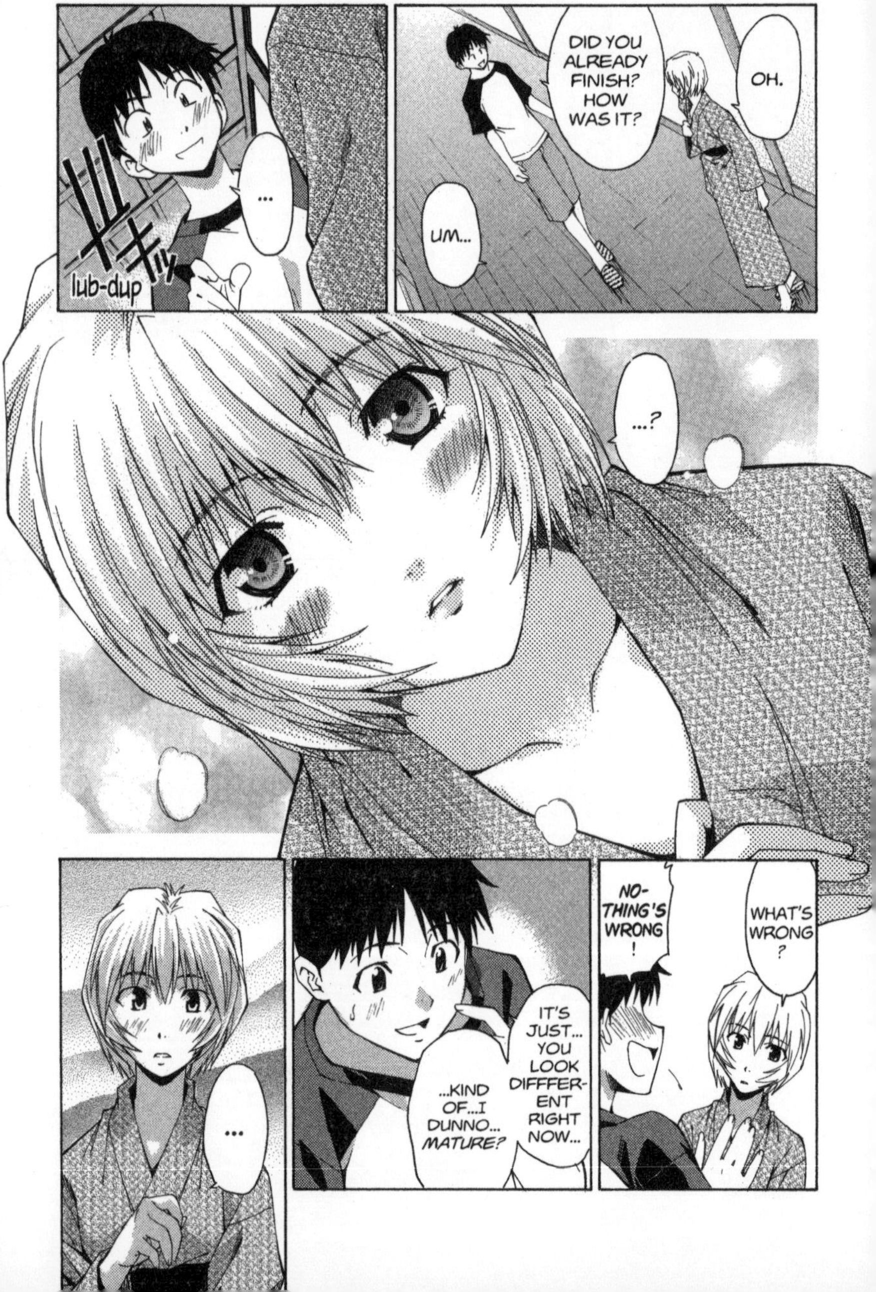
OH.
DID YOU ALREADY FINISH? HOW WAS IT?
UM...
...
lub-dup
...?
WHAT'S WRONG?
NO-THING'S WRONG!
IT'S JUST... YOU LOOK DIFFFER-ENT RIGHT NOW...
...KIND OF...I DUNNO... MATURE?
...

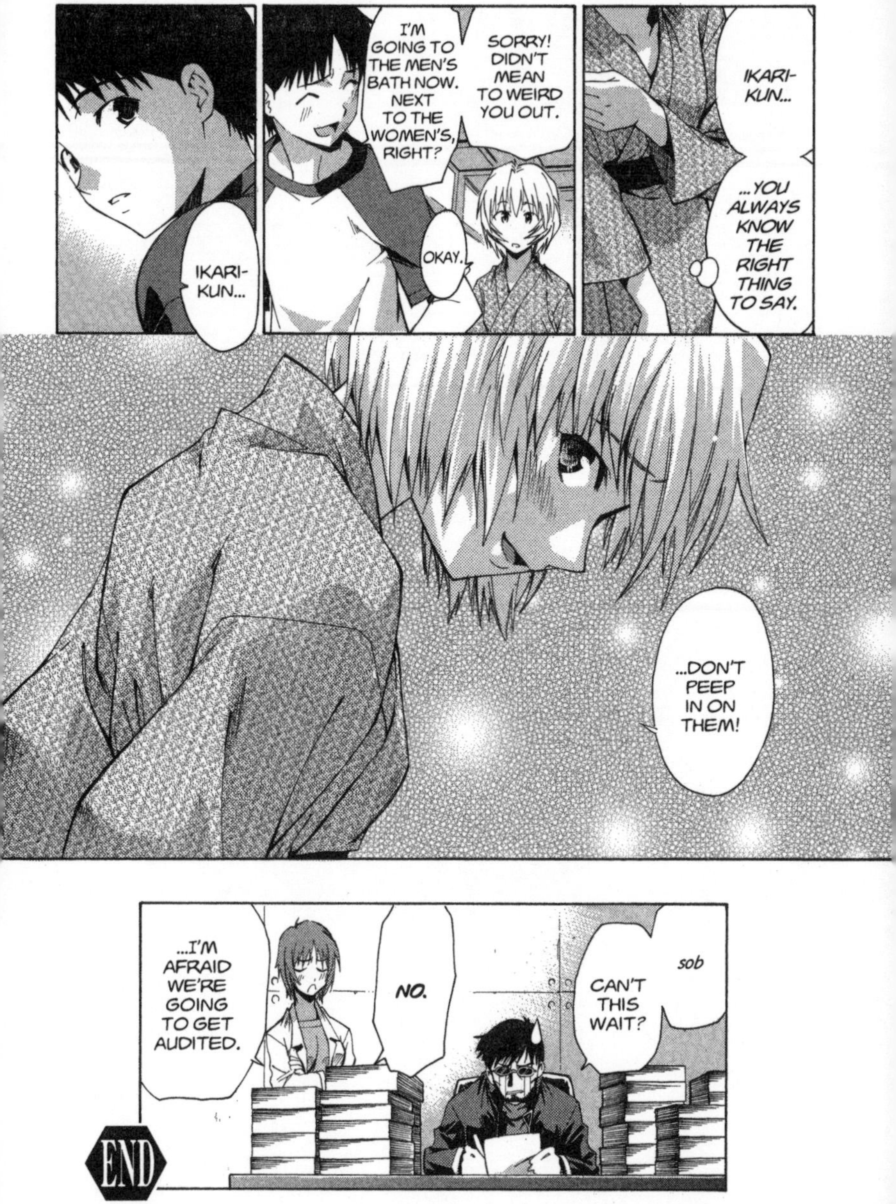
IKARI-KUN...
...YOU ALWAYS KNOW THE RIGHT THING TO SAY.
SORRY! DIDN'T MEAN TO WEIRD YOU OUT.
I'M GOING TO THE MEN'S BATH NOW. NEXT TO THE WOMEN'S, RIGHT?
OKAY.
IKARI-KUN...
...DON'T PEEP IN ON THEM!
sob
CAN'T THIS WAIT?
NO.
...I'M AFRAID WE'RE GOING TO GET AUDITED.
END

AFTERWORD

Well, here we are at volume 5 already.

We count the time passed here in volumes, but of course, the arrival of vol. 5 also coincides with the fact I've been working on this story for three years now [in Japan, vol. 5 first hit the stands in March of 2008—the first chapter of the story appeared in the June 2005 issue of "Shonen Ace" magazine; but of course, the chapter itself was drawn several months before that—ed.].

Surely, it hasn't really been that long? But I want to keep going on longer still, so please stick around for more!

-Osamu Takahashi

~STAFF~
Kasumiryo
Miki
Takuji
Keiji Watarai
Michio Morikawa

COVER DESIGN
Seki Shindo

see you in vol. 6 . . .

EDITOR
CARL GUSTAV HORN

EDITORIAL ASSISTANT
ANNIE GULLION

DESIGNER
STEPHEN REICHERT

PUBLISHER
MIKE RICHARDSON

English-language version produced by Dark Horse Comics

Neon Genesis Evangelion: The Shinji Ikari Raising Project Vol. 5

First published in Japan as NEON GENESIS EVANGELION IKARI-SHINJI IKUSEI KEIKAKU Volume 5. © OSAMU TAKAHASHI 2008 © GAINAX • khara. First published in Japan in 2008 by KADOKAWA SHOTEN Publishing Co., Ltd., Tokyo. English translation rights arranged with KADOKAWA SHOTEN Publishing Co., Ltd., Tokyo, through TOHAN CORPORATION, Tokyo. This English-language edition © 2010 by Dark Horse Comics, Inc. All other material © 2010 by Dark Horse Comics, Inc. All rights reserved. No portion of this publication may be reproduced or transmitted, in any form or by any means, without the express written permission of the copyright holders. Names, characters, places, and incidents featured in this publication either are the product of the author's imagination or are used fictitiously. Any resemblance to actual persons (living or dead), events, institutions, or locales, without satiric intent, is coincidental. Dark Horse Manga™ is a trademark of Dark Horse Comics, Inc. All rights reserved.

Published by
Dark Horse Manga
A division of Dark Horse Comics, Inc.
10956 SE Main Street
Milwaukie, OR 97222

darkhorse.com

To find a comics shop in your area, call the Comic Shop Locator Service toll-free at 1-888-266-4226

First edition: July 2010
ISBN 978-1-59582-520-9

1 3 5 7 9 10 8 6 4 2
Printed at Transcontinental Gagné, Louiseville, QC, Canada

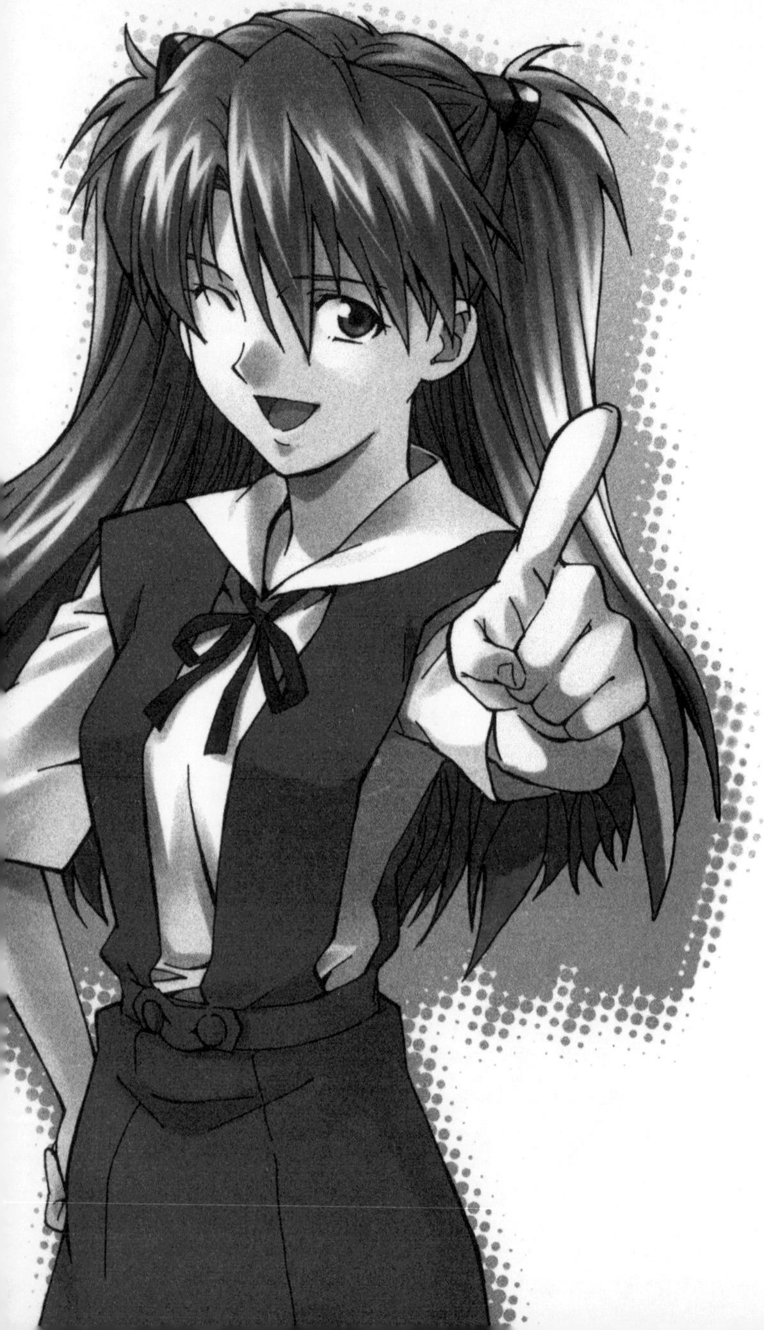

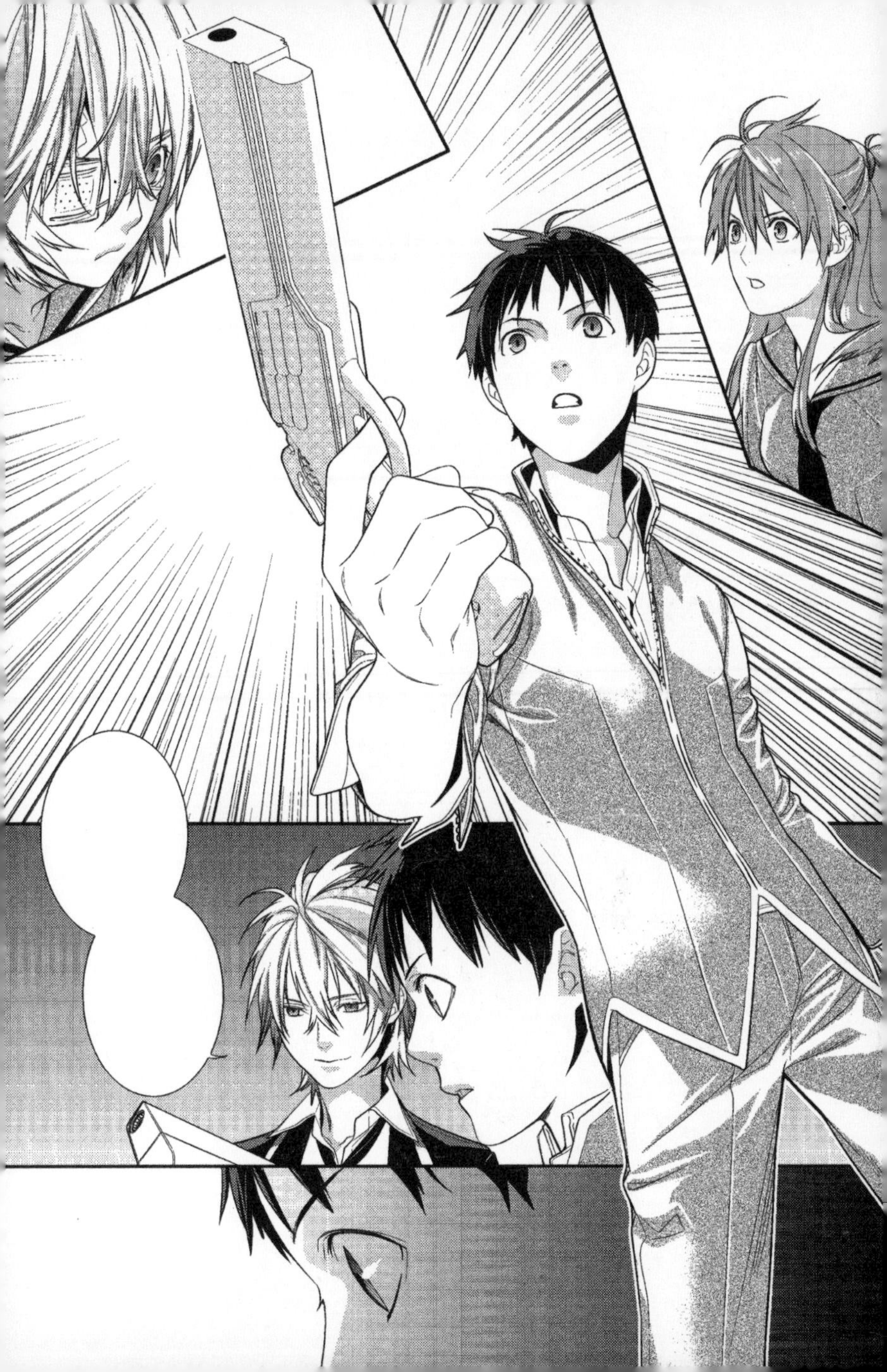

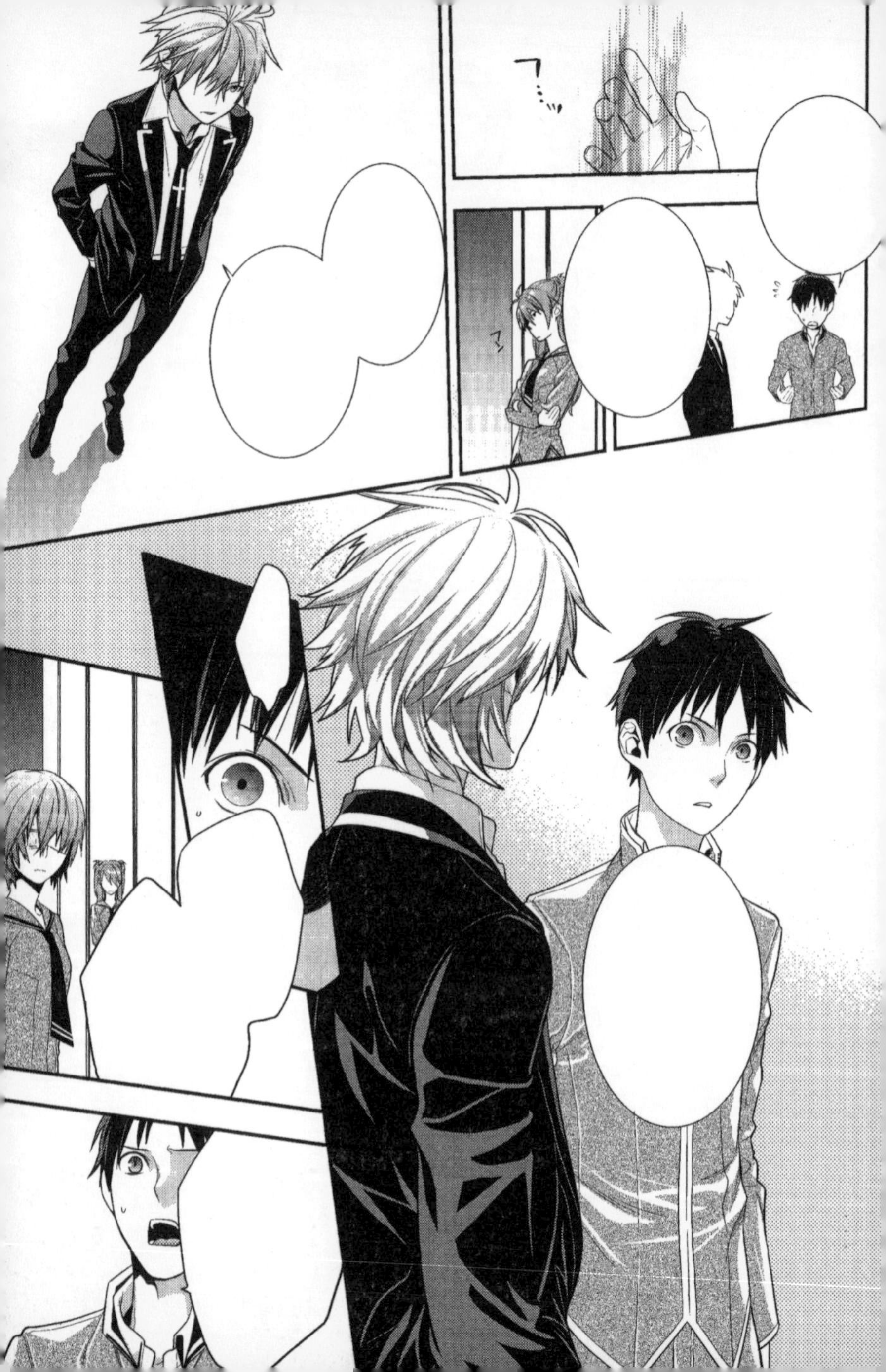

STOP!

止 ま れ

THIS IS THE BACK OF THE BOOK!

This manga collection is translated into English, but arranged in right-to-left reading format to maintain the artwork's visual orientation as originally drawn and published in Japan. If you've never read comics this way before, take a look at the diagram below to give yourself an idea of how to go about it. Basically, you'll be starting in the upper-right-hand corner, and will read each word balloon and panel moving right to left. It may take a little getting used to, but you should get the hang of it very quickly. Have fun! If this is the millionth manga you've read this way, never mind.

1
WELL, THERE IS A CUTE GIRL SITTING NEXT TO YOU...
2
...SO I SUPPOSE IT'S UNDER-STANDABLE YOU CAN'T CONCEN-TRATE--
3
--BUT IF I CATCH YOU SPACING OUT AGAIN, YOUR NOVEL WILL BECOME REQUIRED READING.
4
MISATO-SENSEI...!!
5
JUST KIDDING! ♡
THUD!!
6
A NOVEL.

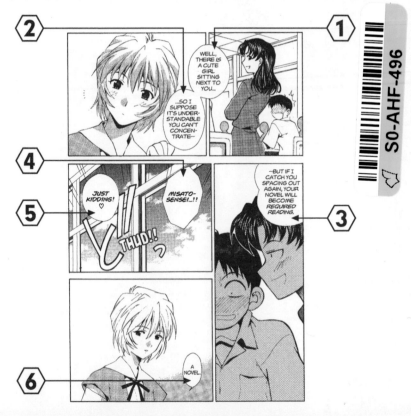